The Best Bargain

FAMILY
VACATIONS

in the U.S.A.

Also by Laura Sutherland and Valerie Wolf Deutsch

Innocents Abroad: Traveling with Kids in Europe

By Laura Sutherland

Great Caribbean Family Vacations

The Best Bargain

FAMILY VACATIONS

in the U.S.A.

LAURA SUTHERLAND
and
VALERIE WOLF DEUTSCH

St. Martin's Griffin ❧ New York

Library of Congress Cataloging-in-Publication Data

Sutherland, Laura.
    The best bargain family vacations in the U.S.A. / Laura Sutherland and Valerie Wolf Deutsch.—1st rev. ed.
        p. cm.
    Includes index.
    ISBN 0-312-15062-8
        1. United States—Guidebooks. 2. Family recreation—UnitedStates— Guidebooks. I. Deutsch, Valerie Wolf. II. Title.
    E158.S95   1997
    917.304'929—dc20   96-38558
                                                                                        CIP

10   9   8   7   6   5   4

CONTENTS

Preface   vii

Acknowledgments   viii

Introduction   1

Resorts   17

Dude Ranches   62

National Parks   89

Family Camps   144

Lakeshore and Riverside Vacations   165

Beach Vacations   201

Learning Vacations and Day Trips   283

State Park Cabins and Resorts   321

Appendix I: Budget Motels   342

Appendix II: U.S. Tourist Offices   344

Index   353

Reply Form   360

PREFACE

We are parents who rely on at least one yearly getaway for a special time together with our families. But like many families today, we need to stretch our vacation dollars as far as possible. Other guidebooks we consulted listed spectacular destinations that were fun to fantasize about, but many were too expensive for the average family. We started asking friends to tell us about their favorite "bargain" family vacations. We wanted to learn about different types of vacations—from secluded spots where we could leave our busy lives behind to places packed with activities to fill our days. The criterion was "the best for less." Friends referred friends, who in turn referred their friends, and soon we found suggestions coming in from all over the country. All information about rates, types of accommodations, and special features were current at press time, but always confirm them when you call for a reservation.

ACKNOWLEDGMENTS

This book was inspired by our young traveling companions, Madeleine, Walker, Silvie, and Rebecca, who continue to reinforce our motto: You *can* take them with you. Special thanks to our agent Vicky Bijur and our editor Anne Savarese. We are especially grateful to the many families who eagerly shared their favorite bargain vacations and hideaways with us. And of course, our heartfelt appreciation goes to our wonderful husbands, Lance Linares and Richard Deutsch.

INTRODUCTION

*Y*ou *can* afford a terrific family vacation this year, once you know about the surprising vacation bargains awaiting you and your family. There are reasonably priced cottages at the beach and rustic cabins along the shores of tranquil lakes and wildlife-filled rivers throughout the country. Take a trail ride through high mountain valleys or read a book by the pool at a dude ranch with a price tag that won't break the bank. Drift across a lake on your own private houseboat, or sleep all day while your children are safely entertained in the kids' club at an inexpensive full-service resort. Even if your budget is modest, there's a vacation out there that your family will remember for years to come.

CHOOSING WHERE TO GO

Your budget, more than anything else, will determine how and where you go: whether you fly or drive, stay in an upscale villa or a simple motel, or go white water rafting through the Grand Canyon or river tubing closer to home. But just as important as how much money you have to spend is what your family enjoys doing and how much vacation time you have available.

The McGuires of Philadelphia are long-range planners. They made a wish list with every type of vacation they hope to take with their two-year-old twins: a tropical beach resort this year, Cape Cod when the kids are four, Disney World when they are six, river rafting when they are eight, houseboating the summer they are nine. On the other hand, the Jacobsens of Madison, Wisconsin let their child's current interest determine their vacations: when their son was dino-crazy at age four, they sought out dinosaur digs in Utah and Colorado. When he was nine and a baseball fanatic, they surprised him with a trip to the Baseball Hall of Fame in Cooperstown, New York. Many other families choose to return to the same cabin by a lake or cottage at the shore year after year; some vacation at the same place for several generations. Other parents prefer to have time to themselves while keeping their kids as involved as possible in a full-scale children's program with plenty of sports and games. The most successful vacations take every family member's needs and personalities into consideration.

It helps to keep the abilities of your youngest child in mind as you plan where to go. When the Jackson family took a trip to Washington, D.C. with their six-, ten-, and twelve-year-olds, the youngest had a difficult time with the long walks to the various museums, which put a damper on the entire trip. Be realistic about what your children can do and will enjoy; their ages and the type of holiday you select can make or break a vacation. Farm stays are big hits with toddlers and preschoolers; resorts with kids' programs are popular with children who like organized activities with others their own age; dude ranches require kids seven or eight and older be mature enough to manage a horse; learning and adventure vacations are most successful with ages eight or nine and up; and teenagers like to be with other teens, with time away from their parents, while their parents just want them as busy as possible. *Every* age seems to enjoy a holiday near the water, whether it's the ocean, lake, or river.

Since vacations nurture the health and well-being of our family, it is important to plan and budget for them. Many excellent values, true bargains, and just plain great vacation spots throughout the country are described in this book. They provide you with a broad range of economical choices, recognizing that one family's A-list vacation is another family's vacation bomb.

EARLY PLANNING PAYS OFF

Advance planning and thorough research can save you hundreds of dollars on your vacation, as many of the best bargains in family travel are snapped up quickly. By planning your summer vacation in January, February, or March, you'll have first choice at many of the good values listed in this book. If you find it's June and you haven't done a thing, don't be discouraged; last-minute cancellations do often occur at the most desirable places.

Some of the Best Family Vacations Start in the Library

Head to your local library to check the guidebooks, travel and family magazines, travel videos, and newspaper travel sections to help you decide where you want to go. Family travel experts keep files with clippings of destinations they think their readers might like to know about, and you should, too. Save articles about areas that interest you for your family travel files.

Call, Question, and Collect

Call or write the tourist office or Chamber of Commerce in the areas you are considering visiting. Addresses, phone numbers, and Web sites of state tourist offices are listed in the back of this book. They can help direct you to addresses and phone numbers of regional and local tourist offices, as can the reference librarian. If your children write the inquiries, they will soon receive lots of colorful brochures and photo-filled pamphlets in the mail. Once your travel plans are set, ask for maps of the area.

Find out the slowest days of the week and the least crowded hours of the day to visit the blockbuster attractions. Ask about family-friendly restaurants and hotels that offer special deals. Talk to trusted friends whose children are close in age to yours and who share your ideas for family fun. Many of the best vacations are based on recommendations from friends.

The World Wide Web

Many larger properties and vacation operators have their own Web page on the Internet with photos and descriptions of their resort, ranch, or classes. Type in their Web address and you'll get an on-line photo-filled "brochure" with the most current rates and packages. The Internet also allows discounters for airline tickets, cruises, and package vacations to offer travel bargains at the very last minute. Commercial services, such as American Online or CompuServe, have travel sections and bulletin boards that include reviews of destinations and guidebooks as well as readers' tips.

YOUR TRAVEL BUDGET

After you've set your travel budget, estimate your expenses to determine what destination, mode of transportation, and type of vacation is affordable for your family:

Transportation

Gasoline
Airplane, train, or bus fare (round-trip)
Airport-to-destination fare
Car rental
Public transportation
Car entertainment, new toys, audiotapes

Food and Lodging

Accommodations
Meals and snacks
Tips and service charges

Activities

Sports
Entertainment
Equipment rental
Excursions
Lessons

Miscellaneous

Souvenirs
New clothing
New luggage
Film purchase and development
Unexpected expenses

CUTTING COSTS: STRATEGIES FOR GETTING THE BEST DEAL

Track Travel Bargains

Subscribe to a publication that tracks travel bargains, such as *Consumer Reports Travel Letter* (800–234–1970; PO Box 53629, Boulder, Colorado 80322-3629; subscriptions $39 per year for 12 issues) or *Travel Smart* (914–693–8300; Dobbs Ferry, New York 10522; subscriptions $37 per year for 12 issues). They can keep you up-to-date on the best airline buys, special resort packages, and hotel discounts.

Travel Off Season

Most families travel in June, July, and August, when resort area prices are at their peak. Off-season travel allows you to take advantage of much-lower prices and fewer crowds. If your kids get out of school in early June, or begin school in mid-September, take advantage of "shoulder season" (spring and fall) prices and save hundreds of dollars. If your youngsters are preschoolers or have an unusual school schedule, plan to travel at times when most children have their noses in the books.

Even if your children have traditional school holidays, off-season prices can work in your favor. Ski resorts have an abundance of recreational activities in summer, and accommodations prices often drop to less than half of what they are in winter. Prices in Florida, Arizona, and Hawaii can be as much as seventy percent lower in their summer off-season.

Some families take advantage of off-season travel by taking their kids out of school for a week or two. Many teachers agree with parents that travel is broadening and are happy to send along homework. To make home schooling successful, set aside a certain time each day for school work. Find books about the places you'll be visiting, and have your child keep a journal noting the geographical features, historical facts, weather, and flora and fauna.

Never Pay Retail

Always ask about discounts and packages, no matter where you are going. Seek out coupons; many state and local tourist publications contain dollars-off coupons for attractions in their area. Local weekly and daily newspapers may offer some, too. Call an attraction you plan to visit and ask where you can find their discount coupons. Follow the example of the Dugan family of Portland, Oregon, who saved $20 on their visit to

Marine World Africa USA in the San Francisco Bay area by calling and finding coupons for $5 off per ticket at a local supermarket chain. Many hotels, such as those we list in San Diego and Hawaii, offer packages with a nightly rate that also includes a rental car or discounted entry to major attractions. It pays to check.

Discount Books

Discount books can save you up to fifty percent on hotel bills, restaurant meals, and admission fees to entertainment and recreational activities. The largest publisher of directories and coupon books, *Entertainment Publications*, offers a book called *Travel America at Half Price*, along with individual city or regional guides that include numerous two-for-one and 50-percent-off deals at hotels, motels, restaurants, and attractions. A special book for teenagers called the *Gold C Saving Spree* covers more than forty different vacation destinations. Call 800-285-5525 for information.

Taste Publications offers a book for $19.95 that lists more than 1,200 hotels and motels coast to coast that offer discounts (subject to availability) at participating hotels, motels, restaurants, and car rentals. *America at 50% Discount* is available by calling 800–828–5004 or 410–825–1002; or by writing 1031 Cromwell Bridge Road, Baltimore, Maryland 21286.

Frequent Flyer Miles

Most airlines offer frequent flyer miles to encourage travelers to remain loyal to the airline. Once you accrue a certain number of miles, you're eligible for free trips and upgrades. You get additional miles for doing business with partner companies, such as long distance telephone and credit card suppliers, and car rental and hotel chains. Many airlines now offer frequent flyer miles for children. It's an excellent way to save money on airplane tickets. You must plan ahead to use the tickets, especially if you are flying during peak vacation season and to popular destinations. Airlines limit the number of seats on each flight for frequent flyer mile holders to use.

Do Overdo

Spontaneity needs to be a part of travel once you're on the road, but detailed planning before you go can insure that you don't get stuck buying full-price books at an airport concession stand, lunch at an overpriced amusement park snack bar, or expensive sunblock on the beach in Maui. Anticipate what you'll need and stock up at discounted prices before you go. Make sure you have plenty of snacks, gum, drinks, wipes, adhesive bandages, and entertainment—books, games, stickers, tapes, and toys—before leaving home.

Penny-Pinching Souvenirs

Kids are natural collectors. Encourage them to search out lower-priced souvenirs, such as decals, pencils, pennants, or postcards. T-shirts make practical souvenirs, but give your kids an allowance or a limit on the number you will buy through the trip. Here are the best tight-fisted souvenir tips we've come across:

- Give kids their own money to budget and spend. All parents know what tightwads children are when it's their own money, not yours, they may spend.

- Bring a blank scrapbook and steer the kids toward collecting free souvenirs such as imprinted napkins, brochures, paper coasters, and matchbooks.

- Purchase an inexpensive journal book, and have family members take turns keeping a family vacation log of impressions, experiences, and drawings.

- Have children pick out a postcard at every stop and surprise them with a photo album to fill with the postcards when they get home. If you've got the room, give them the album at the beginning of the trip. They'll spend many happy hours organizing the postcards and looking at them.

- Stop at a local discount store and let the kids select an article of clothing that will be suitable for school. It will save you time later and they will remember their vacation every time they wear it.

STARVE YOUR FOOD BUDGET
(BUT NOT YOUR KIDS)

Make Your Own Meals

The Day-Farnsworth family of Seattle, Washington took a five-week car trip across the country and adhered to their plan of making their own breakfast and lunch every day. They sought out low-priced ethnic restaurants and neighborhood cafes for dinner. Their savings allowed them to splurge on theater tickets in New York at the end of their trip and a special birthday dinner at a well-known restaurant in Washington, D.C.

Cool It!
Bring a cooler. Even if you're flying to a big-city destination, you can take a small folding cooler for lunches on the go, and to store milk for morning cereal. Many car travelers take two coolers—one hard-side for the car, and one smaller soft-side for overnight stops and day trips. You'll picnic more, giving your kids a chance to stretch their legs and run around.

Find Restaurants With Kids' Menus
Children's menus are usually inexpensive and offer reliable favorites, such as peanut butter and jelly sandwiches, macaroni and cheese, hamburgers, and hot dogs. Fruits and vegetables can be conspicuously absent, but many families make up for this at a different meal.

Restaurants Where Kids Eat Free
"Kids Eat Free" or "Kids Stay and Eat Free" seems to be the latest gimmick in attracting family business, and more and more businesses are expected to jump on the bandwagon. Look for restaurants and resorts that advertise this feature.

LOWER YOUR LODGING COSTS

Get Out Of Town!
If you are planning to visit a major city, seek out hotels or motels on the outskirts of town and take public transportation into the city center. The Jameson family of Cleveland saved quite a bit by staying in Arlington, Virginia and heading into Washington, D.C. on day trips. Staying outside of a major resort area made it possible for the Levitz family of Dallas to ski Aspen for a full week rather than just a few days. Because they had their own car, they headquartered at a budget motel 35 minutes away in Glenwood Springs and paid one-fourth of what they would have paid for "budget" lodging in the Aspen area. They also had a microwave oven and a small refrigerator in their motel room.

Weekend In The City

If it doesn't make sense to stay outside the city, plan your big city visit to include a weekend. Many business hotels in the heart of a city drop their prices considerably on Friday, Saturday, and Sunday nights.

Investigate/Interrogate

"Are there any family discounts or package deals?" should be a standard part of your inquiry. Call a hotel or motel's direct phone number in addition to the 800 number to get the lowest possible price. Find out the latest you can cancel your hotel or motel reservation without a penalty. Ask the reservation desk about parking fees if you are driving your own car, and if you are flying, find out if the hotel offers a free shuttle service to and from the airport. Inquire about free local phone calls. Don't be afraid to bargain.

Budget Motels

No-frills budget motels generally offer little in charm and personality, but the price is right and they are clean and comfortable. The industry's criterion for "budget" is a single room rate of less than $50 per night; many cost much less. Most major chains have toll-free numbers and will send you a directory of their motel locations free of charge.

Well-priced "double doubles" (two double beds in one room) can easily accommodate a family of four. Kids under twelve (and often, eighteen) are usually free, and cribs and rollaways are available at most motels for a nominal fee or free of charge. Reservations are not always required, but it's best to stop early for the night, especially in season. If you're planning to use budget motels in resorts or popular areas, definitely reserve in advance. We list a number of the larger budget motel and hotel chains in appendix I.

Home Exchanges

Exchanging your home for someone else's can completely eliminate your lodging costs, and if the family you exchange with happens to have kids similar in age to yours, you may get a houseful of appropriate toys and books, too. Home exchanges can be lined up for a few days, a week, or a month; details are between you and the other party. To arrange, contact a home exchange service (see below), pay your fee, list your house, and write letters or call everyone with a home that appeals to you. Once you get a response, ask lots of questions (the exchange services give you a list) and ask for references of people who have used the home before.

The two oldest and biggest home exchange firms in the United States are **Vacation Exchange Club,** PO Box 650, Key West, Florida 33041, telephone 800–638–3841 or 305–294–3720. This club publishes four catalogs per year; if you join, your home is listed in each one. Listings cost $50, or $62 with a photograph. **Intervac U.S.** (PO Box 590504, San Francisco, CA 94159, telephone 800–756–HOME or 415–435–3497; fax 415-435-7440; e-mail Interracks® AOL.COM.) charges $78 for a listing in one of its catalogs, but you receive all three of its catalogs over the period of a year.

State Park Cabins and Resorts

State park cabins and resorts offer excellent vacation values. More than twenty-five states have resort facilities and inexpensive cabins along rivers, lakes, and beaches throughout their state park system. The cabins range in style from rustic, which require you to bring your own linens and cooking equipment, to downright elegant, with every amenity included. Because state park cabins and resorts are set in protected areas of natural beauty, most of the parks have hiking trails, naturalist programs, swimming, boating, playgrounds, and picnic areas. Prices of extra recreational activities such as horseback riding and boat rentals tend to be far lower than those at private resorts and parks. We devote a chapter to state park cabins and resorts and list of few of the best throughout the book. Early reservations are essential.

Rental Homes

Home rentals typically are less expensive than hotel stays and offer more value and privacy for the money. Additional savings are met by vacationing with friends and sharing expenses and chores. If you do share a home with friends, your kids will have playmates, and the adults can take turns watching each other's children. Most homes, cottages, and condominiums are rented by the week. Local tourist offices and chambers of commerce often keep lists of real estate agencies that handle short-term rentals. The classifieds section of the local newspaper in the area you are visiting is another good resource.

Family Hostels

Does the term "youth hostel" conjure up images of a dingy, cavernous room jammed with bunk beds, sullen teenagers, and dusty backpacks? Try this instead: clean, private rooms for families in historic lighthouses, tree houses, farms, and lakeside inns. Family hosteling, long favored in northern Europe, is gaining popularity in the United States, and many

American youth hostels have added family rooms so families can bunk down together. To keep costs low, hostelers provide their own food, bed linens, and towels. Many hostels offer kitchen facilities and some offer meals; bathrooms are shared. In addition, many hostels provide a variety of programs for guests, ranging from slide shows and programs on an area's natural history to walking tours of historic neighborhoods.

You do not need to be a member of Hostelling International to stay in a hostel, but nonmembers pay an extra $3 per person per night. If you plan to use more than one hostel in the course of a year you will find it more economical to join. Adult members can expect to pay from $8 to $15 per night, and children ordinarily pay half the adult rate. Family memberships cost $35 per year.

We list a few hostels with family rooms but there are many more to choose from. Members receive a complete listing of all facilities in the United States and Canada. For information, contact Hostelling International, 733 15th St. NW, Suite 840, Washington, D.C., 20005; 202–783–6161.

SURVIVAL TIPS

Pack Smart

We play "Twenty Questions" when we pack for a family vacation, but often don't get past the first three when it comes to clothes:

- Will it show ketchup, chocolate ice cream, or orange soda spills?

- Will it serve as a layer and coordinate with everything else in the child's suitcase?

- Does my child really need it or will something else do double duty?

Other reliable packing tips:

- Pack a carry-on bag with items you can't risk losing.

- When traveling by train or plane take more food and entertainment than you think you'll ever need, to guard against the inevitable delays. It doesn't hurt to pack an extra set of clothes, either.

- A supply of plastic bags comes in handy for wet clothes, souvenirs, and trash.

- Always pack a small first aid kit with plenty of adhesive bandages and children's pain reliever.

- A generous supply of premoistened towelettes help maintain hygiene when there are no sinks.

Slush Funds

Unfortunately things do go wrong on vacations. You may be faced with an expensive car repair bill, medical expenses, or an unexpected airline ticket. Tuck away some extra travelers checks or confirm the limit on your credit card before departing.

Protect Yourself From Backseat Terrorism

Car travel can get monotonous, and everyone knows familiarity and close quarters can breed contempt. Expect your kids to fight, but be prepared with some secret weapons in your arsenal. Here's a battle plan:

- Give each child a bag of nickels (or dimes or quarters). Each time they fight, take a nickel away. If your children are bankrupt within hours, you can start again fresh each morning.

- Pull off the road and stop until they stop fighting. Or, drive to a safe spot and ask them to get out of the car until they've settled their dispute. Many children know their parents will give them plenty of attention if they fight; ignoring them can get results. So can threatening.

- Keep things lively. Audio story tapes offer hours of entertainment for toddlers and elementary school-aged children, and some stories can be interesting for adults, too. For example, all of the *Indian in the Cupboard* series by Lynne Reid Banks, most of Roald Dahl's stories, and many Newberry Award–winning authors have been recorded and can be purchased through **Harper Audio** (call 800–242–7737 to get a catalog). **The Listening Library** (800–243–4504 or 203–637–3616 to get a catalog or place an order) is another excellent source. Many public libraries contain books on tape for kids. For older children or families with a wide span of ages, consider purchasing individual tape players to keep arguments at bay.

- Stop for picnics at rest stops, parks, and school yards.

- Bring balls, Frisbees, and jump ropes to help work off steam when you stop.

- Bring a small supply of inexpensive wrapped gifts to hand out when the going gets tough.

- Rotate seats.

Play It Safe

Pick a designated meeting place at each of your stops, in case you are separated. Teach kids to approach a staff person or official if they are lost. Make sure kids know the phone number of a relative or friend designated to be the contact for messages in case of difficulties. Some parents have a secret whistle to help family members signal each other or to tell children when it's time to go.

Made You Look!

Children rarely enjoy sightseeing, especially the little ones. Limit or eliminate sightseeing from your itinerary. Instead, plan physical activities in areas of great beauty so that the adults can sightsee while you all ride horseback or climb to the top of a peak. Your children might take in a few vistas in spite of themselves. Older children enjoy taking their own photographs, which can encourage them to observe subtleties and nuances of the landscape they otherwise would overlook.

Relax! You're On Vacation

Be flexible. Allow time to stop, take a detour, and get out of the car. Travel brings unexpected situations and surprises. Cars break down, planes are late, lines are long, hotels are overbooked. Show your children how to make the best of a difficult situation through your own gracious example.

Home, Sweet Home

Once the vacation is over, have your children create (or finish) a scrapbook of photos, paper souvenirs, written memories, and illustrations.

DISNEY WORLD AND DISNEYLAND

Shrewd parents pad their wallets for trips to these American shrines, and no guidebook on budget family travel is complete without mentioning them. Costs to anticipate include transportation, lodging, food, admission, and souvenirs. Disneyland in Anaheim, California, is a much smaller complex than its Florida counterpart, and visitors can see most of the park in one day. Most people combine a trip to Disneyland with visits to other southern California attractions. Disney World in Orlando, Florida, is enormous and can occupy visitors for close to a week.

Here are some tips for both parks:

- Contact the parks for information before you go, and develop a plan with your family so that you visit all the attractions everyone wants to see. Make reservations at any sit-down restaurants before you go.

- Arrive at the park well before the doors open to get a good place in the ticket line or purchase your tickets in advance. Go to the most popular rides first or visit them during a parade.

- Visitors are not supposed to bring in their own food, but tuck a few high-energy snacks (protein-enriched candy bars, nuts, and raisins) into your backpack or purse. That way you'll avoid buying expensive snacks and you can postpone lunch until after the peak lunch crowds have left. You'll have fewer people on the rides during the lunch hour and waste less time in lines. One family we interviewed ate an enormous breakfast at their hotel, snacked during lunch, and then splurged on a mid-afternoon dinner at the park. Back at the hotel Mom and Dad fixed a healthy evening snack before the group retired for the night. If you're staying inside the park, head back to your hotel for a rest and snack midday and return later in the afternoon when it's a little less crowded.

- Discuss souvenirs with your children in advance. Many parents recommend buying an article of clothing, such as a T-shirt or sweatshirt; knickknacks, mouse ears (although they are a lot of fun), and other keepsakes will eventually collect dust.

- Check the travel section of your local newspaper and with your travel agent for any package deals that might work for you and compare the costs with a do-it-yourself arrangement.

Disney World

In the last few years, Disney World has added two economy resorts, Disney's All-Star Sports Resort, and Disney's All-Star Music Resort, where rooms cost about $75 per night and guests can use the Disney transportation system to get to various attractions. American Automobile Association members, Florida residents, and senior citizens get a slight discount on admission tickets. Many larger employers offer the Magic Kingdom Club, which has discounted tickets, as an employee benefit.

Weekends tend to be less crowded at Disney World (unless there is a Florida resident special; be sure to check), as Saturday and Sunday are travel days for many people. The park is more crowded at the beginning of the week than toward the end of the week. The general information number (407-824-4321) will keep you informed. Value seasons, when resort and hotel prices drop, are usually January through early February, late April through early June, and late August through mid-December. The park is less crowded during these times.

Explore options for tickets to find the one that best suits your family. There are four- and five-day passes, a "Worldhopper" pass that is good for admission to Disney World and other Orlando attractions, and a Length-of-Stay pass.

Many mid-range motels and hotels offer free transportation to and from Disney World. These hotels charge more for rooms than those with no transportation services, but the cost is worth it if you don't have your own car; many shuttle companies charge $10 per person each way. If you have your own car, expect to pay $4 a day for parking.

Disneyland

Unlike Disney World, California's Disneyland can be "done" in a day or two. For visitors who want to see other attractions in the greater Los Angeles area, Disneyland offers a package deal during the "value season" (January through mid-March, early April through mid-June, and mid-September through mid-December) which includes a passport that allows you to go in and out of the park over a five-day period and a two-night stay at a value hotel in the area. If you stay at a Disney property you get early admission (one and a half hours) before the general public.

Mid-week is the least busy time at this park. Visit Toontown early in the day as it is full at the end of the day. Obtain the schedule of character locations if your children have a special favorite; general information, 714-781-4565.

RESORTS

*A*ssemble a beautiful setting, a glimmering pool or lake, plentiful sports and games, and lively entertainment in one location, and you've got a resort vacation. Resorts usually mean big bucks, but in this chapter we've tallied an impressive number of resorts that offer good values or low prices. A number of them have supervised children's programs, perfect for parents who need a vacation both with *and* from their children.

Resort prices vary considerably. The more amenities the resort offers and the more the staff does for you, the more it will cost. Comparing prices for resorts can be a bit like comparing apples and oranges. "American plan" resorts include three meals a day in the price. Many others offer housekeeping cabins that allow you to cook your own meals. Some resorts charge for everything from canoes to shuffleboard equipment, but just as many offer guests the free use of all recreational facilities. The best choice will depend on your budget, your family, and what you like to do.

Some people we interviewed found it economical to share cottage resort accommodations or a condominium with another family. Larger units often cost much less per person than smaller ones, and can make the most desirable resorts affordable. In addition to the lower cost per family, families staying together have their own kitchen, playmates for their kids, and companions and built-in baby-sitters for themselves.

We list every type of resort, from enormous ones with a laundry list of diversions to serene lakeside places with a boat or two and a game of horseshoes. Take note of the state park resorts found in a number of lucky states. They offer excellent prices, numerous recreational facilities, naturalist programs, and magnificent settings. Because they are among the very best in bargain vacations, you must book them as far in advance as possible. See page 323 for more information on other states with resort parks. Many oceanfront resorts are covered in our Beach Vacations chapter.

Here are a few questions to ask:

- Are there package deals for families?

- Are there seasonal discounts?

- What is and what is not included in the price?

- What about taxes and gratuities?

WEST COAST

RICHARDSON'S RESORT

Address: PO Box 9028, South Lake Tahoe, California 95731
Telephone: 916–541–1801

Kids never stop moving at this full-service resort on the south shore of Lake Tahoe. If they're not speeding along a trail on a horse, bike, or in-line skates, they're racing across the water on a jet ski, motorboat, kayak, or paddleboat. The resort's sandy beach is open to the public and can get crowded during periods of peak use; other good beaches are nearby. You can choose accommodations that are elaborate or simple: lakeside cabins, a hotel, condominiums, and campsites are available. The resort is on Forest Service land next to a nature center and several historic estates, all of which run programs during the summer months. The resort's restaurant and bar overlook a popular broad sandy beach where tame geese occasionally roam, looking for a handout. Families visit in winter to enjoy the many excellent downhill ski resorts nearby.

Season: Year-round, but the best selection of cabins is available in July and August.

Accommodations: Cabins, which sleep between two and eight people, are the best value for families. Four-person rustic cabins, rented by the week, are open in summer only; they provide fully equipped kitchens and all linens, and have porches and small bedrooms, but no insulation or heat. Larger, more deluxe cabins also are available. Two-bedroom, two-story condominiums sleep six.

Special Features: Bike rental shop (the resort is on a bike trail), horseback riding rentals, in-line skate rentals, horseshoes, croquet, pool table, tennis, volleyball, hiking, ice-cream parlor, and playground are all part of the facility. A marina at the resort rents motorboats, paddleboats, kayaks, and jet skis, and includes parasailing and a water-ski school.

Cost: Cabins $496 to $1,095 per week, condos $1,260 per week. Bike rentals $7 per hour, horseback riding $20 per hour.

Nearby: Emerald Bay and Fallen Leaf Lake offer excellent mountain bike riding, and the Forest Service's Tallac Historical Estate, right next to resort property, has festivals, art shows, and concerts in the summer months. The Forest Service's visitors center just down the road has an information display, and sponsors guided nature walks, other naturalist programs, and amphitheater concerts.

KONOCTI HARBOR RESORT AND SPA

Address: 8727 Soda Bay Road, Kelseyville, California 95451
Telephone: 800–862–4930; 707–279–4281

Parents can pamper themselves at Konocti's health spa and fitness center while the kids make friends their own age at the daily summer children's program. Activities for youngsters ages five to fourteen run from mid-morning to midafternoon, then start up again at 5 P.M. Konocti is known for its concert series by Clear Lake, with a full spectrum of entertainers that have included Willie Nelson, Kenny Rogers, and B. B. King. The evening children's program is timed so that parents can attend the first show of the night. Concert ticket holders get reductions on room rates. There's plenty for the family to do together, too, with two Olympic-size swimming pools, water-skiing lessons, tennis courts and miniature golf.

Season: Year-round.

Accommodations: Standard rooms have two double beds. Family units have a double bed and a set of bunk beds in the bedroom and a couch, desk, chair, and TV in a small sitting room. Apartments contain two full-size beds, a queen-size sofabed, kitchen, and barbecue area. The "Big House" family unit has a large kitchen, living room, three bedrooms, three baths, washer/dryer, and eight-person Jacuzzi tub.

Special Features: Two swimming pools (lessons available), two wading pools, playground, miniature golf course, waterskiing, parasailing, golf, shuffleboard, badminton, basketball, horseshoes, volleyball, Ping-Pong, children's video arcade, and tennis. The children's day camp offers arts and crafts, miniature golf, swimming, tennis, and lunch. The evening children's program runs from 5 to 10 P.M. with movies, miniature golf, and more. The 19,000-square-foot fitness center/health spa has a sauna, steam room, Jacuzzi, aerobics classes, weights and exercise equipment, and a lap pool. Massages and treatments are available for an extra charge, and a beauty shop is next door.

Cost: Children under twelve stay free in parents' room; teens $10 per night. Standard rooms and family units $69 per night; apartments start at $140 per night. Big House two-night weekend stays $750, five-night stay midweek $1,750. Children's program $20 per child per day and $20 per child per night; session includes lunch or evening snack. Miniature golf $3 per person. Use of the health spa $7.50 per day if staying in room; free for apartment guests. Ask about multiday and other packages.

TRINITY ALPS RESORT

Address: 1750 Trinity Alps Road, Trinity Center, California 96091
Telephone: 916–286–2205

This well-loved rustic resort, in continuous operation for seventy years, is a perfect vacation spot for families who like a back-to-nature experience with numerous recreational options and certain important trappings of civilization—like espresso, ice-cream cones, and gourmet dining. It's the perfect place to relive the gloriously lazy days of summers past. Forty-three private cabins are tucked among the trees along both banks of the Stewart Fork River, with several charming pedestrian bridges (and one for cars, too) connecting the two sides. A sandy beach right next to the swimming hole in the river is centrally located to all of the cabins, and its gentle slope makes it ideal for both toddlers and older children. Other favorite daytime activities include tubing down the river and trail riding. The resort's stable offers one- and two-hour trail rides, an all-day ride, and a special breakfast ride that should not be missed. When you're tired of cooking, visit the excellent restaurant, which serves dinner on a patio above the river; you can often see an osprey family fishing for its dinner. Many families book for the following year before they leave, but cancellations are often available; call early to get on a waiting list.

Season: May 15 to September 30. May, June, late August, and early September are the easiest times to get reservations.

Accommodations: Very basic cabins have equipped kitchens, dining areas, outdoor barbecues and picnic tables, and private bathrooms. Most of them also have a covered outdoor sleeping veranda overlooking the river. Cabins along the far side of the river are the most private. Apartments are smaller and have one or two bedrooms and a big sleeping porch.

Special Features: The resort has a small general store, a soda fountain with an espresso machine, and a community center that offers complimentary family movies, bingo, square dancing, and talent shows in the evening, and aerobics classes five mornings a week. On the grounds are tennis, badminton, volleyball, horseshoes, basketball, fishing, Ping-Pong, tubing, bonfires, and sing-alongs.

Cost: Apartments sleeping four $455 per week; cabins $585 to $865 per week depending on number of people and size of cabin. Bring your own bed linens or rent them for $20 per week per bed. Bring your own towels. Horseback riding $20 for one hour, $27 for two hours, and $40 for a 3 ½-hour breakfast ride. Pony rides $2.

Nearby: Trinity Lake is one and a half miles away. Golf courses and numerous hiking and bike trails are a short distance from the resort.

KA-NEE-TA RESORT

Address: 100 Main Street, PO Box K, Warm Springs, Oregon 97761
Telephone: 800–554–4SUN; 503–553–1112

Your kids might never forgive you if you don't stay in one of Ka-Nee-Ta's brightly painted canvas tepees. Parents might prefer one of the other types of accommodations—from hotel rooms to camping—that this full-service resort offers, but our advice is to go for the tepees. Big enough to sleep six to eight people, the tepees are set on cement bases and have a built-in picnic table and a fireplace in the center. This experience isn't luxurious resort living, but it's one your children are not likely to forget. Ka-Nee-Ta has numerous recreational facilities, all for an extra fee. A river runs through the property for exploring, fishing, and rafting; there is also horseback riding, an eighteen-hole golf course, a large hot mineral springs–fed swimming pool, bike rental, and much more.

Season: Year-round.

Accommodations: Choose from the tepees, cottages, hotel rooms, RV hookups, or primitive tent camping. Tepees have eighteen square feet of enclosed space and use bathhouse facilities nearby. Bring foam pads, sleeping bags, and food. One-bedroom cottages sleep up to three people and do not have kitchens. Two-bedroom cottages have fully equipped kitchens; lodge rooms range from doubles to deluxe suites.

Special Features: Pool, giant water slide, horseback riding, golf, hiking trails, badminton, volleyball, horseshoes, fishing, tennis, kayaking, laundry facilities, snack bar, restaurant.

Cost: Tepees $50 per night for up to five people; $10 per person above that. One-bedroom cottages $85 per night for two people; two-bedroom cottages $100 per night for two. Each additional person age six and up $12 per night. Tent camping $15 per night; lodge rooms $95 to $235 per night. Cottage and lodge accommodations include free use of the swimming pool.

Rental bikes $6 to $10 per hour; guided horseback rides $20 per hour; kayaking $17 per three-mile trip.

ROCKY MOUNTAINS AND SOUTHWEST

RECAPTURE LODGE & PIONEER HOUSE

Address: Box 309, Bluff, Utah 84512 (Close to the Four Corners where the borders of Utah, Arizona, New Mexico and Colorado meet, Bluff is about eighty-five miles south of Canyonlands National Park and 115 miles south of Arches. Monument Valley is forty-eight miles away.)
Telephone: 801–672–2281

Adventurous families can headquarter here to explore Indian ruins, go llama trekking into the backcountry (guided or on your own), take river raft trips, or simply relax around the pool. Your hosts will give you topographical maps and suggest places to go. Kids can lead llamas on lunchtime treks to ruins—a great motivator for kids who hate to hike! The homey lodge, in the tiny hamlet of Bluff (population 250) offers slide shows during the peak season, naturalist-guided tours, desert cookouts, and bird watching tips. Its Pioneer House is on the National Register of Historic Places.

Season: Year-round.

Accommodations: There are twenty-eight rooms in the main lodge and six in Pioneer house. The lodge has motel rooms and a one-bedroom kitchenette unit that sleeps four in a queen-size bed and a sleeper sofa. Pioneer House has an apartment that sleeps up to ten, and six private rooms that sleep two to six people.

Special Features: The lodge offers a geology slide show and naturalist-guided tours; overnight llama pack trips; an outdoor pool, hot tub, sauna, horseshoe pits, basketball court, and playground; vehicle shuttles for river runners, hikers, and bicyclists; and laundry facilities.

Cost: One-bedroom motel units with kitchenettes and private rooms in the Pioneer House $46 to $60 per night for a family of four. The Pioneer House apartment, which sleeps ten, $80 to $85 per night for four people; each additional person $5.

Llama treks $35 per llama per day. Overnight llama pack trips $150 per person per day; includes all meals. Interpretive tours of area $70 per day per person; shorter tours $40 per person. Four-wheel-drive tours $70 per person; includes lunch at a Navajo camp.

Nearby: You can hike to the Navajo Reservation and Fourteen Window Ruin, a 1,000-year-old Anasazi cliff dwelling, reached by a creaky suspension bridge over the San Juan River. The river runs through town and borders one edge of the lodge. Sand Island, four miles away, is the launch point for raft trips (the lodge can help you make reservations) and has a good swimming area for children. Comb Ridge, four miles west of town, is composed of eroded slickrock riddled with canyons and easily lends itself to independent exploring and climbing for all ages.

HOMESTEAD

Address: PO Box 99, 700 North Homestead Drive, Midway, Utah 84049
Telephone: 800–327–7220; 801–654–1102

Located just an hour from downhill ski resorts such as Snowbird and Alta, and just thirty minutes from Park City, Deer Valley, Sundance, and Wolf Mountain, Homestead is a classic country resort with cottages, condominiums, rooms, and suites scattered about beautifully landscaped grounds. It offers all-inclusive ski packages during the winter months, all-inclusive golf packages during the summer months, and other value packages throughout the year. Cross-country skiing trails head out from the resort and a trail pass is complimentary for guests in the winter, along with sleigh rides and snowmobile tours. In summer, an eighteen-hole golf course is a featured attraction. Guests can soak in the natural hot springs mineral pool, swim, ride horseback, explore the country lanes of rustic Heber Valley on bicycles, or play tennis and lawn games. Two restaurants and two casual eateries draw people from as far as Salt Lake City who come for the excellent food and pastoral ambiance. The original building on the Homestead property, the Virginia House, is on the National Register of Historic Places; guests can book a room in the 110-year-old structure. The Homestead is working with the Audubon Society to turn itself into a wildlife refuge.

Season: Year-round.

Accommodations: Over 122 guest rooms, suites, and condominiums are available. Guest rooms are furnished with king, queen, or double beds and full bath; suites are furnished with king-size bed, mini-refrigerator, and full bath; bed-and-breakfast rooms are furnished with king, queen, or double bed and bathroom with shower. Condominiums, a pricier option, have two to four bedrooms, two baths, fireplace, and kitchen.

Special Features: Eighteen-hole golf course, horseback riding, mountain bike rentals, private and group buggy rides, group wagon rides, indoor and outdoor pools, sauna, outdoor mineral bath, fitness room, lighted tennis courts, outdoor lawn games, video game room, children's play area, scuba diving, snowmobiling, group and private sleigh rides, snowshoeing, cross-country skiing, two full-service restaurants, and more.

Cost: Guest rooms $86 to $138; suites $155 to $304; bed-and-breakfast $85 to $139; condominiums $215 to $500. Golf $26 to $36 for 18 holes; horseback riding $16 per hour; mountain bikes $6 per hour; buggy wagon rides $6 per person; snowmobiling $35 per hour; sleigh rides $10 per person. Cross-country skiing is complimentary for lodging guests (does not include equipment rental).

Nearby: Boating, waterskiing, fishing, hiking, and downhill snow skiing.

YMCA OF THE ROCKIES

Address: Membership Office, Schlessman Center Executive Offices, Estes Park, Colorado 80511-2800
Telephone: 970–586–4444

People have been coming to the YMCA of the Rockies' two centers for three and four generations to enjoy one of the best-loved family vacation destinations. It is popular in winter months for skiing, ice-skating, snowshoeing, and sledding. During the summer families can take advantage of swimming, hiking, hayrides, horseback riding, and a supervised children's day camp. The YMCA of the Rockies has facilities in two locations in Colorado: Snow Mountain Ranch, built in the 1960s, in Winter Park, and Estes Park Center, in operation for more than eighty years, adjacent to the Rocky Mountain National Park.

Snow Mountain Ranch

An absolutely breathtaking setting on nearly 5,000 acres filled with lodgepole pines and spectacular views of the Indian Peaks and Gore ranges,

Snow Mountain is popular in winter for its cross-country skiing on more than sixty miles of groomed trails. Summer recreational pursuits include mountain biking, swimming, horseback riding, and a youth day camp. The program is supervised by college-age counselors trained by the center, and activities for children are organized by age group. Kids hike, take nature walks, play games, swim, play miniature golf, do arts and crafts projects, and much more.

Address: PO Box 169, Winter Park, Colorado 80482
Telephone: 970–887–2152
Season: Year-round.

Accommodations: More than forty cabins have kitchens and fireplaces and sleep five to twelve people. Four different lodges have rooms sleeping four or five people, and most have private baths. Many lodge rooms have two queen-size beds. Campsites and RV hookups also are available.

Special Features: In summer select mountain biking, hiking, horseback riding, pony rides, swimming in an indoor pool, a crafts center, miniature golf, and hayrides. Evening activities include campfires, movies, and square dancing. During the winter a ski rental shop is on the premises, downhill skiing is nearby, and the ranch offers sleigh rides and snowshoeing.

The children's program runs during the summer from 8:30 A.M. to 3:30 P.M. Half-day rates are an option.

Cost: Two-bedroom cabins $98 to $102. Blue Ridge Lodge unit (a room that sleeps five in bunks and a twin bed with a half bath and shared showers) $30 per night. Aspenbrook Lodge rooms (two double beds and one set of bunks, full bath, and phone) $39 to $59 per night. Indian Peaks Lodge rooms (two queen-size beds and a sofabed, full private bath and balcony) $86 per night. Discounts of up to twenty-five percent available for cabins and lodge rooms in early December and from April through the end of May.

Children's program $14 per day for the full-day program, $7 for half day. Horseback riding $15 per hour, white water rafting about $35 for a half-day trip; mountain bike rental $10 for a half day.

Nearby: Downhill skiing is available at the Winter Park and Silver Creek ski areas. Grand Lake Shadow Mountain Lake and the Lake Granby are a few miles away for fishing, sailing, and other water sports.

Estes Park Center

Estes Park is at a lower elevation (8,010 feet) amid mountain peaks, and hiking is popular here on trails that head into Rocky Mountain National Park, which borders the center's grounds. Other recreation options exceptional for their low prices include horseback riding, swimming, golf, and tennis, to name a few. In summer the children's programs for ages two-and-a-half through senior year in high school are a big draw with arts, crafts, swimming, horseback riding, miniature golf, rock climbing, rafting, ropes course, and an overnight camping trip. Teens plan their own activities with an emphasis on outdoor adventure and leadership development. White water raft trips and guided hikes into the national park can be arranged.

Address: 2515 Tunnel Road, Estes Park, Colorado 80511-2550
Telephone: 970–586–3341
Season: Year-round.

Accommodations: Two hundred housekeeping cabins are available. Many two- to four-bedroom housekeeping cabins have kitchens and fireplaces and sleep four to ten people. Five different lodges have rooms sleeping three to six people, all with private baths. Each lodge has a lounge with a stone fireplace where families can gather.

Special Features: Horseback riding, hayrides, indoor swimming pool, miniature golf, square dancing, tennis, arts and crafts, cross-country skiing, ice-skating, summer concerts.

Cost: In peak season, cabins $51 to $207 per night. Simple two-bedroom family cabins (with complete kitchen and fireplace) sleep five for $98 per night. Eastside Lodge $45 per night for three sets of bunks. Five-person rooms in the Wind River Lodge $84 per night. Discounts of up to twenty-five percent available off-season.

Prices for children's programs vary from $8 per half day to $130 for a week-long adventure, with extra charge for horseback riding, rafting, and mountain biking. Cost for these activities vary with the length of the activity.

Reservations: Both centers use a system of priorities in making reservations. "Cabin donors," people who have contributed to the cost of a cabin, get first priority. Second priority goes to members who pay $125 per year per family. Reservations are then open to nonmembers. Most requests are for July and August, so if you can plan your vacation for another time of year you will improve your chances of getting what you want. Be as flexible as you can by requesting either location and several options for date and cabin types.

PAHASKA TEPEE RESORT

Address: 183-R Yellowstone Highway, Cody, Wyoming 82414
Telephone: 800–628–7791; 307–527–7701

Put your own ranch vacation together, stage a family reunion, or just use this resort as headquarters on a visit to Yellowstone or the historic town of Cody. The original Pahaska Lodge was built by Buffalo Bill Cody himself and is listed on the National Register of Historic Places. A restaurant and tavern in the original lodge display some fascinating Buffalo Bill memorabilia, and the resort's convenient location is minutes from the entrance to Yellowstone and an hour from Cody. Guests can choose from hotel rooms in log cabins, a housekeeping cabin, or a family reunion lodge, and they can rent horses, play in the river, or book a river-rafting trip nearby.

Season: Year-round.

Accommodations: There are eighteen log buildings in the property, each divided into several hotel rooms with private entrances and private baths. Rooms in the main lodge and cabin rooms sleep one to six people. One housekeeping cabin is available with a fully equipped kitchen and two queen-size beds. A family reunion lodge has seven bedrooms and eleven queen-size beds as well as a deluxe kitchen, Jacuzzi, and more.

Special Features: Fishing and swimming in the cold river, horse rentals, rafting a few miles down the road. The resort also contains a restaurant and tavern, gift shop, gas station and grocery store, and rents snowmobiles for touring Yellowstone in the winter.

Cost: Lodge and cabin rooms $65 or $110 per night, depending on time of year. Simple housekeeping cabin $120 to $130 per night. Family reunion lodge $650 to $750 per night, $3,500 to $3,750 per week; it can sleep up to seven families in its seven bedrooms, so is well priced if you have a big group. Make reservations for reunion lodge about a year in advance. Horse rentals $15 per hour, half-day rides $50.

CHICO HOT SPRINGS

Address: PO Box 127, Pray, Montana 59065 (Twenty-five miles from Livingstone and thirty miles from the north entrance to Yellowstone; the nearest airport is at Bozeman, ninety minutes away.)
Telephone: 406-333-4933

Even on winter nights, you will find guests floating about in Chico Hot Springs' enormous pool and gazing at the spectacular canopy of a star-filled mountain sky. Miners used these springs in Montana's spectacular Paradise Valley for bathing and laundry when gold was discovered nearby in the late 1800s. A hotel was built in 1902 so that guests visiting Yellowstone could "take the waters." Part of that hotel still stands, but now guests stay in more modern facilities. Many families visit Chico on their way into or out of Yellowstone, but it is well worth visiting on its own merits. The warm, steamy waters of the Olympic-size pool and smaller, hot soaking pools are available to guests year-round, as are various types of soothing massages. If you tire of lazing around the pool you can rent horses or mountain bikes, take white water rafting trips, or go hiking or fishing. Mealtime possibilities include the resort's celebrated gourmet restaurant and a poolside grill and pasta bar. Motel-like units are available, as are housekeeping condominiums and a log house.

Accommodations: Lodge rooms have two double beds and either shared or private baths. A small condominium has a loft with three double beds plus a fully equipped kitchen, washer, dryer, and sauna. One larger condominium has a loft with three double beds and a private bedroom downstairs. The log house has a fully equipped kitchen and sleeps up to ten people in two private bedrooms with double beds, a sofabed, and rollaways.

Special Features: Horseback riding and mountain bike rentals, Olympic-size hot springs–fed mineral pool, and a smaller hot soaking pool next to it. White water rafting and fishing trips are available for an extra fee. The excellent restaurant serves breakfast and dinner with dishes such as roast duckling Grand Marnier, smoked trout, and beef wellington. The prices match the high-quality menus, but it is worth the splurge for a special treat. A poolside grill serves simpler and less expensive fare. Guests can dance to live music on weekends and go cross-country-skiing or dogsledding in winter.

Cost: Lodge rooms with two double beds and shared bath $39 to $60 per night for two people, $5 for each additional person over age five. Children five and under stay free. Rooms with private baths $69 to $85. Small condominiums or the log house $125 to $145 per night; large condominium $129 to $189. If you stay six nights you get the seventh night free. Horseback riding $12 per hour; river rafting $35 for adults, $20 for kids twelve and under for three-hour ride; mountain bike rental $5 per hour, $25 for all day; children's sizes available.

CHAIN-O-LAKES RESORT AND CONFERENCE CENTER

Address: One Country Lane, Cleveland, Texas 77327
Telephone: 713–592–2150

Twelve lakes with names including Camp Lake, Swim Lake, Skillet Lake, Corral Lake, and Crystal Lake offer some of the best family swimming and boating in the Lone Star State. The kids will want to spend most of their time at Swim Lake, a three-and-a-half-acre spring fed lake with inner tube rentals and a long, slippery water slide. Boats and canoes can be rented for use on the other lakes, and the facility also has guided horseback rides, nature trails, and excellent fishing. Low-priced cabins let you do your own cooking, or you can eat at the Hilltop Restaurant. Campsites and RV hookups are scattered throughout the lake areas. Tame alligators in the lakes can be spotted and love to be fed.

Season: Year-round.

Accommodations: Three types of cabins are available; all have kitchens, air-conditioning, and full baths. Rustic cabins and duplexes do not have dishes, utensils, or linens and are a bit tired, but are well priced; each accommodates up to six people. Duplexes can accommodate six people in one large room with two double beds and one set of bunks. Log cabins are pleasantly decorated and popular, especially on weekends. Wilderness campsites, RV hookups, and campsites with water and electricity are available as well. Because the various accommodations at this resort are spread out among twelve different lakes, it never feels as crowded as you might expect.

Special Features: An immense swimming lake, water slide, guided trail rides, pony rides, hayrides, golfing, horse-drawn carriage rides, boat and tube rentals, restaurant.

Cost: Rustic cabins $45 to $75 per night; duplex cottages $60 per night and lake area cabins $80 to $110 per night year-round; log cabins $120 to $150 per night in peak summer months, slightly less the rest of the year. Reservations required for all accommodations and for the restaurant. Guided trail rides $10; canoe and boat rentals $12.50 for four hours, $16.50 per day, $22 for twenty-four hours.

CENTRAL UNITED STATES

STILL WATERS CONDOMINIUM RESORT

Address: HCR 1 Box 928, Branson, Missouri 65616
Telephone: 800–777–2320, 417–338–2323

Branson, Missouri, is famous for its nonstop entertainment, and its country music shows, water parks, theme parks, and craft villages are only minutes from this well-equipped lakeside resort. Accommodations range from hotel rooms to spacious condominium suites. Families headquarter here to see the sights of Branson and fish and boat on Table Rock Lake. Most accommodations are a few steps from the water. There are fishing and water ski boats, pontoons, Waverunners and guided fishing trips right off Still Water's dock, or families can play in one of the three swimming pools complete with slides, diving boards, kiddie pools, and hot tubs. Tickets for the shows and other attractions can be purchased through the resort's "welcome center" at the same time that guests make room reservations.

Season: Year-round.

Accommodations: One-bedroom condominium suites sleep up to four, two-bedroom condominium suites sleep up to eight, and cottages sleep four to twelve people. Hotel rooms are also available. Most units have whirlpool baths.

Special Features: Game room, basketball, two playgrounds, horseshoe pits, two boat launches, tennis courts, sand volleyball courts, and a pavilion with barbecue grills.

Cost: Summer: one bedroom condominium suites $69 to $120 per night, double occupancy; two-bedrooms $129 to $159 for four people. Spring and Fall: one-bedroom $55 to $105; two-bedrooms $85 to $125; winter season about 15% less. Children five and under free, kids six and up $7 per child or adult per night.

OZARK MOUNTAIN RESORT SWIM AND TENNIS CLUB

Address: Route 4, Box 910, Kimberling City, Missouri 65686
Telephone: 800–225–2422, 417–779–5301

If you're bound for Branson, Missouri, the new country music capital of the world, you can stay at this full-service resort and fish, swim, boat, and play your heart's content all day long. Or, you can head to Silver Dollar City, a few miles away, or any number of fun family attractions and shows just minutes from your comfortable condominium. The resort is situated on a mountainside on the shores of Table Rock Lake. You can explore the beautiful Ozark countryside on horses from the resort's stables, hike, play miniature golf, tennis, or any number of games. Swimming is in the Olympic-size pool, or at the lakeside swimming beach. Golfers can enjoy a course at sister property Holiday Hills Resort and Golf Club.

Season: Year-round.

Accommodations: One-, two-, and three-bedroom condos have private patios and balconies, air-conditioning, and fully furnished kitchens.

Special Features: Covered boat dock, rental boats, stables and trail rides, children's play area, activity center, boat launch, walking trails, shuffle board, basketball, volleyball, archery range, fishing guide services.

Cost: One-bedroom condos $55 to $95 per night depending on season; two-bedroom condos $75 to $105; three bedroom luxury condo $135 to $175.

POTOWATOMI INN

Address: No. 6 Lane 100 A, Lake James, Angola, Indiana 46703
Telephone: 219–833–1077

The Potawatomi Inn, in Pokagon State Park on the shores of Lake James and Snow Lake, is a water lover's utopia with abundant opportunities for boating, swimming, and fishing. The Inn has been renovated recently and the complex has motel rooms, cabins, and inn rooms in several adjacent buildings. During the summer months you can go horseback riding, play tennis, and participate in the park's cultural arts programs. A fast and thrilling 178-foot twin toboggan run operates on winter weekends, reaching speeds of thirty-five to forty miles per hour! Once you've had your fill of zooming down the toboggan track, you can ice-skate, ice fish or cross-country ski. A full-time naturalist staff conducts activities throughout the park year-round.

Season: Year-round.

Accommodations: All units are air-conditioned and have private baths. Cabins, motel rooms, and inn rooms all have one or two double beds. Cabins are set in a wooded area; the three-story inn has an indoor pool and restaurant, and the motel units open on the parking lot. No accommodations have cooking facilities, but there is full-service restaurant in the inn for all guests.

Special Features: An indoor swimming pool is available for inn and cabin guests only. A lakeside swimming beach with diving boards and floats is supervised by lifeguards. The park's other amenities include tennis courts, playgrounds, picnic areas, hiking, fishing, naturalist programs, boat and horseback riding rentals. The toboggan slide operates from Thanksgiving through February.

Cost: Room rates are the same for inn and motel rooms with two double beds and cabins: $52 to $58 depending on day of week. Cribs and rollaway beds available for a small charge. Trail rides $10 per hour; rowboats $3 per hour; paddleboats $5 per hour.

FRENCH LICK SPRINGS RESORT

Address: French Lick, Indiana 47432 (One and a half hours from Indianapolis, three hours from Cincinnati.)
Telephone: 800–457–4042; 812–936–9300

Pamper yourself in the spa or pump up your cardiovascular system with a brisk game of tennis while the kids are amused and well-cared for in the Pluto Club, a program for five- to twelve-year-olds that operates from 11 A.M. to 5 P.M. daily during the summer and holidays. This enormous resort in a picturesque setting first started taking guests in 1842, and the current hotel was built in the early 1900s. It offers golf on two different eighteen-hole courses, and bowling in the 2,600-acre resort's very own bowling alley. During the warm-weather days you can swim in an Olympic-size outdoor pool; a retractable glass-domed indoor pool offers evening and year-round swimming. Thirty miles of horse trails extend from the fully equipped stables. There are five different restaurants to choose from but your kids will most appreciate the casual pizza joint for dinner and a stop at the old-fashioned ice-cream parlor for dessert.

Season: Year-round.

Accommodations: Standard hotel rooms have two queen-size beds; most have the same low price. Two-room suites can accommodate four or five people.

Special Features: Full scale spa, ten outdoor and eight indoor tennis courts, tennis clinics for adults and children, golf clinics, surrey rides, bicycle rental, miniature golf, chuck wagon dinner rides, children's activities, video game room, shuffleboard, badminton, volleyball, horseshoes, pool, pony rides, petting zoo.

Cost: Kids under 18 stay free in parents' room: double rooms, per night $79, suites $129. Golf $18 to $35 for eighteen holes; tennis $20 per hour (indoor), $10 per hour (outdoor); bowling $2 per game; riding $18 per 45-minute ride per person, $27 per 45-minute ride for adult and child. Pony rides $6; surrey rides, family $16, kids $4, adults $8.

Nearby: Boating and fishing a few minutes away on Patoka Lake.

CRYSTAL MOUNTAIN RESORT

Address: 12500 Crystal Mountain Drive, Thompsonville, Michigan 49683
Telephone: 800–968–7686; 616–378–2000

The Crystal Mountain area is a year-round paradise for outdoorsy families. It is best known as a winter ski area, with excellent downhill and cross-country skiing, but spring and summer have plenty of activities to keep you busy—swimming, canoeing, fishing, golfing, and hiking, to name a few. Crystal Mountain Resort is a full-service resort catering to families. It features a state-of-the-art conference center, twenty-seven holes of golf, a golf practice center, children's programs, tennis, mountain bike rentals, and trails for summer guests. Up to three children, age fifteen and under, sleep free when sharing two paying adults' accommodations from April through October.

Season: Year-round.

Accommodations: Hotel rooms, deluxe hotel rooms with kitchens, one-, two-, three-, and four-bedroom condominiums, and private homes.

Hotel rooms have two queen-size beds, microwave oven, and mini-refrigerator. Cots are available at no extra charge.

Special Features: Indoor pool and fitness center, outdoor pool, conference center, hiking and mountain biking trails, restaurant, chairlift rides, horse-drawn carriage rides, and children's programs. The children's programs include art projects, environmental activities, hikes, scavenger hunts, pond explorations, and local beach trips. Children between ages eight and thirteen can go on an overnight campout, leaving at 6 P.M. and returning the next morning.

Cost: Hotel room rates begin at $55 during the slow season and go up to $99 per night during the peak summer season. Extended stay discounts start with a four-night stay.

Nearby: Sleeping Bear Dunes is about 45 miles away (see page 182 for more on this area), Lake Michigan is 17 miles away, and Crystal Lake is 12 miles away. Horseback riding and river tubing about 30 minutes away, Interlochen Arts Academy is 16 miles away, and Traverse City is 30 miles away.

MISSION POINT RESORT

Address: 1 Lakeshore Drive, Mackinac Island, Michigan 49757
Telephone: 800–833–5583; 906–847–3312

Mission Point Resort crowns the southeastern shore of Mackinac Island, overlooking the Straits of Mackinac. The island is accessible only by ferry or private plane, and encompasses the nation's second-oldest park with lush pine forests woven with hiking and biking paths leading to vistas overlooking Lakes Huron and Michigan. With no cars allowed, horse-drawn carriages fill the streets. The resort has a complimentary children's program during the late spring and summer, and in the evening, entertainment overlooks sprawling green lawns that spill down to the shore. Kids twelve and under always eat free (off the children's menu with a paying adult), and kids eighteen and under stay free in their parents' room. The "Kid's Klub" is situated in a 3,000-square-foot activities center that contains a twelve-foot tepee and wooden climber. Children take excursions to the fort on the island, see live theater, play games, hear storytellers, and enjoy arts and crafts. Nightly horse-drawn wagon rides around the island are a specialty of the resort. The Family Adventure Package is a particularly good buy for families.

Accommodations: Standard rooms have two double beds; family doubles have two connecting bedrooms, one with a king-size bed and the other with two twins.

Special Features: Health club, fitness center, in-line skates, heated swimming pool, hayrides, bike rentals, kids' activity center and playground, kids' program, video arcade, live theater performances, restaurants, delis, volleyball.

Cost: The Family Adventure Package during the spring and summer offers two nights in a family double, tickets to Fort Mackinac, round-trip ferry tickets, one dinner, two breakfasts, and a sunset hayride around the island (from $95 per adult per night, kids twelve and under free, $40 per night for each teenager). Standard rooms $115 to $190 per night depending on day of week and season. Family doubles $155 to $245 per night.

Nearby: Horseback riding, historical sightseeing, golf courses.

THE VILLAGE INN AND RESORT

Address: 371 Ski Hill Road, PO Box 99, Lutsen, Minnesota 55612–0099
Telephone: 800–642–6036; 218–663–7241; fax 218–663–7920

Originally a downhill and cross-country ski resort, the addition of an eighteen-hole golf course and alpine slide that twists and turns down the ski mountain has turned this action-packed resort into a four-season destination. Week-long stays in two-bedroom townhouses offer the best value, giving families enough time to enjoy the many activities on the resort grounds as well as visit the nearby Boundary Waters Canoe Area (see page 180 for more on this area) and the charming town of Grand Marais. The alpine slide is indisputably the favorite with kids; you can't ride it just once. A chairlift takes you to the top of the slide, which is similar to a concrete luge track. There's a slow lane and a fast lane, and if your cart goes too fast, you can put on the brakes. A free children's program, Mountain Kids Camp, is available for four- to twelve-year-olds; check for days and times when you make your reservation, as the schedule changes throughout the season.

Season: Year-round.

Accommodations: Three types of accommodations are available. Two- to four-bedroom townhouses sleep six to twelve people and come fully equipped with all kitchen essentials and linens. Condominiums range from a one-room efficiency unit that sleeps four to a one-bedroom unit that sleeps six with loft, kitchen, fireplace, deck, and two full baths. The resort's lodge has the atmosphere of a bed-and-breakfast establishment, with each room decorated differently.

Special Features: In summer recreational amenities include the alpine slide, outdoor pool, indoor pool, whirlpools, sauna, tennis, volleyball, gondola rides, horseback riding, hayrides, pony rides, eighteen-hole golf course, hiking trails, and mountain bike rental. A free children's program includes arts and crafts, nature talks, and hikes. Naturalist programs operate during the summer. Bonfires are held nightly, depending on weather. Downhill skiing, snowshoeing, cross-country skiing, and sleigh rides are available in winter.

Cost: Week-long stays in two-, three-, and four-bedroom townhouse units $725 to $1,600, depending on size; nightly stays $115 and up. The condominiums cost $75 to $165 per night, depending on size, time of year, and day of week. Lodge rooms $55 to $125, depending on time of year and day of week. One-day activity pass that includes alpine slide, gondola, and mountain bike rides $20; alpine slide $3.75 per ride, five-ride pass $12.50; horseback riding $20 per person; pony rides for $5 children under seven; hayrides $8 adults, $6 kids.

BAREFOOT BAY RESORT

Address: 279 South Lake Street, Elkhart Lake, Wisconsin 53020
Telephone: 800–345–7784; 847–816–7800 (reservations office); 414–876–3323 (resort); fax 414–876–3484

If your ideal vacation is to lounge around the pool with a great novel or take a leisurely sail around the lake while the kids are off having fun with others their own age, this could be the place for you. Barefoot Bay has a supervised kids' program with activities each morning, afternoon and evening. Two meals a day and all recreational activities (except boating) are included in one low price. This old-fashioned family resort often hosts family reunions.

Season: Memorial Day to Labor Day.

Accommodations: Standard, superior, and deluxe rooms are available, all with air-conditioning and private baths. Standard rooms have one or two double beds; the larger standard rooms can hold a cot or a crib. Superior rooms, a little larger than standard rooms, usually have two double beds and a sofabed or room for a cot or crib. Deluxe rooms, in the newest building near the pools, have two double beds and plenty of room for a cot or a crib. Barefoot Bay has a total of 150 rooms.

Special Features: Indoor and outdoor swimming pool, lake swimming, tennis, miniature golf, family theme nights with entertainment, aerobics classes, softball, volleyball, croquet, horseshoes, shuffleboard— all are included in the rate. Waterskiing, jet skis, pontoons, tubes, paddleboats, mini-speedboats, and canoes are available at an additional charge.

The children's program is divided by age group with separate counselors for each one: Turbo Tykes (three to five), Happy Campers (six to eight), Tweens (nine to twelve), and Teens. Activities vary by age group but generally include stories, games, nature walks, arts and crafts, field games, and swimming at the beach.

Nightclub shows run every evening, and children three and over are supervised in an evening program until the show's end. Shows vary throughout the week; musical reviews are a staple.

Cost: Several packages are available for two, three, five, or seven nights. Rates vary according to type of room. Seven-night stay for adults $616 to $825 per person. Two-night stays $195 to $255 per person; three-night stays $290 to $385 per person. Daily rates for children sharing a room with parents include two meals and the recreational program: age thirteen to seventeen $21, age eight to twelve $19, age three to seven $15, age two and under free. Discounted rates available at certain times of year; inquire when booking.

THE POLYNESIAN

Address: 857 North Frontage Road, PO Box 388, Wisconsin Dells, Wisconsin 53965-0388
Telephone: 800–272–5642; 608–254–2883

The Wisconsin Dells is partyland for kids. Packed with waterparks, waterski shows, a circus museum, wax museums, boat tours, miniature golf courses, train rides, go-carts, and amusements of all types, it's about as far from a quiet cabin-at-the-lake vacation as you can get, and your kids will love it. The Polynesian is a resort and waterpark rolled into one. For the price of lodging, you get over three acres of outdoor water activities and two 8,000-square-foot indoor pool areas. The Mighty Buccaneer, a forty-foot pirate ship, has cargo nets to climb, water slides, shooting streams of water, and places to explore; there are rock waterfalls with hidden caves, geysers and showers spouting at every turn, a sand area with slides and swings, and much more. Kids are splashed, sprayed, and soaked, while their parents relax in the hot tub, or on a comfortable deck chair. Rates are highest during the summer, but the indoor water fun makes it a great buy the rest of the year.

Season: Year-round. The awesome outdoor pool complex is open Memorial Day to Labor Day only.

Accommodations: All rooms have mini-refrigerators and microwaves. Double queens have two queen-size beds; a double suite is one large room with two queen beds and a living area with a sofa sleeper; a two-bedroom suite has two private bedrooms, one with a king-size and one with two queen-size beds, a living area with a sofa sleeper, and a mini-kitchen. The Polynesian is designed for families, and most rooms accommodate four or more people.

Special Features: Pools, sauna, whirlpool, game room, restaurant and bar.

Cost: Costs vary, depending on season: double queen $80 to $140; double suite $105 to $180; two-bedroom suite $160 to $275.

QUARTZ MOUNTAIN RESORT

Address: Lonewolf, Oklahoma 73655 (twenty miles north of Altus)
Telephone: 405-563-2424

An endless selection of diversions awaits families at this sprawling state park resort. Choose from pool and lake swimming, an eighteen-hole golf course, boating and fishing on Lake Altus-Lugert, tennis, miniature golf, hiking, lawn games, two thrilling water slides, and kiddie rides in the fun park. Kids eighteen and under stay free when sharing their parents' lodge accommodations; families also can stay in one- or two-bedroom cabins. During the summer in-park naturalists and recreation staff offer organized activities, including nature hikes, bird watches, scavenger hunts, dances, movies, arts and crafts activities, water aerobics, evening storytelling, ice-cream socials, and marshmallow roasts around the campfire.

The resort is booked by the Oklahoma Arts Institute for special student programs through most of June.

Season: Year-round.

Accommodations: Lodge rooms sleep two to three people and one- and two-bedroom cabins sleep four to six. They provide full kitchens (with microwaves instead of conventional ovens) and all linens, but you must provide your own cookware and dishes. A dormitory unit for family reunions and other large groups has a kitchen and a living room and can sleep sixty-four people.

Special Features: Many of the recreational activities are free; boat rental, the fun park, water slides, eighteen-hole golf, and miniature golf require a nominal fee (see below). Ping-Pong, badminton, tennis, basketball, archery (with supervision), fishing, paddleboating, go-carts, and other activities are also available.

Cost: Two-bedroom cottages in summer $85 to $90 per night, depending on size; rates lower before May 15 and after September 15. Lodge rooms $60 to $75 per night; suites $125 per night. Family reunion lodge $650 per night. Paddleboats and canoes $3 for thirty minutes; go-carts $3 for five minutes; kiddie bumper boats $1 to $2 for five minutes;

eighteen-hole miniature golf course $3 per person; water slide $3 for thirty minutes. Eighteen-hole golf course $8 to $11.

Nearby: Museum of the Western Prairie in Altus, Wichita Mountains Wildlife Refuge, Anadarko's Indian City.

THE SOUTH

GASTON'S WHITE RIVER RESORT

Address: No. 1 River Road, Lakeview, Arkansas, 72642
Telephone: 501–431–5202

No one ever leaves empty-handed after fishing on a stretch of the White River, known for its prolific rainbow and brown trout. Gaston's Resort, situated on several hundred acres in the Ozark Mountains of Arkansas, is paradise for any family that likes to fish, swim, or float along the water. Bull Shoals Lake, a short distance away, offers small- and largemouth bass fishing. When you tire of reeling in the big ones, head to the swimming pool, tennis court, or sprawling playground. Private housekeeping cottages all have kitchens, but plan to eat a few delicious home-cooked meals in Gaston's award-winning restaurant overlooking the river. Its quirky decor, with antiques of all types lining the walls and vintage bicycles hanging from the ceiling, will silence the squirmiest young diner until dinner is served.

Season: Year-round.

Accommodations: Motel rooms have two double beds and a small kitchen area; maid service is provided. Private housekeeping cottages have kitchenettes. They range in size from a studio to a two-bedroom family cabin with private bath, fully equipped kitchen, and living room with fireplace. All couches in cabin accommodations convert into double beds. Children under six stay free.

Special Features: Activities center on trout fishing; there is also a nature trail, swimming pool with large deck area, conference lodge, tennis court, playground, game room, restaurant, gift shop, and sporting goods shop. Fishing guides can be hired for half- and all-day boat trips.

Cost: Motel rooms $66 to $80 for double. Housekeeping cottages with kitchens $85 (studio) to $95 (two-bedroom). Larger cottages have four to ten bedrooms and cost $225 to $775 per night.

F. D. ROOSEVELT STATE PARK

Address: 2970 Highway 190 East, Pine Mountain, Georgia 31822
Telephone: 800–864–7275 for reservations; 706–663–4584

This 10,000-acre state park on Pine Mountain has a museum that includes Franklin D. Roosevelt memorabilia, tours, and programs. Roosevelt founded the Little White House in nearby Warm Springs after being stricken with polio in the 1920s. Park visitors can stay in stone cottages on a picturesque ridge or cottages perched along sparkling Delano Lake for their stay in this beautiful, history-filled area. Water sports enthusiasts can swim in the large pool or explore and fish in two different lakes. Beginning and advanced riders can take guided trail rides on gentle mounts. Thirty-five miles of hiking trails and interpretive walks wind through the park. The popular Callaway Gardens is a short drive away.

Season: Year-round.

Accommodations: Twenty-one cottages with one or two bedrooms are available. All are equipped with complete kitchens, heat, and air-conditioning. One-bedroom cottages sleep two to five people; two-bedroom cottages sleep four to eight people.

Special Features: Swimming pool, ball fields. A summer-only naturalist program includes family campfires, nature talks, and a hands-on junior ranger program with crafts; trips to lakes, streams, and tributaries; walks in the woods; and bird and reptile identification. Most of the programs are free or have a minimal charge.

Cost: In summer one-bedroom cabins $60 per night Sunday through Thursday and $70 Friday and Saturday nights. Two-bedroom cabins $70 per night Sunday through Thursday, $80 Friday and Saturday; $10 per night less off-season. Reservations are taken eleven months in advance, but those who call thirty days in advance often find cancellations. Flat-bottom fishing boat rental $5 per hour; horseback rides $18 per hour; swimming pool $3 per person.

Nearby: Callaway Gardens has world-renowned rhododendron and azalea gardens, a butterfly center where visitors can walk amid the colorful flying insects, golf courses, exhibits on horticulture, and a vegetable and herb garden. Six Flags Over Georgia is nearby and Atlanta is just over an hour away. The Little White House, about twelve miles away in Warm Springs, is the former home of Franklin D. Roosevelt.

HICKORY KNOB STATE RESORT PARK

Address: Route 1, Box 199-B, McCormick, South Carolina 29835
Telephone: 864–391–2450

Playing eighteen holes at this golf resort, one of the state's finest, will cost you about $15. Many of Hickory Knob's guests are hard-core golfers, but when they're not golfing, you might find them fishing for bass, yellow perch, and crappies in Strom Thurmond Lake, swimming in the pool, or trying their hand at skeet or archery. Lodge rooms, cabins, campgrounds, or the historic Guillebeau House can accommodate guests, but families will find the cabins the most economical and best suited to their needs. A staff "recreator" on the year-round recreation staff organizes children's activities through the summer; these include Frisbee golf, birdhouse construction, nature walks, and various arts and crafts activities.

Season: Year-round.

Accommodations: Lodge rooms have two double or two twin beds. Suites have small kitchens and sleep up to four in a bedroom and a living room. Cabins, which accommodate up to six people with two double beds and a sofabed in the living room, have fully equipped kitchens, and all linens are provided. One-week rentals are available June through August only. The two-bedroom historic Guillebeau House, a log cabin built in the 1700s, has one bedroom downstairs and one upstairs, two baths, a living room, and a front porch; it accommodates four people.

Special Features: Swimming pool, eighteen-hole golf course, putting green, playground, nature trail, badminton, horseshoes, volleyball, skeet range, summer activities for kids, stick ball, Frisbee golf, archery, tennis, restaurant, gift shop.

Cost: May through August, lodge rooms $40, suites $80 per night. September to April, rooms $36, suites $72 per night. Rollaway beds $2 per night. One-bedroom cabins $50 per night, $300 per week. Guillebeau House $80 per night, $480 per week. Children under twelve stay free in parents' rooms. Green fees for golf $12 to $16, depending on season. Johnboats $10 per day, no motor.

HIGH HAMPTON INN AND COUNTRY CLUB

Address: 640 Hampton Road, Cashiers, North Carolina 29717
Telephone: 704–743–2411

High Hampton's pedigree as the quintessential southern resort is a long one. Loyal guests started spending summers at the Blue Ridge Mountain home of a Civil War general in 1922. It has managed to retain much of its tradition-laden charm and all of its hospitality. Guests who vacationed here as children in the thirties, forties, or fifties will find the inn's wide verandas, rocking chairs, gardens of blazing azaleas, and mirror-clear lake invulnerable to the passage of time. An American plan resort, High Hampton offers a children's program during June, July, and August. Parents can enjoy an eighteen-hole golf course, tennis, hiking, sailing, boating, or swimming while the kids keep busy with others their own age. The children's program for ages four to twelve runs from 9 A.M. to 2 P.M. and from 6 to 9 P.M. Supervised daytime activities include games, arts and crafts, nature walks, swimming, boating, donkey cart rides, and more. The evening program includes dinner followed by a hayride, games, stories, or a movie. June is the most economical month to visit, as room prices are discounted.

Season: April through November.

Accommodations: Guests stay at the inn or rent rooms in cottages scattered around the grounds. All accommodations have private baths. Children can share rooms with their parents for reduced fees. Most inn rooms have two double beds. Cottages, rented by the week, have fully equipped kitchens and two baths; they sleep six in two bedrooms and a sleeping loft. Rollaway beds and cots are available.

Special Features: Eighteen-hole golf course, eight tennis courts, lake swimming (with small sandy beach and playground nearby), sailing, canoeing, rowboating and paddleboating, fishing, hiking trail, fitness trail, bird watching, croquet, badminton, darts, volleyball, archery.

Cost: Inn rooms include three daily meals and all tips. On Friday and Saturday, rooms sleeping four $89 per person per night for the first two people, $60 per person per night for the third and fourth person. Sunday through Thursday, $56 per person per night for the third and fourth person. Children under six in room with two adults $48 per night. Two-bedroom cottages $1,600 per week in June, July, and August; $1,162 in April, May, September, and October.

Children's program $2 per child per hour. Golf course $26 per day per person; tennis $5 per person per hour. Paddleboats, canoes, rowboats, and Sunfish $5 per hour.

LAKE CUMBERLAND STATE RESORT PARK

Address: 5465 State Park Road, Jamestown, Kentucky 42629
Telephone: 800–325–1709; 502–343–3111

Fifty thousand acres of shimmering water and miles of virgin shoreline makes this one of Kentucky's finest fishing and pleasure boating areas.

Its marina rents reasonably priced houseboats, ski boats, and pontoons; a stable on the park grounds runs guided trail rides through beech, oak, and hickory forests. Deer, racoons, and squirrels wander through the resort regularly. A planned recreation program with guided nature hikes, movies, arts and crafts, and water games runs from Memorial Day to Labor Day.

Season: Year-round.

Accommodations: Wildwood Cottages have woodland settings. Most have one or two bedrooms with a double and a single bed in each, a fully equipped kitchen, living and dining areas, air-conditioning, and a back porch with an outdoor grill. Linens are provided. Lure Lodge has sixty-three rooms, each with two double beds, a private bath, and a spectacular view of the lake from a private balcony. Camping is also available.

Special Features: Indoor and outdoor swimming pool, exercise room, hot tub, game room, dining room, gift shop, convention center, marina with 100 open slips, fishing, a nine-hole par-three golf course, miniature golf, tennis courts, horseback riding, four miles of hiking trails, planned recreation, nature center, grocery store, picnic shelters.

Cost: Lodge rooms $70; children sixteen and under stay free in parents' room. One-bedroom cottages $85; two-bedroom cottages $95 per night in summer, lower the rest of the year. Miniature golf $2 per game, nine-hole golf $7 for all-day play (club rentals available); horseback riding (Memorial Day to Labor Day) $9 per hour-long guided trail ride. Seven styles and sizes of houseboats are available, all with slides: houseboats that can accommodate eight people; four-night mid-week $805 to $1,410, depending on season. Larger boats priced higher. Weekend stays available.

BLUEWATER BAY

Address: 1950 Bluewater Boulevard, Niceville, Florida 32578
Telephone: 800–874–2128 (U.S.); 904–897–3613 (in Florida)

A low-priced Family Vacation Summer Fun Package makes Bluewater Bay, across the Choctawhatchee Bay from the Gulf Coast, one of the most economical of all full-service family resorts. This gigantic residential/resort development includes condominiums, permanent residences, and villas for rent. A children's program, which operates as part of the Summer Fun Package, has special activities for preschoolers, school-age children, and teenagers during the day and on certain evenings. Beachcombers head across the bridge to an island beach a short drive away. Golf and tennis enthusiasts should look into special package arrangements that combine golf or tennis with lodging and other recreational options.

Season: Year-round.

Accommodations: The family package houses guests in one-, two-, or three-bedroom condominiums with all linens and full-size, fully equipped kitchens.

Special Features: Four championship nine-hole golf courses, nineteen tennis courts with two different playing surfaces, playground, private bayside beach, four swimming pools, nature and bike trails, fishing, deep-water marina with boat rental, bike rentals, a restaurant serving breakfast, lunch, and dinner.

Cost: Family Vacation Summer Fun Packages starting at $700 per seven-day week include accommodations, daily supervised activities for children, free weekly tennis clinics, reduced court and green fees, and breakfast or lunch for the family. For the golfing family, children under sixteen play free with parents.

GULF STATE PARK RESORT

Address: 20115 State Highway 135, Gulf Shores, Alabama 36542
Telephone: 205–948–PARK for cabin information and reservations;
800–544–GULF or 205–948–4853 for resort hotel information and
reservations

One of Alabama's six state resort parks, Gulf State Park Resort has the warm salt waters of the Gulf of Mexico on one side and a large freshwater lake on the other. The resort hotel facility borders two and a half miles of unspoiled white sand beach on the Gulf of Mexico, and every room has a private balcony overlooking the water. Cabin accommodations across from the resort overlook the lake. A number of rooms in the resort have kitchenettes; other facilities include a swimming pool, fishing pier, tennis courts, restaurants, and poolside bar serving drinks and snacks. Across the street on the lake side, guests can enjoy an eighteen-hole championship golf course, tennis courts, a swimming beach, boating, and biking. Special programs for children operate during the summer with nature talks, story time, sand castle building, fishing, beach walks, lake studies, and a junior ranger program. Guests can check out recreation equipment for lawn games free of charge.

Season: Year-round.

Accommodations: Standard rooms in the resort hotel have two double beds; kitchenette units have one double bed and a small kitchen; two-room suites have a kitchen. All have private balconies overlooking the Gulf. Modern cabins on Lake Shelby have fully equipped kitchens and two or three bedrooms; all linens are supplied. Rustic cabins, built in the 1930s, are in the woods and include one big room with a kitchen area, heat, and air-conditioning. Campsites are available.

Special Features: Two and a half miles of white sand beaches, 825-foot fishing pier, swimming pool, 500-acre freshwater lake (with fishing, boating, and swimming), tennis, golf, nature center, playground, bicycling, hiking.

Cost: All hotel and cabin guests have access to lake fishing and boat launching, swimming pool, beach area, and tennis courts.

Resort: Children twelve and under stay free; each child over twelve $6 additional per night. In peak summer season standard rooms $99, and one-room kitchenette units $105; suites (which sleep six to eight people) $199. In spring and fall standard rooms $69, one-room kitchenette units $73, suites $139. In winter standard rooms $49, one-room kitchenette units $53, suites $99 per night.

Cabins: Seven-night minimum stay in June, July, and August. Nightly rates March through October: rustic cabins $55 to $75 per night, modern cabins $85 to $120; price varies by size of cabins. Off-season (November through February) rates are considerably lower, usually by half. Note that cabins fill faster than resort rooms.

Johnboats $7.50 per day; green fees for eighteen holes of golf $18 per person per day, $32 with a golf cart. You need a fishing license to fish, which you can buy at the pier or boathouse.

OGLEBAY RESORT

Address: Wheeling, West Virginia 26003
Telephone: 800–624–6988; 304–242–3000

Oglebay, a 1,500-acre resort in northern West Virginia, started life as a farm and summer getaway of Colonel Earl Oglebay, who willed his property to the citizens of Wheeling for recreational and educational purposes. It has remained strong in both areas, offering guests indoor and outdoor swimming pools, hiking and jogging trails, three golf courses, and eleven tennis courts, plus a zoo, model train display, greenhouse, and nature center. Families can stay in its 204-room lodge or opt for one of its forty-nine comfortable cabins. Oglebay offers many package deals throughout the year. Smart shoppers should always ask what special deals are available when they call.

Season: Year-round.

Accommodations: Lodge rooms and two types of cabins are available. The standard two- to four-bedroom family cabin sleeps up to twelve people and has a fireplace, fully equipped kitchen, phones, and one bath. The Oglebay family deluxe cabins sleep fourteen to twenty-six people. All cottages include a fully equipped kitchen, spacious living and dining area, fireplace, air-conditioning, and color television.

Special Features: Oglebay has golf, tennis courts, swimming pools, Jacuzzi, paddleboats, zoo, miniature golf, nature center, hiking, fishing, riding lessons, train, amphitheater entertainment, arboretum, and cascading waters fountain show. Guests who purchase package deals get free or reduced admission to some activities.

Cost: Oglebay offers many packages throughout the year, but one of the most popular with families is the weekday Summer Package: Adults pay $130 per night, double occupancy, and rates include tennis, miniature golf, par-three golf, paddleboating, zoo admission, swimming, and a buffet breakfast. Kids stay free in parents' room; all-day activity wristbands can be purchased for children for $10 per day.

Standard cottages with four bedrooms sleeping eight to fifteen people $600 to $675 (September through May) or $725 to $850 (June through August) per week. Deluxe cottages with two bedrooms sleeping sixteen $935 (September through May) or $1,050 (June through August) per week. Lodge rooms with two double beds $89 to $109 per night in peak summer season.

CACAPON RESORT

Address: Berkeley Springs, West Virginia 25411
Telephone: 304–258–1022

Families and family reunion groups come back again and again to experience the natural beauty of this well-appointed state park with a range of well-priced accommodations. Its 6,115 acres of open fields, gently undulating mountains, and a sparkling lake offer endless recreational opportunities. An eighteen-hole championship golf course (designed by Robert Trent Jones) and tennis courts keep many parents amused, while children enjoy swimming at the lake under the watchful eye of a lifeguard during the summer months. A summer naturalist and recreation director keeps the kids busy with nature hikes, arts and crafts, organized sports, and a junior naturalist program. Families can rent rowboats or paddleboats and try a little fishing, ride horses, or explore the ridges and valleys of this magnificent natural setting.

Season: Year-round; some cabins are available only in summer.

Accommodations: Three types of accommodations are available: cabins, the Cacapon Inn, and a motel-like lodge. Three styles of cabins can be rented: eleven modern cabins have large living rooms, fireplaces, fully equipped kitchens, heat, all linens, and two or four bedrooms.

Thirteen older "standard cabins" have lofts or two bedrooms, all linens, fireplaces, heat, and fully equipped kitchens. Six one-room "efficiency cabins" have a small kitchen area equipped with all cookware and dishes, built-in bunk beds, all linens, a small bath with a shower, and a screened porch. The Cacapon Inn, built in the 1930s, has eleven double rooms with private or shared baths and is comfortable for families with older kids staying in a room separate from their parents. A group kitchen can be used by all inn guests. The lodge has forty-nine comfortable motel rooms with private baths and a restaurant.

Special Features: Lake swimming with lifeguards on duty (summer only), rowboat and paddleboat rentals, golf, fishing, tennis, horse rental, shuffleboard, volleyball, croquet, hiking trails, year-round nature and recreation program.

Cost: Modern cabins $515 per week for four people, $625 per week for eight people April through October; nightly rates $85 to $120, depending on size of cabin and day of week. Standard cabins $335 per week for two to $475 per week for six April 15 through October; nightly rates $55 to $95. Economy cabins $250 per week for four people Memorial Day weekend through Labor Day; nightly rates $40 to $55, depending on day of week. Cacapon Inn rooms $31 to $40 per night. Reservations are taken up to a year in advance and summer weekend cabin rentals are especially popular.

Guided horseback rides $14 per hour; golf $13 for nine holes and $22 for eighteen holes; rowboat and paddleboat rentals $6 per hour. Small fee for swimming. Lake fishing requires a license, which you can buy from the park office.

THE NORTHEAST

SILVER BAY ASSOCIATION

Address: Silver Bay, New York 12874 (ninety minutes from Albany and twenty minutes from Ticonderoga)
Telephone: 518–543–8833

Amid the forests and wide green lawns along Lake George, Silver Bay has long captivated vacationers with its pristine beauty. Guests originally arrived by steamboat, and their luggage was transported by horse-drawn carriage to their lodgings. Many of the original native Adirondack wood and stone buildings remain and are listed on the National Register of Historic Places. Silver Bay's recreational options rival those of the most costly resorts. You must join the Silver Bay Association in order to use the facilities and participate in programs. Silver Bay books conferences throughout the summer, but families may stay when there is extra space, and two weeks in August are set aside just for families.

Season: Year-round.

Accommodations: An inn, twelve lodges, and twenty-three cottages provide sleeping accommodations for up to 800 people.

Special Features: Two gymnasiums, art center, boating (sailboats, rowboats, and canoes), library, crafts center, chapel, six tennis courts, two beaches, swimming, basketball, field and water sports, lawn bowling, aerobics, volleyball, weight training, archery, boat cruises, and supervised age-group programs for babies through teens (summer only), day care program, fitness center and climbing wall (year-round), shuffleboard, hiking; ice-skating, cross-country skiing, snowshoeing in winter.

Cost: Membership in the Silver Bay Association $50 per year for individuals and $100 per year for families. Housekeeping cottages (with kitchens) $582 to $1,404 per week; includes program fees. When more people occupy a cottage than there are beds, there is a fee of $50 per person. American plan is available in certain facilities (includes room, meals, and program fees) $325 to $575 per adult depending on accommodations. Children four to twelve are half the adult price. Children under four stay free. There is a twenty-percent discount on room and board rates for first-time visitors.

CANOE ISLAND LODGE

Address: Box 144, Diamond Point, New York 12824
Telephone: 518–688–5592

Located on Lake George with its own private island less than a mile away, Canoe Island Lodge has excellent swimming, boating, and a European Alpine atmosphere. A huge flotilla of boats takes guests to the gentle, sandy beach at the island or runs them around the lake. If you want a relaxing ride choose the slow, forty-person flat-bottom passenger boat, or if the wind is up, try one of the thirty-foot sailboats. Thrill seekers will want a turn waterskiing behind the ski-nautique boat. A two-hundred-foot beach on the mainland has excellent swimming, and a gently sloping sandy beach on the island is perfect for young children. Families can stay in chalet-type lodgings or quaint log cabins; one family has come back year after year for five generations to relax at this warm and friendly American plan resort.

Season: Mid-May to mid-October.

Accommodations: Most of the accommodations are chalet or bungalow rooms with private baths and windows on three sides. Many rooms have two twin-size and a queen-size bed and are spacious for families. Families with older children may prefer two rooms with a connecting bath. Two-bedroom log cabins with a fireplace and small kitchen area are perfect for four or five people. There is a three-night minimum.

Special Features: Four large sailboats, cruise boats, and aluminum boats are at guests' disposal (a staff member drives); tennis courts, Ping-Pong, waterskiing, square dancing, variety show, social dancing, fishing on the lake. Directed children's programs include arts and crafts and nature experiences. One night each week, usually Thursday, the island has a barbecue for all guests.

Cost: Peak season rates from July to Labor Day include lodging, breakfast and dinner, and all activities (off-season, lunches also are included). Adults $540 to $900 per person per week, depending on type of accommodations. Family rate: first two people in room pay the full rate; children three to six $190 per week, seven to twelve $285, under two $100. A third adult in a room pays three-quarters of the regular rate.

FIELDSTONE FARM

Address: PO Box 528, Cooperstown, New York 13326
Telephone: 800–336–4629; 315–858–0295

Friendly informality describes Fieldstone Farm's atmosphere, and judging by the number of repeat guests, the staff definitely is doing something right. You can turn the kids loose to explore its 170 acres of fields, ponds, and forests, since it's in such a rural locale. City children enjoy catching frogs and boating around the seven-acre pond on the property and swimming in the pool. Parents enjoy the scenic beauty and the rural atmosphere; parents and kids both like the fact that it's just minutes away from the Baseball Hall of Fame in Cooperstown. Wildlife roams through the area; wild geese swim in the pond; guests can spot deer and turtles, play games, and take hikes.

Season: Accommodations can be booked year-round, but most of the activities are available mid-May to mid-October only.

Accommodations: Six apartments and thirteen cottages have complete kitchens and range from a studio to a three-bedroom unit that sleeps eight. Guests may bring their own linen for greatest economy, or may rent with linens furnished. Most units are set up for families with a combination of queen-size or double and twin beds.

Special Features: Outdoor swimming pool, two stocked ponds for fishing and frog hunting, paddle boats and rowboats, kayaks, tennis,

shuffleboard, playground, grassy games area, basketball, volleyball, Ping-Pong, indoor game room with bumper pool, Foosball, and more.
Cost: During the peak season (Memorial Day through Labor Day weekends) one- to three-bedroom apartments or cottages $60 to $100 per day, $300 to $650 per week. Preference is given to weekly reservations from July 4 to late August, but shorter stays are sometimes available. Boat rental $4 per hour.
Nearby: Baseball Hall of Fame (see page 313).

TIMBERLOCK

Address: Indian Lake, Sabael, New York 12864 (summer); RR1, Box 630, Woodstock, Vermont 05091 (winter). (Timberlake is ten miles south of Indian Lake Village, five hours from New York City, five-plus hours from Boston.)
Telephone: 518–648–5494 (summer); 802–457–1621 (winter)

Rustic but not rough, this small Adirondack summer resort maintains a camp tradition that started in 1922. Timberlock's cabins, heated by woodstoves and lit by old-time gas lamps, are tucked among the pines along Indian Lake's wilderness shore. Seventy-five percent of its guests return year after year for the unpretentious atmosphere, good food, and myriad water sports. In summer the dining room is a covered porch with sweeping views of the lake; farm-style meals are simple, hearty, and healthy. Nightly campfires, sing-alongs and moonlight canoe rides are favorite evening activities. The large log lodge has a huge stone fireplace, games, puzzles, and a small library for guests. Children congregate on the sand beach at the center of camp, which has a giant rubber raft, a rope swing, and several docks. Rates include three meals a day.
Season: Late June through Labor Day.
Accommodations: There are ten cabins right at the water's edge. One-room cabins are available with or without baths (bathhouses are nearby). A family cottage with two to three bedrooms is available for larger groups. Linens are provided for all units, which have comfortable beds, screened porches, and wood stoves, but no electricity.
Special Features: The sandy beach along the lake is perfect for building sand castles, and guests can swim out to a raft. Canoes, sailboats (lessons are available), rowboats, kayaks and windsurfers are complimentary; fishing motorboats can be rented. There are facilities for tennis, badminton, archery, horseshoes, volleyball, and basketball. Waterskiing is free on Sunday afternoon; a fee is charged at other times. Fishing is excellent for rock bass, perch, northern pike, and lake trout. Staff can be hired to baby-sit in the evenings but not during the day. With enough

advance notice, daytime baby-sitting on site can be arranged with a town resident.

Cost: American plan, per person per week: adults $685 in family cottage or one-room cabin with bath, $655 in one-room cabin without bath. Children twelve to fourteen or the third or fourth adult in a cottage $535, ages eight to eleven $440, two to seven $325; under two free. Nightly, $95 to $120 per adult; two-night minimum stay.

Western riding $19 per 45-minute ride; rides offered daily except Saturday. Staff will meet buses in Indian Lake Village.

Nearby: Storytown, ice caves at Chimney Point, beaver pond.

CHALFONTE

Address: 301 Howard Street, Cape May, New Jersey 08204 (at the lower end of the Atlantic Peninsula, three and a half hours from New York City)
Telephone: 609–884–8409; fax 609–884–8409

This Victorian landmark hotel in one of the oldest seashore resorts on the Atlantic coast is known for its dinner theater and classical music concerts and a children's workshop series that runs for two weeks during the summer. It makes for one memorable vacation, rich in cultural exposure and seaside fun for young and old. The entire town of Cape May (see page 264 for more on this area), noted for its gingerbread Victorian architecture and famous lighthouse, is on the National Register of Historical Places, and the Chalfonte is one of its liveliest places for families. Room rates include dinner and breakfast, and children stay free in parents' rooms, with an additional charge only for meals. Dinner might be crab cakes à la Chalfonte or southern fried chicken, and the Virginia country buffet breakfast table is often laden with spoonbread, homemade biscuits, eggs, fresh fish, bacon, juice, and coffee. A separate dining room for children six and under allows adults to enjoy their meals in peace. After the children finish eating, they can play in the backyard playground under the watchful eyes of enthusiastic college-age staff. The children's workshops in July include theater, creative movement, mime, storytelling, music, and kite making. Cape May's beach is three very short blocks away.

Season: Memorial Day through mid-October.

Accommodations: Simple accommodations are old-fashioned (some rooms even have a washbasin), but clean and comfortable. Guests can stay in the main building, built in 1876, or one of three cottages. Baths are in the hallway. One cottage has a kitchen, living room, and lovely porches, while another eight-bedroom cottage is reserved for families with children under the age of six.

Special Features: Live theater performances take place on weekends, and classical music concerts are held one night a week. The concerts are free, but theater tickets must be purchased; guests get a discount. Children's workshops are for ages five and up; baby-sitting is available for younger ones. In addition to the children's program, a series of workshops on watercolor and various crafts is held each summer for adults.

Cost: Double room with breakfast and dinner $83 to $159 in midweek (for two people), $93 to $170 on weekends. Children stay free in parents' rooms but are charged for meals: under one year $3, three to six years $10, seven to ten years $15, eleven to fourteen years $18; fifteen years and over count as adults. The following gratuities are required and added to your bill: adults $7 per day, children $5 per day.

Nearby: Amusements are found throughout the city. Walk the promenade, rent a boat, take a trolley or a walking tour of the town. The nearby Historic Coldspring Village, a nineteenth-century southern Jersey farm village, has a petting zoo and a working farm, and tennis and golf are close. Wildwood amusement pier is one town over.

SMUGGLERS NOTCH RESORT

Address: Route 108, Smuggler's Notch, Vermont 05464–9599
Telephone: 800–451–8752 or 802–644–8851

Guaranteed summer fun for the entire family is the slogan of Smuggler's Notch, and judging by the number of happy families who return each year, it's safe to say that all family members are indeed satisfied. The resort's action-packed summer "FamilyFest" offers a good package vacation value with plenty of complimentary recreational options. Facilities include seven swimming pools, three long water slides, water playgrounds, evening entertainment, miniature golf, bonfires, sing-alongs, and an all-day children's programs for three- to five-year-olds, six- to twelve-year-olds, and thirteen- to seventeen-year-olds included in the price. Even the adults get their own program if they want to follow an organized schedule of activities. Otherwise, they can choose from recreational options that include tennis, exercise facilities, a spa, and guided hikes into the beautiful Green Mountains of Vermont. A few activities such as canoeing, mountain bike rentals, pro tennis clinics, and two specialized three-day camps for kids (one offering intensive arts and crafts for six- to twelve-year-olds, the other an adventure camp for ten- to eighteen-year-olds that teaches ropes courses, canoeing and orienteering) cost extra.

Families with children under three who visit in July and August pay extra for the Alice in Wonderland program, but it's included in the price in June. The program has three different age groups: babies from six weeks to sixteen months, toddlers to two-and-a-half years, and two-and-a-half to three-year-olds.

In winter, Smuggler's Notch turns into a ski resort with downhill and cross-country skiing, ice skating, and sleigh rides.

Accommodations: Studio to five-bedroom townhouses are available; many have fireplaces and balconies and views of mountain or woodland. Studios have an open floor plan with a fully-equipped kitchenette, dining and living area, and sleeping arrangements for up to four.

Special Features: Shuffleboard, volleyball, line dancing, bingo nights, karaoke, basketball, horseshoes, hiking tours, llama treks, canoeing, fishing, mountain biking, art workshops, day trips, Vermont country fair, baby-sitting available, massage, fly casting clinics, day trips, private swimming instruction (teach the parents how to teach the child to swim for ages two and older), pro tennis school in summer ($159 for a five-day program).

Cost: FamilyFest five-day stay for a family of four: June: studio $869, one-bedroom condo $1,095; July: studio $1,085, one-bedroom $1,399; August: studio $1,295; one-bedroom condo $1,665. Arts and crafts camp $90; Ropes and Rafts Adventure Camp $125; Alice in Wonderland infant and toddler program $44; mountain bike rental $5 per hour, $25 per day; fly casting clinic $25; day trips $13 to $22; canoe trips $14 to $24 per adult.

Nearby: Golf, fishing trips.

TWIN LAKE VILLAGE

Address: 21 Twin Lake Villa Road, New London, New Hampshire 03257 (100 miles from Boston)
Telephone: 603–526–6460

Located on two hundred acres of sweet-smelling woods and gently rolling hills, Twin Lake Village offers a little something for everyone; nine-hole golf, tennis, water sports, and a baby-sitting program in the morning for two- to five-year-olds so parents can have some time to themselves. The waterfront area at this quaint family-oriented American plan resort on Little Lake Sunapee has a shallow, sloping beach and a large dock where teens and adults can sunbathe, plus canoes, rowboats, and kayaks for guests to use whenever they wish. More than eighty percent of guests return for the gracious atmosphere, excellent prices, and range of diversions for all ages.

Season: The American plan season runs from late June through Labor Day. Some housekeeping cottages can be rented by the week from mid-May to late June.

Accommodations: Cottages, apartments, and hotel rooms are available. The Victorian-style cottages, built in the 1920s, have two to seven bedrooms, a living room, and a fireplace; some also have a kitchen. Apartments have two or three bedrooms, and there are private rooms in the main hotel. Most families stay in cottages or apartments.

Special Features: A small raft is moored near the shore and a sunbathing dock is nearby. Other recreational activities include shuffleboard, fishing, children's dances, bingo, tennis courts, and a supervised children's playhouse, open every morning except Saturday. Sailboats are available for an additional fee.

Cost: For four people sharing a two-bedroom suite, $335 per person per week; children two to five fifteen percent less, children under two $50. Rates include three meals a day, use of all facilities (including tennis courts, rowboats, canoes, kayaks, supervised children's playhouse, nine-hole golf course), and housekeeping service. Sailboats $16 for a half day. Housekeeping cottages $750 per week from mid-May to mid-June. Tips (15 percent, not included in the rates) are expected.

LOCH LYME LODGE

Address: 70 Orford Road, Lyme, New Hampshire 03768
Telephone: 800–423–2141; 603–795–2141

Families have been coming to Loch Lyme for the past seventy years to enjoy the blue water, green fields, flickering fireflies, and whispering wind in the pines. Without any noisy interruptions from television, telephones, or video arcades to distract your kids, you can all enjoy the wholesome pleasures of an old-fashioned family vacation. Even the most active of kids will be happy with the full spectrum of sports and games available here, and the most sedentary of parents will be immensely satisfied, watching the world go by from the comfort of the Adirondack chairs along the lake. Built in 1919, the resort's comfortable rustic cabins are scattered along a wooded hillside and down by the shore.

Season: Memorial Day to late October.

Accommodations: There are three types of accommodations. Four bed-and-breakfast rooms in the main lodge have shared bathrooms. Thirteen housekeeping cabins have fully equipped kitchens. Eleven modified American plan (breakfast and dinner included) or bed-and-breakfast cabins have living rooms, fireplaces, porches, and one or two bedrooms. Housekeeping services provided daily for the bed-and-breakfast rooms and modified American plan cabins; weekly for housekeeping cabins.

Special Features: A shallow beach is perfect for toddlers, and more accomplished swimmers enjoy diving off a float into deep water. Boats, kayaks, canoes, and a sailboard are available at no extra charge. A baseball field, tetherball, badminton, clay tennis courts, and good fishing are near the lodge. If you miss the 8 to 9 A.M. full breakfast, a continental breakfast is served between 9 and 10 A.M. This is a very popular resort that has been enjoyed by multiple generations of families, many of whom book a year in advance.

Cost: Housekeeping cabins (accommodate four to five people) $450 to $675 per week. Cabins with modified American plan $58 per person for the first and second adult, $46 for the third and fourth adult; children five to fifteen staying in a regular bed $32, or $25 on a cot or daybed per night. Lodge rooms with modified American plan $45 per person per day. Children four and under stay free. Ask about Loch Lyme Lodge's many discounts and packages for further reductions.

ROCKYWOLD-DEEPHAVEN CAMPS, INC.

Address: PO Box B, Holderness, New Hampshire 03245
Telephone: 603–968–3313; fax 603–968–3438

Tucked along the shore of unspoiled Squam Lake, the Rockywold-Deephaven family vacation camp has been open to people of all ages since 1897. This classic Yankee summer resort still harvests ice from the lake, delivering frozen blocks to cottage iceboxes each morning. Its sixty cottages and two lodges accommodate from two to fourteen guests each. The lodge dining halls, which look out over the lake, have tall stone fireplaces and tables with legs made of tree branches. A daily schedule of organized activities, which might include mountain climbs, talent shows, square dances, water sports competitions, or capture-the-flag games, is posted near the dining halls. A supervised morning program for children ages three to five operates during July and August, giving adults the chance to explore the lake's inlets and beaver dams and swim along the winding shore. The camp's serenity and respect for nature bring families back year after year.

Season: June through mid-September.

Accommodations: Each cottage has a living room with fireplace, screened porch, private dock, and icebox. Cottages are rented by the week only and sleep two to fourteen people. Rooms have one or two twin beds, and living rooms have daybeds. Lodge facilities for single or double occupancy can be rented by the day. All have daily housekeeping service.

Special Features: Eight Har-tru tennis courts are spread throughout the camp, along with an athletic field, reading rooms, and libraries. Children enjoy the wading beaches, toddler playground, recreation hall, indoor play areas, and miles of hiking trails. Games and outings are organized for all ages, and baby-sitting is easily arranged with advance notice. Canoes, rowboats, sailboats, and kayaks can be rented.

Cost: Weeks run Saturday to Saturday, and cottages are priced according to the number of people assigned to them. Full American plan rates cover room, board, and use of recreational facilities, including tennis courts. Six-person cottages (which can sleep up to fourteen) $3,763 per week; four-person cottages (which sleep up to six) $2,740; and two-person cottages (which sleep up to four) $1,615 per week; extra person in any cottage $446 per week; $223 for two- to five-year-olds; children under two stay free.

Canoes and kayaks $15 per day, $60 per week; rowboats $20 per day, $80 per week; Sunfish sailboats $35 per day, $140 per week. Limited private sailing, tennis, and swimming lessons are available.

FRANCONIA INN AND HILLWINDS LODGE

Address: Franconia Inn, Easton Road, Franconia, New Hampshire 03580; Hillwinds Lodge, Route 18, Franconia, New Hampshire 03580
Telephone: 800–473–5299, 603–823–5542 (Inn); 603–823–5551 (Lodge)

Spend the lazy days of summer at this gracious country inn, which has facilities for swimming, hiking, riding horses, and bicycling through forests and meadow. If your budget is particularly tight, opt for the Franconia's sister lodging, the Hillwinds Lodge, which is more like a no-frills motel. Guests have use of recreational facilities at both places, regardless of where they stay. The location is perfect for invigorating outdoor fun in adjacent Franconia Notch State Park, and the area is filled with such vacation musts for kids as Alpine slide rides, the Mount Washington Cog Railroad, Santa's Village, and Story Land. The inn offers a modified American plan (rates include breakfast and dinner), and bed-and-breakfast arrangement, or a European plan (lodging only). The Hillwinds Lodge provides motel rooms only.

Season: Year-round except April and early May.

Accommodations: The Franconia Inn has thirty-five guest rooms, all with private bath. Several rooms have a double and a single bed, and larger families can use the family suite of two bedrooms connected by a common bathroom. The inn has two porches, one situated for watching the sunrise, the other for viewing colorful sunsets. The plain and simple Hillwinds Lodge has thirty rooms with private baths and two double beds, a restaurant, and a lounge. Rollaway beds are available at both.

Special Features: Most of the leisure-time amenities are at the inn; clay tennis courts, riding stable, library, nightly movies, board games, heated outdoor pool, hot tub, trout fishing, croquet, bicycling, fifty kilometers of hiking trails; in winter, horse-drawn sleigh rides, ice-skating, cross-country skiing on the premises, and downhill skiing nearby.

Cost: Rates include use of tennis courts and equipment, swimming pool, bicycles, hot tub, croquet, golf course, badminton, movies, cross-country trails ticket. Inn: standard double rooms $85; $95 bed-and-breakfast; $150 modified American plan. Children three and under stay free; four to eleven $5 additional; over eleven $10. Rollaways and cribs are available free of charge. Lodge: rooms with two double beds $42 for up to four people. Horseback riding $20 per person per hour; thirty-minute sleigh ride $10 per adult, $5 per child two to eleven.

INN AT EAST HILL FARM

Address: Troy, New Hampshire 03465
Telephone: 800–242–6495 (reservations); 603–242–6495

With cows to milk, eggs to collect (young guests can put their names on the eggs they collect and have them cooked for breakfast), and ponies to ride, the Inn at East Hill Farm has kids persuading their families to return year after year. Horse-drawn hayrides with ice-cream parties take place weekly. Water recreation for all ages includes swimming pools, a pond with paddleboats, a toddlers' wading pool, and an outdoor beach party with waterskiing. Other options include lawn games, hiking trails, and animals to pet and feed. Families with preschool age or young school-age children particularly enjoy this resort, and parents appreciate the adult swimming hours, the nightly bring-your-own cocktail party, and the healthy food selections.

Accommodations: Simple cottages have two or three bedrooms and a bath; some also have a living room. Motel-type units are comfortable but not fancy. A "deluxe" unit with air-conditioning is available. The inn has a total of sixty rooms.

Special Features: Two outdoor pools, indoor pool and sauna, and tennis court. Barns with goats, chickens, pigs, bunnies, ducks, turkeys, a donkey, cows, and sheep (plus baby pigs, calves, and bunnies in the summer). Pond with paddleboats, beaver house, swings, sandbox, and wading pool. Summers and winter holidays have at least one organized children's activity; a list is posted each morning. Selections might in-

teddy bear pancakes are included in the room rate. Games and books are available in the main living room and other common rooms. The inn serves a snack bar lunch and dinner in their restaurant. The inn is so family friendly that parents can order dinner from the front desk, and round up the kids to sit down when the dinner is ready to be served. Younger children love visiting the barn with its pony, donkey, sheep, calf, and bunnies, and draft horses who pull wagons and sleighs. In winter the hiking trails turn into cross-country ski trails, and the duck pond freezes over for skating. Sledding is spectacular since the inn sits in hilly country.

Season: Year-round.

Accommodations: Twenty-two guest rooms, some with kitchenettes, have a variety of bed configurations. There are several family-size suites, one-room units with a double bed and bunks, and two-room family suites.

Special Features: Indoor sauna and hot tub, duck pond, maple sugar house, game room, children's rec room with Foosball, bumper pool, reading loft, and children's toys; videos shown in evening; hot tub and sauna.

Cost: Rates include an afternoon snack and full country breakfast. Doubles $89 to $105. Suites with kitchenettes $130 to $150 depending on size. Children in same room(s) as adults: under five free; six to eleven $8; twelve and older $15.

Nearby: Glacier-carved Lake Willoughby is about twenty minutes away.

ALDEN CAMPS

Address: RFD 2, Box 1140, Oakland, Maine 04963
Telephone: 207–465–7703

Quaint cottages are scattered in a sweet-smelling pine grove along the cove of a sparkling lake where waterskiing, fishing, and canoeing are a regular part of each day. Meals are served in an old-fashioned farmhouse in an open area near meadows and fields. Alden Camps, known for its outstanding food, employs a special chef, an assistant chef, and a pastry cook. A changing menu includes six to ten entrées. The resort is small enough so that everyone is friendly and cordial, but privacy is respected if you want to get away and quietly read a book. The resort has been in business for eighty consecutive years, and guests who came here as children now bring their grandchildren along.

Season: Memorial Day through Labor Day.

Accommodations: Eighteen rustic cottages on the shore of the lake range in size from one to three bedrooms; all have private baths and screened porches facing the lake. Two-bedroom cottages have a double bed in one bedroom and two twin beds in the other. Bed linens, towels, and daily housekeeping service are provided. Cribs are available on request. Cottages are heated by wood-burning stoves or gas heaters, and firewood is supplied.

Special Features: East Lake, known for its excellent bass fishing, has a gently sloping sandy beach perfect for youngsters, and a dock and float for sunbathers. Waterskiing, tennis, basketball, Ping-Pong, shuffleboard, a swing set, croquet, horseshoes, volleyball, badminton, and beautiful hiking trails are available. Small fishing boats can be rented at the resort and sailboat and sail board rentals are available nearby. A canoe is available to guests at no extra charge.

Cost: Two-bedroom cottages $90 per adult per night, $540 per week. One-bedroom cottages $85 per night, $510 per week. Three-bedroom cottages $105 per night, $630 per week. Children under one year $10 per night, $60 per week; kids one to three $20 per day, $120 per week; four to six $30 per day, $60 per week; seven to nine $45 per day, $270 per week; ten and eleven $60 per day, $360 per week. Fifteen-percent tip strongly encouraged. Daily boat rental $10 for boat, $15 for motor; reduced rates for weekly rental.

OAKLAND HOUSE SEASIDE INN AND COTTAGES

Address: Herrick Road RR 1, Box 400, Brooksville, Maine 04617
Telephone: 207–359–8521 or 800–359–RELAX

In a gentle rural setting along a half-mile of oceanfront, Oakland House is located off the paved road 25 miles from the nearest traffic light. Jim Littlefield's family has owned this property since the 1770s and has operated it as a hotel since 1889 when the Eastern Steamboat Line brought guests right to Herrick's Landing near what is now called the "Lobster Picnic Beach." The property includes both warm lake and cooler saltwater beaches, miles of hiking trails, sprawling lawns set up with lawn games, and play areas with gym sets for children. There are complimentary rowboats and life jackets for guests to use on both waterfronts, and it's not uncommon for oceanside rowers to spot a curious seal eyeing the people in the boat.

This retreat particularly welcomes families with children; a special family dining room allows parents and kids to eat with others their own age. More than half of its guests are repeat customers. Some have been coming back for more than 50 years and children of past guests now bring their own children.

Season: Open early May through October; summer season runs mid-May through August.

Accommodations: Fifteen uniquely styled log or clapboard cottages containing between one and five bedrooms are rented by the week. All have fireplaces, private baths, kitchens or kitchenettes, and are right on the water, in the woods, or on the lawns.

Special Features: A lobster picnic is served on the beach every Thursday night. The barn has two pianos, fireplace, casual seating, and a video monitor for family-oriented videos shown on summer evenings. Boat moorings are available to guests at no charge.

Cost: During summer peak season breakfast and dinner are included in the rate: the lowest rates are $1,747 per week for a family of four to a high of $3,059 (including 15 percent service charge and 7 percent sales tax). Rates vary depending on season and accommodation. Discounts are available during specified periods. Children ages two to five half-price, ages six to eleven two-thirds price, infants up to two years $42 per week. During the off-season, meals are not included and prices drop. Cribs are available.

Nearby: Deer Isle Country Club Golf, whale watching trips, Holbrook Island Sanctuary, The Mailboat to Isle au Haut, Bucks Harbor, and sailboats for rent.

DUDE RANCHES

$\mathcal{D}$ude ranch vacations offer families old-fashioned fun. Besides riding until your backside gets sore, your family will spend time together exploring the wide-open spaces on the ranch, working up a chuck wagon–size appetite. Both guest ranches and working ranches take in visitors, and most of them offer families a complete package that combines good old-time hospitality with lodging, horseback riding, and three hearty home-cooked meals a day. Extra activities such as swimming, hayrides, fishing, river rafting, and campfire gatherings are regular features at many. Guest ranches offer the most complete vacation packages. Nestled at the base of majestic mountains or set alongside creeks and rivers, many have been run by the same family for years. Working ranches, where guests can help with daily chores, give families a vivid picture of the lives of modern cowboys and ranch families. They are often less elaborately equipped than guest ranches, and lower in price as well. The majority of dude ranches are in Colorado, Wyoming, and Montana, but they can be found throughout the rest of the country, too. Some host one or two families at a time while others can accommodate more than one hundred people at a time.

Most ranches offer two rides a day; one in the morning and one in the afternoon. No experience is necessary; instruction on horse care and riding is given at the beginning of a guest's stay. Children under six usually ride with supervision in a corral or are led around on ponies while older kids and adults go trail riding. Some ranches allow young children to ride in front of a parent's saddle on trail rides. Be sure to bring proper riding boots or find out if the ranch has loaner boots: sneakers and sandals won't do.

Most of this chapter's listings are packages that include all meals and riding. We list a few ranch vacations where meals are included but riding is purchased separately, and a few where both meals and riding cost extra. If some of your family members don't plan to ride, these will be more affordable options.

We established our price criteria for all-inclusive ranches using an imaginary family of four people: two adults and two children ages eight and ten. Most of the ranches listed cost less than $3,000 for a full week of horseback riding, lodging, meals, recreational activities, and in some instances a supervised children's program. Many of them cost far less. This may sound expensive, but it's actually quite a bargain when you add up the cost of lodging, three meals a day, twice-daily guided horseback rides, breakfast rides, barbecues, swimming, fishing, square dancing, western music shows, sports, games, and more. Best of all, unlike a do-it-yourself vacation, someone else is planning the activities and making the decisions.

Shop around for the ranch that suits your family's ages and interests, as prices vary considerably from ranch to ranch. Some offer a special teenagers' rate while others consider anyone over twelve an adult. Prices for younger children can also vary from ranch to ranch by hundreds of dollars a week. If you're bringing a baby or a toddler, select a ranch that has no charge for children under two or three. Amenities and extras vary as well. Some ranches include supervised children's programs in the price; others have no such programs. Some are located on lakes with boats available or on rivers with tubing and rafting included in the price.

If you are flying to your destination, inquire about fees for airport pickup and delivery. Some ranches offer complimentary transportation, while others request a payment. Most ranches require week-long stays in the summer, although some have nightly or half-week rates. Most ranches add a ten- to fifteen-percent gratuities fee to your bill, while some include it in the quoted price. Still others strongly suggest that you leave a tip of that size for the staff upon your departure. Be sure to inquire when booking and build it into your budget. A number of ranches offer better deals in May, early June, September, and October. If this fits your schedule, you can save even more.

In selecting a ranch that fits your budget, ask:

- Is there unlimited riding? How many trips are planned each day? How long are they?

- What is the minimum age for trail riding? What do little ones do when the adults and older kids are on a trail ride?

- Are loaner riding boots available?

- Will I get the same horse for the entire week?

- Will the ranch provide guests' names for reference?

- Does the week run Sunday to Sunday or Sunday to Saturday? (Keep this in mind when you compare prices, as you might be getting one less day's worth of meals and activities.)

- What is and what is not included in the price?

- What about taxes and gratuities?

The Dude Ranchers' Association has a directory available that describes all of its member ranches. Many of them are well above our price limit, but it's a fun publication to peruse. We include some of their lower-priced ranches. Contact Dude Ranchers' Association, PO Box 471, LaPorte, Colorado 80535; telephone: 970-223-8440.

WEST COAST

GREENHORN CREEK

Address: 2116 Greenhorn Ranch Road, Quincy, California 95971-9204
Telephone: 916-283-0930

A comfortable, casual atmosphere and a magnificent setting along a spring-fed pond in the Sierras keep families coming back to Greenhorn Creek Ranch year after year. Its prices are low and everything's included: two rides per day, horseback riding instruction for greenhorns, separate rides for beginners and experienced riders, a children's program, a swimming pool, pond fishing, and the "rainbow ballet" at sunset, when the lake starts to vibrate with jumping fish. Children ages three to six are entertained in the Kiddie Corral program from 9 A.M. to 4 P.M. by a special activities director. They enjoy brushing the horses, pony rides, arts and crafts projects, nature hikes, and games. Kids age six and over can go on trail rides and drop into the chldren's program whenever they like.

Season: Year-round.

Accommodations: Couples and small families stay in one of eleven lodge rooms, which accommodate one to three people. Larger families opt for one of sixteen duplex-style cabins that can be connected to house families of any size; all have front porches and swings, daily housekeeping service, and private baths.

Special Features: Fishing and swimming in the front yard creek and pond; swimming pool; hayrides; weekly evening bonfire; several cookouts; hiking; mini-rodeo with barrel races, obstacle courses, and egg tosses; saloon; square dancing; frog race; horseshoes; volleyball; rec room with video games, Ping-Pong, pool.

Cost: Weekly, adults $750, teens thirteen to nineteen $650, children seven to twelve $550, four to six $300, three and under free. Rates are lower in early to mid-June and lower still for the rest of the year. Daily rates are available. A fifteen-percent gratuities fee is added to your total bill.

DRAKESBAD GUEST RANCH

Address: Chester, California 96020 (in Lassen Volcanic National Park, seventeen miles from Chester; the last four miles are on a dirt road)
Telephone: 916–529–1512, November through April. (From May through October, call 00 for long-distance AT&T operator and ask for Drakesbad 2 via Susanville operator in the 916 area code.)

Cowboy coffee? Not a chance. Try cappuccino and cafe mocha instead while you linger over chocolate cream pie after dinner. Then wander on over to your knotty-pine lodge room, stopping to roast a marshmallow by the outdoor bonfire. Nature lovers return year after year to this secluded and rustic hundred-year-old ranch surrounded by thousands of acres of forests crammed with lakes and streams. The lodging may be old-fashioned, lit by old-style kerosene lanterns, but the food is up-to-date, with delicious gourmet dinners and colorful and healthy lunch and breakfast buffets. A small trout stream cuts right through the middle of the ranch for fishing and splashing, and its large balmy swimming pool is heated by natural volcanic heat. Since Drakesbad sits in a geologically active landscape in Lassen Volcanic National Park, horseback rides (rented by the hour) take you past bubbling mudpots and hissing steam vents to places like the Devil's Kitchen and Boiling Springs Lake. The ranch's lack of electricity makes for skies packed with brightly glowing stars.

Season: June through October.

Accommodations: Nineteen units can house a total of forty to fifty people. Lodge or cabin bedrooms have a private sink-and-toilet half bath, with shared shower facility nearby. Bungalows and annex units are one large room with two double beds and full baths; duplex rooms have bathrooms with showers and are reserved for parties of four or more.

Special Features: Hiking trails, fishing, volleyball court, horseshoes, evening bonfires, and western barbecues. Lunch is a buffet; there is table service at breakfast and dinner. Vegertarian entrées are offered at all meals and special diets can be accommodated.

Cost: Adults in lodge rooms and cabins $98 nightly, $590 weekly; each additional adult (over age eleven) $81 per night. Children two to eleven $62 per night, $385 per week. Adults in bungalow or annex rooms are $105 per night or $659 per week; each additional adult is $83 per night. Children two to eleven $59 per night. The duplex houses a minimum of four people: adults $110 per night and $679 per week. Each additional adult $79 per night; children two to eleven $59 per night. Includes use of the pool, three meals a day, and housekeeping service. Saddle horses $26 per hour.

COFFEE CREEK RANCH

Address: HC2 Box 4940, Trinity Center, California 96091
Telephone: 800–624–4480; 916–266–3343

Coffee Creek Ranch is surrounded by the high, snow-capped peaks, towering pines, wilderness lakes, and alpine meadows of the Trinity Alps of Northern California. The ranch lies along Coffee Creek, an excellent trout fishing stream with abundant swimming holes. Its secluded cabins are tucked into the woods and apple orchards that surround the heated swimming pool, patios, and main ranch house where breakfast, lunch, and dinner are served. Take the foot bridge across the creek and road to get to the riding stables and grazing meadow, pond, archery range, trapshooting station, and "ghost town." A natural river rock slide, Big Boulder Sluice is a two-minute walk from the ranch house. Horseback riding costs extra, making this ranch a great buy for families who have a mix of riders and nonriders. The ranch is open year-round and has special seasonal activities such as cider pressing and "haunted happenings" in the fall, a grandparents week in September, and cross-country skiing, an inner tube run, snowshoeing, ice fishing, and sleigh rides in winter.

A supervised kids' program for three- to seventeen-year-olds takes place during the summer season from 9 A.M. to 5 P.M. Saturday through Thursday. Little ones under three are supervised by baby-sitters during riding times. Cowboys and cowgirls (three to seven) have pony rides, games, and story time; Junior Wranglers (eight to twelve) have two free riding lessons, horsemanship instruction, swimming in the creek, and fishing in the pond; Bronc Busters (thirteen to seventeen) have roping lessons, rifle instruction, hikes, and an overnight campout.

Season: Year-round.

Accommodations: Cabins have one or two bedrooms and one or two baths, and are individually decorated with western themes.

Special Features: Trout-stocked fishing pond with canoes, guided hikes, hayrides, arts and crafts, badminton, Ping-Pong, volleyball, horseshoes, rifle range, gold panning, health spa, hiking, bonfires, shuffleboard, basketball, gymkhana, archery range, live music, talent show, bingo, square and line dancing, pool table, washers and dryers.

Cost: Prices depend on size of accommodations. Seven-day stays mid-June through Labor Day: adults $740 to $760, teens thirteen to seventeen $720 to $740, children three to twelve $620 to $640, under three $250. Spring, fall, and winter priced lower; shorter stays can easily be arranged. Riding: week-long package $250 per person, $55 per all-day ride, $27.50 for a two-hour ride, $15 for a half-hour lesson. Minimum riding age is five.

HUNEWILL CIRCLE H GUEST RANCH

Address: PO Box 368, Bridgeport, Mono County, California 93517 (summer); 200 Hunewill Lane, Wellington, Nevada 89444 (winter) Telephone: 619–932–7710 (summer); 702–465–2325, 702–465–2201 (winter)

This 4,500-acre ranch borders a range of mountains, giving guests many choices of trails to follow through the rolling foothills and scenic mountain valleys. Children under ten are half price, making Hunewill a good buy for families with younger children. Several crystal-clear streams that run through the ranch are ideal for swimming and splashing on hot days. Kids over six can go on trail rides, and a special children's wrangler is available for lessons and rides appropriate to their ability. Free child care for kids under six is offered during riding times in the summer season.

Season: Late May through mid-September.

Accommodations: Twenty-four cottages each have a private bath and separate entrance. Most have a porch and two twin beds or a queen-size bed; families take units with connecting doors. The main ranch house was built at the turn of the century when Bridgeport was being settled by gold miners seeking their fortune.

Special Features: Two rides per day. A special breakfast ride and all-day trip are offered each week; children take a shorter day-trip ride. Between rides, guests can spend time playing horseshoes, Ping-Pong, and volleyball; hunting for rocks and arrowheads; hiking or fishing; and doing folk and square dancing. Campfires are held on many evenings and there is a weekly hayride.

Cost: Rates include three meals a day, lodging, private saddle horse, twice-daily rides, and all activities and facilities. Adults $760 to $890 per week; children ten to twelve $570 to $650, children under ten $380 to $435, under two $150. There are special rates for nonriders or people bringing their own horse.

BAR M RANCH

Address: 58840 Bar M Lane, Adams, Oregon 97810–3003 (thirty-one miles east of Pendleton)
Telephone: 541–566–3381

In operation by the Baker family for more than fifty years, Bar M Ranch is for families with children age six and older. The ranch was originally a stagecoach stop in the 1800s, and you can still see the markings from the old stage road that traveled through the hills just above the ranch. Riding instruction is offered to beginners, and all guests are encouraged to learn to curry and saddle their own mounts. Trail rides take you through the Blue Mountains, including the North Fork Umatilla Wilderness area. There's fishing on the Umatilla River, and the clear waters of a large swimming pool are warmed by a hot geothermal spring. If you visit during July, you can enjoy the Bakers' spectacular raspberries in the delicious home-cooked meals.

Season: May through September.

Accommodations: Thirty-two riding guests can be housed in several different facilities. The main lodge, built during the Civil War, has rooms with shared bathrooms. The Homestead building has four two-room apartments with private baths, each with a queen-size bed in one room and two twin beds in the other. Two large three-room cabins accommodate up to six people. Laundry facilities are available.

Special Features: Swim in the forty-by-sixty-foot natural heated swimming pool, or swim and fish in the river nearby. A private fishing pond is stocked for kids under fourteen, and other activities include volleyball, square dancing, hiking, and bird watching.

Cost: Adults $800 per week in rooms with private bath, less for lodge room. Children eight to fifteen $600, under eight $500. Prices include lodging, riding, meals, and all ranch activities. Campouts $35 extra per person per night. Transportation from Pendleton $60 per family. Try to book by March for the summer season.

ROCKY MOUNTAINS AND SOUTHWEST

CANYON RANCH

Address: 9820 Transfer Road, Olathe, Colorado 81425 (thirteen miles south of Delta)
Telephone: 970–323–5288

This comfortable, rustic ranch operated by the friendly Mrs. B. B. Frisch has the lowest prices of any we found. Guests have plenty of opportunities to ride, hike, fish, and search for Indian arrowheads, or hunt for frogs in the pond. People come back year after year to enjoy the simple beauty of the surrounding area along with Mrs. Frisch's hospitality and good home cooking. This is a ranch without all the bells and whistles of other ranch resorts, but it's a mighty satisfying place to spend some time riding and relaxing. A canal a short hike away has swimming and tubing, and kids love to splash and wade in the "crik." One or two rides are offered each day, according to guest preferences. Parents can take younger children on the front of their saddle or lead them around on a gentle pony.

Season: Year-round.

Accommodations: Families of three to four stay in the Wickiup, a log house divided to accommodate two parties. One side has a large room with a queen-size bed, a sofabed, and a twin bed. The other side has a double bed and sofabed. Each side has a private bath. Larger families can sleep in the eight-bed log bunkhouse; a bathhouse is just outside the door. Home-cooked traditional meals are served in the main house; a typical dinner is roast beef, mashed potatoes, rolls, green salad, and apple pie. The beef is raised on the ranch with no added hormones.

Special Features: Cattle, geese, peacocks, guinea hens, and dogs roam the ranch. Activities include cookouts in the mountains, horseshoe games, apple picking in season, and observation of deer, marmots, and eagles.

Cost: Weekly, adults $350, children under twelve $300. Includes three meals a day and all ranch and riding activities.

Nearby: Indian caves and artifacts are within walking distance. The

Black Canyon of the Gunnison, Grand Mesa, and the hot springs of Ouray are all nearby.

COULTER LAKE GUEST RANCH

Address: PO Box 906, Rifle, Colorado 81650
Telephone: 970–625–1473

Located on the scenic western slopes of the Rockies with a sparking blue lake for swimming, fishing, and boating, Coulter Lake Guest Ranch has eight cabins scattered along the lakefront and among aspen trees. The owners were annual guests at this ranch for eight years before buying it twelve years ago. Twenty-eight hours of horseback riding are offered each week, along with square dances, bonfires, corral games, and sing-alongs. The trout-stocked lake has rowboats available to guests, and kids can jump into the lake from a dock. Any trout you catch you can eat for dinner on Friday night.

Season: Riding season is June through early October; the ranch is open again mid-December to April 1 for snow sports.

Accommodations: Eight different-size cabins, all with private baths, sleep two to ten people. Three of the cabins have individual bedrooms and are best for smaller families, while one large cabin can sleep ten people in three bedrooms.

Special Features: Daily rides (except Sunday), square dancing twice a week, cookouts, a twilight ride, two all-day rides, sing-alongs, horseshoes, hiking, four-wheel-drive trips.

Cost: Sunday to Sunday, two or more people per cabin from $930 per adult; children five to eleven $705; four $450; under three $360. Rates include meals, housekeeping service in summer, riding, horseshoes, lake fishing and swimming, use of rowboats, and all other activities. Airport pickups $90 round-trip from Grand Junction, $50 round-trip from Glenwood Springs Amtrak station. Three-day minimum stays with reduced rates available in June and September.

HARMEL'S RANCH RESORT

Address: PO Box 399, Almont, Colorado 81210 (four and a half hours from Denver and three and a half hours from Colorado Springs)
Telephone: 800–235–3402; 970–641–1740

This family ranch, set in the middle of the Rocky Mountains, has a variety of options available for families who want to tailor a ranch vacation to their specific interests and abilities without having to pay for a total package. All plans in the summer are modified American (two meals a day included in the price), but one plan allows you to buy activities such as horseback riding and river rafting as you want them, and the other charges one price that includes everything except the overnight pack trip. From mid-May to mid-June, and late August through September, you can rent housekeeping cottages.

Season: Mid-May through September.

Accommodations: Individual cabins or duplexes have a living room, private bath, and one, two, or three bedrooms. Some units have kitchens and all have refrigerators, coffeemakers, daily housekeeping service. Guests make their own lunches or buy box lunches from the resort. Total capacity is 150 people.

Special Features: Two trout streams have excellent fishing. Other facilities and programs include a heated swimming pool, playground, hiking, cookouts, a kids' program, square dancing, horseshoes, hayrides, and an overnight pack trip. Children's menu available.

Cost: Full week all-inclusive package includes lavish breakfast and dinner, horseback riding, mountain biking, rafting and all activities: adults $850 to $925; children six to twelve $600; children two to five $450.

Nearby: Old mining sites and ghost towns, and boating on Blue Mesa Resevoir, forty-five minutes away by car.

DEER FORKS GUEST RANCH

Address: 1200 Poison Lake Road, Douglas, Wyoming 82633 (seventy-five miles from Casper, Wyoming and twenty-five miles southwest of Douglas)
Telephone: 307–358–2033; fax 307–358–4454.

Deer Forks Guest Ranch is a working ranch with herds of cows, sheep, and horses on 14,000 acres. The ranch takes two or three groups of families at a time so that guests really can participate in ranch life. Cabins are furnished with kitchens, but guests can choose a modified American plan package that provides breakfast and dinner. Riding costs extra. Two trout streams are on the property, so bring your fishing gear—or just wade, swim, and watch birds by the water. A spring-fed pond on the lawn has trout and provides entertainment for children. Kids also can feed orphan lambs from a bottle as well as other pets. It's unscheduled ranch-style living.

Season: June through mid-September.

Accommodations: Guest houses are equipped with kitchen, and those not eating on the meal plan need to bring their own food supplies.

A trailer hookup and two furnished cabins are available. One cabin sleeps nine in a sleeping loft, bedroom, and sofabed; the other cabin sleeps six in two bedrooms and a sofabed. Bedding and towels are provided.

Special Features: Horseshoes, volleyball, hiking, riding costs extra.

Cost: Cabin rental fees depend on number of people in a unit: adults $40 per night or $250 per week, children under sixteen half price. Modified American plan (two meals per day), adults $65 per day or $390 per week, children under sixteen half price. Rates include all on-ranch activities except riding.

Morning horseback rides $30 per person, afternoon rides $10 per hour per person; $30 per day minimum. Trailer hookup available (price includes sewer, water, and electricity): adults $20 per day or $120 per week, children under sixteen half-price. Airport pickup in Casper $60.

Nearby: The Wyoming State Fair and Pioneer Museum in Douglas, a stop on the Oregon Trail, rodeos, historical sites. Mount Rushmore, Devil's Tower, and Ft. Laramie are all close enough for a day trip.

LAZY L AND B RANCH

Address: 1072 East Fork Road, Dubois, Wyoming 82513 (sixty-eight miles west of Riverton, on the east wing of the Wind River next to the Wind River Indian reservation)
Telephone: 800–453–9488, 307–455–2839; fax 307–455–2634.

Lush green cottonwood river bottoms, high desert plateaus, alpine meadows, and aspen groves are some of the riding country you'll pass through. There is a riding program for children five years and older including three early dinners followed by supervised activities such as roping, corral games, scavenger hunts, and a hayride barbecue. The hundred-year-old ranch has unlimited rides to old frontier homesteads, across prairies, and into the high country. Kids can create original works of art in a leather tooling and bead shop, go on a hayride, swim in the solar-heated pool, or learn to square dance if they tire of riding. An overnight ride lets guests sleep under the stars.

Season: Memorial Day through mid-September (September, adults only).

Accommodations: Eleven casual western log cabins—all with private baths, heat, and refrigerators—are situated around a common yard. Most cabins have porches or decks, and simple interiors with a small sitting area. Cabins can accommodate one to eight people.

Special Features: Heated pool, tubing on the river, crafts shop, rifle range, fishing, hiking, hayrides, cookouts.

Cost: Sunday afternoon to Saturday morning, adults $895 per person (double occupancy); children twelve and under $795 per person. Book three to four months in advance.

Nearby: Old miners' ghost town of Atlantic City, Sacajewea's grave, Jackson Hole, the Grand Tetons, and the gateway to Yellowstone are an hour away.

EARLY GUEST RANCH

Address: Crowheart, Wyoming 82512
Telephone: 800–863–1105, 307–532–4055

The Wind River cuts through Early Ranch's property, which sits inside Wyoming's only Indian Reservation. Guests who love to fish can learn to fly or spin fish, but for those who crave a little more action, two-and-a-half-hour raft trips down the river are offered as often as guests wish. Two horseback rides a day are featured and explore hilly areas and gentle terrain with helpful wrangler guides. The ranch has a rodeo arena where guests can learn barrel racing, pole bending, calf typing, roping, and ribbon tying in addition to basic western riding. Rates include square dancing in town, all you can eat meals (homemade pies are a specialty), and the "little Buckaroos" program during riding times for children too young to ride.

Accommodations: Log cabins have a total of eight units with a double bed and a private bath in each. Many of the units have connecting doors, and rollaways can be added. One cabin particularly comfortable for families has two bedrooms.

Special Features: Evening campfires and sing-alongs, spa with exercise machines, hot tub, tanning machine and aerobics classes, hiking trails, horseshoes, volleyball.

Cost: Adults $790 per week, children three to nine $650. Overnight pack trips $100 extra. Round-trip airport pickup at Jackson $30 per adult; one child accompanied by each adult is free.

RIMROCK DUDE RANCH

Address: 2728 North Fork Route, Cody, Wyoming 82341 (twenty-six miles west of Cody and east of Yellowstone's east gate)
Telephone: 307–587–3970; fax 307–527–5014

You'll ride with the cowboys at Rimrock, with plenty of time to master all of the gaits in western riding. Guests can ride twice a day or opt for the all-day ride with a pack mule carrying their lunch. Rimrock's rates include riding, river float trips, tickets to the Cody Nite Rodeo (see page 289), breakfast rides, and a tour of Yellowstone National Park. Three hearty meals are served daily, and you can say "please pass the potatoes" as many times as you wish. Many guests return each year, so reserve early.

Season: Late May through early September.

Accommodations: Nine log cabins with western decor have private baths and daily housekeeping service. Most have two queen-size beds or a queen and twin. Four-room cabins accommodate eight people and have two baths.

Special Features: At least two rides are offered per day. Other activities include fishing in the pond on the ranch or in nearby streams, half-day float trips, hiking, tours of Yellowstone, ranch entertainment, square dancing, Ping-Pong tournaments, shuffleboard, and movies. The minimum riding age is five, and a wrangler takes children on special picnic and trail rides.

Cost: Rimrock's prices are higher than our average, but they include extras—such as float trips, tickets to the rodeo, and airport pickup— that make the ranch an excellent value. Seven-day minimum stay. Two people $1,000 each per week, three people $950 each, four people $900 each, more than four $700 each per day. Kids under four stay free. Discounts available for two- and three-week stays.

TWO BARS SEVEN DUDE RANCH

Address: Virginia Dale, Colorado 80548; Tie Siding, Wyoming 82084 (the ranch sits on the Colorado-Wyoming border, twenty-seven miles south of Laramie and I-80)
Telephone: 307–742–6072

The hosts raise and train their own saddle horses at this 7,000-acre working ranch made up of meadows, streams, and lakes. The week begins with a basic orientation to the horses, since many guests have had no riding experience. Two rides are offered each day, and depending on the time of year, guests can help with the ranch chores such as moving cattle, taking out salt, and mending fences. In the evening, head for a beaver dam and watch them busily gnawing down aspen trees, enjoy a hearty ranch-style barbecue, or take an overnight trail ride.

Season: Late May through November.

Accommodations: Six of the fourteen lodge rooms have private baths; others share a bathroom. Rooms and baths are heated and have outdoor entrances. Families of four or five often stay in two adjoining rooms with two baths.

Special Features: Two rides are offered each day. Children must be six years old to ride their own horse on the trail; little ones can sit in front of their parents' saddle. Four nearby lakes are stocked with trout; the lake nearest the ranch has brook trout. You'll see plenty of wildlife in summer, including deer, marmots, prairie dogs, 160 different species of birds, badgers, and porcupines. Breakfast is ranch-style with pancakes, hash browns, and eggs; the afternoon meal is heavier than guests might be used to, but after they've been out riding they welcome a big lunch and dinner. Book early in the year for July.

Cost: May through November, adults $775 to $825 each per week (nonriding adults deduct twenty-five percent); kids seven to fifteen $675. Daily rates available. Fifteen-percent discounts offered in May and November; ten-percent discounts available June 1 through June 15 and Labor Day through October 31. Hosts are flexible in booking arrangements and will pick up guests at the Laramie airport free of charge.

SWEET GRASS RANCH

Address: HC 87, Box 2161, Big Timber, Montana 59011 (twenty miles west of Melville, forty miles northwest of Big Timber, 120 miles northwest of Billings)
Telephone: 406–537–4477; fax 406–537–4477

Warm and gracious hosts Bill and Shelly Carrioccia encourage guests to get involved in the way of life on their ranch. The Carrioccias particularly love to host families, people who help work the cattle, take care of the horses, and do farm chores. The kids can feed the calves, pigs, and horses and learn to milk cows; fresh milk is served at every meal. When you tire of ranch activities, relax around the property, swim in the creek, go fishing, or watch the local beavers go about their business. The Sweet Grass River runs through the ranch, located in a valley in the foothills of the Crazy Mountains. Horseback rides take you up into the mountains, where you'll catch expansive 300-mile views, or down into the lower, flatter open country. The hospitality at this ranch simply can't be beat.

Season: Mid-June through Labor Day.

Accommodations: Guests are housed in rustic log cabins or in the main ranch house. There are cabins with two twin beds and a bathhouse less than a hundred yards away, and one- or two-bedroom cabins with private baths, some with living room and fireplace. Four bedrooms are upstairs in the main house; large families can use the entire unit, which includes a living room and bath. Most rooms have double beds, with the exception of the two-bedroom cabins, which have a double in one room and bunks in the other.

Special Features: Daily half-day rides and long and short all-day rides cover a wide variety of trails. Horses are matched to the rider's ability, and get a rest on Sunday. There is no minimum age for riding; if parents aren't comfortable riding with little ones in the front of their saddle, the wranglers will take them. The Sweet Grass River is suitable for fishing, as are the creek, beaver ponds, and mountain lakes. More swimming holes and five mountain lakes are above the ranch, about a three-hour horse ride away.

Cost: Cabins without bath $645 per person. Two-bedroom cabins with private bath and fireplace $780 per person when four share it. Room in upstairs of main ranch house $700. Children three to five $350, under three free. Overnights and pack trips $40 extra per person. Airport pickup $125 per car trip from the ranch to Billings and back, divided among those going each way.

Nearby: Trips to Yellowstone National Park, ghost towns, float trips, Indian ceremonies, and rodeos can be arranged from the ranch.

KAY EL BAR GUEST RANCH

Address: PO Box 2480, Wickenburg, Arizona 85358 (one hour and twenty minutes from Phoenix)
Telephone: 520–684–7593

Riding season at the Kay El Bar is during the winter, when Arizona desert temperatures cool to a comfortable 75 to 80 degrees. While the East and Midwest are shivering under a blanket of snow, guests at this small ranch saddle up a horse and ride into scenic mountain foothills, along a flat dry river bed, through little canyons and past towering cliffs. Two rides a day are offered (except on Sunday) and riders are separated by ability, so that more serious riders can take faster, more spirited rides, and beginners can amble safely and slowly. The ranch is a national historic site with old adobe buildings. Its main lodge has eight guest rooms and a large great room with a bar, fireplace, games, books, and big over-stuffed furniture. The dining room and kitchen are in another historic adobe building. Grass lawns, big shade trees, flowers, and saguaro cactus cover the grounds. You'll see deer, javelinas, coyotes, and jackrabbits. The minimum age for riding is seven.

Season: Mid-October to May 1.

Accommodations: Lodge rooms with private baths have king or twin beds; one rollaway can be added to king-bedded rooms. One large family cottage has two bedrooms, two baths, and a living room with a fire-place. It can sleep up to seven people and families with children under age seven stay here rather than the lodge.

Special Features: Heated swimming pool, board games, books, hiking.
Cost: Three meals a day, lodging, and riding included in the price. Adults: lodge rooms $1510 per week for two people; cottage $1640 for two people, $3150 for four people per week. Kids two to seven $225 per week; seven to thirteen $400 per week; thirteen and over $500. Shorter stays can be arranged. Taxes and 15 percent gratuity added on.
Nearby: The ranch is four miles from center of historic Wickenburg, and guests enjoy exploring its museums and shops and touring an old gold mine. Two 18-hole golf courses are a short drive away.

LAZY K BAR RANCH

Address: 8401 North Scenic Drive, Tucson, Arizona 85743 (ranch is sixteen miles northwest of Tucson)
Telephone: 800–321–7018 or 520–744–3050

Riders mosey into the desert foothills of the Tucson Mountains warmed by the winter Arizona sun. When you pull off your boots in the evening, feast on barbecued ribs and mesquite-grilled T-bone steak, take a hayride, listen to a cowboy singer, or learn country-western dancing. Little ones love the petting zoo with a pot-bellied pig, pygmy goat, and calf. Out of the saddle there are mountain bikes, a heated swimming pool, golf courses nearby, and a lodge with a library, big screen TV, and dining room. Ten different species of hummingbirds are spotted around this ranch and there are several bird feeding stations and bird identification areas for guests to enjoy. Trail riding is for children ages six and up; rides go out twice a day.
Season: September 15 to June 15.
Accommodations: Rooms are in single-story adobe buildings with two to four rooms per building. Some rooms connect and can accommodate singles to families of five or six. Suites have bedroom and living room with a fireplace.
Special Features: Heated pool; outdoor spa; two lighted tennis courts; horseshoes; recreation room with shuffleboard; billiards; Ping-Pong; mountain bikes.
Cost: Rates depend on season with February, March, and April the highest price: adults double per person $95 to $150, single $115 to $175, special weekly rates available. Children under six $25, six to seventeen $68, over seventeen $85. Three-night minimum stay. Mountain bikes $5 per hour.

MAYAN RANCH

Address: PO Box 577, Bandera, Texas 78003 (forty-five miles northwest of San Antonio)
Telephone: 210–796–3312; fax 210–796–8205

The Mayan has entertained city slickers for more than forty years with a low-priced package deal that includes two rides a day, three Texas-size meals, swimming in an Olympic-size pool, and a complimentary children's program during the summer months. Three generations of the gracious Hicks family run the show year-round, and a week at the Mayan is action-packed. Its rates for children are lower than at many other ranches, and the proximity to San Antonio allows families to spend a week or so at the Mayan and a few days exploring one of the most interesting cities in Texas. An expert roper teaches kids to lasso, and a snake handler gives a heart-stopping rattlesnake demonstration. Families can swim in the "swim corral" (aka the pool) or go tubing down the clear Medina River when they want to cool off.

Season: Year-round.

Accommodations: Thirty-four individual stone cottages sleep one to four people. The Mayan Lodge is a motel-like unit with adjoining rooms. All rooms are air-conditioned and heated.

Special Features: Two trail rides are offered daily, with horseback-riding instruction for beginners. Cowboy cookouts take place every day except Sunday. Other activities include hayrides, cookouts, tennis courts, volleyball, fitness room, shuffleboard, tubing on the river, swimming, fishing, and hiking. A children's program and nightly entertainment are offered during summer months.

Cost: Adult $675 per week; children twelve and under $280; thirteen to seventeen $480.

CENTRAL UNITED STATES

FLINT HILLS OVERLAND WAGON TRAIN

Address: PO Box 1076, El Dorado, Kansas 67042
Telephone: 316–321–6300

Ride in an authentic wagon through the Flint Hills with other "pioneer families" on this overnight wagon train experience. Since these trips are short, leaving at 9 A.M. in the morning and returning at 1 P.M. the following day, the cost is relatively low. You'll eat hearty pioneer-style meals. A chuck wagon lunch is served at noon on the first day, a cowboy-style dinner is cooked over an open fire at the evening campsite, and a huge breakfast (with fresh ground coffee brewed in a sock, cowboy-style) and light lunch are served on Sunday. Transportation is in 1870s-style wagons. You'll either camp out under the stars (bring your own sleeping bags—and tents, if you want to be under cover) or sleep under the wagons. Cowboy music, sing-alongs, and tall tales about the early days are all part of the evening entertainment. Ten to eleven trips are offered each season.

Season: June through September.

Cost: For one night and two days, adults and children age twelve and up $150 each, children under twelve $80, and children under four, free. If you wish to go for one day you can participate until after the evening campfire and entertainment for twenty percent less.

OREGON TRAIL WAGON TRAIN

Address: Route 2, Box 502, Bayard, Nebraska 69334
Telephone: 308–586–1850

Ride in a covered wagon just as the pioneers did when they traveled west by wagon train along the Oregon trail. Guests are encouraged to try their hand at driving the team or take a turn riding the scout horses on this one-, four-, or six-day living history trip. Meals are cooked on the open fire along the way; chow down on stew, hoe cakes, spoon-bread, sourdough bread, vinegar pudding, pioneer coffee, and tea. Multi-day trips start with a two-hour bus trip that takes guests to places along the trail they wouldn't get to by covered wagon today such as an old pony express station, and Chimney Rock and Castle Rock, important landmarks along the way. They learn to set up their own tents, make pioneer bonnets, and grease the wagons the first afternoon; that night there's a steak supper and square dance before they leave on the trail the next day. Bathroom facilities (the potty wagon) are part of the wagon train.

If you can't spare time for the treks, you can attend one of the nightly chuck wagon cookouts held at the base camp along the Platte River where there are also RV hookups and log cabins for overnight stays.

Season: June, July and August.

Accommodations: Wagon train riders sleep under the stars in a sleeping bag or in a covered wagon or tent. Sleeping bags are provided. One-room rustic log cabins sleep five or six and have baths and electricity but no air conditioning.

Cost: Treks, adults: one-day $150, four-day $479, six-day $579; children under twelve: one-day $125, four-day $399, six-day $484. Log cabin $40 per night. Pioneer cookout: adults $13, children under twelve $7, children under six $1 per year of age.

EAGLE HURST RESORT AND DUDE RANCH

Address: HC 88, Box 8638, Huzzah, Missouri 65565 (two-hour drive from St. Louis, sixteen miles east of Steelville)
Telephone: 314–786–2625

If the kids have any energy left after horseback riding along wooded trails and tubing down the clear Huzzah River, they can play lawn games, swim in the spacious swimming pool, or amuse themselves on the play equipment placed throughout the resort. A supervised morning program in summer is available for three- to ten-year-olds so that parents can play in shuffleboard, horseshoes, and Ping-Pong tournaments. This American plan resort provides three delicious meals a day, but the children we interviewed like the hot dog cookout the best. Reasonably priced riding is purchased separately.

Season: Memorial Day through September.

Accommodations: Thirty cabins and duplexes accommodate families of different sizes in one, two, and four bedrooms. Most of the cabins have a combination of double and single beds and all have airconditioning, daily housekeeping service, and small refrigerators for between-meal snacks.

Special Features: Swimming pool, tubing on the river, shuffleboard, horseshoes, Ping-Pong, badminton, pony rides for kids under ten (kids must be tall enough to reach the stirrups in order to go on trail rides), bingo, hayrides, a song fest, a talent show, square dancing, tennis.

Cost: In one-bedroom cottages: week-long stays, adults $279 to $300, children three to ten $150. Stays of three to six nights, adults $50, children three to ten $27 per night. In two-bedroom cottages: weekly stays adults $279 to $305, children three to ten $155. Nightly rate adults $57, children three to ten $30. Children under three always stay free.

Memorial Day and Labor Day packages available; 10 percent discount for reservations between late May and mid-June and after the middle of August. Horseback rides $12 per hour and two breakfast rides $18 each.

CIRCLE K RANCH

Address: 26525 Gay-Dreisbach Road, Circleville, Ohio 43113 (thirty miles south of Columbus)
Telephone: 614-474-3711

Circle K has a large family cottage for rent by the week in the summer and on weekends in the spring and fall. Guests do their own cooking, but a one-hour morning horseback ride is included in the price of a week-long stay. The ranch has plenty of animals; children can help feed the horses, ducks, chickens, goats, and rabbits. This peaceful 200-acre farm has fifteen acres of woods, a fishing and boating pond, a creek running through it, and an above-ground pool. It's a family enterprise with the hosts' four adult children helping out during the summer.

Season: Open mid-May through mid-October. The cottage is rented by the week (Sunday to Saturday) only in June, July, and August and on weekends in spring and fall.

Accommodations: The six-room cottage sleeps six people comfortably but can sleep more; one family of nine has come for many years. Two upstairs bedrooms contain three double beds and a crib. Downstairs is a living room, dining room, kitchen, and bathroom; there is a daybed and chaise in the dining room. All linens are provided.

Special Features: Rides, offered daily in the summer, are included in the price. Children must be nine or ten (tall enough to reach the stirrups) to go on guided trail rides; younger ones stay behind and are led around on gentle ponies. The ranch has a cookout on Sunday when people arrive and serves homemade ice cream on Friday night. Guests have unlimited use of the tennis court, above-ground pool, farm pond for boating or fishing, and hiking trails around the property.

Cost: Week-long stays in the summer $350 for four people, $25 for each additional person, regardless of age. Weekend stays in spring and fall (from as early as you want on Friday to as late as you want on Sunday) $25 per person per night (minimum $75). Horseback riding $10 per person for one-hour trail ride. Book early for summer.

Nearby: Columbus Zoo; outdoor theater in Tecumsa; many caves within an hour's drive.

WOODSIDE RANCH

Address: W4015 Highway 82, Mauston, Wisconsin 53948 (two and a half hours from Milwaukee, four hours from Chicago and Minneapolis)
Telephone: 608–847–4275; 800–626–4275

With eighty-five horses, this 1,400-acre ranch perched on the side of a pastoral river valley has a steed to match any riding ability. After the morning ride when the horses are resting, guests can paddle boats around the fishing pond, take a covered wagon ride, or play a game of volleyball. Supervised child care in the little red schoolhouse runs during the summer months, so parents can ride while their young ones are safely entertained with activities that include arts and crafts, stories, sports, and swimming. Saturday night barn dances are held year-round.

Season: Year-round.

Accommodations: Twenty-two log cabins and cottages with one, two, or three bedrooms all have private baths and fireplaces and house two to ten persons. Twelve rooms in the main ranch house can accommodate two, three, or four people. All units are air-conditioned in summer and heated in winter (firewood is provided). Bedding is provided, but you must bring your own towels.

Special Features: Trail rides are offered every half hour during the day, and small children can ride ponies in a ring. The minimum age for trail riding is about eight, depending on the child's ability to control a horse. The supervised play school for children has morning and afternoon sessions. Other features include a swimming pool, game room, outdoor cookouts, tennis, paddleboats, rowboats, volleyball, horseshoes, miniature golf, shuffleboard, Ping-Pong, sauna, and square dancing.

Cost: High-season summer (July and August), in cabin, adults $575 per seven-day week; kids eleven to twelve $480, eight to ten $377, three to seven $186, one to two $90. June through September, adults $410, children eleven to twelve $350, eight to ten $260, three to seven $140. All cabins have minimum charge of two adults per bedroom. You can also arrange for shorter stays with a two-night minimum. Seven-night stays in ranch house, adults $510; kids eleven to twelve $432, eight to ten $328, three to seven $164, one to two $75.

Fall, winter, and spring offer bunk-and-breakfast getaways that include breakfast and all riding and recreational activities. Fall and spring weekends: cabin adults $199; kids ten and under half price. Winter weekend, $99 per person in cabin and half price for kids, includes use of cross-country trails and breakfast. Equipment rentals extra; horseback riding $20 per forty-five-minute ride; sleigh rides $5.

HOBSON'S BLUFFDALE VACATION FARM

Address: Eldred, Illinois 62027 (seventy miles north of St. Louis)
Telephone: 217–983–2854

In operation for more than thirty years, Hobson's Bluffdale is a sprawling 320-acre working ranch where kids can help with such daily chores as tending the animals; feeding the pigs, chickens, or geese; and collecting eggs. An 1828 stone house has a dining room with a huge fireplace and cozy indoor activities. Horseback riding is available for all ages, and the farm also has a heated pool, boat rides and fishing on a pond, campfires, and even a trip to a nearby water park for the kids. Young archaeologists can visit the site of an archaeological dig. This ranch may not be out in the wild, wild west, but its low, low price and warm hospitality make it an especially good buy.

Season: Mid-March to mid-November.

Accommodations: Hobson's accommodates up to thirty-four guests; three different family rooms have a full-size bed and a set of bunks. The two-bedroom suites can sleep five to six. All are air-conditioned and have private baths. A new hideaway cottage in the woods has an outdoor private whirlpool spa, fireplace, and deck, and can sleep families up to six.

Special Features: Horseback riding begins after breakfast every morning. Younger children ride in the corral, while kids over nine can take trail rides with the adults. Once a week, guests are taken to a nearby lake for canoeing and paddleboating. Evening activities include a hayride, a cookout, bonfires, an ice-cream social, and a square dance. A special excursion to Raging Rivers Water Park is always tops with the kids.

Cost: Sunday to Sunday (includes three meals a day, daily horseback riding, and all activities and recreation), adults $375; children nine to fourteen $255, three to eight $205, under three $140. Daily, adults $65, children nine to fourteen $43, three to eight $35, under three $25. Cottage in the woods, daily rates (includes all meals, horseback riding, and all activities), adults $82, children nine to fourteen $59, three to eight $45, under three $30. Two-night minimum for weekends May through October; three-night minimum Memorial and Labor Day weekends.

WOLF LAKE RANCH RESORT

Address: Route 2, Box 2514, Baldwin, Michigan 49304
Telephone: 616–745–3890

Riding lessons are offered for novices at this popular ranch resort on sparkling Wolf Lake. The lake's sandy beach slopes so gently that volleyball games are set up in the clear water. Little ones can splash and swim without worrying about going out too deep. Two rowboats and a canoe are available for guests to use, or bring your own boat and use their dock. Summer packages run for three, four, or seven nights, and weekend packages are available for spring and fall. All packages include all-you-can-eat meals, two rides each day, and use of the recreational facilities at the ranch.

Season: Late April to early November.

Accommodations: Eight two-room units have a double or king-size bed in the front room and bunk beds in the back room. The Frontier House can sleep eight to sixteen people in four rooms with double beds and two sets of bunk beds. There is a washroom between the rooms and a large living room with a fireplace. All units are heated and bed linens are furnished, but guests must bring their own towels.

Special Features: Horseback riding is conducted on trails; children under six ride in the corral. The ranch has volleyball, tennis, basketball, water volleyball in the lake, a rec room with Ping-Pong, video games, jukebox, stereo, and fireplace; and evening campfires, hayrides, and square dancing. A launderette is available for guests' use.

Cost: Children five and under always stay free. Saturday-to-Saturday stays June through August, adults $470, kids eleven to sixteen $350, six to ten $240. Three-day stays (Wednesday to Saturday) in summer, adults $230, kids eleven to sixteen $190, six to ten $130. Four-day summer rates slightly higher. Spring and fall weekends (Friday to Sunday), adults $129, kids eleven to sixteen $99, six to ten $69. Includes meals, lodging, riding, use of all facilities, a campfire on Friday night, and a hayride on Saturday night.

THE SOUTH

SCOTT VALLEY RESORT AND GUEST RANCH

Address: PO Box 1447BBV, Mountain Home, Arkansas 72653 (two hours southeast of Branson, Missouri)
Telephone: 501–425–5136; fax 501–424–5800

Rated three times by *Family Circle* magazine as one of the best family ranches of the year, Scott Valley has a pastoral setting in the middle of the Ozarks with lots of horseback riding and recreational fun. Experienced and novice riders take separate trail rides, and summer months feature evening activities and ferryboat dinner trips. World-class trout fishing and canoeing (not wild water, just scenic and family-friendly) is available just ten minutes away on the famous White and North Fork Rivers. Ask about Arkansas' special "free fishing" weekend from noon on Friday to midnight on Sunday, when you may fish without a license. Young children are given pony rides and supervision while parents ride; baby-sitting for children under two years is available for an additional fee.

Season: March through November.

Accommodations: Sixteen two-bedroom units and twelve one-bedroom units have air-conditioning, private baths, and housekeeping service. Two-bedroom family units have a double bed in one room, two twins in the other.

Special Features: Five to six horseback rides are offered daily, and children age seven and over can take their own horse on trail rides. Younger ones can either ride double with a parent or go on a pony ride back at the ranch. Facilities include a swimming pool, whirlpool spa, petting zoo, playground, tennis, volleyball, shuffleboard, cookout, hayride, and complimentary launderette. The fishing and boating lake is a ten-minute drive from the ranch.

Cost: Rates include riding, use of fishing boats and canoes, meals, music shows, and all recreational and sporting activities. Three-day minimum stay June 11 to August 15, daily price for adults $107.50; children seven to twelve $88, two to six $57. Seven-night stays in summer $650 per adult; children seven to twelve $530, three to six $340. The rest of the year adults $95 per day; children seven to twelve $75, two to six $47.50. Four people sharing one unit get a ten-percent discount; children under two always stay free. Special family reunion rates. Airport pickups from Mountain Home free of charge.

Nearby: Ozark Folk Center (see page 302); Silver Dollar City; Branson, Missouri; Mountain Village 1890; Blanchard Springs Caverns; Laura Ingalls Wilder Museum; and more.

THE NORTHEAST

GOLDEN ACRES FARM AND RANCH

Address: Gilboa, New York 12076
Telephone: 800–847–2151, 800–252–7787, 607–588–7328; fax 607–588–6911.

Golden Acres is known for family fun in the Catskills, with riding and a variety of other things to do. If the weather turns bad, steer your horse to the indoor riding arena to practice walking, trotting, and cantering.

There are plenty of farm animals to pet—cows, horses, goats, sheep, ducks, chickens, rabbits, dogs, cats—and baby animals in the spring and summer. Children can milk a cow, collect eggs, and help feed the animals. A children's program that runs during the summer months keeps four- to twelve-year-olds busy all day, and a nursery is provided for infants and toddlers ages three months to three years.

Season: Late May to early September.

Accommodations: Families can choose between individual family rooms, two-room suites, or an apartment with a kitchen and two rooms. Golden Acres has a guest capacity of four hundred, so activities can get crowded on busy summer weekends.

Special Features: Large children's playland area, nine-hole miniature golf, children's day camp and nursery, horseback and pony riding and instruction, indoor and outdoor pools, fishing, tennis, basketball, Ping-Pong, hayrides, badminton, movies, softball, fossil hunting, arts and crafts, berry picking, archery, boating, a you-pick vegetable garden.

Cost: All rates include the use of all facilities, horseback riding, nursery, and daycamp. "You-cook" vacation apartments are the best deal if you don't mind doing your own cooking, but you must bring your own towels, cookware, and dishes. One-room unit with kitchen $775 per week for four people, $660 for three people. Two-room suites $900 for four people, or $370 for a three-day, two-night stay. Lowest price for American plan lodging (includes breakfast and dinner for adults and three meals for children) has a shared bath: adults $360 per week, kids eleven to sixteen $215, four to ten $180, toddlers one to three $100, infants free. The farm also has campgrounds.

PINEGROVE DUDE RANCH RESORT

Address: Kerhonkson, New York 12446
Telephone: 800–346–4626; 914–626–7345

Pinegrove is practically a three-ring circus when it comes to dude ranches, with six hundred acres of fun in the sun, snow, or rain. The ranch has one of the largest indoor facilities (choose from tennis, swimming, archery, volleyball, basketball, bocci, and miniature golf) as well as plenty to do outdoors. Winter activities include downhill skiing on two slopes, ice-skating, and tubing. (Ski equipment is complimentary and snow is guaranteed since the ranch has its own snowmaking equipment.) Daily riding in summer, a supervised children's program, and reasonable prices make this ranch a favorite of many who don't want to make the trip out to the "real West."

Season: Year-round.

Accommodations: One hundred twenty rooms have private baths and climate control. Most rooms have either two double beds or two double beds and a sofabed. There are country cottages on the property for larger families that have one to four bedrooms.

Special Features: A full-time children's day camp has arts and crafts, games and sports, and a special nursery for children under two years. There's a complete teen program and baby-sitting available. There's a baby animal farm, leather workshops, steer roping practice, cattle drives, fishing and boating on the lake, and evening entertainment. The Indian Village includes tepees, campfires, totem poles, and local Iroquois Indians demonstrating dances and telling legends. Big eaters will love the all-you-can-eat meals plus free unlimited snack bar.

Cost: Children under four stay free, and children four to sixteen pay half the adult rate. You can opt for a stay of any length; the longer you stay the better the daily rate. Many package deals are available throughout the year. The Family of Three special offers six days and five nights for three people for $999; each extra child $59 per day.

ROCKING HORSE RANCH

Address: Highland, New York 12528–2217
Telephone: 800–647–2624, 914–691–2927; fax 914–691–6434

Just 75 miles from New York City, year-round Rocking Horse Ranch offers 500 acres of cowboy fun. Its resort activities center around daily horseback rides (and pony rides for little ones), but its all-inclusive package features supervised day and evening children's programs, waterskiing, banana-boat rides, fishing, archery, arts and crafts for all ages, three heated swimming pools, sporting facilities, and evening entertainment for adults and children. You can stay for as long or short a time as you like; the prices drop the longer you stay.

Season: Year-round.

Accommodations: One hundred twenty rooms in the main lodge and "Oklahoma building" all have private baths and are air-conditioned. Most rooms can accommodate four to six people in two double beds and a sofabed.

Special Features: The children's program runs daily from 9 A.M. to 4:30 P.M. and again in the evening from 8 to 10 P.M. Kids do everything the adults do, but the activities are supervised and tailored to their abilities. Indoor and outdoor opportunities for children and adults include waterskiing, target shooting, fishing, hiking, riding, playground, Ping-Pong, horseshoes, badminton, squash, tennis, hayrides, paddleboats, miniature golf, bocci courts, fitness gym, sauna, arts and crafts, talent shows, and such nightly entertainment as bingo tournaments, limbo contests, music, and dancing. Older kids get their own evening entertainment several times a week, which might include bonfires, disco parties, and sing-alongs. In winter add skiing and ice-skating to the long list of things to do.

Cost: Many package deals are available, especially during certain weeks of the fall and winter when kids stay free. Regular prices, seven-night stay: adults $615 to $685, children four to sixteen $300 to $325. Two-night, three-day weekend package, adults $220 to $275, children four to sixteen $105 to $125. Third adult in room pays child rate. Rates include everything except lunches and a fifteen-percent service charge added to your bill.

NATIONAL PARKS

*O*ur country's national parks, although spectacular, do not have the automatic kid appeal of Disneyland. Their attractions can be as small as the rustle of a fast-moving snake or the deep purple of a spring-blooming violet. While a mirror-clear glacier lake might not dazzle your children, the parks have loads of thrilling outdoor activities, from trail rides to float trips, that will inevitably win them over. An eagle-eyed twelve-year-old can hunt for arrowheads in Utah's Canyon Country, ride cowboy style in Wyoming's Grand Tetons, or take up the challenge of learning to rock climb in the High Sierras.

If you are not entirely convinced, how about this: compared to other destinations, national parks have dirt-cheap lodgings, from rustic tent cabins and family hostels to midpriced historic lodges. It's actually a challenge to spend money in some. There aren't many fancy places to eat, so you can save your money for outdoor sports and activities.

Camping is obviously the least expensive way to experience our national parks, as campsites cost only a few dollars per night. If your family thrives on spending time outdoors, nothing tops sleeping under an open sky. The sheer beauty of nature works wonders on alleviating the stress of everyday life. A helpful and inexpensive resource is the *Complete Guide to America's National Parks*, with camping and hiking information, climate charts, and state and regional maps; it is available from the National Park Foundation, 800–533–6478. Another informative book is *National Parks: The Family Guide* by Dave Robertson (On Site

Publications, 1993) with first-hand descriptions of kids' activities, best bets, and recreational activities.

Some recommended pretrip reading materials include *Sharing Nature with Children* and *Sharing the Joy of Nature*, with activities and games designed to get you and your children in touch with the out-of-doors, by Joseph Cornell (Nevada City, Calif.: Dawn Publications, 1979; $6.95 each) and *The Young Naturalist* by Andrew Mitchell (Tulsa: EDC Publishing, 1982; $6.95). These books and many others designed for children are available from the Rocky Mountain Nature Association, Rocky Mountain National Park, Estes Park, Colorado 80517 (970-586-1258).

In this chapter we list cabins, motels, inexpensive lodges, and family hostels either in or near national parks where families can enjoy a bit more comfort than camping in a tent provides. If you are planning a summer visit, be prepared: it is crowded out there. The biggest crush occurs in the middle of summer. To protect the quality of these treasured sites, development is closely controlled, and there aren't enough rooms to meet demand. It is wise to make reservations nine to twelve months in advance for the least expensive and most desirable rooms or cabins.

WEST COAST

YOSEMITE NATIONAL PARK, CALIFORNIA

Renowned for its magnificence, Yosemite is the country's most-revisited national park. Its towering granite domes and peaks, cascading waterfalls, glacial lakes and giant trees attract close to four million visitors annually, including many families who return year after year, so advance reservations for all accommodations are essential. Smart travelers can avoid the crowds. Seventy percent of the park's visitors arrive during summer, and most never venture outside the seven square miles of Yosemite Valley. The secret to discovering an uncrowded Yosemite is to visit between October and April (spring will find you knee-deep in wildflowers when the waterfalls are at their crashing best) and avoid holiday weekends. If you do visit in the summer, try the less-traveled but equally attractive areas of the Park, such as Tuolumne and Wawona (see pages 93–94).

All hotels will accept reservations one year before your intended date of arrival, so if you plan ahead you will have a good chance of getting the schedule you want. Other tips from veteran Yosemite visitors: if you want to stay over a weekend, plan your arrival for a weekday; be flexible and have several arrival dates in mind; call to make reservations on weekends, when Yosemite Reservations receives the fewest calls; call thirty, fifteen, or seven days in advance of your planned arrival date, as these are common times when previously reserved rooms become available through cancellations. Your efforts will be worthwhile—the park is truly spectacular.

The park has many programs for families, from campfire talks to guided nature walks. For children five through seven, a special hour with a ranger is offered each day in summer, while eight- through twelve-year-olds can join a national park ranger in search of "secret places" in Yosemite. There are also ranger-led family discovery walks. Sign up for all at the Happy Isle Nature Center (shuttle stop no. 16), which sponsors many other programs designed especially for children. You can leave kids at the center for these free programs on Feathered Friends, Art in Nature, and many other subjects. At the Happy Isle Bookstore (or any visitor center) pick up an Explorer Pack, a day-pack filled with guide-books and activity suggestions for families. Each pack has a theme, such as "Rocking in Yosemite" or "Featuring Feathers."

During spring and summer, guided saddle rides for children seven and up depart from the Yosemite Valley Stables (Easter to mid-October) and at Wawona, White Wolf, and Tuolumne Meadows (summer only). Rides range from two hours ($35) to half a day ($45) to all day ($67). Four- and six-day rides to the High Sierra Camps are available, too. Call 209-454-2002 for information.

The Indian Cultural Museum, next to the Yosemite Valley Visitor Center, has an authentic recreated Ahwahneechee Indian village. The Art Activity Center holds free art classes next to the village store from spring through fall; the Yosemite Theater offers live performances and movies. The Pioneer Yosemite History Center, at Wawona, has historic park buildings from the 1800s, and rangers and docents in period costume lead participatory crafts projects such as candlemaking during the summer and at Christmas time.

Among the many tours of the park are a two-hour tour in an open-air tram and a full-day tour of Glacier Point, 3,214 feet above the valley floor. Stop by a tour desk at any hotel or call 209–372–1240 for information. Tour costs range from $16 to $42; children twelve and under are half price, and those under five are free.

River rafting on the Merced River is a wonderful experience, especially in Yosemite Valley, where at every river bend there's another spectacular view. In early summer, rental rafts complete with life jackets and paddles are available at Curry Village. The Merced has many sandy beaches open mid- to late summer. You also can swim at the Curry Village and Yosemite Lodge swimming pools. The valley has miles of bike paths; bike rental is $5.25 per hour or $20 per day at Yosemite Lodge or Curry Village.

The park is renowned for rock climbing, an excellent sport for building teamwork. Children under fourteen participate in a group lesson; older kids can enroll in a private class. Classes are offered daily from June through September at the Yosemite Mountaineering School in Tuolumne Meadows. Classes are held at Curry Village from October through May.

A winter visit to the park is your chance to soak up its grandeur during a more peaceful season. Coyotes and mule deer are easy to see, hotel rates drop twenty-five percent, low-cost ski packages are available, and the park has far fewer visitors. Take advantage of Yosemite's Midweek Ski Lesson Package: lift tickets and ski lessons at the Badger Pass resort, cross-country ski lessons, bus transportation from one point to another, ice-skating, ski area baby-sitting, and ranger-led nature, history, and wildlife programs are available at a fraction of the cost for similar services at other ski centers. Downhill skiing at Badger Pass, a small resort with a gentle terrain, is great for beginners. The Midweek Ski Lesson Package and children's Badger Pups Package is $25 per day added to the price of the lodging you choose; lodge rooms with the ski package start at $73 per night, double occupancy. There is also a "Ski Free" program; hotel guests receive coupons redeemable the next day at Badger Pass for all-day lift tickets. Many of the 350 miles of trails for cross-country skiing in the park also begin at Badger Pass. Trail passes are free. Call 209–372–1000 for ski information.

The Curry Village Ice Rink is an outdoor rink where families can skate in the shadow of Glacier Point with a spectacular view of Half Dome. An open fire next to the rink is ideal for warming chilled little hands and wet bottoms. Open daily November through March; call 209–372–8341 for information. Winter is also time for ranger-led snowshoe walks and the evening "Discover Yosemite" talk, an interactive program suitable for the entire family.

Note: In addition to the lodgings listed on the next page in Yosemite, there is a family camp in the Sierra Nevadas near the park run by San Jose Family Camps. See page 148 in our chapter on family camps.

WAWONA HOTEL

Address: Yosemite Concession Services Corporation, Yosemite National Park, California 95389. **The hotel is twenty-seven miles from Yosemite Valley on California 41, seven miles from the park's South Entrance and Mariposa Grove of the Giant Sequoias. Telephone: 209-252-4848. Book one year ahead or be flexible about dates.**

Families who plan ahead can escape Yosemite Valley's summer crowds by visiting the park's less-visited Wawona section. This southern section of the park is loaded with historic architecture and great swimming spots along the Merced River. Families with small children love Wawona for the fun Mariposa Grove tram ride through some of the world's oldest and tallest trees and for the Pioneer Yosemite History Center, where costumed docents reenact nineteenth-century life. Anchoring Wawona is the gracious Wawona Hotel, one of California's oldest mountain resort hotels. A beautifully restored Victorian white clapboard, the hotel is reminiscent of early Adirondack resorts with wide covered porches, green wooden rockers, and expansive lawns.

Season: Easter week through Thanksgiving. Re-opens mid-December through January. During January, February, and March, open Thursday through Sunday only.

Accommodations: The 104 rooms are small and simple, but comfortable. Most rooms sleep four with one double bed and two twin beds. Those with private bathrooms have clawfoot tubs with showers. Rooms open onto wide, covered porches. In addition, there is a separate building ideal for family reunions where individual guest rooms share a common area.

Special Features: Swimming pool, daily housekeeping service, tennis courts, nearby snow skiing, golf (nine-hole course), horseback riding, and a variety of hiking trails lead from the hotel. The main lodge lobby has board games and a piano player in the evening. Mealtime is family-oriented at the hotel's dining room, and a Western lawn barbecue is held on summer Saturdays. No televisions or telephones in rooms.

Cost: Rooms with central bath, $71 per night double occupancy. Rooms with private bath, $95 per night double occupancy. Additional adult $13; children stay free when sharing a room with their parents.

Nearby: A short walk leads to river swimming holes and the engaging Pioneer History Center with nineteenth-century crafts and stagecoach rides. About 200 yards upstream from the Center's covered bridge are small swimming and wading pools with big, flat rocks for sunbathing. Winter is especially enchanting; the area surrounding the hotel is perfect for cross-country skiing and snowshoe walks. Less than an hour away is downhill skiing at Badger Pass. Mariposa Grove of the Giant Sequoias is a short drive from the hotel.

TUOLUMNE MEADOWS LODGE

Address: Yosemite Concession Services Corporation, Yosemite National Park, California 95389 (at an elevation of 8,575 feet, this lodge is situated in a large subalpine meadow)
Telephone: 209–252–4848

Families who plan ahead can escape Yosemite Valley's summer crowds by also visiting the park's less traveled Tuolumne area. The Tuolumne high country lies off Tioga Road, which bisects the park from southwest to northeast. Along the road are lakes and the spectacular wildflowers of Tuolumne Meadows, surrounded by peaks and glacier-polished domes. Campfire gatherings are held nightly, often with special children's songs and stories. Eight- to twelve-year-olds can participate in a Junior Ranger program. Tuolumne is a favorite base camp for people heading to the High Sierra Camps or for day hikes in the Tuolumne Meadows area.

Season: Mid-June through Labor Day.

Accommodations: The lodge has sixty-nine canvas tent cabins with beds (all bedding is provided) and centrally located restrooms.

Special Features: Breakfast and dinner are available in a central dining tent beside the river.

Cost: Tent cabins $43 per night, double occupancy. Additional adult $7; additional child $3.

Nearby: Within walking distance are a grocery store, stables, the mountaineering school, gas station, post office, and a hamburger stand. The one and a half mile hike from Tuolumne to Dog Lake is a bit of a climb at first, but there is good swimming and fishing at the end. A great half-day hike to Lembert Dome from Soda Springs at Tuolumne, past many bubbling springs, leads to easy rock climbing on the dome and views of all the major peaks in this area. For older children, an evening guided walk, the Night Prowl, begins at Tuolumne Meadow at 9:30 P.M. to see and hear owls, bats, and other nocturnal animals.

WHITE WOLF LODGE

Address: Yosemite Concession Services Corporation, Yosemite National Park, California 95389 (hotel is in the high country, just off Tioga Road)
Telephone: 209–252–4848

Another great way to escape the summer valley crowds is White Wolf, between Tuolumne and the Valley off Tioga Road. The lodge is a popular base for day hikes or half-day guided horseback rides to Lukens and Harden lakes. There are riding stables near the lodge.
Season: Mid-June through Labor Day.
Accommodations: The lodge has twenty-four rustic canvas tent cabins with beds (all bedding is included) and four cabins with private bath.
Special Features: There are no cooking facilities; simple meals are available in a lovely old clapboard dining hall.
Cost: Cabins with private bath $71 per night, double occupancy. Canvas tent cabins $43 per night, double occupancy. Additional adult $7; additional child $3.
Nearby: Camp store, easy access to lakes. A popular guided four-hour picnic hike to Lukens Lake leaves once a week from the trailhead 1.8 miles east of White Wolf on Tioga Road. Check for the schedule when you arrive.

YOSEMITE LODGE

Address: Yosemite Concession Services Corporation, Yosemite National Park, California 95389 (hotel is in Yosemite Valley near the base of Yosemite Falls)
Telephone: 209–252–4848

If it is your first visit to the park—no matter what season—the famed Yosemite Valley will no doubt be part of your itinerary. El Capitan, Cathedral Spires, Bridalveil, and Yosemite Falls are all "must-sees." This large, modern hotel is at the eastern end of the valley.
Season: Year-round.
Accommodations: The lodge has 495 rooms ranging from deluxe to the more affordable standard rooms. All rooms offer standard motel-style lodging with telephones and private or central bathrooms, but no televisions. Deluxe rooms have a private patio or balcony, private dressing area, activity table, and views of either waterfalls or mountains. There are also cabins with a private or central bath that accommodate up to five people. Cabins are furnished with beds, blankets, and linens, but do not have kitchens, telephones, or televisions.

Special Features: The lodge is part of a compound that includes a swimming pool; a wide range of dining facilities, including poolside fast food; a post office; an outdoor theater; bike rentals; and a tour desk.

Cost: Standard rooms with private bath $73 to $101 per night, double occupancy, depending on season. Cabins with private bath $72 per night, double occupancy; with central bath $56. Additional adult $7 to $11, depending upon accommodation; additional child $3 to $3.75.

Nearby: The Sunrise Camera walk, a two-hour expedition on flat trails to some of the best valley floor sites and landmarks for snapping photographs, leaves the lodge at 6 A.M. Walk, drive, bike, or ride the shuttle to stop no. 7 near the lodge for a quarter-mile walk on a flat trail to the base of Yosemite Falls, the world's fifth highest waterfall. All the valley sites are within easy reach of the lodge, including the Happy Isles Nature Center, which features exhibits and activities just for kids. Happy Isles is the start of several trails, including the Mist Trail to Vernal Falls, which is best suited for children eight and older. From shuttle stop no. 17, there is an easy one-hour hike to Mirror Lake where you can often see the reflection of Half Dome.

CURRY VILLAGE

Address: Yosemite Concession Services Corporation, Yosemite National Park, California 95389 (hotel is beneath Glacier Point on the valley floor)
Telephone: 209–252–4848

Yosemite Valley's major "must-see"'s—El Capitan, Cathedral Spires, Bridalveil and Yosemite Falls—are all close to Curry Village. Set under cedar trees at the eastern end of Yosemite Valley, this popular compound offers a variety of accommodations.

Season: April through September.

Accommodations: You can choose from cabins with private or central bath, tent cabins with a central bathhouse, or standard motel-type rooms with private bathrooms, which sleep up to four people. The cabins can accommodate up to five people with a rollaway bed or crib.

Special Features: Curry Village has a camp store, restaurants, the Yosemite Mountaineering School (open September through June), a swimming pool, bike rental, boat rental for river rafting, an ice rink, and cross-country ski rental.

Cost: Cabins with private bath $72 per night, double occupancy; with central bath $56. Canvas tent cabins with central bath $41 per night, double occupancy. Additional adult $6; additional child $2.50.

Nearby: All the Yosemite Valley sites are within easy reach; refer to Yosemite Lodge's listing on page 95 for details.

HOUSEKEEPING CAMP

Address: Yosemite Concession Services Corporation, Yosemite National Park, California 95389
Telephone: 209-252-4848

Located on the south bank of the Merced River, this is Yosemite's answer to roughing it without a tent.

Season: Late April through mid-October.

Accommodations: Each unit has three concrete walls, a concrete floor, and a canvas roof. The fourth wall is a canvas curtain separating the sleeping area from a covered cooking and dining area. Units sleep six and have two twin-size fold-down bunks and a double bed, a picnic table with chairs, and a fire ring. There are 282 units with a central restroom and shower facilities.

Special Features: A wide, sandy beach is ideal for swimming and has grand views of Yosemite Falls and Half Dome.

Cost: Units $36 per night. Propane stoves available for $1.50 per day, including propane.

Nearby: Laundry facilities and a small grocery store.

HIGH SIERRA CAMPS

Address: Yosemite Reservations, 5410 East Home, Fresno, California 93727
Telephone: 209-253-5674. *Note:* **Reservations are accepted beginning the first Monday in December for the following summer. Due to space limitations, only 10 percent of those who apply are accepted.**

Merced Lake, Vogelsang, Glen Aulin, May Lake, and Sunrise camps are all located roughly eight strenuous miles apart in spectacular mountain settings. These accommodations are in great demand, as they offer a truly magnificent outdoor experience. Visitors can either hike or ride in on their own or participate in a variety of guided hikes or saddle trips of four to six days. All trips depart from Tuolumne Meadows. Trips are appropriate for children over seven.

Season: Late June to Labor Day, conditions permitting.

Accommodations: Camps have dorm-style tent cabins with guests segregated by sex. Cabins are furnished with beds, a blanket or quilt, and a pillow. Guests bring their own sheets; traveler sheets, which weigh much less than regular sheets, can be purchased when you register. There are central restrooms with hot showers (welcome at the end of a day on the trail). Most cabins are equipped with a wood stove for heat; no electricity or phones.

Special Features: Hearty breakfast and dinner are served in a central dining tent.

Cost: Approximately $90 per night per person includes breakfast, dinner, and showers. Children over seven stay at reduced rates. Four-day moderately strenuous guided hike $375 per person; seven-day guided hike $740 per person; four-day guided saddle ride $565 per person; six-day guided saddle ride $890 per person. Rates include all meals and accommodations.

Nearby: Glen Aulin Camp is four miles from magnificent Waterwheel Fall. May Lake Camp is on the shore of May Lake beneath the eastern wall of Mount Hoffman. Sunrise Camp is located on a long narrow shelf forty feet above Long Meadow. Merced Lake Camp is on the Merced River and is the camp at the lowest elevation. Vogelsang Camp is the highest and the most dramatic, situated above the treeline near many alpine lakes.

CRATER LAKE NATIONAL PARK, OREGON

Whether you are parked at a pullout along Rim Drive, hiking a ridge above the caldera, or cruising to Wizard Island aboard a tour boat, your family will be awed by the intensity of the color of Crater Lake. Its remarkably deep and clear water quickly absorbs all colors in the spectrum except blue, and to simply view the lake is thrilling. At 1,932 feet, it is the deepest lake in the United States, and the seventh deepest in the world—a fact that especially excites the imaginations of children.

The lake is in a caldera left after a series of volcanic explosions, and the resulting landscape is rugged and varied for hikers. Wildflowers begin to blossom as soon as the snow melts and peak in mid-July. The most dramatic display is along the half-mile Castle Crest Wildflower Trail. Only one trail, the one-mile steep descent to Cleetwood Cove, leads down the caldera's steep sides to the lake. From there, boats depart for a two-hour tour of the lake which include views of the caldera from 800 to 1,800 feet below its rim and a stop at Wizard Island (mid-June through mid-September: $12 adults, $7.50 children).

CRATER LAKE LODGE

Address: For reservations write PO Box 128, Crater Lake National Park, Crater Lake, Oregon 97604
Telephone: Mid-October to mid-May: 503–830–8700; fax 503–830–8514. Mid-May to mid-October: 503–594–2511; fax 503–594–2622

Crater Lake Lodge, perched on the rim of the lake, reopened in 1995 after a seven-year closure and a $15 million renovation. The lodge now carries forth the grand and nostalgic architectural tradition of mountain lodges such as Mount Hood's Timberline or Yosemite's Ahwahnee with huge tree trunk columns, black-steel-and-parchment cylinder lights, and massive stone fireplaces.
Season: May through October.
Accommodations: The seventy refurbished guest rooms have private bathrooms, some with claw-foot tubs in front of floor-to-ceiling windows with fantastic views of the lake. Other rooms have views of the forest and meadow. No telephones or televisions, just lots of windows!
Special Features: Board games available to check out; visitors have many dining options at the lodge and in nearby Rim Village, where the Llao Rock Cafe serves cafeteria-style meals.
Cost: Least expensive rooms with forest views, $99 per night, double occupancy; each additional person $15. Children under twelve stay free in parents' room.
Nearby: Summer campfire programs are presented at the Mazama Campground, and the park offers many special activities for children. Check at the visitor center.

MAZAMA VILLAGE MOTOR INN

Address: For reservations write to PO Box 128, Crater Lake National Park, Crater Lake, Oregon 97604
Telephone: Mid-October to mid-May: 503–830–8700; fax 503–830–8514. Mid-May to mid-October: 503–594–2511; fax 503–594–2622

What Crater Lake's motel lacks in historic charm, it makes up for in price and ease for families.
Season: May through October.
Accommodations: Mazama has forty identical units nestled in a wooded setting; each room has two queen-size beds. No telephone or televisions.
Special Features: Convenience store for late-night munchies, groceries, and supplies.

Cost: $78 per night double occupancy; each additional person $6. Children under six stay free in parents' room.

Nearby: Rim Village is seven miles away.

OLYMPIC NATIONAL PARK, WASHINGTON

Olympic National Park is an unspoiled landscape of sandy beaches, serene lakes, glacier peaks, meadows, streams, and forests. Few people totally immerse themselves in the ocean here without wetsuits, but many families play on this popular and particularly scenic stretch of rugged coast in other ways—clamming, hunting for beach glass, kiting, hiking, biking, and fishing for salmon and steelhead on the nearby Quinault and Hoh rivers. The half-hour ferry ride from Port Angeles to British Columbia, Canada, is a fun side trip.

The park service runs wonderful naturalist programs for children that include beach and tide pool walks, meadow explorations, and a program called Sub-alpine Secrets. Children eight and older can earn junior ranger certificates. Check with the visitor center on arrival. A trip to this part of the Olympic Peninsula is not complete without a visit to one of its rain forests. Easiest to reach is the Hoh Rain Forest, eighteen miles up the Hoh River from U.S. 101. Its visitor center provides information about the trails, as well as raft trips on the Hoh and Queets rivers.

KALALOCH LODGE

Address: 157151 U.S. 101, Forks, Washington 98331 (seventy miles north of Aberdeen/Hoquiam and thirty-five miles south of Forks; the lodge is perched on a bluff overlooking the Pacific Ocean) Telephone: 360–962–2271; fax 360–962–3391

Kalaloch is a great base if you want a mix of the beach, mountains, and rain forest. The lodge, built in 1953 to resemble an oceanside fishing village, overlooks the beach, and the trail down is easy to negotiate. Beachcombers can collect driftwood, shells, agates, glass, and fish nets that have washed in from distant places. Bring kites, as the beach has great offshore winds. In April the shore usually is hopping with clammers, and in late March or April you might be able to spot a pod of gray whales migrating. The water is too cold and dangerous for young children to swim in, but a small lagoon right in front of the lodge is ideal for paddling.

Season: Year-round.

Accommodations: The least expensive accommodations are the eight guest rooms in the main lodge (some have ocean views) and the "bluff cabins." Some of the lodge rooms are reported to be noisy, so be sure to inquire about the location of your room. Many of the bluff cabins have ocean views and all have kitchen facilities (utensils not included) and full baths (towels and bedding included).

Special Features: The main lodge has a coffee shop, a dining room with many local Northwest seafood dishes, and a reading room. There is a small grocery store on site.

Cost: Mid-April to mid-May, all lodge rooms $55 to $85 per night double occupancy. During other months, lodge rooms $73 to $105 per night double occupancy, depending on view; each additional person $10. Bluff cabins start at $130 per night double occupancy, depending on view; each additional person $10. Children under five stay free.

Nearby: Protected beach coves farther north are ideal for summer splashing. This is a good base for day trips to the Hoh Rain Forest, a spectacular moss-hung rain forest in the park, or a walk along the three-mile boardwalk from Lake Ozette to remote beaches. Other excursions include a visit to the Makah Indian village at Neah Bay, where artifacts are on display. Also within easy access are the secluded beaches of the Kalaloch area, with sea stacks and tidal pools for viewing anemones and starfish.

LAKE QUINAULT LODGE

Address: PO Box 7, 345 South Shore Road, Quinault, Washington 98575 (From Hoquiam, go north on U.S. 101 for thirty-eight miles to milepost 125 just past Neilton; turn right onto South Shore Road and go two miles.)
Telephone: 800–562–6672 (Washington and Oregon only), 360–288–2900; fax: 360–288–2901

This lodge, geared especially to families, is located at the southern edge of the national park overlooking Lake Quinault. In the midst of one of the few rain forests in North America, its setting is one of the best on the Olympic Peninsula.

Season: Year-round.

Accommodations: Built in 1926, Lake Quinault has a main lodge, lakeside rooms, and rooms with a lakeview and/or a fireplace; all rooms have private bathrooms. The least expensive rooms are located in the Annex, which was built in 1923. Some of the rooms in the Main Lodge overlook the parking lot rather than the lake, so be sure to inquire ahead of time.

Special Features: Adjacent to the pool is a game room with equipment for horseshoes, volleyball, and Frisbee, as well as pinball, Ping-

Pong, and video games. Guests can play badminton and croquet on the meticulously kept lawn overlooking the lake, or rent canoes and seacycles in the summer. Fishing on the lake is highly rated. The lodge's playground has swings and a slide. The lodge has a full-service restaurant year-round and an outdoor cafe during the summer. The staff at the lodge's front desk can inform you about the park's nature programs and will provide additional games and puzzles for indoor play. They also will help arrange baby-sitting; they even have rubber sheets for bed-wetters!

Cost: Rates are seasonal. Rooms start at $52 per night double occupancy in winter, and go up to $130 per night double occupancy in summer. Each additional person $10. Children five and under stay free. The lodge offers many special deals, including midweek or off-season specials, so it pays to inquire.

Nearby: Hiking trails through the rain forest start at the lodge; maps are available at the front desk. There is horseback riding available further up the valley.

LOG CABIN RESORT

Address: 3183 East Beach Road, Port Angeles, Washington 98362 (eighteen miles from Port Angeles)
Telephone: 360–928–3325; fax: 360–928–2088

Log Cabin Resort is on Lake Crescent in Olympic National Park; many of its rooms are either along the shoreline or have beautiful lake views. The resort's marina rents canoes, rowboats, and paddleboats, and there is a swimming area at the lake. Campfire programs are scheduled regularly.

Season: Year-round.

Accommodations: The resort has lodge rooms that sleep four; these rooms have two queen-size beds and private bathrooms, plus lake and mountain views. A chalet located along the shoreline with lake and mountain views sleeps six and includes a small kitchen (no cooking or eating utensils provided), an outdoor barbecue, and a picnic table. Other accommodations include rustic cabins with kitchens and camping log cabins (bring or rent bedding) with outdoor picnic tables and campfires.

Special Features: Restaurant, grocery store, and gift shop.

Cost: Lodge rooms $95 per night, double occupancy. Chalet rooms $108 per night, double occupancy. Cabins with kitchens $80 per night, double occupancy; rustic cabins $66 per night, double occupancy; each additional person age six and above $10. Camping log cabins $42 per night, double occupancy; each additional person $5; children ten and under stay free.

Nearby: Hiking, rowboating, and fishing on Lake Crescent; many picnic areas are around the lake. The trail to Marymere Falls, a spectacular ninety-foot waterfall, is a flat three-quarter-mile walk. The Hoh Rain Forest and the Kalaloch Beach area, with tide pools and clamming, are nearby. Other local beaches are Salt Creek Beach, Park, and Rialto. Nearby Port Angeles has bowling, a public indoor pool, and rollerskating.

SOL DUC HOT SPRINGS RESORT

Address: PO Box 2169, Port Angeles, Washington 98362 (thirty miles west of Port Angeles, twelve miles off U.S. 101)
Telephone: 360–327–3583

Set in a valley of 150-foot evergreen trees on the Soleduck River, families come to Sol Duc primarily for its three hot spring pools, which include a toddler pool. There is also a freshwater swimming pool with lifeguards.

Season: Mid-May through September. The hot springs are open on weekends only in April and October.

Accommodations: The resort has furnished cabins; some have kitchens. All one-room cabins have a full private bath, heat, two double beds, or two queen-size beds, a pull-out couch, and a chest of drawers.

Special Features: Massages are available. There is a family dining room, poolside deli, espresso bar, and grocery store.

Cost: Cabins range from $83 to $98 per night, double occupancy. Additional people age four and above $12.50 each; children under four stay free. Rates include use of the pools.

Nearby: Hiking along the well-maintained Olympic National Park trails and fishing for wild coho salmon, steelhead, and native rainbow trout.

HAWAII VOLCANOES NATIONAL PARK, HAWAII

According to legend, this park in the south-central part of the big island of Hawaii is the home of Pele, the Hawaiian goddess of fire. The Hawaiian goddess of the sea chased her from island to island, destroying each dwelling that Pele created. She finally came to Halemaumau, in Kilauea Calera, where she lives today. She is said to preside over the local volcanoes, from the 13,680-foot Manua Kea to Kilauea Crater, and is considered responsible for the eruptions and lava outpourings over the centuries.

Oval-shaped Kilauea Caldera is two and a half miles wide and about 400 feet deep. Within it is Halemaumau Crater, where you can smell sulfur and hear steam hissing out of fissures in the rock. When Kilauea is erupting you can see seething lakes of molten rock, curtains of fire, and fountains of red hot lava. Being this close to one of the world's most active volcanoes is the experience of a lifetime. For an eruption update, call 808–967–7977. Temporary road signs will direct you to safe vantage points whenever eruptions occur.

From the Kilauea Visitor Center, you can hike through or drive around the edge of the caldera. Also within the park are deserts and rain forests; there are few places in the world where these dramatic extremes coexist. Mauna Loa, the world's tallest active volcano, is thirty-three miles northwest of the park headquarters.

VOLCANO HOUSE

Address: PO Box 53, Volcano National Park, Volcano, Hawaii 96718 (at the rim of the Kilauea Caldera at approximately 4,000-feet elevation)
Telephone: 808–967–7321; fax: 808–967–8429

Season: Year-round.

Accommodations: First built in 1846 as a thatched structure, the hotel has undergone many restorations and incarnations. Its forty-two rooms are currently furnished in a modern style with rare koa wood furniture and Hawaiian quilts. In 1935, *Ripley's Believe It or Not* claimed that the fire in the hotel's fireplace had been burning continuously for sixty-one years.

Special Features: Art display, award-winning restaurant, gift shop, snack bar.

Cost: The least expensive accommodations are in the Ohia Wing; they do not have a crater view. Rooms $82 per night, double occupancy; each additional person $10. Children twelve and under stay free in parents' rooms.

Nearby: Kilauea Caldera, the Kilauea Visitor Center, Volcano Art Center.

NAMAKANI PAIO CAMPING CABINS

Address: PO Box 53, Volcano National Park, Volcano, Hawaii 96718 (three miles beyond the Volcano House [see previous page] at approximately 4,000-feet elevation)
Telephone: 808–967–7321; fax: 808–967–8429

Season: Year-round.
Accommodations: Each cabin sleeps four with a double bed and two twin bunk beds. There are electric lights, an outdoor picnic table, and a barbecue grill. Guests provide their own charcoal and cooking utensils. There is a central bath and shower facility.
Cost: Cabins are $33 per night, which includes linens, towels, soap, and a blanket. It is recommended that you bring an extra blanket or sleeping bag, as the cabins are not heated.

ROCKY MOUNTAINS AND SOUTHWEST

GLACIER NATIONAL PARK, MONTANA

With crystal clear lakes and fifty ancient glaciers, Glacier National Park, along with its Canadian counterpart, Waterton Lakes National Park, spreads across 1.4 million acres of wilderness. Considered to be the wildest national park in the "lower forty-eight," its sights include bighorn sheep grazing, osprey fishing on the surface of a glacial lake, and even mountain goats roaming across a sheer rock wall.

All accommodations have easy access to hiking trails, picnic areas, ranger-naturalist programs, and boating activities on the park's many lakes. Glacier Park Boats provides inexpensive boat tours and boat rentals mid-June through September at Two Medicine Lake, Swiftcurrent Lake, St. Mary Lake, and Lake McDonald (call 406–888–5727 for information). There are riding stables at Many Glacier Stable (406–732–5597) and Lake McDonald Lodge (406–888–5670).

Glacier Raft Company has a full range of offerings from May through September, including white water raft trips (half-day: adults $34, children $24), evening supper rides, and reasonably priced overnight raft trips on the Flathead River or through the Great Bear Wilderness. The company also has teamed up with the Bear Creek Ranch for reasonably priced combined horseback ride and raft excursions. Year-round reservations can be made by calling 800–332–9995.

Ideal guides for family backpacking are Glacier Wilderness Guides at

800–521–7238; they will select the best trails for your family's ability levels, point out wildlife, pick out campsites and erect tents, and prepare meals. They will even wash dishes and carry your gear. Overnight trips average $90 per person per day, including food and tents.

MANY GLACIER HOTEL

Address: Glacier Park Inc., Dial Tower, Station 1925, Phoenix, Arizona 85077 (winter); East Glacier, Montana 59434-0147 (summer). The hotel is on the shore of Swiftcurrent Lake, at the foot of Grinnell Glacier.
Telephone: For reservations: 602–207–6000

Season: June through September.
Accommodations: Built in 1914, this historic Swiss-style hotel is the park's largest resort. The least expensive rooms at this resort are the "value" rooms, which sleep up to four people with either two double beds or one double bed and two twin beds. They have a private bathroom and mountain views.
Special Features: Broadway musicals, concerts, sing-alongs by recruited college drama and music students entertain guests. There is a full-service restaurant and a snack bar.
Cost: Value rooms $95 per night double occupancy; each additional person $10; children under twelve stay free in parents' rooms. Rollaway beds $10 per night; cribs $3 per night.
Nearby: Lake cruises, horseback riding, hiking.

LAKE MCDONALD LODGE

Address: Glacier Park Inc., Dial Tower, Station 1925, Phoenix, Arizona 85077 (winter); East Glacier, Montana 59434-0147 (summer) (hotel is on the west side of the park, along Going to the Sun Road).
Telephone: For reservations: 602–207–6000

Season: June through September.
Accommodations: This complex of one hundred rooms has cabins, a motel, and main lodge accommodations. Built in 1913, it has an Old West atmosphere.
Special Features: Full-service restaurant and a snack bar.
Cost: The least expensive rooms at this lodge complex are the motel rooms, which sleep up to four people with either two double beds or one double bed and two twin beds. They have a private bathroom: $82

per night double occupancy; each additional person $10. Cabins $66 for two; each additional person $10. Children under twelve stay free in parents' rooms. Rollaway beds $10 per night; cribs $3 per night.
Nearby: White water raft trips, lake cruises, horseback riding, hiking.

GLACIER PARK LODGE

Address: Glacier Park Inc., Dial Tower, Station 0925, Phoenix, Arizona 85077 (winter); East Glacier, Montana 59434-0147 (summer) (hotel is two miles east of the park at the foot of Squaw Peak Mountain).
Telephone: For reservations: 602–207–6000

Season: June through September.
Accommodations: Built in 1913, this historic lodge has 155 rooms and a full range of activities. It is a magnificent structure, supported by sixty enormous timbers which were five hundred years old when originally cut and set in place.
Special Features: Outdoor heated pool, nine-hole golf course.
Cost: The least expensive rooms at this lodge are the value rooms: $120 per night double occupancy; each additional person $10. Children under twelve occupying a room with an adult stay free. Rollaway beds $10 per night; cribs $3 per day.
Nearby: Lake cruises, horseback riding, hiking.

RISING SUN MOTOR INN

Address: Glacier Park Inc., Dial Tower, Station 0925, Phoenix, Arizona 85077 (winter); East Glacier, Montana 59434-0147 (summer) (hotel is near the Many Glacier Hotel listed above).
Telephone: For reservations: 602–207–6000

Season: June through September.
Accommodations: The complex includes a seventy-two room motel and cabin facility as well as a campground area with views of St. Mary's Lake.
Special Features: Camp store and a coffee shop.
Cost: Motel room $82 per night double occupancy; each additional person $10. Cabins $66 per night double occupancy; each additional person $10. Children under twelve stay free in parents' rooms. Rollaway beds $10 per night; cribs $3 per night.
Nearby: Lake cruises, horseback riding, hiking.

VILLAGE INN

Address: Glacier Park Inc., Dial Tower, Station 0925, Phoenix, Arizona 85077 (winter); East Glacier, Montana 59434-0147 (summer). The hotel is just inside the park's west entrance in Apgar.
Telephone: For reservations: 602–207–6000

Season: June through September.
Accommodations: Many of the thirty-six rooms in this modern inn overlooking Lake McDonald have kitchen facilities.
Cost: One-bedroom unit with kitchen $110 per night double occupancy; each additional person $10. Children under twelve stay free in parents' room. Rollaway beds $5 per night; cribs $3 per night.
Nearby: Lake cruises, horseback riding, hiking.

SWIFTCURRENT MOTOR INN

Address: Glacier Park Inc., Dial Tower, Station 0925, Phoenix, Arizona 85077 (winter); East Glacier, Montana 59434-0147 (summer). The motel is in the center of the park near Swiftcurrent Lake.
Telephone: For reservations: 602–207–6000

Season: June through September.
Accommodations: Eighty-eight motel rooms and cabin units.
Special Features: Camp store, coffee shop.
Cost: Motel room $82 per night double occupancy. Motel room at Pinetop Motel $72 per night double occupancy. Each additional person $10. Two-bedroom cabin without bathroom $38 per night double occupancy; each additional person $10. Children under twelve stay free in parents' room. Rollaway beds $10 per night; cribs $3 per night.
Nearby: Lake cruises, horseback riding, hiking.

GRAND TETON NATIONAL PARK, WYOMING

For those who want a real western-style adventure, a vacation in the Grand Tetons will most certainly fit the bill. Amid these spectacular craggy, cloud-high peaks, which seem to erupt from out of nowhere into the wide Wyoming sky, are many opportunities to fish, hike, ride horses, visit rodeos, and see some of the wild animals that today's children usually know only from books, including elk, cow, moose, bison, bald eagles, and white pelicans.

The Tetons offer spectacular hiking for all abilities, and despite the fact that nearly four million people visit the park each year, you really won't notice the crowds—even in the height of summer—if you venture out of your car and onto the trails. A popular hike is to Hidden Falls, an easy four-mile round-trip walk along the lakeshore. There is a wonderful picnic site along the way at String Lake where you can spend the afternoon swimming and fishing.

Trail rides lasting from one hour ($18) to half a day ($45) are available at Jackson Lake Lodge and Colter Bay Corrals. Reasonably priced hearty cowboy breakfast rides or dinner rides on horseback or by wagon are great fun for kids eight and older. Check with the activities desk at Jackson Lake Lodge. Bar-T Ranch (307–733–5386) in Jackson leads a chuck wagon ride to a Cowboy Cookout complete with "Indians" pursuing the wagons. For those planning a longer stay, the Grand Teton Science School, headquartered in the park, offers a range of outdoor science programs for children and adults.

Narrated cruises on Jackson Lake cost $10.50 for adults and $6 for children; check with activities desk at Jackson Lake Lodge about the breakfast or evening steak-fry cruises. Motorboats ($15 per hour) and canoes ($8 per hour) are for rent at the Colter Bay Marina. Try Teton Boating Company at 307–733–2703 for boat rides on Jenny Lake. Fishing on the park's clear, cold lakes and streams draw countless aficionados. Guided lake and fly-fishing trips can be arranged at the lodge.

The Grand Teton Lodge Company also leads river float trips down the Snake River in rubber rafts—a scenic, not white water, expedition. Their ten-mile trips cost $16 for kids six to sixteen and $31 for adults; there are also luncheon and evening supper trips. Ask for details at Jenny Lake Lodge or Colter Bay Village. More extended family float trips on the mild-flat waters of the Snake River and on Jackson Lake and white water rafting trips on the lower section of the Snake (suitable for older children) are offered June through September by experienced guides. The Chamber of Commerce (307–733–3316; PO Box E, Jackson, Wyoming 83001) can send you a list.

Summertime alpine slide toboggans, a thrill for older kids, run down the slopes of Snow King Resort (307–733–5200). Just outside the park, kids love taking the tram ride in Teton Village or poking around the town of Jackson. There's an afternoon "shoot-out" in the town square and a twice-weekly town rodeo in the summer. The Jackson Hole Golf and Tennis Club near the park's southern boundary is open to day guests and is renowned for its scenic and challenging eighteen-hole championship golf course and tennis facilities.

Inexpensive publications to help you get acquainted with the park include the *Grand Teton Official Handbook, Short Hikes and Easy Walks in Grand Teton*, and the *Discover Grand Teton* activity book for kids; all can be ordered from the Grand Teton National History Association before your visit. Call 307–739–3403.

JACKSON LAKE LODGE

Address: Grand Teton Lodge Company, PO Box 240, Moran, Wyoming 83013
Telephone: 307-543-3100

This full-service large resort hotel is located in the heart of the park, on a bluff overlooking the marshlands of Willow Flats, with gorgeous views across Jackson Lake to the glacial tips of the Teton range. In spite of its name, the lodge is not located on the lake. Guests can swim in a large heated pool or go on organized float trips, and there's a corral with many different trail rides. Moose can be observed from the lodge in the marshy area of Willow Flats.

Season: Mid-May through mid-October.

Accommodations: The resort has cottages, standard hotel rooms in the main lodge, and larger hotel rooms located on either side of the main building.

Special Features: Full-service fine dining room, casual cafe with grilled food, lunch and evening barbecue by the pool during the summer.

Cost: The least expensive rooms are those in the main lodge: $95 per night, double occupancy; cottages start at $107 per night, double occupancy; each additional person over twelve $8.50. Children twelve and under stay free in parents' room. Rollaway beds $8; cribs free.

Nearby: All the park's activities are within easy reach.

COLTER BAY VILLAGE CABINS

Address: Grand Teton Lodge Company, PO Box 240, Moran, Wyoming 83013
Telephone: 307–543–3100

These cabins, popular with families, are located in Colter Bay Village near the shores of Jackson Lake. Along the lakeshore is a beach and a full-service marina, and registered cabin guests can also use the pool at Jackson Lake Lodge five miles away. Float trips, the Indian Arts Museum, trail rides at the Colter Bay Corrals, and guided fishing are all within easy reach.

Season: Mid-May through early October.

Accommodations: There are 209 log cabins with bathrooms; each cabin sleeps up to six.

Cost: Depending on size, one-room cabin with private bath $58 to $81 per night, double occupancy. Two rooms with connecting bath for up to four people $83 to $104 per night, double occupancy. Each additional person over twelve $8. Children twelve and under stay free in parents' room. Rollaway beds $8; cribs free.

Special Features: The village has a restaurant, grill, laundry facilities, sports shop, corral, and fully stocked grocery store.

Nearby: Families can take a short, easy hike from the Colter Bay Visitor Center to Swan Lake in search of swans. Near the cabins is the National Park Service amphitheater, with naturalist programs and guided nature hikes.

COLTER BAY TENT CABINS

Address: Grand Teton Lodge Company, PO Box 240, Moran, Wyoming 83013 (in Colter Bay Village)
Telephone: 307-543-3100

Popular with families, these cabins are situated in Colter Bay Village near the shores of Jackson Lake.

Season: Early June to early September.

Accommodations: Constructed of canvas and logs, each tent cabin has an outdoor grill, wood stove, two double-decker bunks (without bedding), table, and benches. Sleeping bags, cooking utensils, and ice chests can be rented at a central facility where there is also a shared restroom.

Special Features: Along the lakeshore is a beach and a full-service marina. In the village is a restaurant, grill, laundry facilities, sports shop, corral, and fully stocked grocery store.

Cost: Cabins $24 per night, double occupancy; each additional person over twelve $3. Cots $4.50 per night.

Nearby: See Colter Bay cabins above for suggested activities. Float trips, trail rides at the Colter Bay Corrals, the Indian Arts Museum, and guided fishing are all in easy reach. Also nearby is the National Park Service amphitheater with naturalist programs and guided nature hikes.

SIGNAL MOUNTAIN LODGE

Address: PO Box 50, Moran, Wyoming 83013
Telephone: 307–543–2831; fax: 307–543–2569

Signal Mountain is in the heart of the park on Jackson Lake with magnificent views of the Teton mountain range. The resort has its own marina that rents rowboats, canoes, and motor boats and assists families with arrangements for Snake River float trips and guided lake fishing.

Season: Mother's Day through the first Sunday in October. Make reservations up to eleven months in advance.

Accommodations: Log cabins with one or two rooms or lodge-style rooms set in the trees are available. Lodge-style rooms sleep up to four with two queen-size beds and a small refrigerator. Lakefront retreats sleep six people with two queen-size beds and a sofa-bed. They sit on Jackson Lake and offer views of the Teton range. If you have a large group, a family bungalow right on the waterfront is a good value, as it accommodates up to ten people and has a large deck, outdoor barbecue, living room, bedroom, and a kitchen. Bedding is included.

Special Features: Snake River float trips (adults $27, children $15), guided lake fishing ($48 per hour), rowboats and canoes $7.50 per hour, motor boats $60 per half day. There is also a restaurant and a convenience store.

Cost: The least expensive accommodations at this resort are the log cabins with one or two rooms. One-room cabin with one double and one twin bed $72 per night, with two double beds $80 per night. Lodge-style rooms $90 per night. Lakefront retreats $145 per night. A family bungalow with a kitchen on the waterfront starts at $120 per night.

Nearby: All the park's activities are within easy reach.

ELK REFUGE INN

Address: PO Box 2834, Jackson Hole, Wyoming 83001 (one mile north of Jackson)
Telephone: 307–733–3582

Elk Refuge is across from the National Elk Refuge, which attracts eight thousand elk in winter and a variety of birds year-round. The inn also has horse corrals and a pasture, and the butte behind the hotel is the winter home for mule deer, which often roam the grounds.

Season: Year-round.

Accommodations: A twenty-three unit motel with ten kitchen units. Each room has a full bath, color television, phones, and a private patio with valley views.

Special Features: Picnic tables and barbecue grills.

Cost: Kitchen rooms $90 per night; motel rooms $70 to $125 per night in summer, $45 to $76 per night in fall and winter. Children under twelve stay free in parents' room.

Nearby: Grand Teton and Yellowstone national parks, Snake River float trips, horseback riding, sailboarding, two top-rated golf courses, tennis, fishing, biking. The inn is two miles from Snow King Ski Area and fourteen miles from the Jackson Hole Ski Area.

YELLOWSTONE NATIONAL PARK, WYOMING

Larger than the states of Rhode Island and Delaware combined, Yellowstone was the nation's first—and remains its most famous—national park. As you journey through the park, remind your children that Yellowstone's biggest attraction is actually *below* their feet as the park sits on a giant underground volcano that is still very active! But don't worry—experts say the Yellowstone Caldera won't erupt for several thousand more years. It first erupted about two million years ago with such amazing force that tens of thousands of geothermal features still abound in the park, including hot pools, mud pots, steaming fumaroles, and most amazing of all, three hundred or so geysers.

Many visits take the form of a loop, and you should allow two or three days just to see the park's main attractions. Be sure to build in time to explore on foot; you'll find peace just a few miles off the main roads, which are often overcrowded in the summer with traffic. Once your children get out on a trail, up close to see wildflowers or spot enormous bison, they will begin to appreciate the real Yellowstone.

Old Faithful, the world's most famous geyser, sends thousands of gallons of water thundering into the sky and is definitely worth seeing. To avoid summer crowds plan a visit early in the day. En route to Old Faithful, at the end of short scenic loop called Firehole River Drive, is a park-service-approved swimming hole warmed by hot springs; it makes for a great side trip.

The park has many programs for families, from campfire talks to guided nature walks. Check the publication *Discover Yellowstone* (available at all visitor centers) for schedules; it also lists the summer workshop schedule for the Madison Museum Art Center, with excellent hands-on classes covering topics from printmaking to sculpture. Also pick up a *Junior Ranger* newspaper, which suggests such activities as predicting geyser eruptions and guessing animal tracks, and your kids can try to earn a junior ranger patch. Also recommended is the guidebook *Family Fun in Yellowstone* (Yellowstone Publications, $3.75), available at park bookstores.

Some off-the-beaten-track recommendations from veteran park visitors: Fountain Flat Road, which isn't on the main loop so has little traffic, curves all the way to Midway Geyser Basin and is flat and great for bike riding. You can also bike or hike on the partly paved path for two miles into Lone Star Geyser, whose twelve-foot-high cone is constantly splashing and gurgling. Emerald, Rainbow, and Opalescent pools are all located in the Black Sand Basin and worth a visit.

Western-style activities in the park include horseback riding, stagecoach rides, and dinner cookouts via covered wagon or horseback. Guided horseback rides for children age eight and older (one hour $17, two hours $27) are available June through August at Mammoth, Roosevelt, and Canyon. An Old West Cookout and stagecoach rides are available at Roosevelt (see Roosevelt Lodge, page 119).

Yellowstone Lake has excellent fishing and a marina with boat rentals (rowboats, outboards, and charters). One-hour leisurely sightseeing cruises, past an island shipwreck, in June through September on Yellowstone Lake cost $4 for children five through eleven and $7.50 for adults. Rowboat rentals cost $5 per hour, outboards $22 per hour; cabin cruisers can be chartered for $40 per hour (one to six people). You can also hire a guide and fish on the lake for cutthroat trout. If you have a canoe, try the scenic paddle from Lewis to Shoshone Lake. Call 307–344–7311 for information about all activities.

Yellowstone has a variety of accommodations and activities to fit any family's budget. Make summer reservations well in advance; if it is difficult to get through by phone, try calling in the evenings or on weekends.

Note: In addition to the lodgings listed below, see page 173 for a description of the Cliff Lake Lodge, a lakefront resort near Yellowstone featured in the chapter on lake and river vacations, and page 27 in the chapter on resorts for a description of Chico Hot Springs lodge located 30 miles from the north gate of Yellowstone.

OLD FAITHFUL INN

Address: Yellowstone National Park, Wyoming 82190 (in close proximity to Old Faithful, the park's most famous geyser)
Telephone: 307–344–7311

Built in 1903 of local logs and stone and recently designated as a national historic landmark, the original hotel with its six-story atrium lobby, wraparound balconies, and massive four-sided fireplace is the largest known log structure of its kind. Legend has it that at night a ghost walks the creaky floors of the hotel.

Season: May through mid-October.

Accommodations: Although the hotel is expensive, moderately priced rooms that sleep four people with private baths are available.

Special Features: In the summer, classical music concerts take place in the lobby. Guests can watch Old Faithful blow from the second-floor balcony. A full-service dining room and fast food outlet are located directly off the lobby.

Cost: Moderately priced hotel rooms with private baths $68 per night, double occupancy. Rooms without private baths $47 per night, double occupancy. Additional person or bed $8 per night. Children eleven and under stay free.

Nearby: There is a very easy hike on a paved trail and boardwalk through the Upper Geyser Basin, the area around Old Faithful, which has one-quarter of the world's geysers. A walk around the geysers at night is memorable. At the far end of the walk is the brilliant turquoise Morning Glory Pool geyser, one of the park's most exquisite.

OLD FAITHFUL LODGE AND CABINS

Address: Yellowstone National Park, Wyoming 82190
Telephone: 307–344–7311

Rebuilt in 1927, these vintage cabins are in close proximity to Old Faithful, the park's most famous geyser.

Season: Late May through mid-September.

Accommodations: Cabins have private bathrooms or shared bath facilities a short walk away. Frontier cabins will sleep up to five with two double beds and a rollaway bed. Family cabins will sleep up to five and have a toilet and sink in the room.

Special Features: The lodge's lobby has a giant fireplace and a spectacular view of Old Faithful.

Cost: Cabins $22 to $38 per night, double occupancy, depending on shared or private bathroom; additional person or bed $7 per night. Children eleven and under stay free.

Nearby: See activities listed with Old Faithful Inn.

OLD FAITHFUL SNOW LODGE CABINS

Address: Yellowstone National Park, Wyoming 82190
Telephone: 307–344–7311

This is an intimate facility near Old Faithful Geyser. Winter activities include cross-country skiing, snowmobiling, and guided tours in en-

closed snow coaches. When Old Faithful erupts in the winter, the spurting water quick-freezes and falls to the ground like glass.
Season: Mid-December through mid-March; late May through late October.
Accommodations: Standard motel rooms and cabins.
Special Features: The main lodge has a dining room.
Cost: Hotel rooms with private baths $47 per night, double occupancy. Cabins $41 to $63 per night, double occupancy, depending on shared or private bathroom. Additional person or bed $8 per night. Children eleven and under stay free.
Nearby: See activities listed with Old Faithful Inn.

LAKE YELLOWSTONE HOTEL AND CABINS

Address: Yellowstone National Park, Wyoming 82190 (situated near Bridge Bay Marina and the shores of Yellowstone Lake)
Telephone: 307-344-7311

A classic old hotel on the northern shore of Lake Yellowstone, the lodge was completed in 1891 and remodeled in 1903 with its current Colonial look. Fifty-foot Ionic columns are its trademark. The hotel's sitting room has a sweeping view of the lake, and a string quartet and pianist often entertain in the hotel's large sunroom. Summer marina activities include scenic cruises and hourly outboard and rowboat rentals. Guided fishing boats are available for charter.
Season: Late May through late September.
Accommodations: In addition to the hotel's deluxe accommodations, there are moderately priced private cabins, which all have their own baths. Cabins sleep up to five with two double beds and a rollaway bed.
Special Features: Lake-view dining room with reasonably priced meals; kids can order hamburgers.
Cost: "Frontier" cabins with private bathrooms $63 per night, double occupancy; additional person or bed $8 per night. Children eleven and under stay free.
Nearby: The lake has several picnic sites and swimming spots; ask at the hotel. North of the lake, don't miss thundering Mud Volcano and Dragon's Mount, a turbulent hot spring inside a cavern.

LAKE LODGE AND CABINS

Address: Yellowstone National Park, Wyoming 82190
Telephone: 307-344-7311

Situated near Bridge Bay Marina and the shores of Yellowstone Lake, rustic Lake Lodge's cabins are within walking distance of the Lake Yellowstone Hotel. The lodge is built of logs and is nestled in the trees with a magnificent view of the lake and surrounding mountains.
Season: June through September.
Accommodations: All accommodations are cabins. The "western" and "frontier" cabins have private bathrooms with showers.
Special Features: Summer marina activities include scenic cruises and hourly outboard and rowboat rentals. Guided fishing boats are available for charter. The central lodge has a cafeteria.
Cost: Western cabins $84 per night, double occupancy; frontier cabins $43 per night; additional person or bed $8 per night. Children eleven and under stay free.
Nearby: Grocery store, gas station, cafeteria. See attractions listed for Lake Yellowstone Hotel.

GRANT VILLAGE

Address: Yellowstone National Park, Wyoming 82190
Telephone: 307-344-7311

Situated on the shore of Yellowstone Lake, this is the park's newest and southernmost facility, completed in 1984.
Season: Late May through late September.
Accommodations: All accommodations are standard hotel rooms with private bathrooms and showers.
Special Features: Summer marina activities include scenic cruises and hourly outboard and rowboat rentals. Guided fishing boats are available for charter. A dining room overlooks the lake and a steak house is perched over the water's edge.
Cost: Hotel rooms $68 to $84 per night, double occupancy; additional person or bed $8 per night. Children eleven and under stay free.
Nearby: See attractions listed for Lake Yellowstone Hotel.

CANYON LODGE AND CABINS

Address: Yellowstone National Park, Wyoming 82190
Telephone: 307–344–7311

Canyon's cabins are near the spectacular Grand Canyon of the Yellowstone, Hayden Valley, and Lower Falls, which are twice as tall as Niagara Falls.

Season: Early June through early September.

Accommodations: All accommodations are single-story cabins in clusters of four or more, with private bathrooms.

Special Features: The main lodge has a dining room and a cafeteria. Horseback rides (one and two hours) are available at its corrals from mid-June through August.

Cost: Cabins with private bathrooms $48 to $84 per night, double occupancy; additional person or bed $8 per night. Children eleven and under stay free.

Nearby: Look out of your car on the road between Canyon and Tower, and you might see grizzly bears in the broad meadow to the east of Dunraven Pass. At Tower, a short walk leads to the base of pounding Tower Falls. East of Tower, a short hike leads to acres of a 55-million-year-old stone forest; during July and August naturalist-led hikes are scheduled. West of the highway is the Children's Fire Trail, which leads through a burned forest for a kid's-eye-view of how the forest is affected by fires.

MAMMOTH HOT SPRINGS HOTEL AND CABINS

Address: Yellowstone National Park, Wyoming 82190
Telephone: 307–344–7311

Built in 1937, this hotel is in the region of Mammoth Hot Springs, a thermal area where abundant hot springs have formed the tinted limestone terraces. The hotel's Map Room contains a large wooden map of the United States made of fifteen different woods from nine countries.

Season: Mid-December through March and late May through mid-September.

Accommodations: The hotel has both cottage-type cabins as well as hotel rooms. Four of the cabin units have private hot tubs. Frontier cabins sleep up to five with two double beds and a rollaway bed. Budget cabins sleep up to four and have a central, shared bathroom. Linens and towels are included.

Special Features: One- and two-hour guided horseback rides are available from late May through mid-September. There is also a full dining room.

Cost: Although the hotel is expensive, moderately priced rooms are available for $47 to $65 per night, double occupancy. Cabins $34 to $63 per night, double occupancy. Rates vary depending on whether rooms have a private bathroom. Additional person or bed $8 per night. Children eleven and under stay free.

Nearby: A boardwalk meanders through Mammoth Terraces, a collection of unusual geothermal features. Twelve miles south of Mammoth is a roadside exhibit that explains Obsidian Cliff, a cliff made of volcanic glass. Native Americans traded the obsidian for arrowheads and tools. Farther south is Norris, the site of the world's largest geyser, Steamboat Geyser, which erupts twice as high as Old Faithful.

ROOSEVELT LODGE AND CABINS

Address: Yellowstone National Park, Wyoming 82190 (in the northeast region of the park)
Telephone: 307-344-7311

So named because it was a favorite campsite of President Teddy Roosevelt, this lodge retains the rustic charm of another era. Roosevelt Corral offers horseback riding during the summer and stagecoach rides for families through rolling sagebrush-covered hills. Roosevelt also serves as the departure point for the Old West Cookout, a steak dinner cookout via wagons or horses through the mountains to historic Yancey's Hole, located two miles away.

Season: Early June through early September.

Accommodations: There are a limited number of rustic cabins—most are "Rough Riders," with woodburning stoves and no bathrooms, or rustic shelters, which are the least expensive in the park. Rustic shelters have no bathrooms or running water. (There is a central bathhouse, although no linens or towels are provided.) There is wood heat. Frontier cabins have electric heat and full baths. The main lodge has a giant fireplace at each end and a cozy atmosphere.

Special Features: Horseback riding (one- and two-hour rides) and stagecoach rides June to August; Old West Cookout $17 to $41 per person depending on mode of transportation and age of child. Children under five ride free.

Cost: Cabins with private bath $63 per night, double occupancy; family cabins with toilet and sink $41 per night, double occupancy. Budget or Rough Rider cabins with bath facilities nearby $27 per night, double occupancy; rustic shelters with bath facilities nearby $24 per night, dou-

ble occupancy. Additional person or bed $8 per night. Children eleven
and under stay free.

ROCKY MOUNTAIN NATIONAL PARK,
COLORADO

Rocky Mountain National Park is less than a two-hour drive from Denver,
but it seems worlds away with three hundred miles of hiking trails plus
wildlife, including mule, deer, elk, bighorn sheep, coyotes, black bears,
mountain lions, and bobcats. Families can choose from a range of inexpensive accommodations and activities. To start, at the Park Village
North (at the park's entrance on U.S. 34) young kids can ride a miniature
train and climb the observation tower.

Estes Park, just outside the park, offers a hub of activities for families.
Horseback and pony rides are available at the National Park Village Stables (970–586–5269), Sombrero Stables (970–586–4577), and Cowpoke
Corner Corral (970–586–5890), and at Hi Country Stables in the park at
Glacier Creek and Moraine Park (970–586–2337). River rafting is available through Rapid Transit Rafting (303–586–8852). Golfing is available
at Regulation 9 (970–586–8146) or at two public courses. In town there
is an aerial tramway (970–586–3675). Dick's Rock Museum (970–586–
4180) has rocks, geodes, and crystals. The Estes Park Aquatic Center
(970–586–2340) has an Olympic-size pool, kiddie pool, diving tank, and
lap areas. You can rent all the equipment you need for boating, fishing,
or windsurfing at the Lake Estes Marina (970–586–2011).

Walking and hiking trails abound in the park. Easy trails recommended for families include the walk around Bear Lake, East Inlet to
Adam's Falls, and the hike to the pool at Fern Lake. A helpful book to
order before you go is *A Family Guide to Rocky Mountain National
Park* by Lisa Evans (Seattle: The Mountaineers, 1991; $12.95), which
lists family hikes and activities. It is available from the Rocky Mountain
Nature Association, Estes Park, Colorado 80517, 970–586–1258.

Note: In addition to the lodgings listed below there are two family
camps adjoining Rocky Mountain National Park in a magnificent alpine
setting. For details about these accommodations, the YMCA of the Rockies at Estes Park Center and at Snow Mountain Ranch, see page 24 in
the Resorts chapter.

GRAND LAKE LODGE

Address: Summer reservations: Box 569, Grand Lake, Colorado 80447; off-season: 4155 East Jewell Avenue #104, Denver, Colorado 80222. Located at the west gate to the park.
Telephone: Summer, 970–627–3967, fax: 970–627–9495; Off-season, 303–759–5848, fax: 303–759–3179

This national historic landmark, which has attracted returning families for decades, has unbeatable views of Grand Lake and Shadow Mountain. All accommodations are in cabins located in the pines above the main lodge. The national park's hiking trails surround the resort.

Season: June through September.

Accommodations: Cabins have modern conveniences yet are rustic in design. Aspen and Pine Cabins each sleep up to six people and have two rooms, a fully equipped kitchenette, gas heat, full bath, bedroom with bunk and double bed, and a queen-size bed in the living room. Larger parties can choose the Ford Cabin, which sleeps up to eight people, or the Elk Lodge, which sleeps up to fourteen. No televisions or telephones in cabins.

Special Features: Heated pool, playground, picnic areas with grills, riding stables, volleyball, horseshoes, recreation room with games, Ping-Pong, pool table, and laundry facilities. The lodge lobby has musical entertainment, a circular fireplace, a restaurant, and a veranda with swings and food service.

Cost: Aspen and Pine Cabins $100 per night for four people; extra person or rollaway $10 per night. Cribs $5 per night.

Nearby: Lake and stream fishing, boating, golf, tennis, horseback riding, water sports, and white water rafting are all available close by. During the summer there is a children's day camp in Grand Lake, and August brings rubber duckie races, a reptilian ball, turtle races, and a festival of the arts. Call Grand Lake's chamber of commerce at 800–531–1091 for details.

VALHALLA RESORT

Address: PO Box 1439, Estes Park, Colorado 80517 (right on the edge of the park, off Highway 66)
Telephone: 970–586–3284

Season: Year-round.

Accommodations: Each cabin has a living room with a fireplace, color TV with cable, a fully equipped kitchen, a bath with tub or shower, beds of various sizes and numbers, a private deck with barbecue grill, and outdoor furniture.

Special Features: Guests can hike into the national park right from the resort's property. There is a heated outdoor swimming pool and a hot tub, miniature golf, shuffleboard, Ping-Pong, and laundry facilities.

Cost: In summer, cabins for four people $90 to $107 per night, $583 to $690 per week; additional person $15 per night. There is an $8 per night charge for cribs, but if you bring your own, babies stay free. Cabins that sleep as many as twelve are available. Continental breakfast included. Rates are lower from mid-October to Memorial Day. Five-night minimum stay in summer and from Christmas through New Year's.

Nearby: See the descriptions of Estes Park and Rocky Mountain National Park on page 120.

H-BAR-G RANCH HOSTEL

Address: 3500 H-Bar-G Road, PO Box 1260, Estes Park, Colorado 80517 (adjacent to the park in the Roosevelt National Forest) Telephone: 970–586–3688; fax: 970–586–5004 (fax summer only). Reservations essential in July and August. Phone reservations accepted with a credit card; call between 5:15 and 9:00 P.M. Rocky Mountain time zone.

A former dude ranch, this 130-bed hostel has family rooms available. At an altitude of eighty-two hundred feet it offers a spectacular view of the park's entire front range. The history of the ranch, which dates back to 1892, is captured in a collection of photographs and other memorabilia displayed in the hostel's common room.

Season: June through mid-September.

Accommodations: Private family rooms and family cabins can be reserved.

Special Features: Kitchen, linen rental, tennis, volleyball, barbecue, game room, and fireplaces. Hiking trails lead from the grounds into the Roosevelt National Forest. The hostel also provides visitors with information about nearby attractions including old mining towns. Rental cars are available.

Cost: HI members $9 per night for adults; children under fifteen are half price. Nonmembers purchase a membership as they check in ($25 adults, $10 youth under 18). Private family room priced according to number of occupants; family cabin $24.

Nearby: The hostel manager shuttles guests to and from town. In addition to the park's diverse hiking trails, bike trails are close by.

MOAB, ARCHES, AND CANYONLANDS
NATIONAL PARKS, UTAH

Dinosaurs once roamed the rocks and prehistoric earthscapes of the southeastern corner of Utah, from Moab to the San Juan River, an area that now awaits adventure-seeking families. Arches and Canyonlands are down the road from one another; together they form a landscape where the earth's crust reveals itself in layer upon layer of sedimentary rock, stacked and swirled into strange spires and pinnacles. Spring and fall are the best time to visit, as summer temperatures can top one hundred degrees. An excellent book to order before you go is *Best Hikes with Children in Utah*, which highlights trails in and around Arches and Canyonlands ($12.95; order by calling Canyonlands Natural History Association at 801–259–6003). The city of Moab is the gateway to these two parks.

Activities in Arches
Trails lead off from the eighteen-mile main park road. One of the best for young children is the walk to Sand Dune Arch; it is short and flat but thrilling. At one point, you squeeze through a crevasse so narrow, your shoulders barely fit. Youngsters also enjoy the quick hike around Balanced Rock, a huge boulder (the size of 1,600 cars) that teeters atop an eroding stone pedestal. A highlight for children is viewing the dinosaur tracks along the "Potash" road (Highway 279); along this same route are also a number of Indian petroglyphs. Lin Ottinger Tours (801–259–7312) and Tag-A-Long Tours (800–453–3292, 801–259–8946) both lead guided tours of the park's backcountry by jeep while Pack Creek Ranch (801–259–5505) offers horseback tours into the park.

Activities in Canyonlands
Young science buffs will like the short hike to Upheaval Dome; one theory asserts that the dome's giant crater was formed by the impact of an ancient meteorite. There are many companies authorized by the National Park Service to lead white-water river tours, calm water jet boat tours, backcountry vehicle trips, and mountain bike and backpack tours of the park; for a complete listing write to Canyonlands National Park, 2282 South West Resource Boulevard, Moab, Utah 84532, or call 801–259–7164.

We found the canoe treks offered by Tex's Riverways (PO Box 67, Moab, Utah 84532, 801–259–5101) to be an especially good deal. Tex's offers canoe treks on the Green and Colorado Rivers through desert canyons, including the remote and wild parts of Stillwater Canyon in Canyonlands. Floats on the Green River last from four to ten days; the floating is safe and the water calm. You are ferried to your starting point by ground shuttle. The Colorado River floats are shorter, lasting from a half day to three days, and a wide variety of trips take you through natural arches, Indian ruins, and scenic canyons. Deer, beaver, desert bighorn sheep, coyotes, and birds are common sights. The Labyrinth Canyon of the Green River trip (four to five days) costs $40 per person for ground shuttle and $15 per day for the canoe, paddles, and life vests. Stillwater Canyon trips through Canyonlands National Park past Indian ruins and Anasazi Indian petroglyphs cost $110 per person for jetboat return to Moab and ground shuttle and $15 per day for canoe paddles and vests.

Mountain Biking in Moab

Moab has long been a taking-off point for Arches and Canyonlands National Park, but in the past few years it has become the mountain bike center of North America. Not only is its slick-rock bike trail a demanding, technically thrilling route, but it also runs through magnificent high desert country through canyons, unusual rock formations, and dramatic drop-offs. Its mountain bike competitions are world famous, and mountain bike enthusiasts from all over the world come to try this challenging trail.

If your children love to ride but are not up to the demands of this particular trail, there are plenty of other great rides to try. The U.S. Bureau of Land Management's public lands have marked trails and dirt roads. Be sure to stay on roads, trails, slick rock, or sand, as the fragile desert environment takes a beating from bike tires; it can take several years to recover. There are helpful mountain biking maps and books available at local bike shops and bookshops in Moab.

Spring and fall are the best times to ride in Moab, as this high desert location gets very hot in the summer. Bring plenty of water whenever you go. Several outfitters rent mountain bikes, or you can bring your own; shuttle services are available to take you to the top of a trailhead or pick you up at the bottom. Try Poison Spider Bicycles (497 North Main Street, Moab, 800–635–1792, 801–259–7882); rentals start at $28 per day, which includes a helmet, a rear rack, two water bottle cages, and complimentary water bottle. This shop also repairs bikes, stocks accessories and parts, and can recommend a shuttle service to suit your needs. Shuttles will take you to your beginning point and then will drive your car to your final destination. The cost depends on how far you go. Day-long trips cost about $30, two-day trips $60.

Activities in and near Moab

Slam on the brakes! Now back up and get out of the car and pay to see the five-thousand-square-foot "tribute to Albert and Gladys Christenson," carved and sculpted out of a rocky cliff outside of Moab. This World Famous Hole 'N The Rock (fifteen miles south of Moab on La Sal Route on U.S. 191, 801–686–2250) was an intensive project of Albert's; he spent twelve years on these fourteen rooms, excavating 50,000 cubic feet of sandstone.

No bones about it: Vernal, a few hours' drive from Moab in the northeastern part of the state, is the dinosaur capital of the world. Dinosaur National Monument, twenty miles east of Vernal, has a fossil bone deposit in a sandbar of an ancient river. At the Dinosaur Quarry, you can see the fossilized remains of more than 2,000 bones in relief in the 200-foot-long wall. Other exhibits and displays help explain the life and times of the types of dinosaurs whose remains were preserved in the Quarry. Tours are available.

The Dinosaur Gardens in Vernal (801–789–3799) have life-size replicas of dinosaur superstars such as Tyrannosaurus Rex, Brontosaurus, Stegasaurous, and "Dinah"—a twelve-foot-tall orange dinosaur that wanders around the grounds posing for pictures with children. Adjoining the gardens is the Utah Field House of Natural History, which offers a walking tour through re-created prehistoric and geologic time with Indian artifacts, fossils, rocks, and minerals. Kids will enjoy re-created dinosaurs "Big Tooth," "Thunder Lizard," and "Run Faster." Don't miss the museum's gift shop, where a machine will crush a fresh penny into a copper medal bearing a likeness of T. Rex. If you visit in the evening the statues are lit with colored lights; at Christmas they are draped with tiny Christmas lights.

ENTRADA RANCH

Address: PO Box 567, Moab, Utah 84532. The ranch is 35 miles from Moab.
Telephone and fax: 801–259–5796

A beautiful 400-acre ranch set along the Dolores River in a wild, remote, slick-rock location, Entrada Ranch has two and half miles of private river beaches, a wonderful swimming hole, and private red rock canyons. With three houses, three cabins, and two sleeping shelters, the ranch accommodates 32 people. Fresh, organic fruits and vegetables from the ranch's bountiful gardens and eggs from its chickens are available in season.

Season: Year-round.

Accommodations: Families tend to stay in one of the rustic but comfortable houses, which are spaced apart for privacy and equipped with full kitchens and bathrooms. Susan's House has three bedrooms, one queen-size bed, four twin beds, a large living area, and a big screened porch. All houses have barbecue areas, rugged slab floors, clean white sheets, and stacked wood for a wood stove or fireplace.

Special Features: The ranch caretaker can make breakfasts and dinners for additional cost.

Cost: $125 per night for four people; each additional person $20 per night. Discounts for stays of five days or more.

Nearby: Many hiking and biking trails lead from the ranch. Horseback riding and tours to look for dinosaur bones, petrified wood, and agates can be arranged. Organized river trips, rock climbing, canyoneering, calm water float trips, and white-water raft trips are available from Coyote Expeditions near the ranch. The Kokopelli bike trail, which extends to Moab, is ten miles away.

CEDAR BREAKS CONDOS

Address: Center and Fourth East, Moab, Utah 84532
Telephone: 801–259–7830; fax: 801–259–4278

These convenient condominiums are in a residential area within walking distance to Moab, five miles from Arches. The upstairs units have views of the La Sal Mountains.

Season: Year-round.

Accommodations: Six newly furnished suites have one or two bedrooms with king- or twin-size beds, full baths, and fully equipped kitchens.

Special Features: The living area has cable TV, a stereo, books, and maps of the area. Laundry facilities are available.

Cost: Two-bedroom suite $75 per night for three people, $100 per night for four; each additional person up to six people $12.50 per night. Includes full breakfast (ham, eggs, fruit, juice, and more) that you prepare in your own kitchen. Lower rates off-season.

Nearby: The condos are four blocks from Main Street and a short distance from the main shopping area, tennis courts, library, museum, information center, and municipal swimming pool. An eighteen-hole golf course is four miles away. Raft or jet boat trips on the Colorado River and jeep rides in Canyonlands are popular organized activities. For more activities in Moab and this general area, see pages 123–125.

GRAND CANYON NATIONAL PARK, ARIZONA

An amazing panorama to behold, the Grand Canyon is deservedly one of the seven wonders of the world. With so much to see, it will be tempting to zip around the park and try to take it all in by car, but to bring the canyon down to a more memorable size for your kids, try to take time together to walk, linger, and savor its many subtleties and nuances. One way to have children spend time looking is to have them photograph what they observe. Point out to them how the cliffs change color with the sun or how clouds create shadows on the gorge.

The park is divided up geographically into the Inner Rim, the two main rims (South and North), and the two rim drives (East and West). Pick up a *Young Adventurer* newspaper at any of the park's visitor centers for suggestions on how to plan your tour and activities such as becoming a "rock detective" for children between the ages of four and twelve. Junior Ranger Badges are earned by attending ranger-led activities and exploring the geology and zoology of the park. The Grand Canyon Association at 800–858–2808 has many publications to order before you go. *Exploring the Grand Canyon* by Lynne Foster ($15.95) offers fascinating geological information and activities; it is also available at all park bookstores. Activities include creating a sketch pad of animals and their tracks or folding a raven origami.

Numerous organizations lead guided river raft trips along the Colorado River through the Canyon from one to twelve days, but most are quite costly. An affordable way for families to have a taste of the more lengthy white water trips is the four- to five-hour smooth water raft trip through Glen and Marble canyons with picnic-style lunch offered by Fred Harvey Tours; the entire tour takes a full day (520–638–2631). To plan a white-water raft trip, contact the park's River Permit's office at 520–638–7843 for a list of all concessioners. Two recommended for families are OARS (800–346–6277) and Hatch River Expeditions (800–433–8966). Plan a year in advance to get your choice of dates and types of rafting.

Horseback rides are offered at Moqui Lodge and in Tusayan outside the park. Choose from one- or two-hour rides through Kaibab National Forest, or take a four-hour ride to the East Rim through Long Jim Canyon. Evening horseback and wagon rides are also available. Contact Apache Stables at 502–638–2891. The authentically restored 1900s-era Grand Canyon steam train chugs the sixty-four miles from Williams to the South Rim in about two hours (adults $50, children $20) with time allowed to explore the rim; it's a great sightseeing splurge. Call 800–843–8724 to reserve.

Mule rides from two-hour treks ($30 per person) to a one-day trip to Plateau Point ($100 per person, including lunch), or a one- to two-day overnights into the canyon to Phantom Ranch ($250 per person for one night; $450 per person for two nights; $206 per additional person, which includes all meals and accommodations) are run by Grand Canyon National Park Lodges. Riders must be at least four feet seven inches tall. Trips depart daily from the Stone Corral at the head of Bright Angel Trail; the more extended trips need to be arranged at least eleven months in advance. Call 520-638-2401 to reserve.

Some must-see recommendations from veteran park visitors: Go to Yaki Point, off East Rim Drive, an hour before sunrise for an unbelievable view. Likewise, Hopi Point, off West Rim Drive, provides the best sunset spot. One of the best views of the canyon is from Lipan Point on the East Rim Drive.

As many will share your desire to peer into the canyon's larger-than-life depths, be sure to secure accommodations well in advance. If you miss out on in-park accommodations, try lodgings in nearby Tusayan (call the Chamber of Commerce at 602-635-4061).

BRIGHT ANGEL LODGE AND CABINS

Address: Grand Canyon National Park Lodges, PO Box 699, Grand Canyon, Arizona 86023
Telephone: 602-638-2401; fax: 602-638-9247

Season: Year-round.

Accommodations: This rustic lodge on the South Canyon Rim has a wide range of moderately priced rooms and cabins; some cabins have fireplaces.

Special Features: There are two restaurants on the premises; the kids' lunch and dinner menus at all park lodges offer burgers, chicken nuggets, and other kids' standards for $2 to $3.

Cost: Standard lodge rooms $53 per night, double occupancy; each additional person $6. "Historic" cabins $61 per night, double occupancy. Cabins along the rim start at $89 per night, double occupancy; each additional person $7.

Nearby: West of the lodge is the Bright Angel Trail; try hiking a portion, however small, for an up-close canyon view. Along the three-mile round-trip hike to the Mile-and-a-Half Resthouse you'll see many fossils and Indian pictographs. Mule rides depart from the Stone Corral at the head of this trail. An even easier walk with young children is the Rim Trail, which hugs the South Rim for about three miles from the Yavapai Observation Station; the station has dramatic canyon views and geological exhibits.

THUNDERBIRD AND KACHINA LODGES

Address: Grand Canyon National Park Lodges, PO Box 699, Grand Canyon, Arizona 86023. Lodges are at the edge of the south rim.
Telephone: 602–638–2401; fax: 602–638–9247

Season: Year-round.
Accommodations: What these modern two-story lodges lack in charm, they make up for in family conveniences. Both are just steps from the canyon's South Rim and have rooms with two double beds, a sofa-bed, full bath or shower, television, and telephone.
Cost: Park-side rooms $96 per night, double occupancy; canyon-side rooms $106 per night, double occupancy. Each additional person $9 per night.
Nearby: See Bright Angel Lodge on page 128.

MASWIK LODGE

Address: Grand Canyon National Park Lodges, PO Box 699, Grand Canyon, Arizona 86023 (a five-minute walk from the Canyon's South Rim in Canyon Village)
Telephone: 602–638–2401; fax: 602–638–9247

Season: Year-round.
Accommodations: The complex has both rustic cabins and modern lodge rooms. Maswik Lodge rooms have two double beds, full bath or shower, television, and telephone. Cabins have two double beds, shower, and telephone.
Cost: Cabins $55 per night, double occupancy; each additional person $6. Lodge rooms at Maswick South $71 per night, double occupancy; at Maswick North $103 per night, double occupancy; each additional person $7 to $9.
Nearby: See Bright Angel Lodge on page 128.

YAVAPAI LODGE

Address: Grand Canyon National Park Lodges, PO Box 699, Grand Canyon, Arizona 86023 (in the woodlands between Yavapai Point and the El Tovar Hotel; the lodge is a short drive from the Canyon's South Rim)
Telephone: 602–638–2401; fax: 602–638–9247

Season: Year-round.
Accommodations: Yavapai East is a modern two-story complex; its

rooms have two double beds, full bath or shower, television, and telephone. Yavapai West is situated in pine and sagebrush; its rooms have two queen-size beds, full bath or shower, television, and telephone.

Cost: Rooms at Yavapai West $80 per night, double occupancy. Rooms at Yavapai East $94 per night, double occupancy. Each additional person $9 per night.

Nearby: From the Yavapai Observation Center, you can drive twenty-five miles to Desert View; the highlight here is the Watchtower, a 70-foot-tall 1930s interpretation of what an ancient Native American tower might have looked like. There are Hopi murals and petroglyphs. Climb the winding stairs for a spectacular vista. Three miles west of Desert View are the Tusayan Ruins, an Anasazi Indian site. A great rimside picnic spot is the Buggeln Picnic area, about one mile east of Grandview Point on East Rim Drive. Hiking a portion of the South Kaibib Trail, which begins near Yaki Point on East Rim Drive, will offer you and your children another up-close canyon view.

MOQUI LODGE

Address: Grand Canyon National Park Lodges, PO Box 699, Grand Canyon, Arizona 86023 (just outside the park entrance in the Kaibab National Forest)
Telephone: 602–638–2401; fax: 602–638–9247

Season: Mid-February through November.
Accommodations: Most rooms have two double beds; all have full bath or shower, television, telephone.
Special Features: Horseback riding, cook-out areas, dining room on the premises.
Cost: $93 per night, double occupancy; each additional person $9 per night.

PHANTOM RANCH

Address: Grand Canyon National Park Lodges, PO Box 699, Grand Canyon, Arizona 86023
Telephone: 602–638–2401; fax: 602–638–9247

Built in 1922, the ranch is at the bottom of the Canyon's inner gorge and is accessible only on foot, by mule, or by raft. Most of its cabins and dormitory rooms are reserved by mule riders spending the night, but a few can be reserved by hikers.
Season: Year-round.

Accommodations: The ranch has rustic cabins, made of wood and uncut river boulders, and a main lodge. Each cabin has from four to ten bunk beds, a sink, and toilet. Dormitories are segregated by sex; each has ten bunk beds, a shower, and a restroom. Bedding, soap, and towels are provided in the cabins and dormitories.

Special Features: Meals, served in the Beer Hall, must be reserved in advance. There is also a canteen with snacks and supplies. Bring your own pole and reel for good trout fishing at Bright Angel Creek and the Colorado River; tackle and supplies are available.

Cost: $25 per night. Meals are available at an additional cost of $12 for breakfast, $22 for a stew dinner.

Nearby: Swimming in Bright Angel Creek and many day hikes.

GRAND CANYON LODGE NORTH RIM

Address: Mailing: Amfac Parks and Resorts, 14001 East Iliff Avenue, Suite 600, Arora, Colorado 80014
Telephone: 303–297–2757

Grand Canyon National Park's more remote North Rim is in northern Arizona, two hundred and fourteen miles from the park's more popular South Rim. This lodge, a national historic landmark, was designed in the 1920s by Gilbert Stanley Underwood, who was also the architect of Yosemite National Park's Ahwahnee Hotel. Constructed of massive limestone walls and timbered ceilings, it features dramatic vistas of the canyon.

Season: Mid-May through late October. The North Rim is closed in the winter.

Accommodations: "Western" cabins feature a fireplace, two double beds, a full bath, telephone, and private porches. "Frontier" cabins are more rustic, with a double bed, single bed, and a bathroom with a shower only. These cabins are a short walk from the canyon's rim. "Pioneer" cabins have two rooms that are separated by a bathroom with a shower. Motel rooms have double beds and a bathroom with a shower. There are no cooking facilities in any of the rooms.

Special Features: Dining room in the lodge, outdoor grills in the park's picnic areas, laundry facilities, and a grocery story on the premises.

Cost: Western cabins $75 per night double occupancy; $86 per night for four people; $92 per night for five people. Pioneer cabins $70 per night for up to five people. Frontier cabins $57 per night double occupancy; $62 per night for three people. Motel rooms $66 per night double occupancy; $71 per night for three people; $75 per night for four people. Children under twelve stay free.

Nearby: Along the Bright Angel Point Trail, there is an easy one and a half mile self-guided nature trail, which leads to a spectacular view of the Canyon; it begins by the Lodge. Summer activities at the North Rim include pack tours and ranger programs.

BIG BEND NATIONAL PARK, TEXAS

CHISOS MOUNTAINS LODGE

Address: Big Bend National Park, Texas 79834
Telephone: 915–477–2291

Known as the Last Frontier of Texas, Big Bend National Park is in the center of the western part of the state. It is a land of dramatic contrasts— from the lush vegetation of the Rio Grande flood plain to the high country of the Chisos Mountains, which rise from the surrounding stark Chihuahuan Desert. A flavor of Old Mexico pervades, especially in the village of Boquillas, with its backdrop of the Sierra del Carmen and the Fronteriza mountain ranges.

Season: Year-round.

Accommodations: Seventy-two units of varying types and prices include motel-style rooms, lodge rooms, and stone cottages that accommodate up to six people. All have mountain views.

Special Features: Dining facilities and a camp store on the premises.

Cost: Rooms with two double beds and private bath in the thirty-eight room Casa Grande Motor Lodge or motel $68 per night, double occupancy. "Lodge units" with one room, one double and one single bed, private bath, and covered porch $65 per night, double occupancy. The most requested park accommodations are the six stone cottages, which were constructed by the Civilian Conservation Corps and have stone or native adobe walls. They are $73 per night for three people. Each additional person in any accommodation $10.

Nearby: Raft trips down the Rio Grande, from a short ten-mile jaunt through Colorado Canyon to a seven-day camping expedition through the park's Lower Canyons, are available through Far Flung Adventures (800–359–4138). Specialty float trips for children and their parents, from half a day to ten days, are run by Big Bend River Tours in Lajitas (800–545–4240). The guides are very well educated about the area; families can request a specific focus such as geology or birding.

Trips that combine float trips on the Rio Grande with backcountry hiking to old ghost towns, Indian camps, cavalry camps, canyons, and springs are run by Outback Expeditions (915–371–2490). On the east boundary of the Park, the town of Lajitas on the Rio Grande has re-created the history of the Old West and has many accommodations set in realistic reconstructed buildings.

CENTRAL UNITED STATES

ISLE ROYALE NATIONAL PARK, MICHIGAN

ROCK HARBOR LODGE

Address: PO Box 405, Houghton, Michigan 49931 (on the shores of Rock Harbor)
Telephone: Mid-May through September, 906–337–4993; October through early May, 502–773–2191

Set on an island in the northwestern section of Lake Superior, Isle Royale has no roads or cars. It is accessible by boat from Grand Portage, on Minnesota's north shore, or from Houghton and Copper Harbor in the copper country of Michigan's Upper Peninsula. Summer water activities here include boating along 600 square miles of waterways, swimming, and hiking through moss-carpeted forests and ridges with panoramic views of Lake Superior and Canada. Kids especially enjoy the hike to explore the island's old copper mine. In the middle of Isle Royale there are remote lakes to explore, and moose roam all over the island. The lake trout fishing here is superb.

Season: June through September.

Accommodations: Families prefer staying in one of the twenty housekeeping cottages, which have one room with a kitchenette (uten-sils are supplied), one double bed, and two bunk beds. There are also hotel rooms in the lodge.

Special Features: The island is known for blueberry picking (the din-ing room serves delicious pancakes). In August many people swim in the harbor, and there are motorboats and canoes for rent. Cottage guests can eat at the lodge dining room; a grocery store and laundry facilities are nearby.

Cost: Housekeeping cottages $68 per night, double occupancy; ad-ditional person $34.

Nearby: In addition to the many hiking trails, there is a marina with boat rental. Guided fishing tours can also be arranged. Superior Trips (612–788–4560) offers scuba-diving explorations of ship wrecks for $80 per day for a group of six, meals included.

BADLANDS, SOUTH DAKOTA

CEDAR PASS LODGE

Address: Box 5, Interior, South Dakota 57750 (eight miles south off I-90 at exit 131 on the South Dakota Loop 240)
Telephone: 605–433–5460; fax: 605–433–5560

You will feel like you've made a trip to the moon when visiting this landscape of strange and eerie eroded buttes, ridges, and canyons. Bison, pronghorn, mule deer, prairie dogs, and coyotes drift across the old homesteads and hunting grounds of the Sioux Indians. The ranger-led children's programs and fossil trails are worth joining, as the park has preserved 37- to 23-million-year-old fossils of extinct animals as well as sites important to Indian history.

Season: May through mid-October.

Accommodations: These twenty-four air-conditioned knotty pine cabins are operated by the Ogala Sioux tribe.

Special Features: The central dining room features Sioux Indian fry bread, buffalo burgers, and Indian tacos made with buffalo meat. The lodge shop sells authentic Indian crafts.

Cost: Cabin with two double beds, shower, and air-conditioning for two is $43 per night, double occupancy; each additional person $4. Two connecting bedrooms $62 per night for three people, $66 per night for four people.

Nearby: This is a convenient stopover for trips to the Black Hills and Mount Rushmore (114 miles away) or Wind Cave National Park (161 miles away).

THE SOUTH

EVERGLADES NATIONAL PARK, FLORIDA

Only one hour south of Miami, the Everglades encompass 1.5 million acres of watery subtropical wilderness. The park is made up of vast saw-grass prairies, deep mangrove swamps, pinelands, and the warm waters of Florida Bay. Among its wildlife are three hundred species of birds, the elusive Florida panther (which still stalks in the bush), crocodiles, woodstorks, otters, and alligators. The major tourist season is from mid-December through mid-April, due to rainstorms and abundant insects in the summer.

The Anhinga Trail, like many other trails throughout the park, has a boardwalk so that you can safely observe alligators, otters, snakes, turtles, herons, anhingas, gallinules, and many other birds and animals. Bicycles can be rented year-round at the Flamingo Marina store and the Shark Valley visitor center. The best place to see birds are at ponds, such as Eco Pond and at Mrazek and Coot bays; go in the early mornings or late afternoons in the dry winter months.

Because more than one-third of the park is comprised of marine areas and estuaries, boating is the best way to explore. Canoe trails are plentiful. Almost every type of marine organism native to the Caribbean is found in these waters. Throughout the park, naturalists lead hikes, canoe trips, and tram tours. Backcountry cruises and sailing tours are available through TW Recreational Services; call the Flamingo Lodge (below) for details. Other privately operated sightseeing boat tours include Everglades National Park Boat Tours (941–695–2591), which lead boat trips through the mangrove wilderness and islands.

At the Chekikia Recreation Area you'll find a swimming lagoon, campground, and nature trails. On Tamiami Trail, just west of Shark Valley in the park, don't miss the Miccosukee Indian Village (941–223–8380), which gives a realistic view of the traditional Miccosukees, who lived amid thatched-roof cypress huts. Its museum has artifacts and canoes carved from trees; you can watch Chekikia women weave baskets out of sawgrass. Visitors like to watch the alligators wrestle; alligators once were caught by the Indians for their hides and meat.

FLAMINGO LODGE MARINA & OUTPOST RESORT

Address: #1 Flamingo Lodge Highway, Flamingo, Florida 33034 (thirty-eight miles southwest of the park entrance on Florida Bay) Telephone: 800–600–3813, 941–695–3101; fax: 941–695–3921

Season: Year-round for lodge, cabins, and marina. November through April for other facilities. Winter is the peak season, when rainfall and mosquitos are at a minimum. The weather from June through November is very uncomfortable.

Accommodations: Twenty-four spacious air-conditioned cabins each have fully equipped kitchen, separate living room, and bedroom overlooking Florida Bay. The recently remodeled lodge has 102 air-conditioned rooms with two double beds, television, and a private bathroom. The resort also offers two types of fully equipped houseboats: 37-foot air-conditioned Gibson Sport which sleeps six and a 40-foot pontoon which sleeps eight.

Special Features: Guests can go on sightseeing cruises on Florida

Bay, take a white water bay cruise, or a two-hour wilderness tram tour. Motorized skiffs rental $60 per half day, $80 full day; canoes $22 per half day, $27 full day, $30 overnight; single and tandem kayaks are also available at reasonable rates. Bikes $7 per half day, $13 full day, $16 overnight. There is a pool for lodge and cottage guests as well as a dining room, marina store, and laundry facilities.

Cost: April (excluding Easter) and November through mid-December, lodge rooms $74 per night, double occupancy; cabins $99 per night for up to four adults. Mid-December through March, lodge rooms $87 per night, double occupancy; cabins $125 per night for up to four adults. May through October lodge rooms $65, double occupancy; cabins $79 for up to four adults. Each additional person $10. Children under twelve stay free; cribs are free. Air-conditioned Gibson Sport (sleeps six) $575 for two nights November through April; pontoon (sleeps eight) $475 for two nights November through April.

MAMMOTH CAVE NATIONAL PARK, KENTUCKY

The world's longest network of underground corridors extends for more than three hundred miles beneath Mammoth Cave National Park's picturesque hills and valleys. Guided tours will show you colorful stalactites and stalagmite formations, huge cavern rooms, and spectacular pits and domes. Families can dine in the gypsum-clustered Snowball Room, 267 feet underground. The cave's temperature is a steady fifty-four degrees. The park has many interpretive programs around a campfire. Guided horseback rides through the park are offered by Jesse James Riding Stables (502–773–2560), and bicycle trails range from easy to strenuous. Boating and canoeing on the Green and Nolin rivers are popular April through October.

MAMMOTH CAVE HOTEL

Address: Mammoth Cave, Kentucky 42259 (right by the park's entrance, connected to the park's visitor center by an arched bridge)
Telephone: 502–758–2225

Season: Year-round.
Accommodations: This nondescript brick hotel overlooks a ravine and has simple air-conditioned rooms with private bathrooms.
Special Features: Rooms have televisions, private patios, and balconies. Tennis and shuffleboard courts are adjacent to the hotel.

Cost: Rates $45 to $68 per night, double occupancy, depending on the season; each additional person $8.

SUNSET POINT MOTOR LODGE

Address: Mammoth Cave, Kentucky 42259 (located near the Mammoth Cave hotel at the edge of the forest overlooking Sunset Point Bluffs)
Telephone: 502-758-2225

Season: Year-round.
Accommodations: Each room has a shower and tub bath, electric heat, air-conditioning, and a television.
Cost: Three-person room $74 per night, four-person room $80 per night; each additional person $8. Two parents and children under sixteen can stay in a one-room family unit for $68 per night.

WOODLAND COTTAGES

Address: Mammoth Cave, Kentucky 42259 (secluded cottages in the forest, a short distance from the Mammoth Cave Hotel)
Telephone: 502-758-2225

Season: May through October.
Accommodations: Forty individual cottages with two, three, or four rooms; all have private bathrooms with showers.
Cost: Two-room cottage $46 per night for three people; $52 per night for four; each additional person $6. Two parents and children under sixteen can stay in a one-room family unit for $46 per night.

SHENANDOAH NATIONAL PARK, VIRGINIA

This park is a protected mountain wilderness with deer, bears, bobcats, and untouched forests. Hiking trails lead to numerous waterfalls and old homesites. The Stony Man and Whiteoak Canyon trails are easy and beautiful, and there are naturalist programs for children.

Shenandoah River Outfitters (540-743-4159) have tube and canoe rentals for rides down the Shenandoah. The Mountain Heritage Festival Days, held the last Saturday and Sunday in July, feature dancing, games for children, craft demonstrations, and exhibits. The Camp Hoover Days festival is held the second weekend in August.

Near the park at Luray Caverns (540–743–6551), fifteen minutes from the junction of the park entrance and U.S. 211, the "Great Stalacpipe Organ" actually plays concert-quality music. The Skyline Caverns, known for flower formations called anthrodites, are a five-minute drive from the junction of the park entrance and U.S. 340 in Front Royal. Forty minutes from the junction of the park entrance and U.S. 211 is the New Market Battlefield Historical Park (540–740–3101), a 240-acre park with a museum focusing on the history of the Civil War.

Note: In addition to the accommodations listed here, Bears Den Lodge is a beautiful stone hostel with private family rooms located thirty-five miles southwest of the park. Overlooking the Shenandoah River and Appalachian Trail, there is rafting, canoeing, swimming, and fishing. Call 540–554–8708. HI members, adults $12 per night; nonmembers $15 per night. Children are half-price.

SKYLAND LODGE

Address: PO Box 727, Luray, Virginia 22835 (set at the highest point along Skyline Drive with majestic views)
Telephone: Information: 540–999–2211; reservations: 800–999–4714

Season: Late March through early December.
Accommodations: The least expensive accommodations at this lodge, founded in 1894 as a summer retreat, are the quaint and rustic cabins. New lodge rooms are also available. Cabins sleep two to eight people. Most have twin and double beds. Bed linens and towels are provided. Lodge rooms sleep four and have two double or two queen-size beds.
Special Features: Guided horseback riding for children taller than four feet ten inches from April through October; pony rides $4 for thirty minutes. The playground has swings, bars, and seesaws; the restaurant is known for its blackberry ice-cream pie.
Cost: Cabins $46 to $77 per night, double occupancy; lodge units $77 to $88 per night, double occupancy. Each additional person $5. (The higher rates are for Friday and Saturday nights.) Rates are slightly higher during the peak fall foliage season in October. Special two-day consecutive weekday packages (in late March through July, September, and November through early December) can cost as little as $63 per night.
Nearby: Fishing with barbless hook (the fish are returned to the stream).

BIG MEADOWS LODGE

Address: PO Box 727, Luray, Virginia 22835 (on a high plateau overlooking Shenandoah Valley, in grassy meadow)
Telephone: Information: 540–999–2211; reservations: 800–999–4714

Season: Late April through early November.
Accommodations: The least expensive accommodations are the rustic cabins and the rooms in the main lodge, built in 1929. Cabins sleep two to four people; most have double beds. Linens and towels are provided. Lodge rooms sleep two to four people.
Special Features: Campfire programs, a playground, and a restaurant on the premises.
Cost: Cabins $65 to $69 per night, double occupancy; main lodge rooms $60 to $100 per night, double occupancy. (The higher rate is for Friday and Saturday nights.) Each additional person $5. Rates slightly higher during the peak fall foliage season in October. Special two-day consecutive weekday packages from late April through July, and again in September.
Nearby: The cascading waterfall Dark Hollow Falls is an easy hike away. Fishing with barbless hook (the fish are returned to the stream).

LEWIS MOUNTAIN

Address: PO Box 727, Luray, Virginia 22835 (milepost 57.6 in the park)
Telephone: Information: 540–999–2211; reservations: 800–999–4714

Season: Early May through early November.
Accommodations: These rustic heated and furnished cottages sleep two to four people with one to two double beds, a bathroom, towels, linens, an outside cooking-and-living area with a concrete floor, a fireplace, and a picnic table with an outdoor grill. Families stay in one- or two-room cabins that are connected by a private bathroom. Bathrooms have a sink, toilet, and shower.
Special Features: Camp store and laundry are on the premises.
Cost: One- or two-room cabins $52 to $80 per night, double occupancy. (The higher rate is for Friday and Saturday nights.) Each additional person $5. Rates are slightly higher during peak fall foliage season in October.

THE NORTHEAST

ACADIA NATIONAL PARK, MOUNT DESERT ISLAND, MAINE

Acadia National Park is one the most varied family destinations. In summer you can hike, swim, canoe, cycle, take carriage rides and hayrides, and go horseback riding. Winter visitors can cross-country ski and snowshoe. The park encompasses more than 38,000 acres of Mount Desert Island, where lobster cookouts, hikes, and miles of dramatic coastline are all within easy reach.

Acadia has miles of hiking trails as well as bicycle and bridle paths. A trail of less than one mile leads to outstanding views from the summit of Cadillac Mountain, the highest peak on the East Coast. There is also a Junior Ranger Program for kids; check with the visitor center. Lifeguards are on duty in the summer at Echo Lake (fresh water) and Sand Beach (salt water). Tide pooling is a special way to experience Acadia; check a local tide chart and plan your visit as close to low tide as possible. Carriage and hay wagon rides can be arranged at Wildwood Stable (Park Loop Road, 207–276–3622).

The Mount Desert Oceanarium on Clark Point Road in Southwest Harbor (207–244–7330) has touch tanks, a lobster room, a scallop tank, whale exhibits, and more. In Bar Harbor, the Abbe Museum features Maine Indian artifacts. Half- and full-day canoeing trips are a quiet and invigorating way to experience Acadia; call National Park Canoe at 207–244–5854. Coastal Sea Kayaking Tours glide across the clear waters leading eastward to Frenchman Bay or westward to Bluehill Bay. Half-day and full-day excursions as well as island camping outings are available; call 800–526–8615 or 207–288–9605. Inexpensive scenic cruises, including a daily nature cruise to the Cranberry Islands to watch seals, leave from Northeast Harbor; call the Islesford Ferry Company at 207–276–3717. Whale-watching tours depart from Bar Harbor; call 207–288–9794 or 207–288–9776.

In addition to the lodgings listed here, families who enjoy camping can avoid the crowds by basing their stay in one of the five lean-tos on Isle au Haut, an island within the park accessible only by mail boat. Potential visitors must enter an annual lottery in the spring. Obtain an application before April 1 by calling Acadia Ranger Headquarters at 207–288–3338.

SEASIDE COTTAGES

Address: RFD 1, Box 2340, Bar Harbor, Maine 04609 (at the head of Clark's Cove)
Telephone: 207–288–3674

These quaint cottages are separated for privacy and set on nicely landscaped lawns on a secluded, private beach at Clark's Cove. Less than eight miles away are Acadia National Park and downtown Bar Harbor. The ocean water of Clark's Cove is warm and pleasant for swimming in summer. Rowboats and canoes for fishing or seal watching are available at no charge. At low tide, guests can gather mussels steps from their cottage.

Season: Year-round.

Accommodations: Seaside has eight one-, two-, and three-bedroom heated cottages with modern, fully equipped kitchens. Living rooms have color televisions and beautiful views of the water; some have open-hearth fireplaces. Bedding is provided.

Special Features: Outdoor furniture and gas barbecue grills.

Cost: In summer, two-bedroom cottages $800 per week for three people, $850 per week for four. In spring and fall, two-bedroom cottages $105 per night, $725 per week for three people. Rates are lower in early spring, late fall, and winter.

Nearby: For local activities, see page 140.

HALL QUARRY ROAD HOUSE

Address: Somes Sound, Maine. Reservations: c/o Robert and Janet Brinton, 10 Brinton Road, Bethany, Connecticut 06524
Telephone: 203–393–3608

This house, which sleeps up to eight people, has beautiful views of Somes Sound and the mountains of Acadia from its large deck. The owners frequently rent to more than one family at a time. Its wooded, private acreage is near Acadia National Park's hiking trails, a safe swimming beach at Echo Lake, the ocean, and the stores and restaurants of Southwest Harbor and Bar Harbor.

Season: Year-round.

Accommodations: The first floor has a large, modern eat-in kitchen, a full bath, a living room, and three bedrooms. The refurbished basement has a large bedroom and a family room with a woodstove. The house is heated and completely furnished with dishes, linens, microwave oven, washer and dryer, television, and telephone.

Special Features: Large lawn area, outdoor grill, picnic table.

Cost: In April $350 per week; May and October $450 per week; June $650 per week; July $900 per week; August $975 per week; September $550 per week. Rates are not affected if the house is shared with another family.

Nearby: For local activities, see page 140.

BEECH HILL ROAD HOUSE

Address: Somes Sound, Maine. Reservations: c/o Robert and Janet Brinton, 10 Brinton Road, Bethany, Connecticut 06524 Telephone: 203-393-3608

This house, which sleeps five to seven people, is on a quiet dead-end road near Acadia National Park's hiking trails, Beech Mountain, Somesville Landing, Somes Pond, Long Pond, a good swimming beach at Echo Lake, and the stores and restaurants of Bar Harbor.

Season: Year-round.

Accommodations: The first floor has a modern kitchen, full bath, dining room with balcony, and living room with fireplace. The second floor has three bedrooms and a half bath. The house is heated and completely furnished with dishes, bedding, television, telephone, stereo tape deck, washer and dryer, and microwave oven. Its private rear deck has an outdoor grill and a picnic table.

Special Features: Large private yard.

Cost: In April $350 per week; May and October $400 per week; June $550 to $600 per week; July $800 per week; August $875 per week; September $450 per week.

Nearby For local activities, see page 140.

HARBOUR WOODS

Address: 410 Main Street, PO Box 1214, Southwest Harbor, Maine 04679 Telephone: 207-244-5388; fax: 207-244-7156

These fully equipped housekeeping cottages, set in a lightly wooded area across the street from the town marina, are within walking distance of lobster pounds, shops, museums, and restaurants. Some of the cottages are set around a pond that freezes for ice-skating in winter.

Season: May through October.

Accommodations: Cottages have separate living and sleeping areas. A one-bedroom cottage for four has two double beds, galley kitchen, shower bath, and deck or picnic area. A two-bedroom cottage for four has a double bed and two twins, living area with galley kitchen, and deck. A cottage for six has one bedroom with two double beds, shower bath, living area with double sofabed, galley kitchen, and large deck. Bedding and cookware are provided.

Cost: Cottages for three people $75 per night low season, $105 per night high season; cottages for four people $95 per night low season, $115 per night high season. Each additional person $15 per night.

Nearby: The national park, Echo Lake, the Bass Harbor Head Light, and Swan's Island Ferry are a short drive from Harbour Woods.

FAMILY
CAMPS

$\mathcal{C}$all them resorts without the room service, turned-down sheets, or gourmet restaurants—family camps often offer the same range of recreational activities but without the fancy price tag. Mom and Dad won't have to cook, as three meals a day are served in the dining hall. Many family camps also have supervised children's programs, which allow parents time to themselves and kids the chance to be with others their own age.

Growing numbers of traditional children's summer camps are adding family weekends or weeks throughout the summer; close to 400 American Camping Association accredited camps offer family camping throughout the year, and a few now devote their entire summer to family camping. Family camp sponsors range from YMCA and 4-H organizations to university alumni associations, city parks departments, and private owners. The degree of luxury and types of accommodations vary considerably. Most camps have simple cabins with a common bathhouse, but others range from modern two- or three-bedroom suites to shared bunkhouses and tent cabins. Many ask that guests bring their own bedding and towels.

Family camps are typically situated in areas of great natural beauty— on lakes, rivers, or seashores. Expect to find swimming, boating, arts and crafts, horseback riding, volleyball, softball, basketball, evening campfires and sing-alongs, and high and low ropes challenge courses. High ropes courses have such elements as tightropes, Indiana Jones–

style hanging bridges, cargo nets, and vertical wall climbs thirty to forty feet in the air. Participants are secured with harnesses and pulleys so that if they fall, they are caught and safely lowered to the ground. Low ropes courses have many of the same elements but are only four or five feet off the ground. If the participants fall, there is a spotter to catch them. Ropes courses are exciting for children and adults and build agility, self-confidence, and trust.

Family camps are one of the most economical vacations around; once you pay, there are no surprises awaiting your checkbook at the end of the week. They provide an opportunity for families to spend time together in a beautiful wilderness setting while enjoying the company of other families. If you wish to vacation in an area that is not listed in this book, contact the American Camping Association at 800–428–CAMP for a list of their members offering family camping.

WEST COAST

FAMILY VACATION CENTER

Address: UCSB Alumni Association, Santa Barbara, CA 93106-1120
Telephone: 805–893–3123

The beach is at your front door at the University of California at Santa Barbara's Family Vacation Center. When you need a break from the sea and sun, choose from golf, tennis, swimming, arts and crafts, and lectures. Children of all ages are entertained and cared for from 9 A.M. to 9 P.M. except at mealtimes, when families eat together. The dining commons serves three all-you-can-eat meals a day with vegetarian options and a special children's menu. Well over half of the families return each year for the range and quality of adult diversions and variety of planned activities for children. Returning guests get first priority for reservations, and the month of August fills quickly. New guests should try to book by February or March, but there can be last-minute cancellations late in the season.

Season: Eight one-week sessions (Saturday to Saturday) during July and August.

Accommodations: Each family stays in a furnished suite of rooms that includes a living room with a refrigerator; two, three, or four bedrooms; and a private bath. Daily housekeeping is supplied. Three meals a day are included in the price.

Special Features: The children's program includes seaside excursions, swimming, bicycling, archery, hiking, team sports, group games, and arts and crafts. Adults can enjoy pool and beach swimming, tennis and golf lessons, day hikes, sunset sailing, a fitness program, and faculty seminars and lectures presented by UCSB faculty members. Among the family activities are a talent show, family picnic and carnival, and beach campfire sing-along.

Cost: $595 for adults, $470 for ages six to eleven; $400 for ages two to five and $265 for ages one month to twenty-three months.

Nearby: See more on Santa Barbara, pages 212–213.

EMANDAL FARM

Address: 16500 Hearst Post Office Road, Willits, California 95490 (140 miles north of San Francisco)
Telephone: 209–642–3720

Family fun on the farm is Emandal's specialty, and it includes three home-cooked meals a day. Kids gather eggs, see a goat milked, feed the pigs, or play in the shallow waters and sandy beaches of the Eel River. Children love helping to plant and harvest in the farm's extensive garden, pick berries, and cook in the kitchen. Parents enjoy swimming, reading, hiking, and resting. During much of the school year, the farm offers environmental education programs for school groups.

Season: Week-long family stays in August; weekends in May, September, and parts of October.

Accommodations: Eighteen rustic redwood cabins set among oaks, firs, and madrones each have a queen-size bed and a set of bunk beds, a washbasin, and screened windows. Modern bathhouses are nearby. Meals might include German apple pancakes for breakfast, fresh bread and farm-fresh salads for lunch and dinner, and a salmon feed along the river one evening.

Special Features: Activities on the farm revolve around seasonal farm chores: baby animals need tending, seeds need planting, and sheep need shearing in May; berries need picking in August; crops need harvesting and cider needs making in September. Many families spend their days lounging around the river or hiking.

Cost: Week-long stays, adults $595 to $650; $390 for kids twelve to seventeen, $98 for age two to eleven. Seasonal weekends of two to four nights, adults $198 to $410; kids age twelve to seventeen $118 to $250; two to eleven $33 to $75.

SKYLAKE YOSEMITE CAMP

Address: 37976 Road 222, #25G, Wishon, California 93669-9714
Telephone: 209-642-3720

Skylake's private waterfront area on Bass Lake has sailing, canoeing, and wind surfing, all free of charge, and waterskiing is available for an extra fee. Six hours of horseback riding are offered each day at the Camp, where families have spent vacations together for the past thirty-five years. Many families never leave the camp during their stay, while others make a fifteen-mile trip to Yosemite National Park's Wawona gate to explore the park (see pages 93–94). "Prime-season" family camp runs for the two weeks before Labor Day of each year.

Season: Early- and late-season family camp runs from late May to mid-June and for most of September. Prime-season family camp runs the second half of August.

Accommodations: Each family has its own screened house set among the trees (no electricity) with centrally located shower houses; bring your own sleeping bags. Cabins sleep up to eight on bunk beds. The camp can accommodate thirty-four families.

Special Features: Children seven and under ride horses in the ring, while older children and adults ride on trails. Other recreational options include arts and crafts, archery, tennis, and team sports such as softball and volleyball. There is a social hour every night on a lakeside porch with hors d'oeuvres; adults bring their own beverages. Evenings close with a campfire featuring skits and toasted marshmallows for the kids.

Cost: Prime season family camp runs seven days and six nights: Adults and teens $350; children five to twelve $274; four and under always stay free. Half-week rates are also available. Early and late season camps are for three or two nights: three nights, adults $110, children five to twelve $85; two nights, adults $90 and children five to twelve $75. Horseback riding $12 per hour; water skiing $8 for a fifteen-minute trip; mountain bikes $6 for two hours. Reservations are open in January, and the first week of camp fills first.

SAN JOSE FAMILY CAMP

Address: San Jose Family Camp, City of San Jose Department of Conventions, Arts and Entertainment, 1300 Senter Road, San Jose, California 95112 (mailing address); San Jose Family Camp, 11401 Cherry Oil Road, Groveland, California 95321 (camp address)
Telephone: 408–277–4666; fax: 408–277–3270

Residents of San Jose get a small price break at this camp near Yosemite National Park, but anyone is welcome. The camp operates from mid-June through August. Families arrive throughout the week and stay for an average of four nights, participating at their own pace in any of the many activities available. Interpretive programs introduce children and adults to the natural history of the Sierra foothills, and a supervised program for three- to six-year-olds allows parents to pursue activities of their own choice.

    Accommodations: Tent cabins have cots with mattresses, benches, a table, a bookshelf, and outdoor decks. Shared restrooms and showers are located nearby. Guests provide their own linens.

    Special Features: Swimming hole in the Middle Fork of the Tuolumne River, nature-oriented crafts projects, guided tours of Yosemite, nature hikes, fishing, volleyball, Ping-Pong, and sports tournaments are among the daily and weekly choices. Evenings feature campfires, talent shows, skits, and socials.

    Cost: Rates include accommodations, three meals a day, and all activities; San Jose residents get a 20-percent discount. Adults $50 per night; children ten to fifteen $38, six to nine $25, three to five $17. No charge for children under three.

    Nearby: The gold country, horseback riding, hayrides, and a golf course are a short drive away. Many families explore Yosemite National Park—the park entrance is eight miles away. See pages 90 to 92 for more information on the park.

MONTECITO-SEQUOIA LODGE

Address: Generals Highway, Kings Canyon National Park, California 93633
Telephone: 800–227–9900 (reservations); 415–967–8612

The spectacular setting, a hand-picked staff of counselors from all over the world, and nonstop activities makes Montecito-Sequoia Lodge a standout in the world of family camps. Distinguished painters and cartoonists have residencies each week of the summer and offer arts experience to both adults and children at this year-round facility. Located between Sequoia and King's Canyon national forests, Montecito offers swimming, canoeing, and sailing on a sparkling lake; elaborate children's programs tailored to different ages; and plenty of sports and games in the summer. Horseback riding and waterskiing cost extra. In winter guests can cross-country ski or ice-skate on the lake. Ski rental and lessons are available on thirty-five miles of groomed trails; if conditions permit you can ski from the lodge door.

Season: Year-round.

Accommodations: Thirteen rustic cabins sleep six to eight people, each in a king- or queen-size bed and two to three sets of bunks. Bathhouses are nearby. Guests bring their own sleeping bags and towels. Thirty-six lodge rooms with a king- or queen-size bed and bunk beds sleep two to six people; all have private baths.

Special Features: The summer children's program is divided by age: kids six months to twenty-three month play in a special yard accompanied by a parent or teenager. Counselors provide activities for all other age groups: "Chipmunks" (ages five and six) and "Tadpoles" (ages three and four) enjoy goodie bakes, nature hikes, pony rides, and more. "Minnows" (age two) have dock walks, creative play, story time, tumbling, and arts and crats. Seven- to eighteen-year-olds participate in age group activities or choose from activities such as canoeing, sailing, archery, arts and crafts, and tennis. Parents and grandparents may join their children or choose activities, too.

Cost: Rates include all meals and activities except riding and waterskiing. In summer, cabins $335 to $495 per adult, $295 to $535 for children two to twelve. Riding $16 per 75 minutes for adults and $8 for children accompanied by their parents; waterskiing $8 per hour. In winter, weekends include two nights' lodging, six meals, trail pass, youth games, and skiers' orientation on Friday night: $198 per adult, $88 per child four to twelve, $16 per child two to three. Special mid-week packages are available. Snowshoes, ski rentals, and instruction are extra. In fall and spring there are no organized activities, but the pool, tennis courts, and boathouse are open and prices are reduced.

LAIR OF THE GOLDEN BEAR

Address: Lair Reservations, Alumni House, Berkeley, California 94720
Telephone: 510–642–0221

Adults like to play hard when they come to the University of California at Berkeley's family camps in the Stanislaus National Forest. Two different camps, Camp Blue and Camp Gold, have active (and restful) things for parents to do and organized programs for children and teens. The children's programs combine organized activities with unscheduled free time, and each group meets several times each day. "Kub Korral," for two- to four-year-olds, takes place under close supervision. Five- to seven-year-olds have nature activities, pool games, hikes, arts and crafts, and the "Lair Olympics." Eight- and nine-year-olds have nature projects, fishing, games, paddleboating, and storytelling. Preteens have water games, paddleboating, hikes, softball games, movies, and arts and crafts. Teen groups have plenty of athletic and social activities. Guests must belong to the University of California at Berkeley's Alumni Association (a $40 membership fee, but members need not be graduates of the university).

Accommodations: Rustic tent cabins have a wooden platform and sides with a canvas top, twin beds with mattresses (bring your own bedding), and electricity. Small cabins sleep two people, medium cabins sleep four, and large cabins sleep up to eight. Bathhouses are nearby. Meals are served in an open-air family-style dining hall.

Season: Mid-June through August.

Special Features: Each camp has its own lodge, swimming pool, and dining hall. Camp Gold is located near a meadow and has a softball field that both camps share; Camp Blue is more heavily forested. Both have tennis, volleyball, Ping-Pong, horseshoes, arts and crafts, hootenannys, family dancing, and bingo. Pinecrest Lake, a twenty-minute walk from both camps, has sailing, swimming, and boat rental. Camps are staffed by students from the University of California at Berkeley.

Cost: Adults $360 per week; kids thirteen to seventeen $320, ten to twelve $260, six to nine $225, two to five $165, under two $80.

Nearby: Boating, fishing, golf, and horseback-riding facilities. Many people use the camp as a base to explore the surrounding area.

ROCKY MOUNTAINS AND SOUTHWEST

ASPEN GROVE FAMILY CAMP

Address: c/o Brigham Young University, PO Box 22460, Provo, Utah 84602-2460
Telephone: 801–378–6739

A summer-long family camp run by Brigham Young University, Aspen Grove is at the base of stunning Mount Timpanogos in the Wasatch

Range, the westernmost outcropping of the Rocky Mountains. Eleven six-day family camps and two family minicamps are offered each summer. Most families stay in their own rustic cabins, but family reunion groups can select from four family lodges that can house a minimum of twenty-six people. Children are separated into age groups for fun activities (seven different groups serve two-month- to twelve-year-olds), while teens have special programs designed just for them. Adults can read a book by the pool, hike, learn orienteering, or participate in various sports tournaments. Buffet meals include fresh salad bars, home-baked breads, fresh fruits, and a "baby bar" that is loaded with food to please the palates of infants and toddlers.

Season: June, July, and August.

Accommodations: Rustic cabins sleep from five to nine people and are included in the basic family camp fees. Each is carpeted and has a queen-size bed and twin bunk beds. Restroom and shower facilities are close by. The Alumni Board cabin has two sides, each with a master bedroom, bath, sitting area, and loft. Each side of the cabin sleeps eight people and rents for an extra fee in addition to the regular camp fees. The two-story family lodges include eight bedrooms, five bathrooms, a living room, small kitchen, and large loft, and rents for an extra fee.

Special Features: Swimming pool, high adventure ropes course, mountain hikes, tennis, basketball, volleyball, horseshoes, Ping-Pong, badminton, shuffleboard, racquetball, volleyball, miniature golf, arts and crafts (painting, ceramics, pottery, and leather work), campfires, country dancing, archery, orienteering, and children's programs.

Cost: Adults 19 and over: six-day camp $345, mini-camp $174; ages thirteen to eighteen: six-day camp $285, mini-camp $145; children nine to twelve: six-day camp $224, mini-camp $115; children five to eight: six-day camp $199, mini-camp $110; children three and four: six day camp $179, mini-camp $92; infants up to two: six day camp $116, mini-camp $58. Each side of the alumni board cabin $300 per week in addition to regular camp fees. Family lodge $1,000 per week in addition to regular camp fees (minimum occupancy twenty-six people). Bring your own bedding or rent it at $5 per set.

THE TRAILS END RANCH FAMILY CAMP

Address: Inquiries: PO Box 6525, Denver, Colorado 80206; Camp: PO Box 1170, Estes Park, Colorado 80517
Telephone: 970–586–4244, fax: 970–586–3020

Each family stays in its very own Conestoga wagon at this unique family camp on the edge of the Rocky Mountain National Park. Guided hikes, tailored to different ages and abilities (minimum age is four), lead campers into the park, where marmots, chipmunks, elk, bighorn sheep, and deer are often sighted. Campers age twelve and over can learn technical climbing at no extra charge. In addition there is western riding, a ropes course, a separate arts and crafts shop, barn, archery range, and rifle range.

Accommodations: Each of the camp's fifteen wagons accommodates four people in comfortable twin beds. Bathhouses are nearby. A log lodge has a dining room and a lodge room with fireplace.

Special Features: Western riding, hiking, archery, riflery, arts and crafts, and a ropes course. The program designed for four- to eight-year-olds has simpler rides and easier hikes. Families are expected to participate in most activities together. There's a campfire each evening, with sing-alongs, old camp movies, and skits.

Cost: Program runs Tuesday through Sunday. Ages nine and up $325 per person, ages four through eight $175 per person. Costs include meals and all activities. The camp begins taking reservations in October for previous participants, and on November 1 for the public; cancellations are often available.

BRUSH RANCH CAMPS

Address: PO Box 5759, Santa Fe, New Mexico 87502
Telephone: 800–757–8821, 505–757–8821

Family campers can try their hand fly fishing in the clear cool water of the Pecos River—a mile and a half of it runs through the middle of camp. If your line gets tangled or the fish aren't biting, instructors will help you perfect your technique. During family camp sessions, children are divided into groups according to their ages and enjoy swimming, fishing, art projects, and games throughout the morning. Parents can take horseback rides and hikes into the breathtaking Pecos Wilderness, play tennis, pick raspberries, or read by the river at this former dude ranch. In the afternoon, activities are scheduled for adults and children to enjoy together. Family camp is offered for one week during the summer, usually in August; the rest of the season youth camps are offered.

Families looking for an invigorating wilderness experience may want to try one of the two different Parent-Child Adventure Camps for families with kids ages ten to fifteen. Groups head out on week-long horseback trips, or a backpacking trip that includes a ride on the Cumbres-Toltec Railroad. Both sessions offer mountain biking, backpacking and day hikes as part of the program, and take place largely in the Pecos Wilderness area.

Accommodations: Families are housed in cabins (usually one family to each cabin) and bathroom facilities are within the cabin. All linens are furnished. All food is provided "on the trail" during the Parent and Child Adventure Camps.

Special Features: Fly-fishing instruction, ropes challenge course, horseback riding, hiking, tennis, pottery studio, arts and crafts, moonlight swim party, campfires, western dance, ice cream sundae party.

Cost: Four-night family camp $425 for adults and children ten and over. Children five to ten $225, two to five $150. Parent and Child Adventure Camp are $725 per person. There is no tipping of staff.

CENTRAL UNITED STATES

SHAW-WAW-NAS-SEE 4-H CAMP

Address: Northern Illinois 4-H Camp Association, 6641 North 6000 W Road, Manteno, Illinois 60950
Telephone: 800–207–7429; 815–933–3011

Camp Shaw-waw-nas-see, in operation for more than fifty years, is primarily a youth camp, but also has weekend family camp opportunities and a "Grand Camp" weekend for grandparents and their grandchildren. The camp covers 120 acres of rolling pine and hardwood forests with hiking trails and open meadows. Crafts projects including leather working, copper enameling, and basketweaving are popular with the kids. The swimming pool and creek see a lot of splashing action, and supervised children's activities give parents or grandparents a break during part of the weekend. Camp runs from Friday night to Sunday at noon, and is usually sometime in mid-July.

Accommodations: Twenty-four wooden cabins with concrete floors have five sets of bunk beds in each; small families can share one with another family. Modern bathhouses are located near each cabin.

Special Features: Swimming pool, creekside swimming, rock climbing, arts and crafts, archery, volleyball, and campfires with singing, skits, and marshmallows.

Cost: Per weekend, adults (thirteen and up) $75; children four to twelve $60, three and under free. Rates include all meals and activities.

CAMP NEBAGAMON FAMILY CAMP

Address: PO Box 429, Lake Nebagamon, Wisconsin 54849 (May 15 to September 15); 5237 North Lakewood Avenue, Chicago, Illinois 60640 (rest of year)
Telephone: 715–374–2275 (summer); 773–271–9500 (winter)

Waterfront activities on Nebagamon Lake dominate the week-long family camp held each August for parents, grandparents, and children age five and up. Canoes, rowboats, sailboats, and windsurfers are available for guests to use and instruction is provided by camp staff. The fishing is fine; you can catch perch, bluegill, crappies, bass, walleye and northern pike. Nebagamon's playing fields and courts offer baseball, basketball, soccer, softball, volleyball and field hockey, and tennis. Plus, there's arts and crafts, bike rides, and a target range. Each year optional day trips are offered: one favorite is a kayak and canoe trip down the nearby Brule River. Breakfast and lunch are buffet-style, and dinner is served to guests. Evening activities include talent shows, council fires, music and square dancing. Three hours a day of special counselor-led programs for kids are offered to allow parents some free time.

Accommodations: Each family group has a cabin that can hold up to ten people in bunks or single cot beds. Washhouses are centrally located to all cabins.

Special Features: Seven tennis courts, riflery, archery, orienteering, crafts, fishing, hiking, talent shows, lake swimming, sports tournaments.

Cost: Adults eighteen and over $275; first and second child $200, third and fourth child $150.

EDWARDS YMCA CAMP ON LAKE BEULAH

Address: North 8901 Army Lake Road, PO Box 16, East Troy, Wisconsin 53120
Telephone: 414–642–7466

A 2,000-foot boardwalk extends over marshland between two lakes, and Camp Edwards offers special nature walks and classes to teach guests about the wildlife and plants that inhabit the marsh. Three summer weekends and one winter weekend are set aside for the family camp along the wooded shores of Lake Beulah in southeastern Wisconsin. There's an additional weekend set aside just for grandparents and grand-children in August. Camps run for two or three days. Water sports include canoeing, sailing, kayaking, swimming, and touring Lake Beulah on a pontoon boat. The special New Year's family camp features cross-country skiing, tubing, ice-skating, and indoor and outdoor games.

Accommodations: Three types of housing are available, each with a different price. The Runge Lodge has rooms that sleep four people in two sets of bunk beds and share a bathroom with an adjoining room. The Hoffer Lodge, the newest of the bunch, also has rooms that sleep four people in two sets of bunk beds and share a bath with an adjoining room. Log cabins sleep up to twelve people each and have restrooms nearby. Meals, served in the dining hall overlooking the lake, include fresh vegetable bars and delicious home-baked desserts.

Special Features: Archery, riflery, arts and crafts, volleyball, softball, soccer, an observatory, game room, tetherball, campfires, special adult canoe trips, and a ropes challenge course.

Cost: Family camp prices are a total combination of accommodations (price depends on facility) and food service. Families sleeping in a cabin, $106 for two nights, $149 for three nights (you get the whole cabin and can house as many people as you choose). In the Runge Lodge, families $136 for two nights, $188 for three nights. Families in the Hoffer Lodge, $158 for two nights, $218 for three nights. Two-night stays include five meals for $39 per adult (age twelve and over); children six to eleven $33, two to five $15, under two free. Three-night stays include eight meals for $63 per adult, children six to twelve $50, two to five $22, under two free. All activities are included. Grandcamp pricing includes food for one grandparent and one grandchild: weekend stay in cabin $85, in either lodge $95; each additional grandparent $45 in cabin or $50 in lodge, and each additional child is $30 in cabin or lodge.

YMCA STORER CAMPS

Address: 7260 South Stony Lake Road, Jackson, Michigan 49021
Telephone: 517–536–8607

Horseback riding is a big attraction at Storer, where family camping has been a tradition for more than thirty years. Children age seven and up take trail rides while younger ones ride in the corral. A special children's activity program keeps youngsters busy with storytelling, pony rides, arts and crafts, and more, while parents enjoy tennis, sailing, swimming, and archery. Teens also have specialized programming. Instruction in various activities is available to adults and children alike. Evening programs keep the fun rolling for the entire family with square dancing, campfires, talent shows, and barbecues. The summer family programs include long weekend theme camps and a week-long camp. A three-day New Year's Eve camp includes winter activities such as broomball, skating, tobogganing, scavenger hunts, cookie-making, night hikes, and sing-alongs.

Accommodations: Families stay in cozy "A-frame" cabins with bunk beds. Bathhouses are centrally located to all cabins. Meals are served family-style and often follow themes, such as Hawaiian luau, western night, or Italian night.

Special Features: Swimming, sailing, canoeing, kayaking, horseback riding, volleyball, tennis, campfires, cookouts, square dancing, and more; cross-country skiing in winter.

Cost: For long weekends (two nights and three days), adults $86, teens $69, children two to twelve $64. For a full-week program (Sunday to Saturday), adults $189, teens $159, children two to twelve $138.

AL-GON-QUIAN FAMILY CAMP

Address: Ann Arbor Y, 350 Fifth Avenue, Ann Arbor, Michigan 48104-2294 (reservations office). Camp is thirty miles south of the Straits of Mackinac on Burt Lake.
Telephone: 313–663–0536

Set on the western shore of Burt Lake in 150 acres of white birch, maple, and pine forest, Al-Gon-Quian offers a family camp with a yoga emphasis for parents. Yoga classes cater to all levels of skill, from beginners to advanced students. The children's programs are supervised, so Mom and Dad are free to stretch, ride horseback, waterski, or just sit and read. Twenty families participate in each week-long session. School-age kids stay entertained with summer camp mainstays such as canoeing, horseback riding, archery, and arts and crafts, and parents are welcome to join their kids. The camp offers child care for preschool children during the activity periods at no extra charge.

Season: Last two weeks of August.

Accommodations: Each family is assigned a wood-frame cabin over-looking the water, with screened windows, bunk beds, and electricity. Bathroom facilities are nearby; meals are served in a dining hall. Guests supply their own bedding.

Special Features: Horseback riding, riflery, archery, arts and crafts, tennis, sailing, canoeing, waterskiing, campfire sing-alongs, swimming, woodworking, volleyball, and baseball. After breakfast, campers are divided into classes according to the activities that interest them.

Cost: Family Camp runs for six days: adults $250, children one to eighteen $100.

CAMP MICHIGANIA WALLOON

Address: Michigania, Alumni Association, University of Michigan, 03006 Camp Sherwood Road, Boyne City, Michigan 49712-9361
Telephone: 616–582–9191

The alumni association of the University of Michigan offers a full summer season—eleven one-week sessions—of family camping on the shore of scenic Walloon Lake in northern Michigan. Their specialty is blending education with recreation, and members of the Michigan faculty are in residence providing seminar discussions in the evening and informal talks throughout the week. Recreational possibilities are endless; along with the more standard riding, archery, boating, and swimming, you can bring your own sailboats or powerboats—mooring facilities are available at no charge. Nursery facilities are available during morning and afternoon hours, and special activities are designed for specific ages along with activities to be enjoyed by the entire family together. Families have been visiting this camp year after year since 1961.

Special Features: Archery, arts and crafts, sailing, windsurfing, canoeing, rowboats, nature study, horseback riding, riflery, trap shooting, swimming, tennis, square dance, volleyball.

Accommodations: Campers stay in cabins near the lake. Each cabin contains several "residential units" with bedrooms and a bathroom with shower. Campers are responsible for their own sheets and towels; blankets and pillow are provided.

Cost: Riding, riflery, and certain arts and crafts activities cost extra. At Walloon, per week: adults $440 children thirteen to seventeen $395; seven to twelve $330; three to six $275; infants up to two $175. You must join the Alumni Association to attend ($40), but you do not need to have attended the University of Michigan.

CAMP LINCOLN/CAMP LAKE HUBERT FAMILY CAMP

Address: 5201 Eden Circle, Suite 202, Minneapolis, Minnesota 55436
Telephone: 800–242–1909; 612–922–2545

Each morning after breakfast, families select their activities for the day: sailing, windsurfing, and swimming on Lake Hubert; horseback riding, archery, riflery; a high and low ropes course; hiking, mountain biking, or arts and crafts. The challenging ropes courses are a big hit: most kids breeze through them and take great pleasure in watching their parents struggle to complete them. Activity directors assist the adults, and the children, too. Founded in 1909, this camp offers a week-long family camp in middle or late August.

Accommodations: Three families share a large, two-story, three-bedroom cabin. Each cabin has a large central room with a fireplace, a bathroom with toilets and sinks, and three separate bedrooms. A shower house is near all the cabins, and most of the cabins overlook one of the lakes.

Special Features: The swimming beach has a sandy bottom and a gradual slope. One of two large lodges is used for dining and the other for recreation and family social time. Drop a line in the adjoining lakes and you might land a walleye, bass, or crappie. Arts and crafts activities take place in a pottery shop and two other craft shops, and there are athletic fields for soccer and tennis.

Cost: Adults $480; children under ten $440; children under two stay free. Enrollment begins in late September and begins to fill to capacity by late April to early May.

CLEVELAND AREA YMCA FAMILY CAMPS

Address: Camps Division, 8558 Crackel Road, Chagrin Falls, Ohio 44022
Telephone: 216–543–8184

Special holiday family camp weekends are offered on the Memorial Day, Fourth of July, and Labor Day weekends, and several other weekends in the early spring. The Centerville Mills camp features horseback riding, canoeing and fishing on a lake, swimming in an Olympic-size pool, basketball, archery, and an individual and group ropes challenge course with a special obstacle course. Three weekends a year, a special horseback riding camp offers riding instruction and trail and ring riding. Families stay in individual cabins with a central bathhouse.

Accommodations: Cabins have ten bunks and are heated: each family has their own private cabin regardless of the number in their group.

Special Features: Sand volleyball court, stable of twenty horses, basketball, waterfall hike, arts and crafts cabin, fishing, swimming.

Cost: Three-day, two-night camp $60 for the first person, $55 for the second, $45 for each additional.

CAMP CHRISTOPHER FAMILY CAMP

Address: CYO Family Camp, 812 Biruta Street, Akron, Ohio 44307
Telephone: 800–CYO–CAMP; 216–376–2267

Horseback riding, four different lakes, and an awesome ropes challenge course are available to campers at Camp Christopher's Family Camp. Adults and children of any age can ride, the lakes are all within a short walk of the cabins, and the ropes challenge area has six high and twenty low elements. Children from infants to teenagers can attend with their parents. Each morning, the young campers and adults are grouped by age and enjoy different activities under the supervision of qualified camp counselors. Parents and children participate together in a camp program each afternoon. After-dinner activities include carnivals, campfires, hayrides, Indian nights, and haunted houses. Camp Christopher Family Camp has been in business for more than forty years on 160 wooded acres in Bath, Ohio.

Season: Six days and five nights in June, July, and August.

Accommodations: Cabins are heated and carpeted; restroom and shower facilities are in a nearby bathhouse. Thirteen duplex cabins sleep six to ten people on each side. Small families (usually fewer than four people) can share a cabin with another small family.

Special Features: Activities include horseback riding, swimming, boating, fishing, hiking, hayrides, crafts and games, sports, and the ropes challenge course. Each age group has a different course, and harnesses are provided for the highest ones. The courses go through the woods and vary with the landscape.

Cost: Adults $150; children $125 for the week.

THE SOUTH

CAMP FRIENDSHIP

Address: PO Box 145, Palmyra VA 22963
Telephone: 800–873–3223; 804–589–8950

Camp Friendship offers lake and river canoeing, lake and pool swimming (swing off a rope into water), pond fishing, a ropes course, horseback riding, tennis, crafts, archery, riflery, and other activities for all ages. During the third week of August and on Labor Day weekend, families can stay for as few as three days. Special canoeing, inner tubing, rock climbing, caving, and waterskiing trips are offered throughout the week, and scheduled activities for children allow parents time to themselves each morning.

Season: Third week of August and Labor Day weekend.

Accommodations: Families stay in cabins of various sizes, sleeping four to ten people; each family gets their own cabin unless they request to share with another family. A few cabins have private bathrooms but most use centrally located shower houses. Cabins have built-in bunk beds and electricity. Bring your own bedding or rent linens for a small fee. Meals are served buffet-style, featuring lots of fresh fruits and vegetables, a salad bar, and locally baked breads. Families are expected to help clear tables. Participants can bring their own tents or RVs with advance arrangement.

Special Features: Tennis, basketball, soccer, volleyball, archery, riflery, pool and lake swimming, arts and crafts, pottery, basket making, river and lake canoeing, ropes course, horseback riding. Supervised children's activities each morning, ages three to ten. Evening activities include such events as a hayride, campfire, games night, water carnival, or talent show.

Cost: Family package for the full six nights: family of four or more, $1,100; two adults and one child, $830; one adult and two children, $730. Daily rate, adults eighteen and over $55 per day; children three to seventeen, $50 per day, under three free. Minimum stay is three nights. If you plan to bring guests who are not immediate family, they are charged the daily rate. Rock climbing, caving, or water-skiing trips, $10 to $15 per person, including transportation. Horseback riding lessons and trail rides, $13 per person, per hour.

SEAFARER FAMILY CAMPS

Address: Route 65, Box 3, Arapahoe, North Carolina 28510-9716
Telephone: 919–249–1212

An extensive sailing and motor boating program on the expansive Neuse River makes this one of the most popular family camps around. A freshwater lake is used for swimming. Kids particularly love the giant airbag in the lake: one person scoots down to its end, and when a second person jumps onto the bag, the first person goes flying into the water. The camp has a nine-hole par-three golf course, a ropes course, and a special supervised program for children under six. Family camp is offered over a spring and fall weekend, and for a week in late August.

Accommodations: The camp can accommodate fifty families. Each lives in a cabin with a private bath and bunk beds with mattresses: guests supply their own linens. Meals are included.

Special Features: The boat fleet includes sunfish, Hobie Cats, flying scots, sailboards, Boston whalers, ski boats, inboard motor boats, and a large cruising boat. The river is about four miles wide. Tennis, golf (an eighteen-hole golf course is nearby), water aerobics, a nature program, archery, riflery, arts and crafts, and softball are also available. A supervised "kiddie corner" with activities for children under six operates in the morning and afternoon. Evening programs include a sunset cruise for parents, a talent show, sock hop, carnival, bingo night, and movies.

Cost: Week-long stays: Adults $400, children six to twelve $325; five and under $250. Rates include everything except arts and crafts projects. Weekend Camp, Friday to Sunday lunch: adults $110; six to twelve $80; under five $25. Reserve as far in advance as possible.

THE NORTHEAST

CAMP CHINGACHGOOK ON LAKE GEORGE

Address: Capital District YMCA, 6 Chelsea Park, Clifton Park, New York 12065
Telephone: 518–373–0160

Two docks and a fleet of canoes, rowboats, sailboats, and sailboards are the center of the action on Chingachgook's 1,300 feet of shoreline on Lake George in Adirondack State Park. Families have private cabins during the three-day family camps over Memorial and Labor Day weekends. The camp, established in 1913, offers tennis, basketball, softball, soccer, and other games in addition to water sports.

Season: Memorial and Labor Day weekends.

Accommodations: Thirty cabins sleep ten each in bunk beds; all have electricity but no heat. Bathrooms with hot showers are near the cabins. Meals are served family-style in the dining hall and there is at least one barbecue during each family weekend.

Special Features: Kids are wild about the camp's ropes course, which includes a rope spiderweb to climb, a 150-foor rappelling line, and ropes that go through trees. Adults are encouraged to try it as well, and all participants are attached to harnesses. Evening activities include campfires, sing-alongs and dances.

Cost: Three-day family camping weekend $122 per adult and $90 per child, and includes nine meals and all programs.

WEONA FAMILY CAMP

Address: 300 Cayuga Road, Buffalo, New York 14225
Telephone: 716–565–6008; fax: 716–565–6007

Camp Weona's one-thousand acres of fields, streams, forests, and lakes about an hour outside of Buffalo give families unlimited opportunities for hiking, swimming, and exploring at their own pace. Or they can participate in the camp's more organized recreational activities, such as canoeing, noncompetitive outdoor games, horseback riding, and the world class high and low ropes adventure course. Home-cooked family-style meals are served in the dining hall.

Season: Three days over Memorial Day and Labor Day weekends.

Accommodations: Families can stay in cabins or lodge rooms: Private cabins can sleep up to ten in bunk beds with a shared central shower and bathroom facilities. The Weona Lodge offers dorm rooms with private showers and bathrooms and a central living room with a fireplace.

Special Features: Swimming in outdoor heated pool, hayrides, horseback riding, archery, rock climbing, nature study of the pond and forest, fishing, campfires, skits, short plays, and sing-alongs.

Cost: Cabin $65 per person; lodge $83 per person. First child over four is full price, each additional child receives a ten-percent discount. Children under four stay free. Additional charges for horseback riding and the high ropes course.

BECKET-CHIMNEY CORNERS YMCA FAMILY CAMPS

Address: Camps and Outdoor Center, 748 Hamilton Road, Becket, Massachusetts 01223
Telephone: 413–623–8991; fax: 413–623–5890

Family camping events take place at two different sites located side by side high in the Berkshire Mountains of Western Massachusetts. Both are operated by the YMCA and together they cover 1,200 acres of land and water. Camp Becket, founded in 1903, hosts families in August and over Labor Day and Columbus Day weekends. The rest of the summer it operates as a boys' camp. Its sister camp, Chimney Corners, offers a New Year's and Memorial Day weekend camp and is a girls camp throughout the rest of the summer. Each camp has a large pond with boating and swimming, and miles of hiking trails and cross-country ski trails. The two camps each have their own low ropes course and rock-climbing tower and share a challenging high ropes course in the middle. All family camps offer daily age-appropriate activities, nutritious meals served family style, special games and campfires. People can do as much or as little of the programmed activities as they desire.

Accommodations: During the warm months, each family has their own cabin that sleeps eight to ten with washhouses located nearby. Heated lodge rooms sleeping four to six people are used during the winter months; baths are in the hall.

Special Features: Nature crafts, canoeing, kayaking, archery, nature walks, ropes course, swimming in summer. Sledding, skating on the ponds, skiing, nature walks in winter. Family cooking such as apple pies on the fall foliage (Columbus Day) weekend and gingerbread creations over New Year's family camp.

Cost: Children under three free. Memorial Day and Columbus Day weekends (Friday afternoon to Monday afternoon): adults (thirteen and over) $99, seven to twelve $72, three to six $60. Three-night New Year's Camp about 15 percent higher. Summer Becket Family Camp: three, five, or eight nights, adults $98, $194, $265, children seven to twelve, $72, $135, $185, three to six, $58, $115, $165.

CAMP MERROWVISTA

Address: 147 Canaan Road, Ossipee, New Hampshire 03864
Telephone: 603–539–6607; fax: 603–539–7504

Adventure-based activities form the backbone of Merrowvista's Family Camp Program, but discussion and problem-solving sessions on family issues make it both educational and recreational for parents. Two five-day family camps have flexible programs with a wide range of activities planned for all ages. The waterfront is equipped with swimming docks, rowboats, canoes, sailboards, and small sailboats. Merrowvista's state-of-the-art high and low ropes challenge courses are exhilirating fun, but also emphasize working as a team and learning together. The camp's extensive acreage includes an idyllic wilderness setting of hardwood forests, the gentle peaks of the Ossipee Mountains, Dan Hole Pond, and rolling meadows.

Accommodations: Guests can stay in screened cabins (with or without electricity) with shared bathhouses. Each family gets its own room or cabin. Meals are served in a dining hall.

Special Features: Hiking trails radiate out from the camp for private hikes. Group nature studies, fishing, self-guided nature trails, and arts and crafts activities are all part of each session.

Cost: Adults $125; children (up to age seventeen) $100 for the session.

CAMP WYONEGONIC FAMILY CAMP

Address: RR1 Box 186, Denmark, Maine 04022
Telephone: 207–452–2051; fax: 207–452–2611

Located on two and a half miles of private forested shoreline with 2,000-foot Mount Pleasant as a backdrop, Wyonegonic offers three popular family camp sessions during the month of August. The freshwater lake is everyone's favorite center of activity where children and adult campers learn to use the fleet of sailboats, canoes, and windsurfers or backstroke out to a raft to lounge in the sun or play on the slide that ends in the water. Water-skiing and riflery are available for ages eleven and up. Wyonegonic is the oldest girls' camp in the United States and has been in operation for nearly one hundred years. A number of its buildings are original and have great charm and character.

Accommodations: Rustic cabins have restrooms and shower houses nearby. Ample meals are served in the main lodge/dining hall.

Special Features: Clay tennis courts, craft shop, library, athletic field, hiking and jogging trails, swimming, sailing, rowboats and canoes, archery, water-skiing, riflery, sail boarding, fishing, games, aerobics, horseback riding (extra fee).

Cost: Three-day session: adults $150, kids five to ten $114; five days: adults $250, children $190, two days: adults $100, kids $76. No charge for kids under five. Limited baby-sitting for toddlers is available for an hourly fee, but parents should consider bringing baby-sitters for this age group. You may combine sessions.

LAKESHORE AND RIVERSIDE VACATIONS

*N*othing compares to the rejuvenating quality of water. It cools you down on a hot day and provides endless entertainment for children. Kids seem most content splashing and swimming, digging in the sand, and running in the sun. Lake and river visits teach children to be silent and still as well, letting the cool water of a creek rush over their bodies or silently watching beavers, turtles, and frogs go about their business. There are canoes and rowboats to paddle, fish to be caught, water skis to master, and sailboats to sail. As long as there is water nearby, most parents find that all family members stay busy and content.

This chapter covers cottages, cabins, rooms, and houseboats on rivers and lakes throughout the country; you'll find even more in the chapter on resorts. Many of the places we list have self-contained kitchens, so families can either do their own cooking or head to a restaurant for a special treat. The type of water recreation can be as simple as a sandy beach and an inner tube or two or as elaborate as a full-service marina supplied with a variety of boats, fishing gear, and scuba-diving equipment. The places we have selected are either right on the water or a stone's throw away. Both privately owned and state-run facilities are listed, and all offer excellent values to vacationing families.

River Rafting

Family rafters report that white water rafting is a thrilling vacation that provides lots of opportunities for togetherness. The following outfitters offer special trips for families, but there are many more. To find specific outfitters in an area you are interested in visiting, contact America Outdoors, a national organization listing outfitters and guides.

America River Touring Association offers family trips throughout the west: 800–323–2782.

America Wilderness Experience is a trip broker that represents many outfitters: 800–444–0099.

Class VI River Runners operate in the Appalachians of West Virginia: 800–252–7784 or 304-574-0704.

Expeditions, Inc. offers trips through the Grand Canyon: 520–779–3769.

OARS (Outdoor Adventure Specialists) runs a variety of trips throughout the west: 800–736–4677 or 800–346–6277.

ROW River Odysseys West offers special "Family Focus" trips; rafters as young as five are welcome. 800–451–6034, 208–765–0841; PO Box 579, Coeur d'Alene, Idaho 83816.

Unicorn Expeditions runs rivers in Maine: 800–864–2676.

WEST COAST

CONVICT LAKE RESORT

Address: Route 1, Box 204, Mammoth Lakes, California 93546
Telephone: 619–934–3800

Named for a group of notorious escaped convicts who holed up in the area many years ago, Convict Lake is now famous for its abundance of trophy trout. Anglers can rent fishing boats, rowboats, canoes, and bicycles from the resort. More than twenty housekeeping cabins are within an easy walk of the lake, where guided horseback rides take young wranglers on a tour. Swimming is a bit chilly during most of the year, although many children splash around in July and August when the water temperature hits fifty-five degrees. An Olympic-size heated pool is a five-minute drive away. The resort's gourmet restaurant is open for dinner only. Proximity to Mammoth Mountain ski area for winter downhill skiing and summer mountain biking makes this resort an excellent choice for sports-minded families.

Season: Late April through October.

Accommodations: Twenty-three cabins and one large house can hold two to twenty people. Many are set up for families, with a combination of twin and double beds. All have private baths, fully equipped kitchens, and linens; just bring your own food and fishing gear.

Special Features: Guided horseback rides, horseshoes, hiking.

Cost: Cabins can be rented by the night or by the week. Week-long stays offer a good value: two-bedroom cabins sleeping four $575 per week; sleeping six $640 to $730. Nightly stays $89 per week night for one-bedroom unit, $109 per weekend night. Three-night minimum on holiday weekends. Fishing boat rentals $45 per day or $10 per hour, canoes and rowboats $22 per day or $5 per hour. Guided horseback rides (for age seven and up), lake ride $20; three- to four-hour meadow or canyon ride $40. Children under seven can be led on horseback around the resort by their parents for $10.

Nearby: Bodie Ghost Town, Mono Lake, Mammoth Lakes Basin, Hot Creek, Fish Hatchery, Devil's Postpile National Monument.

PINECREST LAKE RESORT

Address: PO Box 1216, Pinecrest, California 95364 (several hours' drive east of the San Francisco Bay area, in the Stanislaus National Forest)
Telephone: 209–965–3411

A large sandy beach and clear blue warm waters make for great fishing, boating, and swimming at Pinecrest Lake Resort. Rent a paddleboat, play tennis, or watch movies under the stars in Pinecrest's outdoor amphitheater, and stay in a comfortable cabin, townhouse, or motel room. Some units have a lake view, and all are within walking distance of the lake. The forest service nearby has guided nature hikes, and there is a hiking trail around the lake. In winter, cross-country ski or head to Dodge Ridge (four miles away) for downhill skiing.

Season: Year-round.

Accommodations: Cabins and townhouses have complete kitchens. Linens provided. Fourteen two- and three-bedroom townhouses sleep six to eight people. Seven two- and three-bedroom cabins sleep four to six people. (The townhouse can sleep more, as it has a sofabed.) Motel rooms have two queen-size beds.

Special Features: Sailboats, paddleboats, rowboats, and party boats can be rented at the marina. Other facilities include tennis courts and a restaurant and snack bar. Campgrounds are within walking distance.

Cost: Motel rooms for four people $460 per week in winter, $520 per week in summer; $65 to $80 per night. Two-bedroom cabins sleeping four $650 per week in winter, $745 in summer; $95 per night. Three-bedroom cabins sleeping six $710 in winter, $810 in summer; $100 to $130 per night. Two- and three-bedroom townhouses $720 to $1,075 per week, $115 to $165 per night. In July and August, cabins and townhouses are rented by the week only. Two-night minimum at other times.

Tennis courts $6 per hour. Motor boats $50 for a half day, $70 all day; kayaks $20 half day, $30 all day; party boats $40 to $50 for two hours, $100 to $120 half day, $120 to $150 all day (rates vary according to size of party boat).

Nearby: Restaurant, grocery store, sports shops, and post office are within walking distance. Horseback rentals are three miles up the road.

BONANZA KING RESORT

Address: Route 2, Box 4790, Trinity Center, California 96091 (seventy miles from Redding)
Telephone: 916–266–3305

Bonanza King sits right on Coffee Creek, and every summer an enormous and deep swimming hole is created right in front of the resort by a rock dam. Kids spend hours swimming and splashing, or wading up and down the creek. The simple cabins, which rent by the week in the summer, sit on a quiet grassy meadow. Coffee Creek meets the Trinity River about a mile from the resort, creating a natural swimming hole that is a popular side trip for visiting children. The tiny hamlet of Coffee Creek is about a half mile away from the resort. The Lethbridge family has operated Bonanza King for the past twenty years and many of their guests come back each year to enjoy their warm hospitality and majestic setting.

Season: Mid-April to mid-October, depending on the weather.

Accommodations: Six furnished cabins house three to eight people. Most have a combination living room and kitchen, one bedroom, and sleeping lofts with beds. All pots, pans, and utensils are provided, as are towels and linens. Cabins are heated with wood stove, propane, or electricity.

Special Features: Grassy areas for playing, horseshoe pit, small farm animals, swimming hole, volleyball, children's swing and sandbox, campfire area, fishing. One-mile hike to Trinity River.

Cost: Cabins $75 per night for three people ($525 per week) to $100 per night for eight people ($700 per week). Rates are calculated by size of cabin and number of people in it.

ODELL LAKE LODGE

Address: PO Box 72, Crescent Lake, Oregon 97425 (in the Deschutes National Forest, seventy miles east of Eugene and sixty miles west of Bend)
Telephone: 503–433–2540

Set on the wooded shore of the lake with its own marina, Odell Lake Lodge offers housekeeping cabins and lodge rooms and plenty of recreational activities. Families can rent fishing boats, rowboats, and canoes, or rent mountain bikes to explore the many trails in the area. A lakeside restaurant has views of the wild birds that inhabit the lake, including ospreys and an occasional bald eagle from a sanctuary next door. Fishing is excellent here, with salmon and rainbow and lake trout. In the evening, guests gather around the fireplace in the lodge's Great Room. Families will be most comfortable in the housekeeping cabins tucked into the forest.

Season: Year-round. There is lakeside recreation in the summer and cross-country skiing on groomed trails in winter.

Accommodations: Thirteen housekeeping cabins include kitchens, private baths, linens, and firewood. Several of the four-person cabins do not have ovens. Seven bedrooms are located in the lodge; many are set up for four people.

Special Features: There are barbecue and picnic areas, games, a small playground, family movies, and a wading area and sundeck on the lake. The lake is glacier-fed and most people don't swim until late July or August when it warms up, but kids enjoy playing in Odell Creek, which runs next to the lodge. Boat, mountain bike, and ski equipment rentals are on the premises, and the lakeside restaurant serves homestyle breakfast, lunch, dinner, and snacks. Outdoor recreation includes basketball, volleyball, horseshoes, Ping-Pong, and badminton.

Cost: Lodge room for four people $38 to $50 in summer, $42 to $52 in winter. Housekeeping cabin $50 per night for four people (for four-person cabin) to $195 per night for sixteen people. Winter rates slightly higher, ten-percent discount for stays of more than five days.

Motor boats $35 to $45, canoes $15 per day. Mountain bikes $10 per half day, $15 per full day. Summer reservations accepted from March 1, winter reservations from June 1.

BAKER LAKE RESORT

Address: PO Box 100, Concrete, Washington 98237 (two hours from Seattle)
Telephone: 206–853–8325

Families that like to fish will enjoy dropping a line in Baker Lake, which is filled with rainbow, steelhead, Dolly Varden, and silver trout. When you tire of fishing, take a dip in the lake, rent a rowboat or canoe, or simply take in the views of the snow-topped northern Cascade Mountains. Most of the cabins are situated near the lake and are fully equipped. This is the only development on Baker Lake; campsites and RV hookups are offered as well.

Season: April through October.

Accommodations: Twelve simple studio and one-bedroom cabins are available. Half have private baths and fully equipped kitchens; the other half do not have kitchens and use bathhouse facilities nearby. Each cabin has an outdoor fire pit and picnic table. Guests supply their own bedding.

Special Features: Playground, swimming pool, small store, boat rental, hiking, and laundry service.

Cost: Daily rates $40 to $45 for four-person cabins with shared baths, $55 to $90 for fully equipped cabins. Rowboats and canoes $20 per day on weekend, $15 per day weekdays; paddleboats $5 per hour.

ROCKY MOUNTAINS AND SOUTHWEST

REDFISH LAKE LODGE

Address: PO Box 9, Stanley, Idaho 83278 (at the headwaters of the main fork of the Salmon River, sixty miles north of Sun Valley in the Sawtooth National Forest)
Telephone: 208-774-3536

Deer wander through the grounds of this idyllic lakeside complex in the morning, owls patrol after dark, and a family of ospreys have a nest nearby. Guest can stay in cabins, a lodge, or motel rooms; the lodge has its own marina and white sandy beach that slopes gently into the lake. Boating, swimming, and fishing take up most of the day at Redfish, which is the only lodging available on the lake besides a campground. A vast wilderness area begins at its southern end, and a shuttle service is available to give hikers a head start on exploring its rugged beauty. Guided horseback rides take guests into the Sawtooth wilderness area.

Season: Late May through September.

Accommodations: Each of the twelve log duplex cabins with fireplaces or wood stoves sleep five to six people and have a small sitting room, at least one separate bedroom, and a front porch with furniture. Larger cabins have a loft or upstairs bedroom. Thirteen lodge rooms have shared baths and sleep two to three people. Motel units have two double beds; five lake suites can sleep four people and have a living room, bathroom, master bedroom, and private deck. Only one unit has a kitchen; it sleeps eight people and is rented by the week. The main lodge has a dining room and bar. Bedding and towels are provided.

Special Features: Marina with boat rental, lounge, general store, gas station, public showers, launderette. Restaurant serving breakfast, lunch, and dinner. Hiking and riding trails radiate from the lodge. Horses can be rented by the hour, half day, and day nearby.

Cost: Standard motel rooms with two double beds $82 per night. Lodge rooms with one double bed and one twin, wash basin and shared bath $54 per night. Suites with master bedrooms and sitting room with queen Murphy bed $112 (maximum four people). Duplex units $96 to $120 per night. Lakeside cabins sleeping up to eight $245, four- to six-person cabins $118 to $140 per night. Extra person charge $10 per night, children under three free, cribs $4 per night.

HILL'S RESORT

Address: Route 5, Box 162A, Priest Lake, Idaho 83856
Telephone: 208–443–2251

The fact that Hill's has been owned and operated by the same family since 1946 gives this comfortable resort on the sandy shores of Priest Lake a well-cared-for look. But Hill's changes with the times in areas that are important to many of us—there's a good children's menu that serves vegetables (an endangered item on many other kids' menus), an espresso and juice bar, and a gourmet restaurant overlooking the lake for those times when you tire of cooking. Homemade huckleberry pie with ice cream is a specialty. Accommodations range from deluxe to basic. Water recreation is the big attraction here, with swimming, fishing, kayaking, and canoeing. The broad and gently sloping beach has both sunny and shady spots for reading and relaxing. In winter, hundreds of miles of snowmobile trails start from the resort and cross-country trails abound.

Season: Year-round.

Accommodations: Condominiums, chalets, duplexes, and cabins are available. Lakefront housekeeping units and deluxe lakefront units have fireplaces, dishwashers, and balconies or decks. Individual cabins, which sleep four to ten people, are the most economical.

Special Features: Mountain bike and cross-country ski trails, hiking and jogging trails, boat rentals, tennis courts, gourmet restaurant, laundry (seasonal), and nearby golf course.

Cost: Late June through Labor Day, individual cabins $715 to $1,900 per week, depending on size; other times of year $610 to $1,250. Nightly stays available in fall, winter, and spring. Canoes and rowboats $20 per day, $115 per week; mountain bikes $30 per day, $175 per week; tennis courts $8 singles, $10 doubles.

LAZY J RESORT AND RAFTING COMPANY

Address: PO Box 109, Coaldale, Colorado 81222
Telephone: 800–678–4274; fax: 719–942–4310

Headquarter at the Lazy J in comfortable cabins with panoramic views of the Sangre de Cristo Mountains and the San Isabel National Forest, and take advantage of the half- or full-day river raft trips on the Arkansas River. Mild to wild white water raft trips are offered and can be tailored for any age; the Lazy J has taken people as young as two and as old as ninety-four on the river. Horseback riding is also available by the hour. Guests can swim in the river or a heated pool.

Season: May through September.

Accommodations: Log cabins with one or two bedrooms have kitchens. Motel rooms can accommodate two or three people; rustic chalets accommodate four. Campsites are also available.

Special Features: A restaurant with a deck overlooking the river is open for breakfast and lunch. Raft trips that last from an hour to two days, guided horseback trips, volleyball, horseshoes, launderette, and a heated pool are on the premises.

Cost: $55 to $70 per night, depending on size and number of people. Motel rooms $38.50 per night, chalets $30 to $35 per night. Half day river trips $30 to $55; full-day trip $75 to $85 per person. Children's rates are about ten percent less than adults, multi-day trips start at $135. Group discounts are available. Riding costs $12 per hour and $24 for two hours.

CLIFF LAKE LODGE

Address: PO Box 267, Cameron, Montana 59720
Telephone: 406–682–4982

Popular as a family reunion site, Cliff Lake Lodge allows guests to put together their own vacation package, including fishing, boating, horseback riding, and hiking. Children enjoy wading and fishing in the creek that runs next to the cabins. The lake is several hundred yards from the lodge and cabins, with the boat dock and swimming area about a quarter of a mile away. A national bird refuge sits right behind the lodge and visitors can be assured of spotting golden eagles, bald eagles, osprey, cormorants, pelicans, and many other bird species. River otters and beavers inhabit the lake.

Season: Almost year-round; the lodge closes for part of the winter when snow makes it inaccessible.

Accommodations: Choose from modern log housekeeping homes or rustic cabins. A modern three-bedroom guest cabin sleeps four to eight people, and two modern log cabins can sleep up to twelve people; these cabins have every convenience, including coffeemakers. Seven rustic cabins for two to four people have one or two bedrooms, a front room/kitchen and a tiny porch. Cooking is done on a wood stove or outdoor barbecue. The only running water is out front; a shared bathhouse is nearby. Guests must bring their own cooking gear and towels.

Special Features: Guests can rent fishing boats with motors and canoes (all with life jackets); guided horseback tours are on site, and white water raft trips can be arranged. Several blue ribbon fly fishing rivers are nearby, and hiking trails to mountain lakes abound. If cabin guests do not want to cook they can dine at the resort's Saddlehorn restaurant. Snowmobiling is popular in winter.

Cost: Rustic cabins $30 for one bedroom, $40 for two bedrooms. Modern three-bedroom cabins $80 per night for four people; $15 each additional person (eight maximum). Modern twelve-person cabins $150 per night base rate with additional charge for extra people.

Boats with motors $40 per day. Canoes (holding three people) $25 per day. Full-day horse tours with lunch $50 per person per day; hourly rate $15.

Nearby: Yellowstone National Park is thirty miles away. See page 113 for more on Yellowstone.

HOLLAND LAKE LODGE

Address: 1947 Holland Lake Road, Swan Valley, Montana 59826 (halfway between Kalispell and Missoula)
Telephone: 800–648–8859; 406–754–2282

A waterfall at one end of Holland Lake is about a mile and a half from the lodge. The hike is just the right length for even young children to walk and far enough away to make it a perfect picnic outing. Two wilderness areas surround Holland Lake Lodge, nestled in a valley between two mountain ranges. You can rent canoes or paddleboats for exploring the lake, or explore the surrounding terrain on horseback or on foot. Cabins are available with and without kitchens, and the lodge has a full-service restaurant for guests in the lodge rooms and cabins. Cabins are the best arrangement for families.

Season: Mid-May to mid-November.

Accommodations: Five cabins (four have kitchens) sleep four to nine people. Eight lodge rooms have two shared hall bathrooms. Two of the king rooms can accommodate a double rollaway bed.

Special Features: Swimming, fishing, volleyball, horseshoes, hiking, pool table, piano, sauna. Create your own recreation package by renting canoes and paddleboats. Horseback riding is available by the hour, day, or for pack trips. Breakfast, lunch, and dinner can be purchased in the dining room, and there is a bar.

Cost: Cabins without kitchen sleeping four people $77 per night; cabins with kitchen sleeping four $85 to $90 per night. Cabins with kitchen sleeping nine people $118; cabins with kitchen sleeping six $100. Lodge rooms with shared bathrooms $65, rollaway bed $5. Canoes $5 per hour, paddleboats $6 per hour. Horseback riding $15 per hour, all-day rides $110. Reservations for June, July, and August fill a year in advance,

but there often are cancellations in February when guests must place a deposit for that year; call mid-February to inquire. Reservations for other times are much easier to get.
Nearby: Roadside stands throughout the region sell cherries in July.

SLIDE ROCK STATE PARK

Address: Seven miles north of Sedona, Arizona, on state highway 89
Telephone: 520–282–3034

Slide Rock is one of nature's finest water parks. It stretches over a quarter-mile section of Oak Creek with a slick rock bottom and natural water slides. The current carries swimmers through the grooves and into pools in the creek; little ones can stay occupied for hours in its wide natural wading pools, while its natural rock chutes offer older kids an exhilarating ride. Try to visit on weekdays in the summer; weekends can be crowded, and the number of visitors is limited to the number of spaces in the park's parking lot. Slide Rock was homesteaded in 1907, and visitors can tour the original homestead and apple orchard areas. There are picnic areas and barbecue pits and a volleyball area.

Where to Stay

Located just one-half mile from the Slide Rock swim area, Pfeifer's Slide Rock Lodge offers clean and comfortable rooms. It has a private creekside area just across the road on Oak Creek for fishing, swimming, and sunning, plus a large picnic area with barbecue grills and tables. Twenty knotted pine-paneled motel rooms with one or two double beds can accommodate two to four people each for $69 to $99 per night. The nearest restaurants are two miles away. Address: 6401 North Highway 89A, Sedona, Arizona 86336. Telephone 520–282–3531.

Splash all day in the many natural swimming holes in Oak Creek, across the street from Don Hoel's Cabins, or head back to Slide Rock about six miles away. There's a playground for the kids, spectacular hiking, fishing, horseshoes, and Ping-Pong. Of the eighteen log housekeeping cabins half have fully equipped kitchens, porches, and barbecues, and can sleep two to six people in one, two, or three double beds for $65 to $105 per night, double occupancy; extra person $10 per night. Address: 9440 North Highway 89A, Sedona, Arizona, 86336. Telephone: 520–282–3560.

CENTRAL UNITED STATES

EMINENCE CANOES, COTTAGES, AND CAMP

Address: PO Box 276, Eminence, Missouri 65466
Telephone: 800–224–2090; 314–226–3642

The Ozark National Riverway has several private canoe concessionaires that offer canoe, kayak, and tube rentals, car shuttles, and accommodations to floaters. Eminence is one of the most family-friendly, with special "Quality Time" packages for parents and kids. The camp is on private land about a block away from a long beach where the water is deep enough for diving off "Button Rock," a three-tiered natural diving platform. Guests can take float trips on either the Jack's Fork River or the Current River. Both of these spring-fed rivers are so clear that you can see the fish swimming on the bottom. Turtles abound in these waters; you might also see beaver, deer, turkey, or mink.

Season: March through November.

Accommodations: Nine informal cottages have fully equipped kitchens, living and dining areas, one or more bedrooms, porches, barbecues and picnic tables out front, all linens, air-conditioning, and heat. Twenty-five campsites and six RV sites have bathrooms nearby.

Cost: Cottages $60 for two adults, additional person $10 per night. Children twelve and under $10 per child per stay, whether it's one night or one week. Canoes $30 per day for a Saturday, $27 per day during the week. Kayaks $20 per day; tubes $4 per day, or $8 per day for tube and transportation. Private vehicle shuttles $10 per hour when staff drive your vehicle, 50 cents per mile when you ride in their van.

The Quality Time Family Package combines lodging with canoe and tube rentals. Six days and five nights of cottage accommodations, two days of canoeing, tubing anytime, and the use of facilities $300 for a family of four. Be sure to ask about this arrangement. Horseback riding $15 per hour. Shorter Getaway packages are available, too.

Nearby: The National Park Interpretive Centers offer wildlife hikes, plant identification walks, demonstrations of a three-story grist mill, and cave tours.

FLOAT TRIPS ON THE MERAMEC RIVER

Address: Blue Springs Ranch, PO Box 540, Bourbon, Missouri 65441 (off Highway N); Meramec State Park, PO Box 57, Sullivan, Missouri 63080 (Highway 185 south)
Telephone: Blue Springs, 800–333–8007, 573–732–5200; Meramec 800–334–6946, 573–468–6519

Stay in a comfortable cabin in Blue Springs Ranch or Meramec State Park and get an early start on a tube, canoe, or raft float down the Meramec River. Both places offer bus rides to your starting point; float back five or ten miles to your cabin at your own pace.

Season: Blue Springs is open year-round; Meramec is open from March 1 to October 31.

Accommodations: Both Meramec and Blue Springs have housekeeping cabins with fully equipped kitchens, living rooms, and all linens. They range in size from one to five bedrooms, and many have fireplaces. Less expensive "camper unit" cabins—without living rooms or kitchens, but all with private baths, air-conditioning, heat, coffeepots, cooking griddles, and outdoor barbecues—are available at Blue Springs.

Special Features: Blue Springs offers horseback riding, hayrides, swimming pool, country store, and cave tours and fishing in a natural trout stream. Meramec has marked hiking trails, cave tours, and a dining lodge.

Cost: Meramec State Park cabins $60 to $165 per night, depending on size and number of people. (Most four-person cabins $75 per night.) Blue Springs cabins $65 to $165 per night. Camper unit cabins $40 to $55 per night.

Canoe rentals $28 to $30 per day, rafts $40 to $55 per day, inner tubes $5 per day. Transportation upstream for the five-mile float $7. Guided horseback rides $8 per half hour, $15 per hour. Hayrides, adults $4, children $2.

BLACK PINE BEACH RESORT

Address: HC 83, Box 464, Pequot Lakes, Minnesota 56472
Telephone: 800–543–4714; 218–543–4714

Situated on Lower Whitefish Lake in the Brainerd area, Black Pine Beach Resort offers well-kept cabins, a family-friendly atmosphere, and a sandy beach with good swimming and fantastic fishing. You can rent a boat from the resort and explore the fourteen interconnected lakes of the Whitefish chain; the resort is centrally located so you can boat to all the lakes from the resort's dock. The entire area is a recreation paradise with shops, dining, and different amusements for all ages. Guests can fish for land walleyes, northerns, lake trout, and more; the resort will arrange fish fries for guests at the big barbecue by the beach. On Monday morning, complimentary coffee, rolls, and juice are served on the deck so that new adults and kids can meet each other. The Saturday night newsletter includes a list of guests, where they're from, and the ages of their children.

Season: Year-round.

Special Features: Sand volleyball, beachside barbecue pit, canoes, boats and motors, paddleboats, tandem bicycle, horseshoes, private boat launch. Game room with Ping-Pong, video games, juke box, and pin ball machines.

Accommodations: Cabins with two, three, and four bedrooms have full kitchens and living rooms, decks, and barbecues. All bed linens are provided, but bring your own towels and soap, no housekeeping provided. Most cabins have knotty pine interiors.

Cost: Weekly rates: two-bedroom cabins accommodating four people, $590 to $800 per week during the summer (depending on exact week and location); three-bedroom cabins $700 to $1,100; four-bedroom cabins $1,050 to $1,200. Extra people accommodated for $15 per person per day. Boats $10 per day, $50 per week; motors $25 per day, $125 per week; canoes and paddleboats $5 per hour; tandem bike $5 per hour.

Nearby: Horseback riding, waterslides, antique stores, amusement centers, mini golf, golf courses.

TIMBER BAY LODGE AND HOUSEBOATS

Address: Box 248, Babbit, Minnesota 55706 (May to October); 10040 Colorado Road, Bloomington, Minnesota 55438 (November to April)
Telephone: 218–827–3682 (summer); 612–831–0043 (winter)
Reservations: 800–846–6821 year-round

Whether you stay at the resort or on a houseboat, you will revel in Timber Bay's environs—the twenty-mile-long Birch Lake and Superior National Forest. Hiking and bicycling trails wind through this forest, and the lake can be explored (and fished) by canoe, sailboat, or rowboat. The world-famous Boundary Waters Canoe Area is a short drive or paddle away. A supervised children's program free to cabin and houseboating guests plans activities that use the surrounding natural environment. The group might gather sarsaparilla to make root beer, search for wild roses to make sachets, learn about edible mosses or animal tracking, or row to an island and cook lunch over an open fire. Families can tour the lake on houseboats that sleep two to ten people, have rooftop patios, and are completely outfitted. Birch Lake is well known for walleye, crappie, and northern fishing.

Season: May through September.

Cabin Resort

Accommodations: Twelve log-sided cabins with one to three bedrooms are spaced far enough apart from one another to give real privacy. All have fireplaces, fully equipped modern kitchens, decks, heat, bedding (bring your own towels), deck furniture, and outdoor charcoal grills. They are rented by the week (Saturday to Saturday) from mid-June to mid-August, and daily or weekly in the early or late season.

Special Features: Waterfront activities include swimming, waterskiing, canoeing, and fishing. A children's program for five- to twelve-year-olds (run by a full-time children's activities director) operates from early June through late August and offers nature activities, crafts, hikes, and picnics. A part-time naturalist program for adults and children includes wildlife talks, nature walks, star gazing, and day canoe trips. In addition, guests can play volleyball, horseshoes, badminton, archery, and shuffleboard. A game room featuring Ping-Pong, pool, Foosball, and video games is available for teens and adults.

Cost: Mid-June to late August, one-bedroom cabins $650 per week, larger cabins $1,050 per week. Rates are based on double occupancy; additional person $15 per night or $75 per week; children half-price. Early- and late-season discount of 10 to 20 percent. Fishing boats, motors, and pontoon boat rentals are available on a daily or weekly basis.

Houseboats

Houseboats sleep two to ten people, and all have covered front and rear decks, hot and cold running water, propane gas stoves, ovens, refrigerators, gas heat, twelve-volt electric lights, pollution-free toilets, and showers. Each boat comes equipped with life preservers, cooking equipment, pillows, and blankets. Guests supply their own food and sheets. Aluminum fishing boats and motors or canoes can be towed along at an additional charge. Approximately ninety percent of Birch Lake is Forest Service property, and loons, eagles, deer and bear are common sights on the lake or along the shoreline.

Cost: Houseboat rates range from $450 for two persons for a three-day weekend to $1,500 for a full week for a 44-foot boat (sleeps eight to ten); tax and three-percent service fee additional. Early and late discounts of ten to twenty percent apply prior to mid-June and after mid-August.

GUNFLINT NORTHWOODS OUTFITTERS CANOE TRIPS AND CABINS

Address: 750 Gunflint Trail, Grand Marais, Minnesota 55604
Telephone: 800–362–5251

Glaciers have carved out a series of interconnected lakes in the Boundary Waters Canoe Area where river otters, moose, eagles, deer, bears, and beavers make their homes. Canoers can travel for days into the largest canoeing wilderness in the world. The Boundary Waters area adjoins the Quetico Wilderness in Canada and the two encompass 2,000 lakes, 2,500 miles of canoe routes, and 3,500 boat-in campsites. The region covers 2 million acres in all. Visitors need permits to explore the area, and Gunflint Northwoods Outfitters can arrange it through their guided or do-it-yourself canoe tours of the Boundary Waters. They outfit you with everything you'll need—canoes, life jackets, tents, even packed food—for your trip. Many families stay in simple "canoer cabins" before and after they leave on their excursion, and enjoy the complimentary use of a canoe and other facilities on the grounds, such as the naturalist-led activities during summer months. A gourmet restaurant serves breakfast, lunch, and dinner. Gunflint's family packages cover routes that have short portages and the best stopping spots for children.

Accommodations: Canoer cabins, similar to camping cabins, are one-room units with bunk beds for up to six people (bring your own sleeping bag). There's a grill and sink area for modest cooking. Most people bring their own coolers. More deluxe cabins range in size from one to four bedrooms; most have saunas and fireplaces.

Special Features: Playground, hiking trails, a small sand beach; boats, motor, and canoe rentals; fishing guides, fly fishing school; gourmet restaurant.

Cost: Canoer cabins $65 to $85 depending on number of people; deluxe cabins start at $877 per week, double occupancy; includes breakfast for two adults. Children three and under stay free; age three and up $210 per week.

SUNSET RESORT

Address: Old West Harbor Road, PO Box 26, Washington Island, Wisconsin 54246
Telephone: 414–847–2531

Back-to-nature types will want to take advantage of Sunset Resort's idyllic and quiet setting on Washington Island at the tip of Door County.

Families swim on the lovely sandy beach, hike, relax, and explore the surrounding island. Biking is a popular way to get around the island; if you don't bring your own, you can rent a bike near the car ferry dock on the south side of the island. The resort serves breakfast daily during the summer and specializes in Norwegian grilled toast and Icelandic pancakes. Eleven rooms are available; one is set up just for families.

Season: Mid-May to mid-October. Busiest times are in July and early August.

Accommodations: Room 10 is the best for families; it's actually two connected rooms, with a double bed in one and two twin beds in the other. Cribs are available. All guest rooms are designated nonsmoking.

Cost: Room 10 is $100 per night, double occupancy; additional person $16.

MEADOWBROOK RESORT

Address: 1533 River Road, Wisconsin Dells, Wisconsin 53965
Telephone: 608–253–3201

Just eight blocks from the downtown Wisconsin Dells and 300 feet from the Wisconsin River, Meadowbrook Resort's location gives guests the option of walking to various restaurants, shops, and amusements or relaxing by the river. Children enjoy playing in the huge frontier-style fort and play area, water playland, and swimming pool. The resort is situated on twelve wooded acres, offering privacy and quiet in a bustling vacation hot spot. All of its units have some type of cooking facilities, and there are outdoor grills, picnic tables, and a nightly campfire. Meadowbrook is a popular family reunion site.

Season: Memorial Day to late September.

Accommodations: Motel units have one large room with two double beds, one twin, and either a refrigerator and microwave or full kitchen. One- or two-bedroom family suites have full kitchens. Log lodges and cabins range in size from one large room to three bedrooms; all have fully equipped kitchens and some cabins have fireplaces.

Special Features: Swimming pool with slide, water playland, shuffle board, picnic area, fishing in a natural pond, horseshoe pit, Ping-Pong, tetherball, video games, volleyball, nightly campfires.

Cost: July 1 to mid-August: motel units $89 to $99 depending on type of kitchen; one- to two-bedroom family suites $119 to $139; cabins and lodges $99 to $209 depending on size. Holiday weekend prices subject to slight increase. June and late August: motel units $59 to $69; family suites $79 to $89; lodges and cabins $69 to $129. Rest of year: motel units $29 to $39; family suites $47 to $55; lodges and cabins $47 to $89.

PINE BEACH RESORT

Address: 481 County A, Wisconsin Dells, Wisconsin 53965
Telephone: 608–253–6361

Guests at Pine Beach alternate days swimming and fishing in Lake Delton with visiting the numerous water parks, water-ski shows, museums, and miniature golf courses of the action-packed Wisconsin Dells. The resort is situated on six acres of park-like grounds and has a heated swimming pool and a broad sandy beach with a swimming area that slopes gradually into the water. There's a diving raft a short swim off shore and a wooden pier for fishing and sunbathing. Rowboats are available free of charge for guests to use.

Season: May through September.

Accommodations: Lake view and poolside cottages have two bedrooms with a double and queen bed, and a sofa bed in the sitting area, dining-kitchen areas and baths. Large cottages are similar in layout but have more space and a separate kitchen and dining area. Family suites have one bedroom with a queen bed, and a kitchen/dining area with a sofa bed and can sleep two to four people. All units are air conditioned and heated. All bedding and kitchen utensils are furnished, but you must bring your own beach and pool towels.

Special Features: Playground, sand volleyball, basketball, picnic tables, and barbecue grills.

Cost: Summer: family suites $95 per day, $570 per week, cottages $125 per day, $720 per week. Cots or cribs $5 per day, extra person $10 per day; motor boat rental $30 per day. Off-season (rates depend on exact dates): family suites $60 to $70 per day and $360 to $420 per week; cottages $70 to $87 per day and $420 to $522 per week.

SLEEPING BEAR DUNES NATIONAL LAKESHORE

You'll huff and puff to the top of these steep and rugged sand dunes, but once at the top you'll be rewarded with a fast run down, and your kids will never forget it. At the bottom, walk the rest of the way to Lake Michigan for a picnic or swim, then brace yourself for the climb back up and down the exhilarating slope. The best places to stay are around Big Glen Lake or Little Glen Lake, where the many cottages for rent have boating and swimming in the summer. The area has many magnificent hiking trails leading to scenic views or through more moderately rolling dunes, beech and maple forests, and wooded low dunes. Be sure to take a trip to Leelanau's Fish Town on the wharf and wander through its shops, stopping for a bite at one of the restaurants. Canoeing on the

Platte River, Manitou Island, and the Manitou Underwater Reserve are close by.

Where to Stay

Miller's Cabins has three charming log housekeeping cabins that sleep five to seven people. The cabins are right on Big Glen Lake at the end of a quiet cul de sac, and owner Jeanette Miller prefers families with children. Guests can see the dunes from their cabins; $750 to $800 per week. Call late February for reservations during the peak summer months. Address: Route #2, Maple City, Michigan 49664. Telephone: 616–334–4929.

Maple Lane Motel and Resort has beautifully decorated motel rooms, some with kitchenettes, and two apartments in an old carriage house. The beach is a half-block away, and guests have the use of canoes and rowboats. A park-like area behind the motel has barbecue grills and picnic tables, a volleyball and basketball court, a horseshoe pit, and a firepit. A separate recreation room in the resort has a player piano, puppets for kids, a lounge and seating area, and a kitchen area for guests to use. Rooms accommodating four people with kitchenettes cost $85 per night, and the apartments in an old carriage house start at $85 per night; both are rented out by the week only in the summer, but by the night during the rest of the year. All include a continental breakfast. Address: 8720 South Dorsey Road, Empire, Michigan 49630. Telephone: 616–334–3413.

LAVALLEY'S RESORT AND ANTIQUES

Address: PO Box 99, N7017 H-03 AuTrain Lake Road, AuTrain, Michigan 49806
Telephone: 906–892–8455

Simple rustic cabins on the edge of AuTrain Lake are available year-round. Boating, fishing, canoeing, and mountain biking are popular during the summer months, and the mountain bike trails turn into snowmobile and cross-country ski trails in the winter. Nearby is the AuTrain River, where guests can rent canoes to leisurely explore its waters.

Season: Year-round.

Accommodations: Two cabins and a two-bedroom lodge unit are available. The one-bedroom cabin sleeps up to four people in a double bed and sofabed. The four-bedroom cabin sleeps up to eight people in two double beds, two twin beds, and a sofabed. Both have lake views and fully equipped kitchens; bring your own towels.

Special Features: Cabins have fire rings outside and firewood is available. A paddleboat and rowboats are available to guests. Mountain bike, kayak, and canoe rentals are available.

Cost: One-bedroom cabin $40 to $55 per night; four-bedroom cabin $70 to $115 per night, depending on number of people.

Nearby: Fishing, scuba diving, and underwater reserves with boat wrecks are close by. Lake Superior's sandy beaches are two miles away. Hiawatha National Forest, Pictured Rocks National Lakeshore, and Alger Underwater Preserve are a short drive away.

CHAIN O' LAKES CANOE TRIPS

Address: 2355 East 75 South, Albion, Indiana 46701 (thirty miles northwest of Fort Wayne)
Telephone: 219–636–2654; fax 219–636–2190

Row, row, row your boat through the eight connecting lakes that make up this four-mile-long state park. (Three additional lakes not in the chain can also be explored.) Rent a canoe for two to four people and paddle from lake to lake along connecting natural channels through the chain. Stop to swim and sun for awhile on a sandy beach, then resume your journey to the canoe camping area next to River Lake, where you'll sleep out under the stars in a canoers' campsite. The next day you can paddle back to your starting point at Sand Lake. Simple housekeeping cabins are available for rent by the week during summer months and nightly during the rest of the year. The park also has rowboats and paddleboats for rent (lifejackets are included), plus fishing, hiking trails, swimming beaches, and picnic spots.

Accommodations: The state park has eighteen cabins housing up to six people. Each has two bedrooms, a private bathroom, a wood-burning stove that comes with a supply of firewood in the winter, and a porch with a swing and a picnic table. You can book these cabins up to a year in advance by the night from September through May or by the week through the summer. Bring your own dishes, cooking utensils, and linens. Canoe campsites are primitive and must be reserved in advance. Other campsites are available in the main area of the park.

Cost: Cabins $55 per night, $385 per week. Canoe, $9 (plus tax) per day, can seat two to four people, depending on size. Canoe campsites $5 per night.

PYMATUNING STATE PARK CABINS

Address: PO Box 1000, Andover, Ohio 44003 (in the northeast corner of the state, next to the Pennsylvania border, sixty-five miles east of Cleveland)
Telephone: 216–293–6329

At this park, guests stay in comfortable cabins next to a special swimming beach and boat tie-up area reserved for them. Motorboats and pontoons can be rented by the week or by the day. A family of beavers has been active at this park, and their dams are accessible via a short hike through the woods. Be sure to ask the park office for the latest information on the beavers' whereabouts to see them at work. Swimming, boating, and fishing are popular summer activities, and nature programs (including movies, slide shows, campfires, and junior naturalist programs) are conducted during the summer. A water spillway a short drive away has an area where ducks can be seen walking across the tangle of fish.

Season: Year-round.

Accommodations: Twenty-seven deluxe housekeeping cabins—with two bedrooms, kitchen, bathroom, living room, and screened porch—can sleep up to six people each. Cabins are heated and available year-round. Thirty-five simple housekeeping cabins are available May through mid-September; these sleep up to four people in a living room–kitchen and bedroom combination separated by a curtained divider, with a private bath.

Cost: Deluxe cabins $425 per week, $75 per night. Standard cabins $325 per week, $60 per night. Reservations accepted a year in advance; weekly reservations are given preference in summer. Summers fill up by about mid-March, so be sure to book early.

THE SOUTH

BUFFALO OUTDOOR CENTER

Address: Two locations: PO Box 1, Ponca, Arkansas 72670 (upper river, at the junction of state highways 43 and 74); Route 1, Box 56, St. Joe, Arkansas 72675 (middle of the river at Silver Hill, U.S. 65 south)
Telephone: Ponca, 501–861–5514; Silver Hill, 501–439–2244

The Buffalo River meanders through spectacular sections of the Arkansas Ozark highlands. Multicolored bluffs tower 500 feet or more above the water along with lofty waterfalls, massive boulders, and hairpin turns. Birds skim the water, turtles bask on rocks, and the emerald green water is so clear that you can see to the bottom. The river is so exceptionally beautiful that 132 miles of its course have a protected status as a National Riverway. Float trips down the river can be combined with comfortable cabin accommodations nearby. The best times to canoe are March, April, and May. Most people float for one day, but you can go for overnights if you wish, and camp along the river.

Season: March through June in Ponca, year-round in St. Joe.

Accommodations: Log cabins are equipped with a full kitchen, rock fireplace, barbecue grill, loft bedrooms with two double beds, main floor bedroom, towels and all bedding, all cooking and eating utensils, air-conditioning, and front porch swings. The cabins are designed to accommodate six people.

Cost: Cabins $85 per night for two people; each additional person $15. For up to six people, six-day stays $550. Two children under twelve stay free. Canoes $30 per day, rafts $18 per day, guided jonboats for fishing $90 per person per day, mountain bikes $15 per day. Shuttle service available for an additional fee.

PETIT JEAN STATE PARK

Address: Mather Lodge, 1069 Highway 154, Morrilton, Arkansas 72110
Telephone: 800–264–2462; 501–727–5431

The dramatic ninety-five-foot Cedar Falls, a fishing and pedal boating lake, hiking trails through forests, canyons, and streams, and a log and stone lodge are trademarks of the first state park in Arkansas, which was built in the 1930s by the Civilian Conservation Corps. Many of the park's housekeeping cabins, which share a bluff with the lodge, overlook an impressive canyon. A boat house by the lake houses a snack bar, boat rental, and fishing supplies during the summer. Cabin and lodge guests have free use of the swimming pool at the lodge and cabin area, playground, and tennis courts. Hiking trails to the falls and forests radiate out from the lodge. Petit Jean is home to the Museum of Automobiles, a showcase of antique cars.

Season: Year-round.

Accommodations: Mather Lodge has twenty-four rooms. Nineteen one-bedroom cabins with linens and fully equipped kitchens sleep four to six people, and a honeymoon cabin features a hot tub. Cabins without kitchens sleep four people in two double beds.

Special Features: An interpretive program from Memorial Day to Labor Day has such scheduled events as trail hikes, evening programs, and a junior naturalist program for children under the age of fourteen. The park has a campground, restaurant, playgrounds, recreation hall, public swimming pool, tennis courts, and snack bar.

Cost: Accommodations are priced for two people, but children under twelve stay free in their parents' room. Housekeeping cabins $75, rollaway beds $5 per night. Honeymoon cabins $110 per night. Cabins without kitchens $45 per night. Lodge rooms with two double beds $50 and lodge rooms with one double bed $45 per night. Fishing boats with motor $25 per day, paddleboats $4.25 per hour.

BAYOU SEGNETTE STATE PARK

Address: 7777 Westbank Expressway, Westwego, Louisiana 70094
Telephone: 504-736-7140

Just a thirty-minute drive from the French Quarter in New Orleans, the comfortable cabins of Bayou Segnette State Park seem a quiet world away. Cabins are perched at the water's edge with their own private piers. The natural features of the park include swamps, wetlands, hardwood forests, and a freshwater canal that leads to lakes and eventually to the Gulf of Mexico. An awesome wave pool (open Memorial Day through Labor Day) lures residents of the greater New Orleans area in addition to park guests. It can hold up to 500 people at a time. Built to simulate ocean waves, it features twelve minutes of waves and twelve minutes of calm water. The park supplies rafts with the price of admission.

Season: Year-round.

Accommodations: Twenty air-conditioned and heated cabins can accommodate up to eight people in one double bed, two bunks, and two rollaways. Kitchens are completely equipped but guests must bring their own towels; other linens are provided. All cabins have screened porches over the water.

Special Features: Swimming pool that is separate from wave pool, boat launch, campground, playground, laundry facilities and a large picnic area surrounding a small bayou in the park.

Cost: Cabins $65 per night. Rafts included in price of admission to the wave pool: $8 adults; $6 children 11 and under.

CROOKED RIVER STATE PARK CABINS

Address: 3092 Spur 40, St. Mary's, Georgia 31558 (ten miles north of the center of the town of St. Mary's on the south bank of the Crooked River)
Telephone: Information: 912–882–5256; reservations: 800–864–7275, Monday through Friday, 8 A.M. to 5 P.M. Book eleven months in advance for any holiday stay (Christmas break, Easter); all other times of the year, reserve at least eight weeks in advance.

This five-hundred-acre state park just south of Cumberland Island and Jekyll Island has reasonably priced vacation cottages as well as an Olympic-size pool, bathhouse, and picnic shelters. Eleven charming cottages are located on the Crooked River. Popular park activities include swimming, saltwater fishing, boating, and hiking. The park is forty-five miles from the nearest public access ocean beach at Georgia's Jekyll Island or at Florida's Fernandina Beach.

Season: Year-round.

Accommodations: Cottages have either two or three bedrooms and a living room, kitchen, screened porch, heat, and air-conditioning. The two-bedroom cottage sleeps eight; the three-bedroom sleeps up to twelve. There are two double beds in each of the bedrooms. All linens and cooking utensils provided.

Cost: Two-bedroom cottages $55 per night week night, $65 per weekend night. Three-bedroom cottages $10 more.

Nearby: Visit the nearby ruins of the McIntosh Sugar Works mill (built in 1825 and used as a starch factory during the Civil War). The ferry for the Cumberland Islands leaves from St. Mary's. The park is less than an hour from Okefenokee Swamp.

CUMBERLAND MOUNTAIN STATE PARK

Address: Route 8, Box 322, Crossville, Tennessee 38555
Telephone: 615–484–6138

This park spreads across the Timberland Plateau, the largest timbered plateau in America. Its housekeeping cabins are tucked into the woods or near the shore of Bird Lake, which has a boating marina that rents paddleboats, rowboats, canoes, and motor boats. When you tire of doing your own cooking, head to the restaurant overlooking the sparkling blue water. A supervised nature and summer recreation program includes free activities, nature hikes, sports, and craft programs for children.

Season: Year-round.

Accommodations: Thirty-six cabins with full kitchens accommodate four to sixteen people in one-, two-, or three-bedroom units. Most have fireplaces.

Special Features: Swimming pool and fishing are free to cabin guests. Private boats are not allowed. Other facilities include a swimming pool, playground, hiking trails, tennis courts, badminton, volleyball, horseshoes, shuffleboard, Ping-Pong, softball, and basketball.

Cost: Weekly prices $350 to $650, depending on size of unit. Nightly rates $50 to $95.

BIG RIDGE STATE PARK

Address: 1015 Big Ridge Road, Maynardsville, Tennessee 37807
Telephone: 423-992-5523

Set along the southern shore of Norris Lake, Big Ridge State Park has nineteen rustic cabins, camping, and lots of activity down by the water. It's within an hour's drive of both the Great Smoky Mountain and Cumberland Gap national parks. Children of all ages enjoy the sandy beach on the lake, which has a special enclosed area for little ones and lifeguards on duty during swimming hours. For the older kids, there's a diving area with diving stands, and canoe, paddleboat and rowboat rentals.

Season: Cabins can be rented from April through October. Swimming and boating Memorial Day to mid-August.

Accommodations: Each cabin accommodates up to six people in two double beds and one sofabed. All have fireplaces, screened porches, and full kitchens. Linens and towels are provided.

Special Features: Basketball, volleyball, badminton, horseshoes, tennis (bring your own racquet and balls), picnic areas, hiking trails, and daily activities for families during the summer months, such as arts and crafts, campfires, nature walks, and organized sports activities.

Cost: Cabins, rented by the week only from Memorial Day through Labor Day, $390 for six nights. The rest of the year, $65 per night. Rowboats $2.25 per hour; canoe or paddleboats $3 per hour.

STEPHEN FOSTER STATE PARK

Address: Stephen C. Foster State Historic Park, Fargo, Georgia 31631
Telephone: 912-637-5274

Way down upon the headwaters of the Suwanee River, right in the middle of the Okefenokee Swamp, this state park and nature center provides air-conditioned cottages, boat tours, and boat rental. A half-mile nature trail and boardwalk leads into the swamp where deer, birds, and alligators live. Take the guided ninety-minute boat tour through the swamp to learn more about its history, wildlife, and plants, then head out in your own boat; trails are clearly marked and it's virtually impossible to get lost. On Thursday, Friday, and Saturday evenings naturalists give slide shows, videos, and nature talks. Sunday morning nature walks led by naturalists further inform visitors about the odd flora and fauna of the swamp. The best months to visit are March, April, early May, October, and November. People visit year-round, but summers are hot, humid, and full of mosquitoes.

Season: Year-round.

Accommodations: Nine two-bedroom cottages have living rooms, dining areas, kitchens, screened porches, all dishes and linens, and central heat and air-conditioning.

Special Features: Boardwalk and nature walk, boat tours, boat and bike rentals.

Cost: Cottages $56 per night Sunday through Thursday, $66 Friday and Saturday. Boat tours, adults $8, children under twelve $6, kids under three free. Canoes and jonboats $9 per half day, $13 per day. Boats with motor $21 per half day, $31 per day. Bicycles $5 per half day, $8 per day. Reservations for cottages can be made up to eleven months in advance and reservations for boats can be made thirty days in advance.

HOMOSASSA SPRINGS STATE WILDLIFE PARK

Address: 9225 West Fishbowl Drive, Homosassa, Florida 32646 (seventy-five miles north of Tampa)
Telephone: 352–628–2311; 352–628–5343

Go face to face with a manatee in this rehabilitation center for Florida's native wildlife and endangered species. The high point of the park is the floating observatory with an underwater viewing area, where you can see thousands of fish and the mild-mannered manatees (once thought by sailors to be mermaids) swim by. Manatees that have been injured in the wild, orphaned, or born in captivity are reacclimated here before being returned to the wild. Educational programs focusing on the manatee, alligator, crocodile, native Florida snakes, and other wildlife native to Florida are presented three times daily. Boat tours of Pepper Creek allow visitors to see deer, bobcats, otters, and cougars in addition to dozens of birds.

Season: Year-round.

Cost: Adults $8, children three to twelve $5, under three free.

Where to Stay

MacRae's has motel rooms and apartment units on the Homosassa River, one and a half miles from the springs. A fleet of rental fishing boats is available for anyone who wants to drop a line; the staff will give you a map and point you in the right direction. One-bedroom apartments have fully equipped kitchens and sleep up to six in two double beds and a sofabed for $70 per night. After a day on the river, relax in the front porch rockers. All units are air-conditioned. Address: 5300 South Cherokee Way, PO Box 318, Homosassa, Florida 34487. Telephone: 352–628–2602 (day); 352–628–1315 (night).

ADVENTURES UNLIMITED

Address: Route 6, Box 283, Milton, Florida 32570 (twelve miles north of Milton)
Telephone: 904–623–6197; 904–626–1669

Stay in an air-conditioned cabin on the grounds of Adventures Unlimited and then select the adventure to suit your family. Choose from canoeing, tubing, kayaking, and paddleboating during your visit. Canoe trips range from two hours to three days on spring-fed rivers through pristine state forest property. If you need to stop for a swim or a snack there are plenty of white sandy beaches along the banks. You'll be transported to your starting point and float at your leisure back to your cabin.

Season: Year-round.

Accommodations: Efficiency and one-bedroom cabins are air-conditioned and have fully equipped kitchens, all linens, and private baths. Large family cabins have a full kitchen, bath, and living room. Two styles of rustic camping cabins sleep four people in a double bed and bunk bed. All but one rustic cabin are air-conditioned; shared bathhouses are located nearby. You also can opt to camp at the waterfront tent sites or hook up an RV.

Special Features: Playground, swimming beach, wilderness store, horseshoes, nature trails, volleyball, and picnic areas. You also can rent paddleboats, inner tubes, kayaks, and river rafts.

Cost: Rustic camping cabins $40 for up to four people, $10 each additional person. Efficiency and one-bedroom cabins $60 to $75 per night for up to four people. Group cabin $160 for up to fifteen people, $10 each additional person (maximum sixty).

Kids twelve and under canoe free with two paying adults. A one-day canoe trip costs $13 per person; canoes can hold two adults and two children under age eight. Tube trips $8, kayaks $20 per day, paddleboats $26 per day. Shuttle transportation included.

HUNGRY MOTHER STATE PARK

Address: Route 5, Box 109, Marion, Virginia 24354 (one hundred miles south of Roanoke, four miles north of Marion)
Telephone: 800–933–7275 (reservations); 540–783–3422 (park office)

Hungry Mother, with its sparkling lake set in forested mountains, has been a family favorite for years. Like some of the grand old resorts of the Northeast, people who came here as children are now bringing their own children back every year. Comfortable cabins are at one end of the lake near a sandy swimming beach watched over by lifeguards throughout June, July, and August. A summer program for children and families includes arts and crafts, nature hikes, environmental awareness, survival skills, animal studies, and evening activities. The fun continues with paddleboat rentals, guided horseback rides (at a remarkably low price), and excellent fishing off a wheelchair-accessible fishing pier. When parents need a break from cooking, a restaurant serves lunch and dinner.

Season: March through November.

Accommodations: Rustic log cabins with one or two bedrooms were built by the Civilian Conservation Corps in the 1930s. One-bedroom cabins contain a double bed and can hold a rollaway bed or two. Seventeen two-bedroom cabins have one double bed and two single beds and can hold two rollaway beds to accommodate up to six people. All have fully equipped kitchens, private bathrooms, fireplaces, and all bedding and towels. Hemlock Haven Conference Center, located inside the park, contains eleven additional cabins and is available for group rental. Campsites also are available.

Special Features: Large sandy beach, horse rentals, twelve miles of hiking trails, rowboat and paddleboat rentals, fishing, and a restaurant serving lunch and dinner.

Cost: One-bedroom cabins $300 per week; two-bedroom cabins $412 per week. Rollaway beds, $21 per week. Paddleboats $5 per hour, rowboats $4 per hour; horses $7 per hour. Special off-season rates are available.

BLACKWATER FALLS STATE PARK

Address: Drawer 490, Davis, West Virginia 26260
Telephone: 800–CALL–WVA (reservations); 304–259–5216

Explore the park on one of the many hiking or riding trails during the summer months. Lakeside entertainment includes swimming, sunbathing, rowboating, and paddleboating. A recreation center has arts and crafts projects for kids, and outdoor playing fields have volleyball, horseshoes, basketball, and tennis. Guests stay in the lodge or in house-keeping cabins; cabins require reservations in advance, particularly in the summer, but lodge rooms are easy to get, especially midweek.

Season: Year-round.

Accommodations: Twenty-five cabins of different sizes sleep two to eight people. Heated cabins have fireplaces, full kitchens with modern appliances, and all linens. A fifty-five-room lodge and a campground also accommodate guests.

Special Features: Swimming in the lake, paddleboat and rowboat rentals, horse rentals, playground, tennis, volleyball, and other game courts, horseshoes, nature center, recreation building, sled run, and bicycle rentals.

Cost: Summer cabins $420 (two people) to $625 (eight people) per week, $66 to $116 per night, depending on unit and time of week. Horse rental $18 per hour, boats $3 per hour.

Nearby: A golf course is ten miles away and fishing is nearby.

THE NORTHEAST

MOUNTAIN SPRINGS LAKE RESORT

Address: PO Box 297, Mountain Springs Drive, Reeders, Pennsylvania 18352
Telephone: 717–629–0251

Set in 350 acres of rolling woodlands and open lawns, this resort on the shores of a spring-fed private lake sits in the middle of several ski areas in the Poconos. During the summer, families can swim and play on the gentle sandy beaches, go boating, fish, hike, or play tennis. Year-round Lakeview and Woodside units and seasonal lodging are available. Every accommodation includes a rowboat at no extra charge.

Season: Year-round.

Accommodations: Lakeview accommodations overlook seventy-six-acre Mountain Springs Lake, and Woodside accommodations are set in laurel woods just minutes from the lake. Seasonal accommodations, available May through October, are simpler and less expensive than the others. All units are no more than a five-minute walk to the beach.

Special Features: The beach is perfect for children of all ages, and there are canoes, sailboats, fishing equipment, tennis courts, and toboggans for rent. A snack bar is open during the summer, and a restaurant is open on select weekends.

Cost: Seasonal four-person cottages and apartments range from $500 to $650 for a seven-night stay during July and August, $435 to $650 for the rest of the season. Lakeview and Woodside cottages for four to six people range from $835 to $1,320 depending on time of year and specific cottage. Most accommodations have sofabeds and can take one or two additional people for $20 per night, $75 per week. Canoe $15 per day, $45 per week; sailboat $35 per day, $95 per week; tennis courts $5 per hour; toboggan $15 per stay; safety floatation device $2 per stay.

Nearby: Horseback riding, outlet malls, golf, Pocono Raceway.

HERRINGTON MANOR AND SWALLOW FALLS STATE PARKS

Address: 222 Herrington Lane, Oakland, Maryland 21550
Telephone: 301–334–9180; 301–387–6938

Herrington Manor State Park is adjacent to Swallow Falls State Park; the two are three miles apart by road and five miles by a picturesque hiking trail. Herrington Manor has twenty log cabins near a lake, while Swallow Falls has campgrounds with fully equipped tents and Maryland's tallest waterfall (fifty-five feet). In winter guests can cross-country ski, ice-skate, or go sledding. In summer guests swim at the lakeside beach, fish, and go boating. A naturalist is on hand during the summer months to take guests on guided canoe trips and hayrides and to lead a Junior Ranger program and other activities.

Season: Year-round.

Accommodations: Twenty log cabins for two, four, or six people are available. All have complete kitchens and bathrooms, heat, and a wood-burning stove. Fully equipped campsites have tents, Coleman stoves, lanterns, and sleeping pads.

Special Features: Activities include lake swimming, hiking, fish-stocked lakes with canoes and boats for rent, tennis, snack bar, athletic field with softball, tennis, basketball, and horseshoes. Guests can use athletic equipment free of charge.

Cost: Cabins $65 to $85 per night, $325 to $450 per week. Weekly minimum during summer, two-night minimum during rest of season. Equipped campsites $30 per night. Canoe, paddleboat, and rowboat rentals $4 per hour, $15 per day. Reservations accepted up to a year in advance.

LAKE TAGHKANIC STATE PARK

Address: 1528 Route 82, Ancram, New York 12502
Telephone: 518–851–3631

With 1,500 feet of gently sloping shoreline, rolling hills, hiking trails, and a choice of cabins in the woods or cottages along the lake, Lake Taghkanic is the perfect spot for a family beach vacation. It has two beaches for swimming (with lifeguards during the summer), one with a concession stand that sells ice-cream cones and hot dogs. Summer months have a nature center with such family-oriented programs as nature hikes and arts and crafts. Special weekend programs continue into the fall.

Season: Early May to late October for cottages and cabins. The park is open year-round for day use.

Accommodations: Choose from sixteen one- to four-bedroom cottages along the lake with full kitchens and private bathrooms, or fifteen rustic cabins in the woods with cold running water and shared bathhouses.

Special Features: There is a ball-playing field, a playground, boat rental, and a fitness trail. The nature center has a frog pond with a waterfall, displays, literature, and an arts and crafts area. Programs for families include ecology studies, and special boat rides. In winter you can ice fish, ice-skate, cross-country ski, and snowmobile.

Cost: Cottages and cabins are $50 to $82 per night with a two-night minimum, and $200 to $350 per week (minimum seven days from the end of June to the end of August). You provide sleeping linens, cooking and eating utensils. Rowboats $4 per hour.

HARVEY'S LAKE CABINS AND CAMPGROUND

Address: RR1, Box 26E, West Barnet, Vermont 05821 (eight miles from St. Johnsbury, nine miles from Danville, exit 18 on I-91)
Telephone: 802–633–2213

Owners Marybeth and Michael Vereline continue to add attractive cabins facing the lake to the private cabin and campground resort that combines the quiet serenity of the woods with the pristine beauty of the lake in Vermont's Northeast Kingdom. With 800 feet of shoreline on Lake Harvey and another one thousand feet of canoeable river access, families that enjoy water sports can spend their days swimming in the lake, exploring the waterway in boats, or fishing for rainbow and lake trout, bass, perch and sunfish. There are two different beaches, a grassy play area with a swing set, and picnic areas near the water. A recreation package allows families to experiment with boats and bikes for one low weekly price.

Season: May 15 to October 15.

Accommodations: Ten different cabins overlook the lake; five are just steps from the water. All have living rooms, dining areas, and fully equipped kitchens, and range in size from a large one-story one-room A-frame cabin to a two-story, three-bedroom cabin. Everything is provided except sheets and towels, which can be rented. No smoking is allowed in the cabins. Forty-three campsites are also available. A one-room cabin with equipped kitchen in woods has a shared bathhouse and sleeps two people but you can add sleeping bags on the floor.

Special Features: Recreation hall with pool tables, Ping-Pong, and video games, laundry facilities, horseshoes pit.

Cost: Cabins, rented by the week only in July and August, $495 to $595 per week, each additional person $60 over cabin's base rate up to the cabin's maximum. Children under twelve $35 per week extra. One-room cabin in the woods $250 per week, $45 per night; no extra person charge. Linen rental $10 per person per week. Cabins rent nightly from May 15 to June 30 and from September 1 to October 15, $85 per night, double occupancy; additional person $10; children under twelve $5. Recreation package includes canoe, paddleboat, rowboat, and bicycle rental $25 per week. Rowboat, canoe, and bike rental $4 per hour, $10 per half day, $20 per full day; paddleboat $8 per hour.

Nearby: Maple sugar houses and hiking trails nearby.

INDIAN JOE'S COURTS

Address: Box 126, West Danville Vermont 05873
Telephone: 802–684–3430

The prices at this simple, clean, and comfortable cabin resort with its own stretch of sandy beach on Joe's Pond simply can't be beat. Cabins and cottages, some with kitchens, are situated on a hill overlooking the pond and the peaceful countryside of Vermont's Northeast Kingdom. The private swimming beach is across the road and a public swimming beach is a short walk away. Rowboats, canoes, and paddleboats are available for all guests to use free of charge. Hiking trails are nearby.

Season: May 15 to October 15.

Accommodations: Cabin units have refrigerators but no kitchens; cottages have fully equipped kitchens. All units have private baths, heat, and linen service.

Special Features: Playground with swings, horseshoe pits, basketball hoop, barbecue grills.

Cost: Cabins $40 to $55 per night; cottages $55 to $75 for four people; extra person $10 per night.
Nearby: Stowe, maple syrup farms, cider mill.

LAKESHORE TERRACE

Address: Box 18, Wolfeboro, New Hampshire 03894
Telephone: 603–569–1701

Two miles from the popular resort of Wolfeboro on the shores of Lake Wentworth, Lakeshore Terrace has serviceable family units at excellent prices in a secluded setting. The spacious fifteen-acre property has six cottages cooled by the shade of pine trees; it's just a few minutes from town but feels miles away. Two private swimming beaches are shallow and perfect for little ones; a third, large sunning beach backed by a garden and lawn is for sun worshippers and more accomplished swimmers. Lake Wentworth is much quieter than nearby Lake Winnipesaukee. Guests can expect to see beavers, tame ducks, and Gertrude and Frank, the loons who return year after year. Many families headquarter here to explore the surrounding area.

Season: Memorial Day to Columbus Day weekend.

Accommodations: Six unpretentious cottages house two to five people; all have screened porches and full baths, and four have full kitchens. The largest cottage, called Sandbox, is right on the swimming beach and holds five people. Week-long rentals are preferred in July and August. Week-long guests bring their own linens.

Special Features: Rowboats are free for guests. There is a rose garden and an outdoor cookout area.

Cost: Most cottages $65 (without kitchens) to $75 per night, $375 to $475 per week. Sandbox cottage $110 to $145 per night, $650 to $875 per week, depending on number of people. Ten-percent reduction in June and after Labor Day (except holiday weekends).

Nearby: Steamer trip on Lake Winnipesaukee, eighteen-hole golf course, waterslides, tennis, fishing, sailing, and horseback riding are all nearby. A number of marinas in Wolfeboro rent sailing boats and power boats. Mount Washington is within an easy drive.

ANCHORAGE

Address: 725 Laconia Road, Pilton, New Hampshire 03276
Telephone: 603–524–3248; fax: 603–528–1028

Set along the banks of Lake Winnisquam, the Anchorage has three beaches, playgrounds for children, rowboats, canoes, and paddleboats for guests to use. The entire thirty-five-acre property is situated between the main road and the beach, offering privacy and quiet. Hiking trails lead through forest, orchards, and berry bushes.

Season: Mid-May through mid-October.

Accommodations: Simple cottages range in size from one to eight rooms. All have fully equipped kitchens and views of the lake from a screened front porch. Extended families can stay in the Trapp House (which has its own dock and secluded beach), as it sleeps up to eighteen people.

Special Features: A gently sloped swimming beach is perfect for young ones, and the lawns are groomed for baseball or soccer. There's volleyball on the beach, horseshoes, shuffleboard, badminton, weekly campfires in summer, and cookout areas with grills.

Cost: The Anchorage has three sets of rates by the week: one-bedroom cottages sleeping four people, peak season (July to mid-August) $710; special season (the last week of June and last two weeks in August) $565; off-season (from mid-May through mid-June and September through mid-October) $420. Larger lakefront cottages sleeping five to ten people, peak season $775 to $1,300; special season $615 to $995; off-season $450 to $720.

Nearby: Three miles from outlet mall, waterslides, mini golf, polar caves, Storyland, White Mountains.

SEBAGO LAKE LODGE AND COTTAGES

Address: White's Bridge Road, North Windham, Maine 04062
Telephone: 207–892–2698

Set on the shores of Maine's second-largest lake, Sebago Lake Lodge and Cottages offers cottages by the week and lodge rooms (some with kitchenettes) by the day. The cottages are on a hill that slopes down to the lake, scattered among pines and white birch trees. The White Mountains can be seen in the distance from the lodge rooms. Five hundred feet of lake frontage is yours for swimming or boating, and the use of canoes and rowboats is included with all cottage and room rentals. Lakeside picnic tables are a popular spot for lunch, and in the evenings, families gather around the large outdoor fireplace to cook hot dogs, roast marshmallows, and pop popcorn.

Season: Year-round.

Accommodations: Cottages range in size from studios to two bedrooms. One-bedroom cottages sleep four on a double bed and sofabed in the living room. Most cottages have screened porches and wood stoves. Lodge rooms can accommodate two to four people, and many have kitchenettes.

Cost: Cottages $395 to $695 per week, double occupancy, with 25-percent discounts for off-season rentals; each additional child $25 per week. Lodge rooms $48 to $110 per night. Each additional child under ten $5 per night, over ten, $10 per night. Waterskiing, fishing boats, and Wave Runners $25 to $185 per day.

ATTEAN LAKE LODGE

Address: PO Box 457, Jackman, Maine 04945
Telephone: 207–668–3792

Guests park their cars along the shore of six-mile-long Attean Lake and take a ten-minute boat ride to their own private island, where memories of work and school days fade. They swim, read, or hike a short distance to a stream or pond where canoes have been placed for their use. The woods are veined with walking paths—one family favorite leads to an inlet where moose often are spotted. A large sandy lakefront beach is perfect for swimming with children, or you can find an island beach all your own. Beach cookouts take place on Wednesday and Sunday, and lunches are available in picnic baskets for family outings, which can include salmon and trout fishing, waterskiing, or boating. Fifteen lakefront log cabins with private porches are nestled amid spruce, birch and towering pines, and are lit by kerosene and heated by wood stoves or fireplaces. All have full baths with hot and cold running water, and guests enjoy three hearty meals a day. The Holden family has operated this lodge since 1900.

Season: Memorial Day through September.

Accommodations: Twenty log cabins with private porches overlooking the lake are set amid pine, spruce, and birch trees; all have magnificent views. Cabins are completely furnished and accommodate two to six guests. The main lodge has a large fireplace, library, games, desk, and public phone.

Special Features: A large sandy beach along the lake is perfect for children, and all sorts of boats (kayaks, canoes, low-speed motor boats, sailboats, and paddleboats) can be rented. Beach cookouts take place on Wednesday and Thursday, lunches come in picnic baskets. Hiking trails lead through forests and along rivers.

Cost: Rates include three meals a day. Adults: single person $160 per day, $850 per week; two people $210 per day, $1,325 per week. Third person $95 per day, $525 per week. Children five to twelve $70 per day, $400 per week, children under five $25 per day, $130 per week. Boat rentals $10 to $15 per day.

KAWANHEE INN

Address: Route 142, Weld, Maine 04285 (summer); 7 Broadway, Farmington, Maine 04938 (winter)
Telephone: 207–585–2000 (summer); 207–778–3809

A gradually sloping fine white sand beach leads to the waters of Lake Webb, one of Maine's most beautiful bodies of water. The swimming is perfect, with summertime afternoon lake temperatures of seventy-two to seventy-eight degrees. Cabins and a lodge containing bedrooms and a restaurant line the shore, which is wooded with white birches, pines, and pointed firs. A Maine guide takes guests fishing in the lake. Old-fashioned wooden rocking chairs grace the porches. A discounted rate is possible for guests who wish to provide their own linens and maid service. For a special treat head to the restaurant for an elegant all-American meal.

Season: Early May through mid-October.

Accommodations: Ten cabins have one, two, or three bedrooms. All cabins have living rooms, stone fireplaces, private baths, and screened porches. All two-bedroom cabins have kitchens and one one-bedroom cabin is equipped with a kitchen. Fourteen comfortable bedrooms on the second floor of the lodge have private or shared baths. Minimum stay during the peak summer season is two nights.

Special Features: Canoe and boat rentals; a restaurant, which serves breakfast and dinner in the main dining room or on screened-in porches; many hiking trails that radiate out from the lodge; horseshoes, croquet, volleyball.

Cost: Cabins are rented by the week only, July and August, $575 to $750. Bedding, towels, and housekeeping service included, unless you opt for the "bare-bones" arrangement in which you supply linens and housekeeping for a fifteen-percent discount. Inn rooms $60 to $90 and up double occupancy, per night. Additional person in inn rooms $10 per night. Canoe rental $10 per day, fishing boat $30 per day, paddle-boats $5 per use. In June, September and October, lodging prices drop 15 percent.

BEACH
VACATIONS

*Y*ou can't beat the beach for keeping children amused and content, and parents usually find keeping watch a little more relaxing with the sand and surf in the background. But can you afford the beach-bum fantasy—a Cape Cod–style house overlooking the water, a linen closet brimming with thick white beach towels, salty air, seagulls, fresh lobster, a clean and safe beach where your children can swim and build sand castles?

It need not be out of your price range. To make the most of your beach vacation dollars, think about selecting a stretch of less popular coastline. For example, vacations along the North and South Carolina coast are far less expensive and just as delightful as their New England counterparts. If you can break away in late May, early June, or September, you will find the weather at most beach locales still appealing, the beaches less crowded, and off-season rates generally in effect.

Beach house rental fees vary widely, but houses typically are cheaper than hotel stays and offer more value and privacy for the money. Unfortunately, there is no national association of beach house rentals, so renting an inexpensive beach house takes some sleuthing and some haggling. But even a three-day beach house escape can feel like a week off elsewhere—and there seems to be a beach house for every budget. Additional savings are met by cooking your own meals and sharing expenses with another family. If families double up, renting a large house certainly is cheaper than staying at a hotel for the week. Children will have built-in playmates, and adults can share in watching each other's children, providing one set of parents a day or night off. Privacy is one of the big drawing cards for beach house renters, along with a feeling of homey comfort. Many "beach houses" today are actually condominiums.

It is best to book six months to one year in advance. During peak seasons, such as July, August, Thanksgiving, Easter, and Christmas, it might not be as easy to talk landlords out of enforcing their standard one-week minimum rule. But it is always worth trying to negotiate the list price during the off-season. When selecting a house, ask if bedding, towels, and kitchen utensils are provided. Expect to pay a security deposit (ours was $200, $50 of which was deducted as a cleaning fee).

Here we highlight a selection of great family beach destinations and provide listings of homes and condos for rent, as well as inexpensive hotels with kitchens and/or family amenities, state park cabins, and family hostels. If the area you plan to visit is not mentioned, write or call the local chamber of commerce. They often keep lists of homeowners, real estate agents, or property management firms that handle vacation rentals. The "vacation rental" columns of the area's newspaper's classified section can also be helpful.

WEST COAST

MAUI, HAWAII

A Hawaiian vacation need not cost a fortune, especially on Maui. In fact, if you budget it right, your biggest expense could be your air fare. For longer than a week, a condo unit with a kitchen can result in significant savings on your food bill. When booking a condo, be sure to inquire about discounts for longer stays (usually more than four to seven days) and car/condo packages. High season in Hawaii is generally mid-December through March. However, you'll find that the weather is tropical and great for beaching it during the off-season, when lower rates apply. In fact, some of the best weather is in very late summer and fall, when temperatures are cooler and there is less rain than in the winter and spring months.

Some of the best beaches on Maui are beautiful and safe Kapalua Bay (see Napili accommodation on page 205), and the unspoiled Makena beaches (see Kihei accommodation on page 203). One of Maui's most spectacular sites is Mount Haleakala, a volcanic crater large enough to hold Manhattan. Horse and bike trails descend into the depths of the

crater's sides and meander across its moonlike surface. A visit to touristy
Lahaina is fun, as every block is crammed full of shops, galleries, eateries,
and historic buildings. Maui's idyllic eastern coast, near tiny Hana, has
some of Hawaii's most glorious scenery (see Hana accommodation on
page 206). The four-hour drive to Hana from Lahaina winds along the
ocean past black sand beaches, old lava flows, dense jungle growth, and
lush groves of mango and monkey pod trees.

Snorkelers can rent gear at the Maui Dive Shop, which has many locations around the island, including a shop in Kihei. They will also give
you a map to the best snorkeling spots near the place you plan to swim.
Highly recommended is the snorkeling excursion led by marine biologists to Molokini Crater and the wild dolphin boat trip to the island of
Lanai with the nonprofit Pacific Whale Foundation (808–879–8811); they
depart from Lahaina or Maalaea Harbor. For a splurge, try a day-long
snorkel and picnic to the island of Lanai with the congenial crew of the
Trilogy (808–661–4743).

Your children will not forget the fire dancing and fast-moving hula
dancing at the Hyatt Regency's highly authentic "Drums of the Pacific"
luau held on the beach and available to non-hotel guests in Ka'anapali.
Native Hawaiian crafts are demonstrated and the imu (pig) is unearthed,
which is part of a succulent all-you-can-eat dinner buffet. Adults $55,
children $25, under five free. Call 808–667–4420.

Here we highlight two of our favorite and affordable ground-floor
oceanfront condominiums, which are on opposite sides of Maui—on
the west side at Napili and on the south side in Kihei. A ground-floor
unit allows for easier access to the beach or pool and will save you
energy transporting beach gear or running inside for a snack.

HALE PAU HANA RESORT

Address: 2480 South Kihei Road, Kihei, Maui, Hawaii 96753
Telephone: 800–367–6036; 808–879–2715; fax: 808–875–2038

It doesn't look like much from the road, but once you enter your oceanfront condo at Hale Paul Hana you will be swept away by the spectacular
view of the ocean and the neighboring islands of Molokini, Kahoolawe,
and Lanai. The resort, an unpretentious and small condominium complex fronting uncrowded Kamaole II Beach in South Kihei, has drawn a
steady clientele of loyal families for years. The property extends along a
perfect white-sand beach cove with clear turquoise-blue water. Families
prefer the ground-floor apartments in the smaller two-story complex,
where you have a private lanai adjoining a verdant lawn. All units are
set up for housekeeping. Simply grab your towel, as you are steps from

an expansive and ideal beach for children, with gentle surf and a sandy bottom. You can watch your children swim, snorkel, and frolic from your lanai lounge chair or while barbecuing on your apartment's lawn. The complex also has a small oceanfront pool, and it is a short drive or walk from any possible convenience you'll need. Across the street you can rent snorkel gear at the Maui Dive Shop, which will also direct you to the best snorkel sports nearby.

Season: Year-round.

Accommodations: All units are oceanfront and are fully equipped for normal housekeeping. They range from one-bedroom, one- or two-bath units that sleep four people (there is a sofabed in the living room) to two-bedroom, two-bath units that sleep up to six people. Units are individually owned, so furnishings vary, but they are all clean and modern; they all have a telephone and TV (some have a VCR). Units have ceiling fans, but no air-conditioning.

Special Features: Good snorkeling at resort's cove, tide pools a short walk up the beach, neighboring beach with lifeguard, laundry facilities, daily trash removal, towels changed daily, condo cleaned and bed linen changed weekly.

Cost: April 15 to December 14, one-bedroom, one-bath ground-floor unit $115 per night; one-bedroom, one-bath second-floor unit $110 per night; one-bedroom, two-bath ground-floor unit $120 per night; one-bedroom, two-bath second-floor unit $115 per night; two-bedroom, two-bath upper-floor unit $155 per night. Rates are double occupancy; each additional person $10. Children under five stay free. Rates seventy percent higher December 15 to April 14. Ask about car/condo packages where room and car start at $130 per day.

Nearby: As the island is small, all attractions such as Haleakala Crater, Iao Valley, Lahaina, and Hana are within no more than a few hours' drive. The complex is a ten-minute drive from Wailea, where you'll find tennis, championship golf courses, and lavish resorts that are fun to walk around. A great place for children to learn to snorkel near Kihei is at Wailea's well-marked public beach park, Ulua Beach, with restrooms and showers. Further south is Makena, South Maui's most beautiful and unspoiled stretch of coast, with many public beaches. For more advanced snorkeling, drive past Makena to the coral reefs at the Ahihi Kinau Natural Reserve, and to La Perouse Bay; both are about a twenty-minute drive from Hale Pau Hana.

NAPILI SUNSET

Address: 46 Hui Drive, Lahaina, Maui, Hawaii 96761
Telephone: 800–447–9229, 808–669–8083; fax: 808–669–2730

Napili Bay is a small reef-protected inlet of sea and white sand. This small two-story condominium complex of forty-one units sits right above a half-mile long crescent of beach along the Bay, where the water is calm and picture-perfect blue, and the bottom a gentle slope of white sand. All units are oceanfront and are fully equipped for housekeeping. Ground-floor units have private lanais, twenty feet of grassy lawn with a barbecue, and are steps from the beach, which also happens to be a good snorkeling spot. The hotel shares Napili Bay with a number of other complexes so there are often many families with children. Rising behind Napili Bay are the slopes of the West Maui Mountains and views of Molokai and Lanai.

Season: Year-round.

Accommodations: One-bedroom apartments sleep four people; two-bedroom, two-bath apartments sleep up to six people. All apartments are equipped with full-size and complete kitchens, microwave ovens, TVs, and ceiling fans (no air-conditioning).

Special Features: Daily maid service, fresh beach towels daily, linens changed every other day, small pool across the street from the beach, VCR rental laundry facilities, in-room safe, convenience store north of the complex, fax machine.

Cost: April 15 to December 14, one-bedroom apartment $150 per night; two-bedroom apartment $210 per night, double occupancy. Each additional person $12; children under two stay free. Rates seventy-five percent higher December 15 to April 14.

Nearby: The complex is within walking distance of Kapalua's beautiful beach, tennis courts, championship golf course, and restaurants. A short drive from the complex is a large grocery store and snorkle rental. A great snorkeling beach, and one of Maui's best (except in winter), is also a short drive from the condo at Honolua Bay, north of Kapalua. Walk the jeep road through a rain forest to the beach and follow the right shoreline as you snorkel out to the point. The water never gets deeper than five to ten feet and is loaded with fish and turtles. Fifteen minutes south of the hotel is the busy hotel-packed area of Ka'anapali; twenty minutes south is Lahaina.

HANA'S WAIANAPANAPA STATE PARK CABINS

Address: Department of Land and Natural Resources, 54 South High Street, Room 101, Wailuku, Hawaii 96793 (write for reservations). Approximately fifty-two miles east of Kahului Airport, off Hana Highway, which is about three hours' drive time from west Maui on a spectacularly scenic road. **Telephone:** 808–243–5354. Reserve in writing well in advance.

Operated and maintained by the Division of State Parks, these cabins are located in the wild and breathtaking Hana area of Maui in a 120-acre park of hala groves near the sea cliffs. This is a rustic getaway for picnicking, shore fishing, and hardy family hiking along an ancient Hawaiian coastal trail that leads to Hana. It provides a wonderful opportunity to study a seabird colony and anchialine pools, and there are a number of historical sites and ancient heiaus (temples). Swim in one of the nearby "Seven Sacred Pools," hike through the bamboo forest above the pools, and visit the spectacular waterfalls that tumble into them. On your drive to the pools you will pass little agricultural settlements that have not changed since Hawaii's missionary days, plus spectacular beaches and numerous waterfalls.

Season: Year-round.

Accommodations: Each cabin sleeps up to six people and has a living room with two twin beds and a bedroom with two bunk beds. They are completely furnished with bedding, towels, cooking and eating utensils, electrical lights, hot water, showers, and toilet facilities. Guests must clean the cabins before departing. Clean linens and towels are supplied every third day.

Special Features: The park is on an ancient lava flow with numerous submerged lava tubes, natural stone arches, and other remote, wild low-cliffed volcanic coastal features such as sea stacks and blow holes. You can also explore a native hala forest (bring mosquito repellant!).

Cost: Cabin $45 per night for four people; each additional person $5. Maximum charge $55 per night. Five-night maximum stay.

Nearby: The ocean at the state park is not safe for swimming, but nearby Hana Beach Park is a great beach for kids. The hotel Hana Ranch (808–248–8211, ext. 3) has horseback-riding tours through ranch pastures or along spectacular shorelines. The tours are very popular, so reserve well in advance.

Note: Other state parks with cabins or A-frame shelters on the islands of Hawaii include Kokee State Park on Kauai (PO Box 819, Waimea, Hawaii 96796; 808–335–6061); Hapuna Beach State Recreation Area on Hawaii (PO Box 390962, Kailua-Kona, Hawaii 96739; 808–882–1095); and Makaekahana State Recreation Area on Oahu (808–293–1736). See page 325 for general information on Hawaii's state park accommodations.

SAN DIEGO, CALIFORNIA

San Diego is a perfect destination for a family vacation. Seventy miles of beautiful beaches, an average climate of seventy degrees with little rain, dozens of public parks, and myriad attractions suited for both adults and children will have you coming back again and again. Whether you stay in San Diego, La Jolla, Coronado, or even Tijuana, Mexico, you are within ten to thirty minutes of the beach or any major attraction. At most beaches you can rent boogie boards, surfboards, or bikes. There are many coastal bike routes; for a map, call 619–231–BIKE.

Mission Bay is a hub of aquatic activity. It includes Sea World (619–222–6363), resort hotels (see the Bahia and the Dana Inn on pages 208 and 209, respectively), and is one of the best spots for swimming, bicycling, in-line skating, jogging, kite flying, and simply having fun. Children eleven and older are thrilled with jet skiing at Mission Bay Park; the ski resembles a surf motorcycle and is easy to learn to maneuver. For about $30 per hour, you can rent one at Jet Ski Rentals (619–276–9200). Families can easily spend two days at Sea World, a theme park devoted to creatures of the sea on Mission Bay's south side, as there is so much to take in—from cavorting penguins and a petting pool with dolphins to the killer whale Shamu and an underwater "walk" through shark-infested waters with "The Shark Encounter." Also situated along Mission Bay is Belmont Park, a shopping and entertainment complex with two restored landmarks: the Plunge and the Giant Dipper. The Plunge is the largest indoor swimming pool in Southern California, while the Giant Dipper is a vintage wooden roller coaster with more than 2,600 feet of tracks and thirteen hills.

Balboa Park is the city's cultural center, with many inventive museums set in an expansive and festive park. Highlights include the Natural History Museum (619–232–3821), where kids can get a close-up view of desert life, including replicas of dinosaurs; the Hall of Champions (619–234–2544), with exhibits of San Diego's finest athletes; the Marie Hitchcock Puppet Theater (619–466–7128); the San Diego Model Railroad Museum (619–696–0199); and the Mingei International Museum (619–239–0003), which showcases toys from around the world. Budding scientists will want to visit the park's Reuben H. Fleet Space Theater and Science Center (619–238–1168), which has more than fifty hands-on exhibits and movies in its multimedia planetary center, or the San Diego Aerospace Museum and International Aerospace Hall of Fame (619–234–8291 and 619–232–8322), with seventy aircraft including World War II fighter planes.

Also located in Balboa Park is the must-see San Diego Zoo (619–234–3153), home to nearly four thousand animals, many of which are rare and exotic. In addition to spectacular bioclimatic exhibits like the new

Polar Bear Plunge, Hippo Beach, Gorilla Tropics, Sun Bear Forest, and Tiger River, the zoo features a petting zoo and a nursery where baby animals are cared for by their substitute mothers. Forty-five minutes from downtown is the San Diego Wild Animal Park (619–234–6541). A monorail tram takes you on a fifty-minute safari to view twenty-five hundred animals roaming freely in surroundings similar to their native homelands.

Coronado Island, just a few minutes from downtown, also has its share of gorgeous sandy beaches. Its Hotel Del Coronado is one of the most famous hotels in the world for both its architectural beauty and the famous guests who have stayed there; see the Glorietta Bay Inn (page 211) for a bargain find just across the street! The shoreline of La Jolla is one of the area's loveliest. Its Children's Pool Beach, a sheltered sandy beach at the foot of Jenner Street, has seasonal lifeguards on duty and good conditions for scuba diving and skin-diving. Kids can snorkel at La Jolla Cove. The Stephen Birch Aquarium at 2300 Expedition Way in La Jolla (619–534–FISH) is certainly worth a visit. At La Jolla and Casa Coves and Scripps Park below Prospect Street, gnarled, wind-bent trees invite kids to climb when they are not running the expansive stretch of grass or checking out the underwater caves. Scripps Park is a picnicker's haven, with little thatched beach huts jutting off the rocks.

BAHIA RESORT HOTEL

Address: 998 West Mission Bay Drive, San Diego, California 92109
Telephone: 800–288–0770; 619–488–0551

Although not a "budget" accommodation, the Bahia provides a good value for a full-service destination resort. Set on fourteen beachfront acres on a private peninsula surrounded by Mission Bay, the Bahia's studios and suites with kitchenettes are perfectly suited for families. This large resort of 325 rooms has a private beach where you can rent sailboats, catamarans, or paddleboats. It has a free summertime family activity program called the "Bahia Beach Bunch," a teen water sport program, an Olympic-size pool with a lifeguard, a large pond which is home to a family of seals, children's menus, and Family Hour cruises aboard its sternwheeler catamaran, the *Bahia Belle*.

Season: Year-round.

Accommodations: Beach-view rooms in the one-story building are most popular with families; garden-view rooms are less expensive. Bayside suites are spacious, with one king-size bed or two double beds, a sleeper sofa, and kitchenette.

Special Features: The "Bahia Beach Bunch" is a family-oriented program for children five through fourteen accompanied by their parents. Activities include a variety of beach sports and crafts. The teen program features instruction in sailing a small capri, windsurfing, kayaking, and ocean swimming. Outdoor heated pool has a roped-off shallow area for children, poolside snacks; there is a whirlpool spa, tennis courts, bike and water sport rentals and lessons, marina slip, and the Comedy Isle professional comedy club.

Cost: Garden view rooms $130 per night, beach view $150 per night, double occupancy. Children under eighteen stay free in their parents' room; each additional adult $15. Ask about value packages with discounted admission tickets for Sea World, San Diego Zoo, and the Wild Animal Park.

Nearby: The resort is two blocks from the Pacific Ocean, five minutes to Sea World, and a short drive to San Diego's other attractions such as the San Diego Zoo (see page 207).

DANA INN AND MARINA

Address: 1710 West Mission Bay Drive, San Diego, California 92109
Telephone: 800–445–3339; 619–222–6440

The Dana Inn is a low-rise family-style hotel with 196 rooms—many with bay views—spread across eleven acres on Mission Bay Park right next door to Sea World. It has its own marina, bayside park, paddleboats, bicycle and boat rentals, and tennis courts. A large patio and play area surrounds its heated pool and spa.

Season: Year-round.

Accommodations: Rooms, either bay-view or poolside, have two double beds, air-conditioning, TV with HBO and Disney channels, and refrigerators. The more moderately priced poolside rooms have sliding-glass doors which directly access the pool area.

Special Features: Complimentary transportation to and from Sea World, poolside snacks, Ping-Pong, shuffleboard, family restaurant with children's menu.

Cost: Rooms with two double beds $74 to $129 per night, double occupancy, based on view and season. Children under eighteen stay free in parents' room. Ask about value packages with discounted admission tickets to area attractions.

Nearby: Trails from the hotel lead you throughout Mission Bay Park, and it is an easy walk to Sea World and beaches. Belmont Park is a two-minute drive by car or a ten-minute walk. The San Diego Zoo, Old Town, and downtown are a ten-minute drive.

THE BEACH COTTAGES

Address: 4255 Ocean Boulevard, San Diego, California 92109
Telephone: 619–483–7440; fax: 619–273–9365 (Due to popularity, book well in advance.)

Pacific Beach is a popular beach community not far from downtown. Family-owned and operated, the Beach Cottages offers cottages with real "beach cottage feel," apartments, studios, suites, and motel rooms right on the beach. When your kids are not busy building castles in the sand or swimming in the ocean, there's Ping-Pong and shuffleboard. The accommodations are within walking distance of grocery stores, shops, and waterfront restaurants, and San Diego's major attractions are all a short distance away by car.

Season: Year-round.

Accommodations: Cottages, apartments, studios, and suites all have kitchens, and come equipped with towels, linens, and cooking utensils. Cottages have sandblasted white wood walls and ceilings, hardwood floors, and a semi-private furnished patio with a barbecue; they range from one to two large bedrooms and sleep four to six people. There is a nice-sized fully equipped kitchen, eating area, living room with a hide-away bed, and one small bedroom with a double bed. Also comfortable for families are the deluxe studios with two queen-size beds and a kitchen and the two-bedroom suites which have a full kitchen, barbecue grill, breakfast bar, table and chairs, two bathrooms, and two bedrooms. Motel rooms have two double beds and sleep four people. All units have telephones and TV.

Special Features: Laundry facilities.

Cost: During the summer, cottages $150 to $175 per night for four to six people; rate based on number of bedrooms and location. Deluxe studio for four people $120 per night. Motel room for four people $110 per night. Rates considerably lower for the rest of the year (cottage $95 to $120 per night or $570 to $720 per week off-season), with weekly and monthly discounts.

Nearby: Short drive to Sea World, the San Diego Zoo and Balboa Park, the Historic State Park of Old Town, and Point Loma.

THE GLORIETTA BAY INN

Address: 1630 Glorietta Boulevard, Coronado Island, San Diego, California 92118 (across the street from the famous Hotel del Coronado, the backdrop for the Marilyn Monroe movie *Some Like It Hot*).
Telephone: 800-283-9383, 619-435-3101; fax: 619-435-6182

Although you will feel like you are on your own small island, Coronado and its strand of beautiful sandy beaches is only a short drive across the bridge from San Diego's major attractions. The Glorietta Bay Inn was built as the mansion home of sugar baron John Spreckles; eighty-eight rooms (including family suites) surround the mansion building, and all have views of the bay and hotel gardens. The hotel has a heated swimming pool, spa, and bike rentals along with access to a great swimming beach across the street. Its location next to the infamous Hotel Del Coronado makes for a fun detour: The "Del" 's staff welcome visitors to walk around their legendary historic landmark hotel. Your children will want to make a beeline for the candy shop in the lobby (a sightseeing attraction in itself).
Season: Year-round.
Accommodations: Standard hotel rooms have either two double beds or two queen-size beds, and comfortably accommodate four people; they have either a garden, lanai, or bay view. Family suites are similar to large apartments; they have one bedroom, one or two bathrooms, a living room, and a full kitchen. All rooms have cable TV with movie channels.
Special Features: Pool, spa, bicycle rental, sitting porches, music room with player piano. Breakfast available for small fee. Staff can assist with guided island tour, public golf, tennis, and water sports.
Cost: June through September, garden-view room $109 per night, double occupancy; room with lanai $120 per night, double occupancy; bay-view room $135 per night, double occupancy. Children four and under stay free in room with parents using existing bedding; each additional person $10 per night. Family suites for four people $179 per night; seven-night minimum during the summer. Off-season rates lower.
Nearby: Just across the bridge from San Diego's major attractions, including the San Diego Zoo, the historic district, and Sea World. Mexico is just fifteen minutes south by car.

SANTA BARBARA, CALIFORNIA

THE MIRAMAR RESORT HOTEL

Address: PO Box 429, Santa Barbara, California 93102 (eighty-five miles north of Los Angeles and three miles south of Santa Barbara) **Telephone:** 800–322–6983; 805–969–2203

Santa Barbara is the epitome of a perfect beach town, and you will think that you have uncovered a real bargain when you stay at its only ocean-front resort—until you see that a steady clientele of families has known about it for years. They come for Santa Barbara's warm weather, gorgeous setting, and this resort's casual and well-priced offerings. There are two heated swimming pools, a spa, four tennis courts, grassy areas with children's play equipment, an exercise gym with saunas, and a private life-guarded beach spread over fifteen acres of landscaped tropical gardens.

Season: Year-round.

Accommodations: A horseshoe-shaped motel complex rings the resort's largest pool. Poolside rooms have various bed configurations that sleep up to four. Guests desiring more peace and quiet opt for the nearby blue-roofed cottages or lanai rooms (some with sliding doors that look out to the ocean). Oceanfront rooms are big, with two double beds and an outside patio; they can connect with a parlor that sleeps two and has a full kitchen. Cottages range from one to three bedrooms with living rooms, kitchens, and small decks. A train passes the property in the middle of the night; ask for the quietest location if your group has light sleepers.

Special Features: Five hundred feet of private beach fronted by a wooden boardwalk (in the summer the hotel anchors a raft off the beach for guests), beach umbrellas, backrests and mats available from an ever-present lifeguard; bicycle rental, and family-style dining, including a Santa Fe-Amtrak Railcar diner with fast food. Shuffleboard, Ping-Pong.

Cost: Poolside rooms $80 per night; oceanfront rooms $160 per night; one- to three-bedroom cottages start at $135 per night. Rates depend on size of cottage, kitchen, and location. Children under twelve stay free in parents' room. Two-night minimum May through October weekends.

Nearby: Three miles away, Santa Barbara's three-mile-long beach-front bike path begins at Stearn's Wharf; it has become a haven for in-line skaters. Here you can rent bikes, skates, or pedalinas (four-wheeled Italian surreys) and ride to the popular Santa Barbara Zoological Gardens (805–962–6310) with lions, picnic spots, and a playground. Other kid-pleasing attractions are the Museum of Natural History, the Sea Center on Stearns Wharf, and Kid's World, a park designed by local children based on their earthly model of dreamland. At the end of May, during the I Madonnari festival, the plaza in front of the town's eighteen-century mission blazes with hundreds of vivid chalk drawings ranging from re-created works of Michelangelo and Matisse to funny trompe l'oeil street scenes. For $10 you get a two-foot square and a big box of colorful chalk (805–569–3873).

Note: We cover the University of California at Santa Barbara Family Vacation Center in the chapter on family camps; see page 145.

THE MONTEREY PENINSULA, CALIFORNIA

Summer fog has a way of hovering over much of California's central coast, yet Santa Cruz's protected bayfront location manages to provide many afternoons of hot sun. Located seventy miles south of San Francisco, and an hour's drive from Monterey and Carmel, this laid-back resort community draws families year-round for its spectacular coastal scenery, which ranges from beaches gentle enough for tots to ones only world-class surfers would brave, towering redwood groves, the Pacific Coast's last surviving full-scale seaside amusement park, and many scenic paths to bike, hike and skate. Here families can have the honky-tonk beach boardwalk experience or the chance to really get away from all, exploring redwood forests, tide pools, and wildlife.

The Santa Cruz Boardwalk (408–423–5590) sits right on the main beach and features the classic wooden Giant Dipper roller coaster, a vintage 1911 carousel, and a gently twirling Ferris wheel that looms over the sea. Sea lions lounge on the pilings of the Santa Cruz Municipal Wharf, a short walk from the Boardwalk, which has many seafood restaurants and several stands that rent fishing tackle. Sightseeing cruises and whale-watching tours depart here.

Children rarely seem to mind the chill in Santa Cruz's ocean. Cowell Beach (site of the Dream Inn and Seaway Motel, see page 214), by the Boardwalk and wharf, is Santa Cruz's most protected cove and has the warmest water, along with lifeguards and boogie board rentals. West of the boardwalk is West Cliff Drive, where families can rollerskate and ride bicycles (available for rent near the Boardwalk) along a two-mile path that hugs the rugged coast and winds past Lighthouse Point all the way to Natural Bridges State Beach. En route you'll see hoards of surfers, sea lions, and the tiny memorabilia-filled Santa Cruz Surfing Museum (408–429–3429). Natural Bridges State Beach is a family favorite with spacious picnic areas, rocky tide pools brimming with sea stars and hermit crabs, and a population of monarch butterflies that blanket the park's eucalyptus forests in the winter.

Next door to the state beach is the University of California's Long Marine Lab (408–459–2883), with dolphin and sea lion tanks and an eighty-five-foot whale skeleton on display. Inexpensive tours are available. Should you tire of sun and surf, spend a day six miles north of Santa Cruz in Felton, where there's a six-mile steam train excursion through some of the state's oldest and tallest redwoods. The Roaring Camp and the Big Trees Narrow-Gauge Railroad (408–335–4400) is billed as a way to relive the pioneer days of the 1800s. During the summer, you can ride the train to and from the Beach Boardwalk to Roaring Camp. Easy hiking trails lead from Roaring Camp into Henry Cowell Redwoods State Park (408–335–4598). For an experience in "living history," visit Wilder Ranch State Park (408–426–0505), two miles north of Santa Cruz, with interactive crafts from the 1800s, an amazing low-lying cypress tree to climb, and trails to the beach.

Forty-five minutes down the coast from Santa Cruz is the spectacular indoor/outdoor Monterey Bay Aquarium (408–648–4888), along Cannery Row in Monterey. If you want the place to yourself, go after 3 P.M. and avoid holiday weekends. Kids enjoy the overhead exhibit of full-size models of sea mammals; the three-story-high Kelp Forest; the Touch Pool, where they can touch a variety of starfish and other tide pool life; and the Bat Ray Pool, where they can try to pat the passing bat rays.

SEAWAY HOTEL

Address: 176 West Cliff Drive, Santa Cruz, California 95060
Telephone: c/o the Dream Inn, 800–662–3838; 408–426–4330

A number of accommodations lie within a few blocks of Cowell Beach (Santa Cruz's centrally located and warmest beach), the boardwalk, and the main wharf, but only one resort—the high-rise (and high-priced) Dream Inn—provides direct beachfront access. The resort recently opened the Seaway, a lower-priced annex directly across the street, where guests can use all of the Dream Inn's amenities, including two outdoor heated pools hovering over the ocean, for sixty-five percent of the price.

Season: Year-round.

Accommodations: Rooms have one king- or two queen-size beds; all have an outside patio or deck, and some have ocean views. A "junior suite" has a kitchen, and there are three rooms that accommodate large families.

Special Features: Across the street is an outdoor heated pool and kids' wading pool overlooking the ocean, spa and sauna, and family restaurant. Rooms have TVs with VCR; video rental available.

Cost: Mid-May through mid-September, least expensive rooms $99 per night, double occupancy. Children stay free in parents' room. Junior suite in mid-August $149 per night. Rates drop considerably off-season— to $75 per night at oceanfront Dream Inn.

Nearby: Within walking distance to the Santa Cruz Beach Boardwalk, municipal wharf, West Cliff Drive's skate and bike path, and a short drive to downtown Santa Cruz.

CAPITOLA VENETIAN COURT

Address: 1500 Wharf Road, Capitola, California 95010
Telephone: 800–332–2780; 408–476–6471 (Book early, because many families return to their favorite rooms annually.)

Hovering right over Capitola Beach, just south of Santa Cruz, the family-oriented Venetian Court consists of a quirky melange of pastel-colored stucco apartments that were first built in the 1920s. Although remodeled, they still retain their historic charm. Some of the units have ocean views and balconies; some have fireplaces; all are steps from protected Capitola Beach. The water here is warm and safe for swimming, and there's far less fog in Capitola than the town's more famous neighbors to the south, Monterey and Carmel.

Season: Year-round.

Accommodations: Comfortable one-, two-, or three-bedroom apartments all have kitchens. Cribs are available.

Special Features: The family-oriented beach in front of the Venetian has a lifeguard, and is usually quite active with kids building sandcastles, playing volleyball, boogieboarding, and swimming. The warm and shallow Soquel Creek feeds into this beach; it is dammed up in the summer to create a calm wading lagoon perfect for young children. Paddleboats are available for rent. On the weekend after Labor Day, flower-laden barges float downstream for the nautical Begonia Festival parade.

Cost: June to September, one-bedroom non-ocean view $120 per night for family of four; ocean view $150 per night. Weekly rates available; two-night minimum stay on high-season weekends. Off-season rates considerably lower.

Nearby: The apartments are within walking distance of Capitola Village's shops and restaurants; the town is very informal and compact enough to cover on foot. The Esplanade, which parallels the Venetian's beach, has many fish restaurants and places to grab a quick bite or an ice cream. Just steps away from the hotel is the Capitola Wharf, with a marina and fishing. Capitola is fifteen minutes from the Santa Cruz Beach Boardwalk and forty-five minutes from the Monterey Aquarium.

VACATIONS BY THE SEA

Address: Agent: 215 Monterey Avenue, Capitola, California 95010
Telephone: 408–479–9380 (**Summer weekends can be booked a year in advance.**)

Vacations by the Sea offers beachfront homes, apartments, and condominiums either on Capitola Beach or in quaint Capitola Village, just south of Santa Cruz. Capitola-by-the-Sea is an artsy seaside resort town of beach and craft shops, restaurants, and cafes. The Soquel Creek feeds into its main beach, which is perfect for wading. There's a lifeguard on duty and paddleboats for rent in the summer.

Season: Year-round.

Accommodations: The least expensive accommodations are the one-bedroom, one-bath apartment (for up to three people) two blocks from the beach; a two-bedroom, one-and-a-half-bath apartment (for up to five people), also less than two blocks from the beach; and one-bedroom condominiums (for up to five people) across the street from the beach. All are equipped for housekeeping; guests must bring their own sheets and towels.

Cost: June 15 to September 15, one-bedroom, one-bath apartment starts at $560 per week; two-bedroom, one-and-a-half-bath apartment starts at $770 per week. Rates are lower off season.

Nearby: Refer to the Capitola Venetian Court on page 215 for activities in Capitola. Capitola is fifteen minutes from the Santa Cruz Beach Boardwalk and forty-five minutes from the Monterey Aquarium. For Santa Cruz and Monterey Peninsula activities, see page 213.

SANTA CRUZ COUNTY BEACH VACATION RENTALS

Address: Agent: Bob Bailey Real Estate, 106 Aptos Beach Drive, Aptos, California 95003
Telephone: 408–688–7009 (**Best to call in October to book for the summer; by February it may be too late to reserve a beachfront home.**)

This agency handles vacation homes and condominiums in the beautiful seaside communities of Santa Cruz, Rio del Mar, Capitola, La Selva Beach, and Sand Dollar Beach, which are all beach areas just south of the city of Santa Cruz.

Season: Year-round.

Accommodations: All rentals are completely furnished with the comforts of home, and are equipped with barbecues, telephones, and cooking utensils. Some are oceanfront; others have ocean views. Many have fireplaces, microwave ovens, and cable TVs with VCRs. Homes sleep three to sixteen people, so they can accommodate more than one family.

Cost: During the summer, a two-bedroom home starts at $600 per week; a three-bedroom home $945 per week.

Nearby: Refer to the Capitola Venetian Court on page 215 for activities in Capitola. For Santa Cruz and Monterey Peninsula activities, see introduction on page 213.

THE NORTH COAST, CALIFORNIA

PIGEON POINT LIGHTHOUSE HOSTEL

Address: 210 Pigeon Point Road, Pescadero, California 94060 (fifty miles south of San Francisco on the coast, twenty miles south of Half Moon Bay, and twenty-seven miles north of Santa Cruz) Telephone: 415–879–0633 (call between 7:30 and 9:30 A.M. or 4:30 and 9:30 P.M. Pacific Standard Time); fax: 415–879–9120. Reservations are essential. Reserve by phone; minimum of forty-eight hours' notice if reserving with credit card or ten days if reserving with check. Private weekend rooms tend to be booked three to four months in advance.

Perched on a cliff overlooking the ocean on the central California coast, this 115-foot lighthouse is one of the tallest in America. Guiding mariners since 1872, it was restored in 1981 as a hostel. Several breathtaking beaches close by are ideal for beachcombing, surfing, jogging, horseback riding, and windsurfing. If you visit between November and April you may be lucky enough to see the annual gray whale migration from the boardwalk behind the lighthouse's fog signal building. Staying in a real lighthouse will be quite memorable for kids.

Season: Year-round. The hostel is closed from 9:30 A.M. to 4:30 P.M.

Accommodations: The hostel has fifty-two beds, and private family rooms are available.

Special Features: Outdoor hot tub ($3 per person per half hour), baggage storage, kitchen, linen rental, and on-site parking. One-hour lighthouse tours are available on Sunday from 10 A.M. to 3:00 P.M. ($2 adults, $1 children). Children must be at least forty inches tall to climb the tower.

Cost: HI members, adults $11 per night; nonmembers $14 per night. Children under 17 accompanied by their parents are half-price.

Nearby: One hundred yards north of Pigeon Point is a tide-pool area that's fun to explore. Pescadero Marsh is the feeding and nesting place for more than 150 species of birds. A short drive south is the Año Nuevo State Reserve, the breeding site of northern elephant seals. You must reserve tickets well in advance.

POINT MONTARA LIGHTHOUSE HOSTEL

Address: Sixteenth Street at California Highway 1, P.O. Box 737, Montara, California 94037 (between Montara and Moss Beach) Telephone: 415-728-7177 or 728-5280 (call between 7:30 and 9:30 A.M. or 4:30 and 9:30 P.M.); fax: 415-728-7177. Reservations essential from April to September and on weekends; mail one night's deposit as early as possible.

Overlooking the ocean on the rugged California coast twenty-five miles south of San Francisco is yet another lighthouse accommodation—the Point Montara Fog Signal and Light Station. Established in 1875, these turn-of-the-century buildings have been preserved and restored to serve as a base for exploring this spectacular stretch of coastline and watching the annual migration of gray whales between November and April. Your children will never forget sleeping in a real lighthouse!

Season: Year-round. The hostel is closed from 9:30 A.M. to 4:30 P.M.

Accommodations: The light tower, which sits atop seventy-foot cliffs, and its Victorian-style lightkeeper's quarters, are now part of the hostel's forty-five bed facility. There are six private family rooms.

Special Features: Outdoor hot tub, baggage storage, kitchen, laundry facilities, linen rental, and on-site parking. Staff members present special interpretive programs on the ecology of tide pool and intertidal zones of the San Mateo coast.

Cost: HI members, adults $12 per night; nonmembers $15 per night. Children five to ten with parent half-price.

Nearby: The James Fitzgerald Marine Reserve, a four-mile stretch of tide pools filled with starfish, crabs, mussels, abalone, and sea anemones, is one-half mile north and accessible by a trail. There are also several breathtaking beaches for beachcombing, jogging, horseback riding, and windsurfing.

POINT REYES HOSTEL

Address: Box 247, Point Reyes Station, California 94956 (off Limantour Road)
Telephone: 415–663–8811 (call between 7:30 and 9:30 A.M. or 4:30 and 9:30 P.M.) Reservations are always advisable; mail one night's deposit (credit card numbers accepted) as early as possible; indicate gender of family members for dorm-style accommodations.

This hostel is two miles from the ocean in a secluded valley of the national seashore. Summer at the seashore, a sixty-five-thousand-acre wilderness area, features fresh air, blooming wildflowers, and marshes full of birds. The park is known for its migrating birds as well as abundant flora and fauna, including bobcats, foxes, deer, elk, harbor seals, and sea lions. Many trails in the park lead to wooden hills, rocky coves and long, sandy beaches.

Season: Year-round.

Accommodations: One private family room is available for parents with children under five. (Book by April for a summer stay.) Other families stay in the dorm-style accommodations of this thirty-bed hostel.

Special Features: Kitchen, linen rental, patio with an outdoor barbecue, and on-site parking.

Cost: HI members, adults $12 per night; nonmembers $15 per night. Children under eighteen with parent $6.

Nearby: Limantour Beach, with its rolling sand dunes, is two miles from the hostel and easily accessible by car. It is ideal for summertime wading. At the end of the Limantour Spit you can watch for harbor seals. Drakes Beach (a forty-minute drive) is famous for the high, white cliffs backing its swimming strand, and is the only spot at the seashore with food service. Sculptured Beach is the best for tide pool exploring; check the tide table at the visitor center. Point Reyes Lighthouse, twenty-five miles from the hostel, is the best place in the Bay Area for whale watching from January to April.

The park's Bear Valley Visitor Center has exhibits of the area's animals as well as lists of park activities. Visit the center's Miwok Village, which reconstructs the daily life of the Miwok Indians who first inhabited Point Reyes, and walk the Earthquake Trail along the San Andreas Fault to see remaining evidence of the 1906 San Francisco quake. Behind the visitor center is the Morgan Horse Ranch, where you can learn about the horses' history and see them grazing. Horses can be rented at Five Brooks Stables (415–663–8287); bikes can be rented at Trailhead Rental (415–663–1958).

THE INN AT SCHOOLHOUSE CREEK

Address: 7051 North Highway One, Little River, California, 95456 (on the coast highway, three miles south of Mendocino)
Telephone: 707–937–5525

Even though the water's cold, the craggy coastline, picturesque town, and easy access to state parks and forests makes Mendocino a wonderful family vacation destination. Facing the Pacific Ocean, this cozy historic inn is located on ten acres of flowering gardens, meadow, and forest. It was once part of a large coastal ranch, and there is a forest and shallow creek on the property that is fun for kids to explore. Wonderful tide pools are a five-minute walk away, and children are fascinated by the whales that can be viewed from the property November through March. Mendocino, with its artisan shops and galleries, is three miles away. Also nearby are many rivers, harbors, beaches (the water is cold but the beach is great for kite flying, running, and beachcombing), and spectacular state parks.

Season: Year-round.

Accommodations: The inn has separate cottages with kitchens and decks that were built at the turn of the century. Other accommodations include rooms from the 1930s and more contemporary rooms in small buildings. All rooms have ocean views, private baths, and fireplaces.

Special Features: The inn's "Ledford Home," built in 1862, has a comfortable lounge with a fireplace. Books, games, and puzzles can be borrowed from their large library.

Cost: Rooms dating from the 1930s $80 to $100, double occupancy; cottages $100 to $130 per night, double occupancy. Each additional person $10. Children seven and under can stay in the cottages only. Two-night minimum stay on weekends.

Nearby: Mendocino's visitor center, in the historic Ford House on Main Street, has a calendar of events that lists children's activities, including an annual sand castle building contest held on Labor Day, Easter egg hunts, and Fourth of July carnival. Three miles south of Mendocino is Van Damme State Park, which has a relatively safe beach, hiking trails, and the Pygmy Forest Discovery Trail, where you can see decades-old trees that are only a few feet tall. Mendocino Headlands State Park has surfing, sport diving, and fishing. Its Big River Beach has tide pooling, rocks to climb, and lots of room to romp. Canoe rental is available for rides down the Big River from Catch a Canoe at the Big River Lodge (707–937–0273).

Note: If you plan to stay at least a week in Mendocino, weekly vacation home rentals range from $500 to $700 per week. Call Mendocino

Coastal Reservations (707–937–5033), Pacific Resorts (800–358–9879), or Shoreline Properties (800–942–8288).

THE LOST WHALE BED & BREAKFAST INN

Address: 3452 Patrick's Point Drive, Trinidad, California 95570 (one mile off U.S. 101, fifteen minutes from the Arcata-Eureka Airport)
Telephone: 800 – 677–7859

Unlike most bed-and-breakfast establishments, this Cape Cod–style inn overlooking the Pacific enthusiastically welcomes families. In fact, the owners have children of their own. A wooded path leads to a private beach, which has a secluded cove of jutting rocks, tide pools, and sea lions. On the inn's enclosed grounds children can pick berries or have fun in the toy-stocked playhouse and playground with a jungle gym, seesaw, swings, and fort. There are ducks and goats to feed at the innkeeper's adjacent pigmy goat farm, and books, puzzles, and games to entertain kids at sundown.

Season: Year-round.

Accommodations: The inn has eight suites, all with private bathrooms; five suites have ocean views. Two of the rooms have step-out balconies and sleeping lofts for children.

Special Features: Included in the price is a hearty breakfast of casseroles and quiches, home-baked muffins, fresh fruit, and locally smoked salmon. Sherries and home-baked pastries are available at the end of the day. The hot tub has views of crashing waves. Cribs, bassinets, and high chairs are available.

Cost: November to April, rooms $100 to $140 per night double occupancy; May to October, $120 to $160 double occupancy, depending on type of room. Additional adult $20; additional child ages three to sixteen $15; under three stay free. Rates include breakfast.

Nearby: Patrick's Point State Park is a ten-minute walk away. Also close by is Agate Beach, which has wonderful driftwood formations, sea-tumbled agates, jade, and tide pools. Trinidad is a quaint fishing village with a marina for deep-sea charter boats, surf fishing, lagoons for summer swimming, sailing, and windsurfing. Hiking trails through the redwoods and Fern Canyon, with its thousands of ferns and beautiful waterfalls, are a twenty-minute drive north.

SEASIDE, OREGON

BEST WESTERN OCEANVIEW RESORT

Address: 414 North Prom, Seaside, Oregon 97138
Telephone: 800–234–8439, 503–738–3334; fax: 503–738–3264

Few people totally immerse themselves in Seaside's fifty-five degree water without wetsuits, but many families play on this popular and particularly scenic stretch of Oregon's rugged coast, just above Tillamook Head, in other ways—kite-flying, skimboarding on the hard wet sand, and pedalling around on low-to-the-ground beach tricycles. Children enjoy splashing about, no matter what the temperature, and the waves here are great for more serious boogie boarding and surfing with wetsuits, which can be rented along the beach. The full-service Oceanview Resort is just steps from Seaside's waterfront promenade, which has an aquarium, one and a half miles of broad, flat beach studded with playground equipment, and rides from carousels to bumper cars.

Season: Year-round.

Accommodations: Most rooms have ocean views. A popular room for families is the oceanfront queen room with a queen-size bed, queen-size sofabed, gas fireplace, private deck, fully equipped kitchenette, and TV. Less expensive but equally nice for families are the oceanview rooms with two queen-size beds, microwave oven, snack refrigerator, deck, and TV.

Special Features: Indoor heated swimming pool.

Cost: Oceanfront queen rooms start at $95 per night; oceanview queen rooms start at $75 per night.

Nearby: Surfboards and wetsuits can be rented at Cleanline Surf Shop (503–738–7888). Families enjoy kayaking in the estuary of Nehalem Bay that runs through town. Outdoor Fun for All (503–738–8447) rents kayaks, bicycles, mopeds, and in-line skates. Ecola State Park, seven miles south of town, has scenic hiking.

Note: If you plan to stay at least one week in Seaside, one- to three-bedroom cottages start at $500 per week. Call Beach Realty at 503–738–9068.

ISLANDS IN THE PUGET SOUND, WASHINGTON

Remind your children that the *Free Willy* movies were filmed on the San Juan Islands, north of Seattle in northern Puget Sound, and you'll be off to a great start exploring this magnificent archipelago. The San Juan

Islands have everything for a well-rounded family vacation of active outdoor activities, quiet time, and comfortable lodgings.

There are 172 islands in the San Juan Islands, many of which are a
short ferry ride from either Seattle or Tacoma. If you're planning to drive
onto the ferry in the summer months, arrive hours ahead and be prepared to wait. You may also plan your itinerary so you continue on the
ferry to British Columbia. The San Juan Islands are only 90 miles from
Vancouver. Call the Washington State Ferries at 206–464–6400.

The San Juans are full of hidden coves, quiet roads perfect for biking,
and long stretches of wild beach with plenty of tide pools to explore.
This is the place for outdoor adventure—from fishing for salmon and
trout, camping, sailing, or spotting abundant wildlife. You are bound to
see harbor seals, sea lions, herons, otters, starfish, dolphins and, of
course, the huge black-and-white orca whales who inhabit these waters.

Orcas Island, one of the San Juan's largest, has quiet roads through
rolling countryside dotted with small farms and many accessible
beaches. It is not difficult to find your own quiet lagoon on a sandy
beach with lots of driftwood and brilliantly colored starfish. Moran State
Park, on the island, has two freshwater lakes for swimming, boating, and
fishing. Take time to climb to the top of Mount Constitution in the park;
it's the highest point in the islands and the view is great—you might
spot deer swimming from island to island. Other popular island activities
include biking, kayaking, and if it's warm enough, swimming at Cascade
Lake.

Another popular island is San Juan Island, home of the busy tourist
center of Friday Harbor. Here you can sign up for a whale-watching
cruise, a fishing trip, or wildlife tour. For the best whale watching, come
between May and July, and book hotel reservations well in advance. At
Friday Harbor, don't miss the Whale Museum (360–378–4710), where
your kids can "adopt" an orca to support research.

In the sound near Seattle is primitive Vashon Island, home to one of
Hostelling International's most unusual accommodations: authentic tepees. Both Vashon and Orcas are ideal for bicycle touring; in fact, once
you leave the ferry landing, you will see more bikes than cars.

BEACH HAVEN RESORT

Address: Enchanted Forest Road, Route 1, Box 12, Eastsound, Orcas Island, Washington 98245 (sixty miles north of Seattle, accessible by ferry from Anacortes; west of Orcas lies Vancouver Island and Victoria, British Columbia)
Telephone: 303–376–2288. Book well in advance.

Many families have come to this secluded island retreat, set on ten acres of gentle sloping private pebble beach on Orcas Island, every year since 1942; some couples met here as youngsters and now come with children of their own. At Beach Haven, the water reaches up to the decks of eleven sixty-year-old log cabins and a large three-bedroom A-frame cedar home, which are sheltered by a dense, old-growth forest. Rustic yet clean and very comfortable, the cabins face west for breathtaking sunsets. Beach Haven is a place to really get away; there are no phones or TVs. Deer and river otters freely roam, and there are wonderful tide pools, rowboats and canoes to rent, and miles of beach to explore.

Season: Year-round. There is one-week minimum stay in summer.

Accommodations: All units have private baths and are nicely furnished for full housekeeping with a well-equipped electric kitchen, linens and towels, electric heat, and wood stoves with firewood. Each unit has a deck with a picnic table. Modern apartments have sliding glass doors over the beach.

Special Features: You can walk from the cabins to more than 1,400 feet of beach. An inventive playground behind the cabins has a two-story fort with a bridge spanning to a stockade, swings, and a playhouse. There's also Ping-Pong, horseshoes, and a driftwood "horse."

Cost: Two-bedroom cabin for five people $95 per night; three-bedroom cabin with loft for eight people $145 per night; "Cedar Beachcomber" cabin for ten people $200 per night.

Nearby: Moran State Park has thirty miles of trails and five lakes with swimming, row boats, paddleboats, and freshwater fishing. Oceanfront Obstruction Pass State Park has tide pools. Whale watching and sea kayak tours are available for all levels; call 360–376–4041 or 360–376–4755. A unique way to explore the island is by moped; Key Mopeds (360–376–2474) has a large number of them for rent.

ROCHE HARBOR RESORT & MARINA

Address: PO Box 4001, Roche Harbor, San Juan Island, Washington 98250 (located on the northwest tip of San Juan Island; take the Washington State Ferry from Anacortes to Friday Harbor, if you want your own car on the island)
Telephone: 360–378–2115; fax: 360–378–6809

Registered as a historic site, Roche Harbor is a destination resort with a full-service marina situated beside a picturesque harbor on San Juan Island. In high demand for family vacations are the resort's renovated family-style cottages with water views, which were built in 1910 for the workers when this was a lime and cement company town. The cottages are surrounded by a large lawn with plenty of room for family fun, and are close to a pool, tennis courts, volleyball and badminton nets, and a playground. Canoes, kayaks, and outboards can be rented at the resort, as well as mopeds for touring the island. Three-hour naturalist-guided whale searches and kayak treks leave right from Roche Harbor's docks. Although not a "budget" accommodation, Roche Harbor provides good value for a full-service destination resort.

Season: Year-round.

Accommodations: Two styles of family cabins are available: recently renovated "front row" cottages with outstanding views of the harbor, and more rustic "back row" summer-style cottages. A large "front row" cottage or large "back row" cottage has one double bed in one room and two double beds in another, plus kitchen, bath, and living room. A small "front row" or "back row" cottage has one double bed in one room, two twin beds in another, plus kitchen, bath, and living room. Waterfront condominiums with one, two, and three bedrooms are also available. These units have equipped kitchens with an eating area overlooking the water, fireplace, TV, and large decks with water views.

Special Features: In-season heated outdoor swimming pool, tennis courts, volleyball, hiking trails through nearby limestone quarries, full-service marina for vessels of all sizes. Several dining options including wharf-side cafe, live music and dancing during the summer, general store, post office, laundry facilities.

Cost: During prime season (May 10 through September), large front row cottage $185 per night; smaller front row cottage $175 night. Large back row rustic cottage $125 per night; small back row cottage $115 per night. Waterfront condominiums start at $138 per night, prime season. All rates lower the rest of the year.

Nearby: The Resort's Marine Activity Center offers a three-hour whale-watch cruise ($39 adults, $29 children), open-deck kayak treks ($39 adults, $29 children), kayak rentals ($12 per hour), motor boat rental ($25 per hour), and daily cruises to Victoria, British Columbia ($37). For other activities on San Juan Island see page 222.

VASHON ISLAND RANCH HOSTEL

Address: 12119 South West Cove Road, Vashon Island, Washington, 98070 (a five-minute ferry ride from Tacoma, fifteen-minute ferry ride from West Seattle; also accessible by ferry from the Kitsap Peninsula or downtown Seattle) Telephone: 360–463–2592. Reservations are essential June through August; phone reservations are accepted with a credit card.

This hostel's hand-hewn log cabins and five Sioux Indian tepees with family rooms, set on ten acres, provide an unforgettable getaway. Guests also can sleep in cozy covered wagons that surround a campfire or in a log lodge with an old western facade. In pleasant weather Indian drumming is performed around the fire. Parents who want a special getaway while vacationing with their children can stay on the premises in a private room in the lodge while their older children stay in the tepees. (Parents determine if their children are old enough for this). In the second week of July, Vashon has an annual strawberry festival with street dancing and colorful fanfare.

Season: May through October.

Accommodations: The lodge is a hand-hewn log building crafted from the ranch's own Douglas Fir trees; it sleeps fourteen in bunk rooms, has two bathrooms with showers. The lodge's private room has a queen-size bed and bathroom. Family rooms in private tepees have three to four cots and a firepit.

Special Features: Outdoor kitchen with western facade, indoor kitchen, linen rental, baggage storage, on-site parking, volleyball, horseshoes, horses on site (no riding). Pancakes made from an old family recipe are served each morning. Bikes are available at no charge for touring the island. Free pick-up by hostel managers at the ferry.

Cost: HI members, adults $9 per night; nonmembers $12 per night. Children five to ten half price. Private room in lodge $25 to $55 per night depending on time of year.

Nearby: Vashon Island, twelve and a half miles long and five and a half miles wide, is a paradise for cyclists. Guests can bike to the beach two and a half miles away.

THE WASHINGTON COAST

This area stretches from Neah Bay at the entrance to the Strait of Juan de Fuca south to Ilwaco, where the Columbia River spills into the Pacific. If you want a combined vacation of beaches, the mountains, even a rain forest, your best base is the Kalaloch area near Neah Bay (see page 100 in the National Parks chapter). If endless beaches for beachcombing are your style, head for the area south of Moclips to Ocean Shores, a stretch of about twenty miles with numerous beach turnoffs and small towns that are popular holiday and vacation spots for families. Razor clam digging is a popular sport here, as are kite flying, shell collecting, and driftwood gathering. The Ocean Shores area has golf, tennis, horseback riding, bowling, and ocean fishing.

Further south, the Long Beach Peninsula extending from Ledbetter Point to the Columbia River has more broad, sandy beaches, Beachcombers can hunt for old shipwrecks, glass fishnet balls, and shells. Long Beach and Seaview have amusement arcades and go-carts, many shops and galleries, and two nine-hole golf course. Ledbetter Point State Park has pine forests, salt marshes, and sand dunes.

OCEAN CREST RESORT

Address: Sunset Beach, Moclips, Washington, 98652 (one mile north of Pacific Beach)
Telephone: 800–684–8439, 360–276–4465; fax: 360–276–4149

This resort is in a natural forest setting with views of the Pacific and direct beach access. Although the water is cold and rough for swimming, the beach is sandy and ideal for beachcombing and splashing about. Children will enjoy the resort's playground and indoor heated pool, which is handy on foggy days.

Season: Year-round.

Accommodations: Lodgings consist of apartments or hotel rooms with fireplaces and cable TV.

Special Features: Pool, spa, sauna, exercise room, sun decks, and lounge. Cribs are available for a $3 one-time charge.

Cost: During high season (March 16 to September 30), apartments for up to six people and large studios for up to four people $77 to $125 per night, double occupancy, depending on number of bedrooms and view. Additional adults $11 per day; children under fourteen $5.50 per night, under five free. Rates are much lower during the rest of the year.

Nearby: Ocean Shores, eighteen miles away, has mopeds for rent.

IRON SPRINGS OCEAN BEACH RESORT

Address: PO Box 207, Copalis Beach, Washington, 98535 (three miles north of Copalis Beach, between Copalis and Pacific beaches on Washington 109)
Telephone: 360–276–4230

This rambling hundred-acre oceanfront resort has secluded cabins and apartments among the trees on a low-lying bluff overlooking the ocean. There is a private, although steep, path to the beach. When the tide is high, the beach is accessible along the road as well. The main focus here is the beach; the water is too cold for swimming but wonderful for razor clam digging, crab and surf fishing, beachcombing, and building campfires at night. A shallow creek that runs through to the ocean is especially appealing to small children.

Season: Year-round.

Accommodations: Each apartment or cottage has a fully equipped kitchen, electric heat, and a fireplace. Bedding is provided.

Special Features: Beach, covered heated pool, badminton net, playground for youngsters, coffee shop. Cribs are available. You can purchase home-cooked cinnamon rolls and clam chowder on the premises to take to your room. Bring your own television or rent one here.

Cost: The least expensive accommodations are the apartments for four, $74 to $80 per night. One-bedroom cottages for four start at $80 per night. Additional adult $10 per night; additional child $6.

Nearby: For activities on this stretch of the Washington Coast see page 227.

KLIPSAN BEACH COTTAGES

Address: 22617 Pacific Highway, Ocean Park, Washington 98640 (on Klipsan Beach, which is part of the Long Beach Peninsula)
Telephone: 360–665–4888

The eight comfortable, cedar-shingled Klipsan Beach Cottages are very popular with families, and typically there are many children here in the summer. The beach is two yards from the cottage decks. There is also a small rhododendron forest and a safe stretch of dunes between the cabins and the beach. Beachcombers can hunt for old shipwrecks, glass fishnet balls, and shells.

Season: Year-round.

Accommodations: Eight separate and secluded cottages have two or three bedrooms, fireplaces and firewood, unobstructed ocean views, and fully equipped kitchens.

Cost: June through September, two-bedroom cabin for four $95 per night; A-frame for six $150 per night. October through May, cabins $70 per night, A-frame $125 per night.

Nearby: Long Beach and Seaview have amusement arcades and go-carts, many shops and galleries, and two nine-hole golf courses.

TEXAS

PORT ARANSAS, CORPUS CHRISTI, AND THE PADRE ISLAND NATIONAL SEASHORE

Endless beaches surround the Gulf Coast city of Corpus Christi, which is small enough not to overwhelm but large enough to have a full sampling of seaside pleasures. Less than thirty minutes south of downtown, you can choose between tame or wild shores. The Padre Island National Seashore is the longest remaining stretch of undeveloped ocean beach in the United States. With a vast landscape of wind-sculpted dunes, this sparkling preserve of white sand and shell beach stretches for some eighty miles all the way to the Mexican border. The beaches are ideal for swimming and sunbathing from April through December. Swimming is permitted all along the beach; lifeguards normally are on duty at Malaquite Beach in the summer; at Padre Bali County Park, just beyond the bridge on North Padre Island; and at the day-use beach at the National Seashore. Various nature programs are offered on weekends during the off-season (September through May); in summer they are held daily and include beach walks, campfire programs, and activities such as making fish prints.

Just north of Padre Island is Mustang Island State Park and the laid-back fishing and resort village of Port Aransas, known for its miles of wide, white beaches, and deep-sea fishing. The catches are big—marlin, sailfish, amberjack, and the enormous Gulf shrimp are plentiful. The Gulf water is warm, the strand wide, and tall dunes separate the beach from the myriad beach condominiums that line the shore. Here you can drive your car along the hard-packed sand right to your favorite beach spot; parents with young children prefer Port Aransas Beach near town, which is clean, lifeguarded, and has a no-vehicle zone. A special treat here is to rent horses to ride directly on the beach; call Mustang Riding Stables at 512–749–5055. Downtown Port Aransas has a kitschy nautical motif with waterfront restaurants, souvenir shops with every possible shell creation, and bobbing charter fishing boats which line the harbor.

The Wharf Cat offers a five-hour family fishing trip for king mackerel; call 800–605–5448.

The Padre Island Causeway links Mustang Island back to Corpus Christi in about a twenty-five-minute drive where there are many attractions should you tire of the hot sun. The International Kite Museum (512–883–7456) makes for a fun stop, as does the Texas State Aquarium (800–477–GULF), which focuses on marine life of the Gulf of Mexico and the Caribbean Sea; just down the road is Pirate of the Gulf and Playland at the Beach (512–884–4774), a popular theme park. Kids love to take a ride on the porpoise-feeding boat, the *Dolphin Connection*, which departs daily from downtown March through October (512–882–4126). The ride includes opportunities to pet the dolphins.

Note: In addition to the beachfront accommodation listed here in Port Aransas, the historic Tarpon Inn, located downtown on the waterfront and listed on the National Register of Historic Places, has twenty-four simple rooms that open onto shady porches with rocking chairs. Families return yearly for its comfortable atmosphere. A collection of 7,000 fish scales line the walls of its lobby, including one signed by President Franklin D. Roosevelt. Room with two double beds, $70 per night; call 512–749–5555.

ISLAND RETREAT

Address: 700 Island Retreat Court, Port Aransas, Texas 78373
Telephone: 800–553–9833; 512–749–6222

The Island Retreat's efficiency apartments overlooking the beach provide a good budget option for families. A private boardwalk leads you right down to a wide and safe Gulf beach, and there are two swimming pools on the property in addition to tennis courts, volleyball, shuffleboard, and basketball.

Season: Year-round.

Accommodations: One-, two-, and three-bedroom efficiency apartments are completely equipped with an all-electric kitchen, dishwasher, microwave oven, central air-conditioning and heat, and cable TV. Motel rooms are also available with two double beds, microwave oven, and refrigerator.

Special Features: Light housekeeping provided daily, bed changed weekly, fish-cleaning facility.

Cost: During high season (May 16 to September 6), motel room for four people $58 per night, $348 per week; one-bedroom apartment for four people $89 per night, $534 per week; two-bedroom apartment for six people $105 per night, $630 per week; three-bedroom apartment for eight people $120 per night, $720 per week. Rates are lower the rest of the year.

Nearby: For activities in this area, see page 229.

THE SOUTH

THE OUTER BANKS, NORTH CAROLINA

This region of North Carolina, best known for fishing, encompasses 130 miles of coastal beaches north of Oregon Inlet (Duck through Nags Head), Roanoke Island, Hatteras Island, and Ocracoke. Whatever the sport or activity—swimming, beachcombing, fishing, sailing, or sail-boarding—sand and surf are within easy reach. The communities of Kitty Hawk, Kill Devil Hills, and Nags Head all have access to the beach with bathhouses and lifeguards at many locations. Coquina Beach, south of Nags Head, and the public campgrounds along the Cape Hatteras National Seashore also offer protected beach areas.

The steady breezes that attracted the Wright Brothers to the Outer Banks in 1903 continue to attract kite flyers and hang gliders to the East Coast's highest dunes at Jockey's Ridge State Park in Nags Head. Be sure to visit the Wright Brothers National Memorial and the North Carolina Aquarium, on the north end of Roanoke Island. The sound waters off Roanoke are warm and the sandy bottom is perfect for wading. The best swimming area is the "ole swimming hole" adjacent to the aquarium.

Berthed in Manteo is the *Elizabeth II*, a sixteenth-century English sailing vessel similar to those that brought colonists to the New World in 1584. During the summer this state historic site offers living history interpreters portraying roles of the mariners and colonists.

Cape Hatteras National Seashore, a seventy-mile stretch of open beach that attracts surfers and sailboarders, begins south of Nags Head. A free forty-minute ferry ride from Hatteras takes you to historic Ocracoke Island. Descendents of the banker ponies, the island's first settlers, are cared for by the National Park Service. For more about Ocracoke, see page 235.

Note: In addition to the vacation rentals listed here, the Outer Banks Hostel, located in a former 1920s schoolhouse on ten wooded acres, has two family rooms and efficiency apartments. From this new hostel's location, it is only a four-mile trip to Kill Devil Hills, where the Wright Brothers made their first powered flight. If you want to take to the air yourself, it is eight miles to the dunes, where you can take beginner hang-gliding lessons. Forty miles down the coast, you can challenge the winds on the water by windsurfing at the infamous Canadian Hole. The hostel ($15 per night) also has a picnic area, volleyball, shuffleboard, and canoe and kayak rentals; 919–261–2294.

SUN REALTY'S BEACH VACATION HOMES

Address: Sun Realty, PO Box 1630, Kill Devil Hills, North Carolina 27948 (agent)
Telephone: 800–334–4745

From Duck to Kitty Hawk, Kill Devil Hills to Nags Head, North Carolina's barrier islands have beaches that families return to year after year. Sun Realty represents the largest number of privately owned rental vacation properties on the Outer Banks. Available are condominiums and houses located from the northern beach of Corolla south to Nags Head and Hatteras Island. In addition, they offer several package vacations—such as kayak nature tours and big game fishing—that allow guests to truly experience the Outer Banks.

Season: Year-round.

Accommodations: Upon request, the agency will send you a rental brochure with color photographs and complete descriptions of all their offerings, which include oceanfront properties and those a short walk from the beach. Homes are all equipped for normal housekeeping.

Special Features: Amenities include walkways to the beach, outside showers, sun decks, a screened porch with picnic table and swing, and a roof-level deck with an ocean view.

Cost: During high season, beach homes start at $850 per week.

Nearby: Kite flying and hang gliding on the high dunes at Jockey's Ridge State Park in Nags Head, the Wright Brothers National Memorial, North Carolina Aquarium on Roanoke Island, Manteo's historical sites (for more activities in this area, see the introduction on page 231).

CAROLINA DESIGNS REALTY

Address: Carolina Designs Realty, 1197 Duck Road, Duck, North Carolina 27949
Telephone: Reservations: 800–368–3825; information: 919–261–3934

This agency and property management firm handles finely appointed weekly beach vacation homes in Corolla, Duck, Southern Shores, Kitty Hawk, and Kill Devil Hills. All you need to bring is your bath and beach towels! They will send you a color magazine with an exterior and interior photograph of each home along with full descriptions; floorplans are also available. Among the listings are many palatial whitewashed-wood oceanfront homes that accommodate as many as sixteen people; these properties offer a good value for vacationing with another family or for large family gatherings.

Season: Year-round.

Accommodations: Homes vary from oceanfront and soundfront properties to homes on the canal, in the woods, or near the dunes. Some are set in subdivisions built around a sports complex or an outdoor or indoor pool.

Special Features: All represented properties have central air-conditioning, a washer and dryer, cable TV, a telephone, a fully equipped kitchen, an outside grill, and freshly made beds. Extra amenities vary from home to home but might include a family video and reading library, games, puzzles, a Jacuzzi, a porch swing, a volleyball net, screened porches, decks with beach furniture, fish cleaning tables, and a large outside shower.

Cost: During the height of the summer, an oceanfront home for eight people starts at $1,040 per week; an oceanfront home for ten $1,180 per week; an oceanfront home for sixteen $1,950 per week. Oceanside home for ten $990 per week; for eight $795 per week. Rates are considerably lower off-season.

Nearby: For activities in this area, see the introduction on page 231.

THE CRYSTAL COAST, NORTH CAROLINA

The Crystal Coast and its sixty-five miles of expansive white beaches continues to lure families for swimming, shelling, fishing, and exploring. This stretch of the Carolinas includes Morehead City, Atlantic Beach to Emerald Island, Cape Cateret, Down East, historic Beaufort, and several barrier islands with secluded beaches accessible only by ferry. One of the many fun side trips is going to the Cape Lookout National Seashore, fifty-five miles of barrier islands and home to the Cape Lookout Lighthouse. On Carrot Island, Shackleford Banks, and Cape Lookout, wild banker ponies roam freely.

Long a center for sea adventures, historic Beaufort is a charming, restored eighteenth-century fishing community that is fun to explore. Kids can see navigational instruments and models of historic ships at the North Carolina Maritime Museum (919–728–7317), visit buildings dating back to the mid-1700s in the Beaufort Historic Site, or spend the day hunting for sand dollars at the Rachel Carson estaurine, a complex of salt marshes and tidal flats inhabited by many unusual species of birds.

Linking Beaufort and Morehead City is the bustling town of Atlantic

Beach. Fort Macon State Park, a Civil War fort with nature trails, is the beach here most favored by locals. Kids enjoy playing at the fort, and there are lifeguards at designated spots. If you plan a Sunday morning visit, you will most likely see the Carolina Kite Club engage in their weekly high-flying show. The North Carolina Aquarium at Pine Knoll Shores on Bogue Banks (919–247–4003) gives you a fish's-eye view of the ocean and makes for a great rainy-day outing. Casting off the piers makes Bogue Banks a haven for fishing—it is hard not to catch something.

CRYSTAL COAST RENTALS

Address: 7413 Emerald Drive, Emerald Isle, North Carolina 28594; or 515 Morehead Avenue, Atlantic Beach, North Carolina 28512 Telephone: Emerald Isle Office: 800–367–3381, 919–354–3040; Atlantic Beach Office: 800–334–6390, 919–247–1100

This rental agency handles weekly oceanfront, soundfront, "second row from the beach," and oceanview cottage rentals and condominiums on Emerald Isle, Atlantic Beach, Pine Knoll Shores, and Indian Beach. Upon request, they will send you a booklet with color photographs describing all your options.

Season: Year-round.

Accommodations: A full range of accommodations are available from small cottages to large beach homes that accommodate as many as twenty-one people. Think about sharing an oceanfront home with another family or two, or planning a family reunion! Homes are equipped for housekeeping with everything except linens, paper products, beach or recreational items, and cleaning materials.

Special Features: You will find homes with outdoor showers, private and lighted walkways to the beach, sun decks, Jacuzzis, fireplaces, gazebos, screened porches, outdoor barbecues, and beach furniture.

Cost: During high season, oceanfront homes range from $675 per week (for a duplex on Atlantic Beach that accommodates six people) to $1,900 per week (for an enormous home for twenty-one people on Emerald Isle). Soundfront cottages average $800 to $1,000 per week for homes that accommodate up to eleven people. Cottages that accommodate up to twelve people second row in from the beach and those with ocean views range from $500 to $900 per week. Rates are considerably lower off-season.

Nearby: For local activities, see the Crystal Coast's introduction on page 233.

ALAN SHELOR BEACH RENTALS

Address: Alan Shelor Rentals, PO Box 2290, Atlantic Beach, North Carolina 28512 (agent)
Telephone: 800–786–RENT; 919–240–RENT

Atlantic Beach, located on the eastern end of Bogue Banks, is one of the most bustling beach towns of the Crystal Coast. Families are drawn to the beach at Fort Macon, Jungleland amusement park, and the area's many fishing piers. Alan Shelor Rentals handles a number of reasonably priced vacation rentals in Atlantic Beach, either on the beach or a short distance away. They will send you a brochure with complete rental descriptions and black-and-white photographs.

Season: Year-round.

Accommodations: Examples of listings include the oceanview Anderson Duplex, which sleeps six; it has beach access and an outside shower. The Gangwer Cottage and Buck Cottage are both easy walks to the beach; each sleeps six. Southwinds Condominiums are two-bedroom units near Fort Macon State Park. The units sleep six people and have access to two pools.

Special Features: Linens, cribs, and high chairs available to rent.

Cost: Anderson Duplex $450 per week in summer, $350 per week off-season, Gangwer Cottage $425 per week in summer, $350 per week off-season. Buck Cottage $400 per week in summer, $325 off-season. Southwinds Condominiums $525 per week in-season, $400 per week off-season.

Nearby: For other local activities, see the Crystal Coast's introduction on page 233.

OCRACOKE ISLAND AND HATTERAS ISLAND, NORTH CAROLINA

A highly recommended day trip from Beaufort or Hatteras—or a longer vacation destination—is wild and beautiful fourteen-mile-long Ocracoke Island. From Beaufort, it is an hour's drive to Coast Island, and then an inexpensive two-hour ferry ride to Ocracoke. The island has a few restaurants and shops, and many places to swim, bike, and explore; the beaches here are absolutely beautiful, with wide expanses of sand and clear water. Part of the Cape Hatteras National Seashore, Ocracoke has endless low dunes, wildflowers, loons, and geese. You can walk or bike around the island to see the working fishing village and its glistening lighthouse, go shelling and swimming, and even spend the night at the island's National Park Service campground (800–365–CAMP).

One of the nicest ways to enjoy Ocracoke is by renting a vacation cottage. For rentals call Ocracoke Island Realty at 919–928–6261 or Sharon Miller Realty at 919–928–5711. Another way to see Ocracoke is to rent an oceanfront home on Hatteras Island and take the ferry over for the day. Agencies specializing in cottage and home rentals on Hatteras are Midgett Realty (800–527–2903) and Hatteras Realty (800–428–8372).

WRIGHTSVILLE BEACH, NORTH CAROLINA

CAROLINA TEMPLE APARTMENTS

Address: PO Box 525, Wrightsville Beach, North Carolina 28480
Telephone: 910–256–2773; fax: 910–256–3878

Wrightsville Beach is a peaceful seaside community at the southern tip of North Carolina along the Cape Fear Coast, between the Intracoastal Waterway and the Atlantic Ocean. Families congregate at the three-mile stretch of beach between the town's two fishing piers for long days of shelling, boogie boarding, and swimming. Built just after the turn of the century, the Carolina Temple Apartments offer simple yet immaculate quarters with kitchenettes and, in classic southern fashion, a beautiful wraparound porch with rocking chairs and an occasional well-placed hammock with water views. The property is located on the narrow south end of the beach and spans the island from the ocean to the sound. There are two large plantation-style buildings, the oceanfront Carolina Cottage and the sound-front Temple Cottage. Each two-story structure has eight efficiency apartments.

Season: Late March to early November.

Accommodations: Two- or three-room efficiencies can accommodate four or six guests respectively. Most can also be supplied with an additional crib or rollaway bed. Every unit is air-conditioned, has a fully equipped kitchen, private bath, ceiling fan, and TV. Bed linens included.

Special Features: Ocean- and sound-front beach, private sound-side pier with docking facilities, patio and picnic area with charcoal grills, TV and VCR room with video and book library, shaded sand box play area, laundry facilities, spring and fall breakfast, Easter egg hunt, Thanksgiving holiday flotilla and fireworks display.

Cost: June through August, weekly rentals only; spring and fall, nightly or split-week rentals available. Off-season, $300 to $500 per week, $80 to $100 per weekend night, $60 to $80 per week night depending on size of unit. In-season, $500 to $700 per week depending on size of unit.

Nearby: Johnnie Mercer's Pier and Oceanic Pier are magnets for fishing families. For clams and oysters, try the marsh grass at Masonboro Island. You can purchase fresh fish daily at Mott's Channel Seafood (910–256–FISH). Bert's Surf Shop and Aussie's Island Surf Shop, both in the center of town, rent surfing and beach gear. Boats are for rent through Sea Mark Boats (910–350–0039), or you can take a cruise to Masonboro Island, a nine-mile barrier island packed with wildlife, on a forty-foot pontoon with a marine biologist; call Blockade Runner Scenic Cruises (910–350–BOAT).

When you tire of the beach, spend the day checking out the noted family events at the North Carolina Aquarium at Fort Fisher (910–458–7468), or visit the Wrightsville Beach Parks and Recreation Center, a thirteen-acre park with sports fields and sailing, surfing and kayaking lessons. Wrightsville Beach is a ten-minute drive from the historic center of Wilmington, where kids love the horse carriage rides, the Wilmington Railroad Museum (910–763–2634), or tours of the Battleship *North Carolina* (910–350–1817). Also nearby is the Jubilee Amusement Park in Carolina Beach with three water slides.

Note: Renting a beach house (average price $800 per week) is one of the most economical ways to visit Wrightsville Beach. Bryant Realty (800–322–3764) has many listings which range from little cottages to palatial homes with porches looking eastward to the sea or westward over the Intracoastal Waterway. During high season (April to October), boats line the Intracoastal Waterway and put on quite a flotilla show which is fun to watch from your cottage porch.

THE SOUTH CAROLINA COAST

Bargain hunters will be delighted by the many oceanfront state park vacation cabins along South Carolina's coast, an area also known for its isolated sea islands and miles of sandy beaches. Visitors arriving in the state from the north will find many resort amenities at the bustling vacation hub of Myrtle Beach and the nearby seaside communities along the fifty-five-mile Grand Strand. Myrtle Beach, albeit frenetic, has a broad and beckoning beach; many accommodations, shops, restaurants, honky-tonk carnival-type amusements and kid's activities; and enough golfing, tennis, and water sports to keep every member of the family busy. Accommodations for Myrtle Beach are listed on pages 238–239.

From Myrtle Beach south to Charleston along U.S. 17, Huntington Beach State Park, adjacent to the lush Brookgreen Garden, has one of the best public beaches on the Grand Strand, with picnic facilities, a playground, calm ocean swimming, nature trails, ocean fishing, and in-

terpretive programs. Kids will enjoy touring Charleston's eighteenth-
and nineteenth-century historic district by horse-drawn carriage.

The area around Charleston has some of the east's most pristine
beaches and resorts, especially on Kiawah Island, Isle of Palms, and Seabrook Island. Here you will find long, wide expanses of coastline rich
with dunes, marshes, and wildlife. For rental agencies that rent homes
in these resort areas, see pages 240–243.

South from Charleston, the coast has many sea islands separated from
the mainland by salt marshes. Family-oriented Edisto Island still has remnants of the past with old plantation houses, small fishing villages, abundant wildlife and a shell laden beach—although it, too, is slowly
becoming more developed. Along with state park cabins, there are many
cottages for rent at reasonable rates. These are listed on pages 240–241.
The island has mild weather year-round, with daytime temperatures that
average from the mid-eighties to nineties during the summer and mid-
forties to low sixties in winter. Nearby Hunting Island is a large secluded
barrier island with semitropical beauty and an abundance of wildlife
near historic Beaufort. Its broad, sweeping beach with state park cabins,
listed on page 241–242, is one of its main attractions as well as a great
vacation bargain.

MYRTLE BEACH STATE PARK CABINS

Address: U.S. Highway 17, Myrtle Beach, South Carolina 29577
**Telephone: 803-238-5325. Due to the popularity of these cabins,
it is advisable to book well in advance; they start taking reservations the first Monday in January for the upcoming year.**

This coastal park has five two-bedroom vacation cabins that sleep up to
six people and two apartments that sleep either three or eight. In addition to a great swimming beach you'll find picnic facilities, a playground, a pool, nature trails, ocean fishing, interpretive programs, and
a nature center.

Season: Year-round.

Accommodations: All accommodations are furnished, heated, air-
conditioned, supplied with linens, and equipped with all cookware and
eating utensils.

Special Features: Laundry facilities.

Cost: Cabins $55 per night on weekend nights, $50 per night Monday
through Thursday, $150 per weekend (Friday through Sunday), and
$300 per week. Apartments $39 to $55 per night on weekend nights,
$34 to $50 per night Monday through Thursday, $102 to $150 per week-

end (Friday through Sunday), and $204 to $300 per week. Rates lower November through March.

Nearby: See the South Carolina introduction on page 237 for more area attractions. In addition, children enjoy the Myrtle Beach Pavilion Amusement Park (803–448–6456), which has the largest water flume in the Carolinas.

BEACH COLONY RESORT

Address: 5308 North Ocean Boulevard, Myrtle Beach, South Carolina 29577
Telephone: 800–222–2141; 803–449–4010

A bustling twelve-story Myrtle Beach oceanfront resort, the Beach Colony has a multitude of family activities including family musicals right on site. During the summer, they run a Children's Activities Program, and an exercise room, exercise trail, and racquetball court are available year-round. The resort is not shy of heated pools—it has three spacious outdoor pools which include a kiddie pool, whirlpool, and a pool with a lazy river ride, all with ocean views, and a year-round indoor pool and whirlpool.

Season: Year-round.

Accommodations: Oceanfront or ocean-view suites or condominiums with one to four bedrooms have living rooms, many different sleeping arrangements, private balconies, and kitchens with microwave ovens.

Special Features: Entertainment including family musicals, restaurant, two poolside bars.

Cost: June through September, ocean-view suite for two adults and four children $84 to $115 per night (depending on month); oceanfront suite for two adults and four children $103 to $149 per night; oceanview two-bedroom condominium for four adults and two children $130 to $149 per night; oceanfront two-bedroom condominium for four adults and two children starts at $150 per night. Weekly rates available for the oceanfront condominiums during the summer. Rates significantly lower January through May. Discounts for stays of three nights or longer. Entertainment and golf packages available.

Nearby: Championship golf courses, free tennis at Myrtle Beach tennis club, recreation center including free bowling at nearby Captain's Quarters. See the South Carolina introduction on page 237 and Myrtle Beach State Park Cabins on page 238 for more area attractions.

VACATION RENTALS ON KIAWAH ISLAND, ISLE OF PALMS, AND SEABROOK ISLAND

This area around Charleston has some of the east's most beautiful beaches and world-famous resorts with long, wide expanses of coastline dotted with dunes, marshes, and wildlife. A number of private rental agencies will help you find a home or condominium in these resort areas. Rates can be cheaper than renting directly through the resort; when calling be sure to inquire about charges for outside guests who want to take advantage of the children's programs and pools. Dunes Properties rents homes and condominiums on Isle of Palms, which is the closest major resort area to downtown Charleston; call 800–476–8444. Beachwalker Rentals (800–334–6308) and Pam Harrington Exclusives (800–845–6966) both rent properties on beautiful Kiawah Island. Ravenel Associates rents homes and condominiums on Kiawah, Seabrook, and Wild Dunes; call 800–247–5050.

EDISTO BEACH STATE PARK CABINS

Address: 8377 State Cabin Road, Edisto Island, South Carolina 29438 (on the ocean, fifty miles southeast of Charleston)
Telephone: 803–869–2756. Due to the popularity of these cabins, it is advisable to book well in advance; the park starts taking reservations the first Monday in January for the upcoming year.

This beachfront park is rich in Indian history and has some of the state's tallest palmetto trees. Its five vacation cabins are 1.8 miles from the beach. There is a salt marsh and a beach for swimming and hunting for seashells and fossils. Should you tire of the beach, there are picnic areas, a playground, hiking trails, fishing, boat ramps, and seasonal interpretive programs.

Season: Year-round.

Accommodations: Cabins have two bedrooms and sleep up to six. All are furnished, heated, air-conditioned, supplied with linens, and equipped with all cookware and eating utensils.

Cost: Cabins $52 per night, $141 per weekend (Friday through Sunday), and $282 per week. Rates are lower November through March.

Nearby: See the South Carolina introduction on page 237 for more area attractions.

EDISTO ISLAND VACATION RENTALS

Address: Edisto Sales and Rental Realty, 1405 Palmetto Boulevard, Edisto Beach, South Carolina 29438
Phone: 800–868–5398; 803–869–2527

Family-oriented Edisto Beach and Island still has remnants of its southern past with old plantation houses available for tours, fresh shrimp arriving daily from small fleets, abundant wildlife, and a shell-laden beach. Edisto Sales and Rental Realty handles a number of reasonable vacation rentals either on the Atlantic Ocean or at St. Helena Sound, in addition to homes just a short walk to the beach. They will send you a color magazine that describes all their listings.

Season: Year-round.

Accommodations: A wide variety of homes (oceanfront, ocean view, or a short walk to the beach) are available. The homes are fully furnished with the exception of bed and bath linens. As an example, beachfront "Edistow" has two bedrooms, one and a half baths, air-conditioning, and a sun deck. "Fish Called Wanda," across from the beach, has two- and three-bedroom apartments. The "Bradley" is a block from the beach and sleeps ten people. The "R & R" is a new four-bedroom home, one block from the beach, which also sleeps ten people.

Special Features: Beach chairs, beach towels, and floats are provided.

Cost: During the summer, the Edistow $775 per week, Fish Called Wanda $470 per week, the Bradley $595 per week, the R & R $690 per week. Rates are lower off-season.

Nearby: There is public access to bike paths, an eighteen-hole golf course, tennis courts, and a marina for boat and fish charters. Parasailing and jet ski rentals can be arranged. Edisto is one hour south of Charleston and two hours north of Savannah and Hilton Head. See the South Carolina introduction on page 237 for more area attractions.

HUNTING ISLAND STATE PARK CABINS

Address: 1775 Sea Island Parkway, St. Helena Island, South Carolina 29920 (located midway between Charleston and Savannah)
Telephone: 803–838–2011. Due to the popularity of these cabins, it is advisable to book well in advance; the park starts taking reservations the first Monday in January for the upcoming year.

Hunting Island, near historic Beaufort, is a large secluded barrier island with semitropical beauty and an abundance of wildlife. If you are looking for a beach vacation with a focus on wildlife, this is the place. Expect to see alligators sunning themselves at the Visitor Center pond, dolphins swimming in the surf, and otters playing in the lagoon. The park's broad four-mile undeveloped beach is perfect for swimming, and there are picnic areas, a playground, hiking trails, a boat ramp, a fishing pier, a boardwalk for nature observation, and seasonal interpretive programs. Fifteen two- and three-bedroom vacation cabins sleep six, eight, or ten people. Some of the cabins are oceanfront; others are a short walk from the beach.

Season: Year-round.

Accommodations: A few of the cabins have fireplaces. All are completely furnished, heated, air-conditioned, supplied with linens, and equipped with all cookware and eating utensils.

Special Features: A wooded boardwalk and nature trails lead through varying environments from salt marshes and maritime forests to saltwater lagoons—you are likely to see egrets, alligators, deer, and raccoons. Wading on the beach, you can spot sea combs, blowfish, and hermit crabs. The park runs a sea turtle Carolina Explorer program for adults and children to look for tracks and nests of large reptiles. Other children's programs are offered daily, including a snake program. There is also a pier for surf casting off the beach and fishing at the lagoon; bait can be purchased at the park's tackle shop. Climb the 132-foot-high park lighthouse for wonderful views.

Cost: Cabins $65 to $80 per night on weekend nights, depending on type of cabin; $60 to $75 per night Monday through Thursday; $180 to $225 per weekend (Friday through Sunday) and $360 to $450 per week.

Nearby: The park is sixteen miles east of historic Beaufort, noted for its huge water festival in July. For information about Beaufort, call its Chamber of Commerce at 803–524–3163.

HILTON HEAD ISLAND FOREST BEACH VACATION
VILLAS

Address: Shoreline Rental Company, PO Box 6275, Hilton Head Island, South Carolina 29938
Telephone: 800–334–5012, 803–842–3006; fax: 803–842–8857

We found the Hilton Head Beach Club Villas and Seascape Villas, both on Forest Beach and represented by Shoreline Rental Company, to be a bargain for the popular resort community of Hilton Head Island. The island has twelve miles of pristine sandy ocean beach and a wonderful semitropical climate, and is famous for its championship golf courses and tennis and water sport facilities. Hilton Head Beach Club Villas are two-bedroom apartments on ground-floor level, just yards from a family-oriented beach. The Seascape villas have either two or three bedrooms; they are a short walk from another pleasant beach.

Season: Year-round.

Accommodations: With two bedrooms and one and a half bathrooms, the Hilton Head Beach Club apartments sleep four to six people. The Seascape villas sleep six to eight people in ground-floor units with either two or three bedrooms.

Special Features: The Hilton Head Beach Club has a swimming pool. Seascape Villas have a children's play yard and a pool. Both have free tennis passes for the Van der Meer Tennis Center.

Cost: In summer, Hilton Head Beach Club apartments $695 per week; in spring and fall $475 per week; in winter $450 per week. Seascape Villa's two- and three-bedroom units $650 and $875 per week in summer; $465 per week and $540 per week in spring and fall, respectively; and $450 and $500 per week in winter.

Nearby: Accommodations are close to shopping, restaurants, bike paths, and a water fun park. The beach sand on Hilton Head is hard enough for bicycling; for rentals try Hilton Head Bicycle (803–686–6886). Shore Beach Service (803–785–3494) rents catamarans, aquacycles, boogie boards, and more. See the South Carolina Coast introduction on page 237 for more of the general area's attractions.

THE GEORGIA COAST

Many beautiful and family-friendly beaches are found along the Georgia Coast and its barrier islands; here we list accommodations on Jekyll Island, Sea Island, Tybee Island, and a unique hostel in Brunswick. A fun side trip from any of these destinations is to the magical and tranquil eighteen-mile Cumberland Island National Seashore, the southernmost barrier island in the Georgia Sea Island, which is separated from the mainland by a salt marsh, the river, and the sound. On the ocean side of the island, a vast beach stretches out of sight, speckled liberally with an abundance of shells at low tide. A barrier of high sand dunes protects the island. It is here among the sea oats that the female loggerhead turtles come ashore in summer to lay their eggs. The central part of the island is inhabited by armadillos, deer, raccoons, wild turkeys, and wild horses. The park is accessible by ferry from St. Mary's. Summer temperatures range from the eighties to low nineties; during the summer it is best to visit the beach early and late in the day.

The Okefenokee Swamp Park (912–283–0583), eight miles south of Waycross on U.S. 1, is another wildlife sanctuary of astounding beauty with exhibits, trails, and boat tours on original Indian waterways. Other attractions include the Serpentarium and Wildlife Observatory, a "Swamp Creation Center," the "Living Swamp Center," and Pioneer Island's authentic swamp homestead, complete with rare artifacts. For more on the Okefenokee Swamp, see pages 189 and 190.

Note: Midway between Savannah and Jacksonville, Florida is the barrier island of St. Simons Island, a year-round resort community. The best beaches in this area are right nearby on Sea Island, accessible by boat or ferry. Specializing in home rentals on Sea Island is Sea Island Cottage Rentals at 912–638–5112.

TYBEE ISLAND VACATION RENTALS & LIGHTHOUSE POINT BEACH CLUB

Address: Tybee Island Rentals, PO Box 627, Tybee Island, Georgia 31328
Telephone: 800–476–0807; 912–786–4034

Not as pristine as Cumberland to the south or as upscale as Hilton Head to the north, Tybee Island, just fifteen minutes from Savannah, is a small and unpretentious island community with one main road where your family can vacation at an unhurried pace. Weathered summer cottages and yucca-covered dunes dot the landscape, and there are great beaches for swimming and shelling. The oceanfront villas at the Lighthouse Point Beach Club have pools and easy access to Tybee Island's North Beach, which is a quiet stretch of coastline noted for shelling and shorebirds. Villas have breathtaking views of the Atlantic. Tybee Island Rentals also has cottages and beach houses for rent around the island.

Season: Year-round.

Accommodations: Beach club villas have two bedrooms and two baths and sleep up to six people. They each have a color TV, wet bar, washer, dryer, dishwasher, and a queen-size sofabed in the living room. Homes and cottage rentals vary in size (they sleep as many as fifteen people), amenities, and access to the beach. The agency will send you a brochure with black-and-white photographs and complete descriptions of all its listings.

Special Features: Beach club has tennis courts, swimming pools, and a playground. Many of the homes and cottage rentals are steps from the beach, are air-conditioned, and have screened porches or sun decks and outdoor showers.

Cost: Mid-April to mid-September, oceanview villas at the beach club $125 per night, $875 weekly; poolview villas $115 per night, $805 weekly. Mid-September to mid-April oceanview villas $105 nightly, $735 weekly; poolview villas $95 nightly, $665 weekly.

Mid-April to mid-September homes and cottages are rented by the week; off-season they are available nightly. High-season rates average $800 per week for homes that sleep six people within walking distance of the beach.

Nearby: Sea bass and sea trout fishing is recommended from the jetties at North and South Beach. Guided fishing excursions are available from Chimney Creek Fishing Camp (912–786–5917). The Tybee Island Marine Science Center (912–786–5801) has interactive marine biology exhibits. South Beach is the island's most popular due to its easy access and food stands. Children enjoy the carousel at Tybee Amusement Park and the climb up to the Tybee Island Lighthouse (also a museum); you'll be rewarded with a view from Tybee to Savannah and Hilton Head. Bicycling, tennis, and superb golf courses are also nearby. A half-hour drive brings you to historic Savannah.

BEST WESTERN JEKYLL INN OCEANFRONT RESORT AND VILLAS

Address: 975 North Beachview Drive, Jekyll Island, Georgia 31527
Telephone: 800–736–1046; 912–635–2531; fax: 912–635–2332

In the late 1800s, Jekyll Island, off the southern Georgia coast, was the private getaway of the Vanderbilts, Morgans, and Rockerfellers. The mansions of the old Wall Street families still exist (thirty-three have been restored for public viewing), but today the island is run by the state and is reasonably priced. Set on fifteen secluded acres on a half-mile of beach, the Jekyll Inn is the largest oceanfront resort on the island. The atmosphere is very casual and family-oriented.

Season: Year-round.

Accommodations: A total of 188 oceanfront, oceanview, or courtside standard hotel rooms all have their own deck or patio. There are also seventy-four villas with spacious living and dining areas, fully equipped kitchens with dishwasher, color TV, telephone, and private patio. The one-bedroom villa has one and one-half baths and accommodates four adults. The two-bedroom villas sleep six with a larger living and dining area, a full bath upstairs, and a half-bath downstairs.

Special Features: Half-mile of beach, Olympic-size pool, volleyball, badminton, shuffleboard, playground, fish restaurant, poolside bar.

Cost: Rates vary depending on time of year (May 10 to August 17 is high season; November 15 to February 15 is low season, and there are shoulder seasons the rest of the year). Courtyard rooms $57 to $103 per night and $309 to $520 per week; oceanview rooms $67 to $114 per night and $362 to $572 per week; oceanfront $77 to $145 per night and $414 to $624 per week. Room rates based on double occupancy; additional person $5 to $10 per night.

One-bedroom villas $81 to $166 per night and $446 to $939 per week for four people; two-bedroom villas $98 to $166 per night and $551 to $939 per week for six people. Rates vary depending on time of year.

Nearby: The island is great for bike riding; bike rental is available on North Beachview Drive (912–635–2648). Take a ride out to the island's northern tip, where there are small inlets that are fun for catching crabs. Also a short drive away are four challenging golf courses, a fitness center with membership by the day (912–635–2232), and a thirteen-court tennis center, illuminated for night playing. Golf is cheap here—for about $20 you can play all day. Fishing boats sail daily from the Jekyll Island marina to catch red snapper and black bass or to watch dolphins. There are covered picnic shelters along the beach and organized nature walks led by docents of the University of Georgia Marine Extension Service (912–635–2232). The Jekyll Island Day Camp (912–635–2232) will keep your four- to twelve-year-olds busy with beach games, treasure hunts, swimming, and bike hikes ($8 per half-day, $15 per day, $50 per week, which includes lunch). There is also cable waterskiing (912–635–3802) on a twelve-acre lake without a boat, and an eleven-acre water park called "Splashtacular," with seven slides, an endless river, a huge wave pool, and a children's slide (912–635–2074).

Note: For cottage rentals on Jekyll Island call Parker-Kaufman Realtors at 912–635–2512. They handle reasonably priced one- to six-bedroom cottages either on the beach or a short distance away. Among the listings are three-bedroom houses for eight within walking distance of the beach for $390 to $490 per week in summer.

HOSTEL IN THE FOREST

Address: PO Box 1496, Brunswick, Georgia 31521 (located halfway between Savannah, Georgia and Jacksonville, Florida, two miles west of I-95 on U.S. 82)
Telephone: 912–264–9738; 912–265–0220; 912–638–2623. Reservations are not accepted.

This is one of America's unique and most-photographed hostels. Kids will not forget spending the night in its treehouses or geodesic domes. It also has a swimming pool and a fish pond. The hostel is ten miles from the beaches at Jekyll Island. The Cumberland Island National Seashore and National Wildlife Refuge are also nearby.

Season: Year-round.
Accommodations: Families can sleep together in four of the geo-desic domes, or in three of the seven treehouses.
Special Features: Baggage storage, kitchen, laundry facilities, linen rental, on-site parking, and shuttle service to downtown.
Cost: Adults $9 per night. Children under nine half price.
Nearby: See the introduction on page 243 for specific activities in this area.

AMELIA ISLAND, FLORIDA

Families are drawn to Amelia Island for its thirteen miles of beautiful wide, white beaches with tall dunes, its world-class resorts, vacation cottages, and camping. You can choose to have an active vacation, or to simply relax. Kids enjoy the Eight Flags Water Slide in nearby Fernandina Beach, horseback riding along the beach at Seahorse Stables, or riding bikes along the island's many jogging paths. A fun day trip is to take the ferry from Georgia's St. Mary's to nearby Cumberland Island (see page 243), where you'll find miles of deserted beaches and wildlife.

Specializing in home and cottage rentals on the island are Amelia Island Lodging System (800–872–8531 or 904–261–4148) and Amelia Island Rental and Management Services (800–874–8679 or 904–261–9129).

ST. AUGUSTINE, FLORIDA

Founded in 1565, St. Augustine is the oldest permanent European settlement in the continental United States and is filled with reminders of its Spanish history. This blend of history combined with fine swimming beaches make it a popular family vacation destination. Oceanfront accommodations are primarily condominium/resort complexes. Like many Florida beaches, this one allows cars on the beach. If you are nervous about keeping track of young kids amid vehicles, consider a quiet day by the pool at your condominium resort complex.

Guides in Colonial dress will accompany you on a trip through the carefully restored Spanish Quarter for a re-created glimpse of how this community of Spanish soldiers, settlers, craftspeople, and their families lived in the eighteenth century. History abounds in the country's oldest store, the oldest house, and the oldest wooden schoolhouse, as well as in the narrow cobblestone streets, Colonial-style shops, and classic cathedral. There are many ways to explore the city—on foot, by tram, by horse-drawn carriage (boarded on the bayfront south of the fort), or even from a seventy-five-minute cruise along the bay.

Kids can get the feel of a real castle at Castillo de San Marcos (904–829–6505), built in 1672, with an impressive moat and drawbridge, huge cannons, and sentinel turret. National Park Service ranger tours that explain the fort's history are easy for kids to understand. The Fountain of Youth Archaeological Park (904–829–3168), where Ponce de Leon came ashore in 1513, has a planetarium, Indian burial site, train station, and significant landmarks.

The Oldest House, aka the Gonzales-Alvarez House (904–824–2872), has remnants that span hundreds of years. The kitchen and living areas have relics from as early as Florida's first settlement. Likewise, the Oldest Store Museum (904–829–9729) shows how people shopped for such items as corsets and bicycles at the turn of the century. Students dressed in period costumes show how time was spent in school before the American Revolution at the Oldest Wooden Schoolhouse (904–824–0192). Visitors can also tour an authentic Old Jail (904–829–3800).

Children enjoy climbing to the top of the Lighthouse Museum; as a reward for huffing and puffing you'll find a panoramic view of the city. Replicas of Napoleon Bonaparte and many other historical figures are at the Wax Museum (904–829–9056), and Ripley's Believe It or Not Collection (904–824–1606) is chock full of oddball displays such as a dummy of the world's fattest man. White Bird's Family Fun Resort has an eighteen-hole adventure golf course and arcade games. Zorayda Castle (904–824–3097), modeled after Spain's Alhambra in Granada, has harem quarters, a mummy's foot, and mosaic tiles from an Egyptian mosque. East of the castle, the Museum of Weapons and Early American History (904–829–3727) has unique displays, including items from the Civil War.

Reptile enthusiasts will want to visit the Alligator Farm (904–824–3337) south of the city, where you can watch gators snapping away from an elevated walkway. Twelve miles south of the city is Marineland (904–471–1111), with 1,000 species of marine animals and daily dolphin shows. St. Augustine is less than two hours from Disney World (see page 15) and Sea World, and about two hours from the Kennedy Space Center.

South of Marineland at Washington Oaks Gardens State Park on State Road A1A south is Boulder Beach, a large protected area of stone formations. The rocks are a bit tricky to navigate for children younger than seven. Its outcropping is a rocky mixture of shells, coral, and sand. A museum of natural and cultural history is on the grounds, as are tidal marshes, hiking trails, and a picnic area.

ST. AUGUSTINE HOSTEL

Address: 32 Treasury Street, St. Augustine, Florida 32804 (five blocks east off U.S. 1)
Telephone and fax: 904–808–1999. **Reservations essential for private rooms and are advisable for other rooms January through March. Phone reservations are accepted.**

This clean and homey hostel, located in the city's historic Spanish District behind the Cathedral, is three miles from the beach. It is within walking distance to the City Gates, restored houses, the Oldest Store Museum, the Oldest Schoolhouse, the Old Jail, and the Oldest House.
Season: Year-round.
Accommodations: Family rooms are available in this small seven-room hostel. A family room has a double bed and oversize bunk beds for children as well as its own private bathroom. All rooms are air-conditioned.
Special Features: Spacious and tranquil common room with an organ, fish tank, and couches; roof garden, baggage storage area, well-equipped kitchen, linen rental, on-site parking, surfboard and inexpensive bike rentals. The welcoming managers will arrange sailing excursions for guests.
Cost: Private room $28 per night. Dorm-style room: adults $12 per night; children under ten free; children over ten $6 per night.
Nearby: See the introduction to St. Augustine on page 247 for specific activities.

OCEAN GALLERY

Address: 4600 Highway A1A South, St. Augustine, Florida 32084
Telephone: 800–940–6665, 904–471–6663; fax: 904–471–5994

This forty-acre oceanfront resort complex of four hundred condominiums on a quarter mile of St. Augustine Beach has fully equipped apartments, a weight room, two saunas, four tennis courts, two racquetball courts, two shuffleboard courts, four outdoor pools with hot tubs, one indoor/outdoor pool heated in the winter, and two walkways to the beach.
Season: Year-round.
Accommodations: The condos are completely equipped for housekeeping and have washers and dryers. There are two- and three-bedroom units with two bathrooms on the ocean and less expensive one-, two-, and three-bedroom units a short walk from the beach. The

one-bedrooms sleep up to four people; the two-bedrooms sleep up to six people; the three-bedrooms sleep up to eight.

Cost: March through August, oceanfront two-bedroom, two-bath unit $715 to $770 per week, depending on view. Away from the beach, apartments $480 to $620 per week, depending on location and number of bedrooms. Off-season rates lower. Additional $10 guard fee and $50 to $55 cleaning fee.

Nearby: The complex is a short drive from the downtown historical section and fifteen minutes from Marineland. Golf, fishing, and boating are nearby. See the introduction to St. Augustine on page 247 for specific activities.

VERO BEACH, FLORIDA

THE DRIFTWOOD RESORT

Address: 3150 Ocean Drive, Vero Beach, Florida 32963
Telephone: 561–231–0550

The climate is pleasant at Vero Beach, which is part barrier-island and part mainland, even in the height of summer. Moderate temperatures allow guests to take advantage of Florida's off-season, when prices are low. Some of the state's kid-favorite attractions are within a two-hour drive (the Space Center is eighty miles from Vero, while Disney World and Sea World are one hundred miles away). Established in the early 1900s, the Driftwood is built out of timber that washed ashore; it was recently named to the National Registry of Historic Places. The resort has not only updated its comfortable villas, which are directly on a nice sandy beach with private boardwalk access, but also has preserved many of the building's original antiquities.

Season: Year-round.

Accommodations: The resort's oceanview or oceanfront "vacation villas" are recommended for families on a budget. They are totally self-contained, have one or two bedrooms, and sleep a minimum of four people. All have kitchen facilities and a living room. Some have private Jacuzzis.

Special Features: Swimming pool overlooking the ocean, surf-side restaurant.

Cost: Off-season (Friday following Easter through December 21, January 2 through 31) oceanfront $85 to $110, oceanview $75 to $99, poolview $75 to $99, park or inn view $75, cottage $80, two-bedroom $130 to $140 per night. In-season (December 21 through January 1, February through Easter week and all holiday weekends), oceanfront $110 to

$170, oceanview $99 to $115, poolview $75 to $89, park or inn view $99, cottage $115, two-bedroom $160 to $210 per night.

Nearby: Jaycee Park Beach has an old-fashioned boardwalk, a playground, and a picnic area. Great waves are found at Wabasso Beach, eight miles north of town, where lifeguards, equipment rentals, and a snack bar make for a good day at the beach. In mainland Vero, rent all beach gear at Deep Six Watersports (561–562–2883) and bicycles at Bicycle Sports (561–569–5990). You can ride bikes on the island's seven-mile-long path, or if your family is up for mountain biking, try the unpaved Jungle Trail along the river's edge. Sebastian Inlet State Park (561–589–2147) has a three-mile guided turtle walk during the summer, which is the nesting season for the threatened Atlantic loggerhead turtle. Team up with another family to cruise the Indian River, which is part of the Intracoastal Waterway, on a self-skippered pontoon boat that carries ten people; call Captain Jack's Marina (561–231–0926). The river teems with wildlife; porpoises swim around the boats, and manatees are often spotted along the shore.

THE FLORIDA KEYS

A slice of tropical paradise can still be found in the Florida Keys, a chain of thirty-four subtropical islands connected by the Overseas Highway. Kitsch most certainly co-mingles with wild natural beauty, which will make a beach adventure here all the more varied and fun, especially for your kids. The tacky roadside attractions (Water-skiing parrots? You bet!) run the gamut from thatched tiki bars selling every possible seashell souvenir (there is even a shell "supermarket" called The Shell Man) to fast food stands with Cuban and Spanish fare. As you drive the stretch of highway linking these islands, you are bound to find stretches of land so narrow that sea—the open Atlantic and the turquoise Gulf of Mexico—and sky will almost surround your car.

At Dolphins Plus, a research center in Key Largo (305–451–1993), swimming with the dolphins cost $80 per half-hour for good swimmers ten and older; book at least six weeks in advance. No tricks or amusement park hoops here; this is a serious environmental education center. For more commercial, acrobatic-style dolphin and sea lion shows, visit the venerable Theater of the Sea in Middle Keys (305–664–2431); it has been around since the 1940s.

At Robbie's Boat Rental Marina (mile marker 77.5), children can safely feed tarpon fish that hang out under the dock pilings, jaws outstretched. Sunset cruises are available at Papa Joe's Marina (mile marker 79.7); you may be in luck and spot a wild dolphin! Highly recommended for families are the snorkel cruises on the *H.M.S. Looe* (800–553–0308), which depart daily from Dolphin Marina (next to Big Pine Key at mile marker 28.5) to the coral reefs at Looe Key National Marine Sanctuary; be sure to book in advance.

The Museum of Natural History and the Florida Keys Children's Museum (305–743–9100), located at Crane Point Hammock and run by the Keys Land and Sea Trust, make for an educational stop when you tire of sun and sand. On the other side of the spectrum, Ripley's Believe It or Not! Odditorium in Key West is what you would expect from this kid-pleasing chain. Not to be missed in Key West is the Blue Heaven (305–296–8666), which is not only a restaurant but also a wacky playground filled with local charm.

Note: In addition to the accommodations listed here, the Key West Hostel, a five-minute drive from the beach, has a private room that can accommodate families if reserved in advance. HI members, adults $14.50 per night; non-members $18. Children under sixteen half price. Call 305–296–5719.

CONCH KEY COTTAGES

Address: RR 1, Box 424, Marathon, Florida 33050. Conch Key is at mile marker 62.3.
Telephone: 800–330–1577; 305–289–1377

Set on its own private island, an old-fashioned atmosphere pervades at Conch Key, where many of the oceanfront cottages have screened porches and hammocks. The beach here is sandy-bottomed and lined by mangroves.

Season: Year-round.

Accommodations: Lattice-trimmed cottages with reed, rattan, and wicker furnishings are set amid gardens of allamanda, bougainvillea, and hibiscus. There are three one-bedroom cottages on the beach, and a four-plex with two one-bedroom apartments. All one-bedroom apartments have one king-size bed or one queen-size bed and a sofabed; they sleep four people. There is also a two-bedroom cottage with four double beds for eight people and a two-bedroom mobile home with one queen-size bed, one full-sized bed, and one futon for six people. All units are air-conditioned and have color TVs and full kitchens.

Special Features: Private marina, boat ramp and dock, heated fresh-water pool, barbecue grills, laundry facilities.

Cost: One-bedroom apartments $108 per night or $680 per week high season (mid-December through April 21 and June 9 through September 4), $83 per night or $520 per week off-season (April 22 through June 8 and September 5 through mid-December). One-bedroom beachfront cottage $168 per night or $1,078 per week high season, $128 per night or $840 per week off-season. Two-bedroom mobile home is $181 per night or $950 per week high season, $120 per night or $761 per week off-season. Two-bedroom cottage is more expensive.

Nearby: Easy access to magnificent coral reefs for snorkeling or fishing on the oceanside or to the Gulf for bonefish and tarpon fishing. For activities on the Keys, see page 251.

BAHIA HONDA STATE PARK

Address: 36850 Honda State Parkway, Big Pine Key, Florida 33043 Telephone: 305-872-2353. Cabins can be reserved up to one year in advance, by telephone or in person only.

The cabins at this 524-acre park on Big Pine Key are among the nicest (and least expensive) places to stay in the Keys. Graced with palm trees, pelicans, and abundant marine life of Caribbean origin (including parrot fish and sea turtles), Bahia Honda is unique among other islands in the Keys because of its extensive sandy beaches, which make for great swimming both in the Atlantic and in Florida Bay. Deep waters are close enough offshore to provide exceptional tarpon fishing and snorkeling. Visitors can also go on boating expeditions and take guided nature walks.

Season: Year-round.

Accommodations: In addition to camping sites, there are six duplex cabins on stilts that each sleep up to six people. Cabins have two bedrooms, a living room, a kitchen/dining room, and a full bath. There are two double beds, two bunk beds, and two cots. Basic cooking utensils, kitchenware, linens, and towels are provided. They have central air-conditioning and heat, a deck with picnic table, grill, and outside table. All are boat accessible.

Special Features: A dive shop rents snorkeling equipment, kayaks, bicycles, motorboats, and a miniature glass-bottom boat. The park has beachside picnicking with shaded picnic tables and grills. There are two boat launching ramps at the park's marina, and charter boats and guides are available for hire for tarpon fishing, which rates among the best in the state.

Cost: Mid-December to mid-September $124 per night for up to four family members; mid-September to mid-December $97 per night. Each additional adult $5.50 per night. Children stay free when sharing cabin with their parents. Minimum two-night stay; maximum two-week stay.

Nearby: Daily snorkel trips to Looe Key National Marine Sanctuary can be arranged at the park. Big Pine is also only a short drive into Key West. For more activities on the Keys and in Key West, see page 251.

TRAVELER'S PALM

Address: 815 Catherine, Key West, Florida 33040
Telephone: 800–294–9560, 305–294–9560; fax: 305–293–9130

Key West has many inns and bed-and-breakfast establishments, but few are appropriate for families. Breaking this rule is the Traveler's Palm in Old Town, where the owner's young child will show your kids the pool, the playground, and the lush tropical grounds. Although not a "budget" destination, this hotel's five small cottages and apartments, which offer one- and two-bedroom accommodations, are priced well below the going rate for this expensive area. Cottages are usually rented by the week, and many have decks and hammocks.

Season: Year-round.

Accommodations: One-bedroom, one-bath cottages and apartments, decorated in a tropical style, sleep up to four people. Each has a fully equipped kitchen, is air-conditioned, and has a private outdoor dining or lounging area with an outdoor grill. Two-bedroom cottages sleep up to six; one has a private pool.

Special Features: Spacious common area with a large heated pool and Jacuzzi, playground, hammocks under a thick canopy of trees. The hotel also operates a custom charter service for sportfishing, half- or full-day snorkeling excursions, and private boat trips for swimming, picnics, and bird watching.

Cost: One-bedroom apartment in season (December 21 to Easter) $181.50 per night; off-season $137.50 per night. One-bedroom cottage in season $192.50 per night; off-season $160 per night. Two-bedrooms start at $192 per night. All rates double occupancy. Children $12.50 per night; each additional adult $25 per night. Ten-percent discount for stays of one week or longer.

Nearby: Fort Zachary Taylor's beach, the area's best beach for families, is ten minutes away by car. For more activities on the Keys and in Key West, see page 251.

SANIBEL AND CAPTIVA ISLANDS, FLORIDA

Sanibel and Captiva islands are the southernmost tropical islands in the chain of barrier islands stretching along Florida's Gulf Coast. With towering palms and pristine beaches, the islands are great for swimming, biking along a network of landscaped bike paths, canoeing in bays and secluded bayous, fishing, golf, and tennis.

Over one-third of Sanibel is dedicated as a wildlife sanctuary—the J. N. Ding Darling National Wildlife Refuge and the Sanibel Captiva Conservation Foundation are known for bird watching, and the swooping antics of anhingas will even hold a young child's interest. Sanibel is famous for its shells; in fact, the "sand" here is composed of ground seashells. There are approximately 160 species of shells on its shores. You'll find pamphlets around the island helping you identify your findings. Lighthouse Beach on Sanibel is noted for shelling, Bowman's Beach for wildlife viewing, Turner's Beach for fishing, and Captiva for sunsets. Your children will enjoy taking their findings to the Bailey-Matthews Shell Museum (941–395–2233) and matching them up with more that 10,000 specimens from around the world.

Bike rentals are available at several places on the islands, along with two golf courses, miles of nature trails, in-line skating trails, several fully equipped marinas, and public tennis courts. Fun for families is the "Sealife Encounter" afternoon sea cruise with marine biologists run by Adventures in Paradise (941–472–8443).

GULF BREEZE COTTAGES

Address: 1081 Shell Basket Lane, Sanibel Island, Florida 33957
Telephone: 800–388–2842; 941–472–1626

Gulf Breeze is a small, friendly resort of thirteen individual cottages on its own Gulf of Mexico beach. Gulf Breeze is one of the few island resorts composed of individual cottages; most accommodations along Sanibel's shore are four-story condominiums. Located halfway between the lighthouse and the point on Shell Basket Lane, Gulf Breeze was built on a spot that reportedly has the most seashells on the island. Porpoises swim close to the shore, and you can watch them from your cottage porch.

Season: Year-round.

Accommodations: Units include large motel-style efficiencies with kitchens, one-bedroom cottages for up to four people, and two-bedroom cottages for up to six people. All units are furnished with cable TV, air-conditioning, heat, linens, towels, and dishes.

Special Features: Laundry facilities.

Cost: May to mid-December, efficiency $630 per week; one-bedroom cottage $770 per week; two-bedroom cottage starts at $770 per week. All rates are double occupancy; each additional person $10 per day. Rates higher December 15 through April, but still priced lowest on beach.

Nearby: Fishing piers, marinas, boat rentals, golf courses, wildlife sanctuaries, shops, restaurants, and grocery stores are close by. See page 254 for specific activities.

POINTE SANTO

Address: VIP Realty Group, 1313 University Drive, Fort Myers, Florida 33907
Telephone: 800–328–8318, 941–489–1100; fax: 941–489–3137

VIP Realty handles a vast range of rental properties including condominiums, beach cottages, and private homes in the Fort Myers, Sanibel, and Captiva areas. Among the listings is the four-story Pointe Santo resort's individually owned villas, which are popular with families and priced at an especially good value during the off-season (May through December). The weather is warm, but your kids will be in the water around the clock and all units are fully air-conditioned. The resort is in a ten-acre landscaped setting around a lagoon. Many units have panoramic views of the Gulf of Mexico.

Season: Year-round.

Accommodations: Two-bedroom Mediterranean-style villas sleep four to eight people. They have fully appointed electric kitchens, central air-conditioning, and cable TV. Fourth-floor units have rooftop sun decks.

Special Features: Heated swimming pool, whirlpool, tennis courts, shuffleboard, nearby sailboat and bike rentals.

Cost: Off-season (May through December) $710 to $860 per week for two-bedroom unit; rate depends on sea view and time of year. Rates much higher the rest of the year.

Nearby: All of Sanibel's amenities are close by. See page 254 for specific activities.

GULF OF MEXICO (THE PANHANDLE), FLORIDA

Miles of white, sugar-fine sand beach stretch along the "panhandle" of the Gulf of Mexico in northwest Florida. May to September is the tourist season here, but the weather is pleasant year-round if you can break away during the less expensive off-season. Protected by the St. Joseph Peninsula, which extends into the Gulf like a barrier island, the beaches here are some of the safest in all of Florida. You can swim nearly year-round, although water temperatures in mid-winter might drop too low for all but the hardiest swimmers. Waterskiing, sailboarding, and boating are popular, as are snorkeling and diving among the reefs.

Grayton Beach, seventeen miles east of Destin, is typical of the panhandle beaches with its laid-back town center, pristine white sand, and emerald green water. Uncrowded and secluded, the beach has rolling white-sand dunes and clumps of sea oats. Ranked as one of the country's best beaches, Grayton is one of a number of seaside communities collectively called the Beaches of South Walton. The Grayton Beach State Recreation Area is a park near town with an undeveloped stretch of beach, camping, picnic areas, a lake for fishing, boating, diving, and self-guided nature trails that take you through barrier dunes and piney woods. Rangers lead evening campfire talks on summer Saturdays.

Note: In addition to the accommodations listed here, the Clearwater Beach Hostel has family rooms and fully equipped apartments that can be reserved in advance. Located just across the bay from Tampa and only two blocks from Gulf of Mexico beaches, this new hostel has a swimming pool, landscaped courtyard, volleyball, tennis, shuffleboard, and a barbecue/picnic area. They also provide free use of canoes and rent bicycles for a modest fee. HI members, adults $12 per night; nonmembers $15. Children ages five to twelve half price. Call 813-443-1211.

RIVARD OF SOUTH WALTON

Address: 15 Pine Street, Santa Rosa Beach, Florida 32459
Telephone: 800-423-3215

This rental agency handles weekly vacation rentals including beach homes, condominiums, townhomes, and duplexes in Grayton Beach and its surrounding communities. Among the listings are many traditional cottages and houses, some steps away from the shore. Upon request, they will mail you a brochure with color photographs and complete descriptions, including proximity to the beach, of all their properties. Their rates are either less expensive (especially if you have a large family or share with friends) or comparable to the area's hotels.

Season: Year-round.

Accommodations: All properties have telephones, fully equipped kitchen, washer, dryer, microwave oven, dishwasher, cable TV, and VCR. Most furnish sufficient linens and towels. Housekeeping service is provided upon departure.

Cost: Comfortable family homes start at $800 to $1,000 per week during the summer; rates are lower during the other seasons of the year.

Nearby: Golf and deep-sea fishing can both be arranged nearby. Rent all beach paraphernalia at Beach Chairs 4U (904-231-4448). Your kids will love Big Kahuna's Lost Paradise Waterpark up the coast in Destin

(904–837–4061) or a ride on Destin's Glass Bottom Boat (904–654–7787).

ST. JOSEPH PENINSULA STATE PARK CABINS

Address: Star Route 1, Box 200, Port St. Joe, Florida 32456
Telephone: 904–227–1327. These are popular, so book at least one year in advance.

This 2,516-acre park is nearly surrounded by water and has eight rustic but modern cabins on St. Joseph's Bay. You'll find miles of unspoiled white sand beaches, many sand dunes, forests, freshwater ponds, and salt marshes. The park has nine miles of pristine white beaches perfect for swimming, shelling, and fishing, and eight miles of property on the bay with areas for snorkeling, fishing, and boating. There are two nature trails and an undeveloped wilderness area for hiking and camping.

    Season: Year-round.

    Accommodations: Each cabin sleeps five people and is completely equipped for housekeeping, with all kitchen utensils and bedding provided.

    Special Features: Boat ramp, boat basin, and canoe rentals.

    Cost: March through mid-September, cottages $70 per night for four people; five-night minimum stay. September 16 through February, $55 per night for four people; two-night minimum stay. Each additional person $5.

    Nearby: See page 256 for other activities in this area.

GULF SHORES, ALABAMA

Alabama never gets the attention of Florida's Panhandle, but its small stretch of Gulf coast, with the low-key resort community of Gulf Shores as its center, has thirty-two miles of soft white sandy beaches and water that is comfortable for swimming at least eight months a year. Extensive tracts of coast have been preserved by the state park system; refer to Gulf State Park Resort in the Resorts chapter.

GULF COAST, MISSISSIPPI

GAYLE'S COTTAGES

Address: 143-A Teagarden, PO Box 6081, Gulfport, Mississippi 39507 (located between Gulfport and Biloxi)
Telephone: 601–896–8266

Gayle's Cottages are duplexes two hundred yards from the beach, nestled under giant oaks and magnolias. There is a large deck patio with a barbecue grill, lounge chairs, and dozens of visiting squirrels and birds. The cottage's beach has swimming, jet ski and paddleboat rentals, and a fishing pier. The owners will charter you their twenty-nine-foot twin engine Cris-Craft boat for all-day fishing trips or excursions to West Ship Island, the Mississippi district of the Gulf Islands National Seashore. The island has a white sand swimming beach with lifeguards in the summer.

Season: Year-round.

Accommodations: Furnished cottages have one or two bedrooms (each with a queen-size bed and a double bed), a living room with a sofabed, breakfast bar, cable TV with HBO, and a fully equipped kitchen with a microwave oven. The one-bedroom sleeps four, the two-bedroom sleeps six.

Cost: One-bedroom $65 per night, two-bedroom $85 per night. Ten-percent discount on nightly rate for weekly stays.

Nearby: The cottages are ten minutes from a number of golf courses and coastal restaurants, forty minutes from Mobile, and one hour from New Orleans. A ferry leaves from both Gulfport and Biloxi for the seventy-minute ride to the Gulf Islands National Seashore.

THE MID-ATLANTIC

CHINCOTEAGUE ISLAND, VIRGINIA

Famous for its pristine coastline, national seashore, old-time seafaring town, and wildlife, Chincoteague Island offers families the ideal vacation—a perfect blend of virgin beach alongside many kid-pleasing amusements. The island's small New England–style downtown is not a burgeoning resort, but it will keep everyone in the family content with its surf shops, fish houses selling delicious crabs and renowned salt oysters, and candy kiosks offering the island's famous "Pony Tail" saltwater taffy. Only a few miles seaward, across the bridge, you will find tranquility among the wetlands of the Chincoteague National Wildlife Refuge and the undeveloped dune-dotted beaches of the Virginia section of the Assateague Island National Seashore. Within the refuge's 9,000 acres are miles of beach, rolling dunes, level marshland, channels, and freshwater ponds.

Horse-loving children, especially those who have read *Misty of Chincoteague*, can see her descendants run free at Assateague. Small, shaggy-coated, big-bellied, and squarely built, these hardy animals are said to be related to the horses left here by shipwrecked pirates centuries ago.

The national seashore is a flat and easy bike ride over the bridge from town. If your motel does not rent bikes, try T & T Riding Rentals (804–336–6330). The beaches here are clean; the water temperatures range from fifty-five degrees in May to seventy-five degrees from August through November. There are no concessions on Assateague but you'll find many picnic areas. Lifeguards are stationed at Toms Cove Beach adjacent to the Toms Cove Visitor Center; north of the visitor center the beaches become wilder and more secluded. Rangers lead campfires at Toms Cove Beach in the evenings; children will enjoy their tales of pirates and island lore. You can fish for blue crab at Toms or Swans cove; pick up a brochure at the visitor center with information on how best to catch and prepare them.

There are many trails through the Chincoteague National Wildlife Refuge; guidebooks can help you identify some of the many birds you'll see, which will undoubtedly include osprey, blue herons, egrets, and blue-winged teal. Originally set aside as a resting and feeding ground for the greater snow goose, the refuge now has more than 300 species of birds. An easy trail for biking or hiking is the Woodland Trail—you may be lucky and see a grazing pony. Visitors can also take a one-hour narrated bus safari through the back roads of the refuge or a guided sunset cruise through the serene Assateague Channel to the tip of the island.

Your family will want to spend some time in the village in addition to the great beaches of Assateague. Misty fans can see her footprints cast in the sidewalk at the Island Roxy Theater and update their library with other books from the series at the town's bookshops. Many places rent small boats along Main Street and East Side Drive. Visit the country's only Oyster Museum; watch taffy being pulled at the Pony Tails candy shop.

During the last two and half weeks in July the island holds its annual Pony Penning. On Wednesday, wild ponies are rounded up for the famous Pony Swim to Chincoteague, Thursday morning is an auction, and on Friday the remaining ponies return to Assateague. Reserve accommodations well in advance for this event. You can also see native ponies and miniature horses at the Chincoteague Miniature Pony Farm.

Nearby Wallops Island is home to NASA's Goddard Space Flight Center, which has a collection of spacecraft and flight articles as well as exhibits about America's space program. During the summer there are tours of launch sites; NASA operates its experimental rocket program here.

CHINCOTEAGUE ISLAND VACATION RENTALS

Address: 6282 Maddox Boulevard, Chincoteague, Virginia 23336
Telephone: 800–457–6643, 804–336–3720

This rental agency has a small listing of centrally located private homes either on the water or with a water view. Their rates are either less expensive (especially if you have a large family) or comparable to island hotels. Most of the houses the agency represents are old-fashioned and quaint, with screened porches and sun decks, but they also have been remodeled so that they are equipped with modern conveniences including dishwashers and air-conditioners. Ask for a booklet with descriptions and black-and-white photos of the listings.

Season: Spring, summer, fall.

Accommodations: Among the cottages recommended for budget-minded families are "West Winds," "One Pine Island," and "Big Pine." Across the street from Chincoteague Bay, West Winds is a remodeled three-bedroom house that sleeps eight people. It has a large kitchen, separate dining area, and living room, and it is one mile from town and three miles from Assateague.

One Pine Island is a remodeled house that sleeps six people on Little Piney Island, also a short trip to the beach. It has two bedrooms, one bathroom, a fully equipped kitchen, a living room, air-conditioning, and a screened porch. It also has a dock across its yard for crabbing, fishing, or docking your own boat.

Big Pine is a new home, three miles from the beach and an easy walk to town. It sleeps six and has two bedrooms, one bathroom, a fully equipped eat-in kitchen with a dishwasher and microwave, a living room with a color TV, a washer and dryer, a small deck in back, and central air-conditioning and heat.

Cost: During spring and fall, West Winds $410 per week; in summer $595 per week. During spring and fall One Pine Island and Big Pine $365 per week; in summer $505 per week. Mini-weeks and weekend rates available.

Nearby: All cottages are close by car or bike to the Assateague National Wildlife Refuge, which is famous for its oyster beds, clam shoals, and wild ponies. Big Pine is close to the carnival grounds, where the ponies are corralled during Pony Penning week, and it is also a short ride (about five miles) to Wallops Island.

REFUGE MOTOR INN

Address: PO Box 378, Chincoteague Island, Virginia 23336
Telephone: 800–544–8469 ext. 25, 804–336–5511; fax: 804–336–6134

This unpretentious family-run inn is right outside of town, just before the bridge to Assateague Island. It is within walking distance of the Chincoteague National Wildlife Refuge and a five-minute drive from the national seashore. The motel is secluded amid loblolly pine trees with views of a pasture where some of the island's wild ponies graze.
Season: Year-round.
Accommodations: Queen rooms accommodate up to five people; they have two queen-size beds and a refrigerator. All rooms have a phone, private bath, color TV, and patio or balcony.
Special Features: Bike shop on the premises for renting bicycles, indoor/outdoor heated swimming pool, sauna, hot tub, exercise room, wooded picnic areas with hibachis, spacious playground, pasture with ponies, laundry facilities, large meeting rooms recommended for family reunions. Front desk will handle reservations for the Wildlife Refuge bus safari and for the guided sunset cruises through the Assateague Channel.
Cost: Queen rooms $65 to $80 per night off-season; $80 to $100 per night during the summer, depending upon month. Rates are for two adults with two children under twelve. Third child and children under 17 in same room $5 per night; extra adult $8 per night. Cribs and cots are available at a slight additional cost.
Nearby: National Wildlife Refuge, National Seashore.

ISLAND MOTOR INN

Address: 4391 Main Street, Chincoteague Island, Virginia 23336
Telephone: 804–336–3141; fax: 804–336–1483

All the rooms at the Island Motor Inn have private balconies with spectacular views over Chincoteague Bay. A waterfront boardwalk connects the rooms and provides a great observation deck for viewing island birds and boats as they negotiate the Inland Waterway.
Season: Year-round.
Accommodations: Oversize rooms are popular with families; you can request a variety of bed arrangements including queen- or king-size

beds. Each room has a refrigerator, cable TV with free movies, and a VCR (upon request).

Special Features: Outdoor and indoor waterfront solarium swimming pool, well-appointed fitness center with large hot tub, quiet garden area, coffee shop.

Cost: From July to Mid-August, rooms $88 to $150 per night for a family of four, depending upon view. June and late August, $78 to $135 per night; spring and fall, $68 to $135 per night; winter $58 to $125 per night.

Nearby: National Wildlife Refuge, National Seashore.

LEWES, DELAWARE

THE BEACON MOTEL

Address: 514 East Savannah Road, Lewes, Delaware 19958
Telephone: 800–735–4888, 302–645–4888; fax: 800–735–4888

Families have long convened in the Delmarva peninsula, which separates Chesapeake Bay from Delaware Bay and the Atlantic Ocean. At the dramatic top of this coast, where the Delaware Bay meets the open ocean, is the charming town of Lewes. Lewes offers some of the area's least-crowded swimming beaches and its kitschy Colonial, Victorian-style town center is fun to explore when you are ready for some time away from the beach. Just south of the wharf, this motel is very convenient for families due to its proximity to both the bay and ocean beaches and the historic town center.

Season: April to October; weekends in November.

Accommodations: Of the forty-six standard motel rooms, twenty are larger-sized suite-style rooms with a pull-out sofabed. All rooms have air-conditioning and heat, a refrigerator, private balconies, daily housekeeping service, and cable TV with free in-room family-style movies.

Special Features: Outdoor heated pool with sun deck. Charter fishing can be arranged by motel staff.

Cost: Shoulder-season rates start at $50 per night, double occupancy; summer weekday $85 to $95 per night, double occupancy; summer weekend $115 per night, double occupancy. Each additional person over twelve $5 per night; children under twelve stay free when sharing a room with their parents. Additional $30 per night for suite-sized room.

Nearby: Ten minutes from the motel is Rehoboth Beach and Boardwalk. Bay Beach is three blocks away; ocean beaches are three miles away. Families with young children are drawn to convenient Lewes Beach, which has gentle waves and easy access to town either on foot or by bicycle. Bikes can be rented at Lewes Cycle Sports (302–645–4544). Cape Henlopen State Park, a mile east, has bigger surf and more undeveloped shores with enormous sand dunes that are great fun to explore. Lifeguards are on duty during the summer, and visitors can take nature hikes to observe unusual shorebirds (be sure to check out the park's Seaside Nature Center).

You can walk to town from the motel. Children enjoy touring the historic Shipcarpenter Square in downtown Lewes by old-fashioned surrey; call the Lewes Carriage Company at 302–645–4744 for details. The town also has two museums, the Zwaanendaal and Cannonball House, with artifacts retrieved from the Dutch ship *De Braak*, which sank off Cape Henlopen in 1798.

Note: For stays of a week or more, Jack Lingo Realty (800–331–4241 or 302–645–2207) handles a full range of choices, from single-family homes to townhouses or condominiums, that start at $500 per week. Homes are located on or a short walk from the Delaware Bay.

THE NORTHEAST

CAPE MAY, NEW JERSEY

THE QUEEN VICTORIA

Address: 102 Ocean Street, Cape May, New Jersey 08204
Telephone: 609–884–8702

A hard-packed white-sand beach runs for three miles in this classic Victorian-style seaside resort community, which protrudes into Delaware Bay on the Atlantic Ocean. Meander down quaint streets lined with ginger-bread–styled buildings on your way to the beach, take a horse-drawn carriage ride or a surrey bicycle for a spin, visit one of the nature centers, or spend a day at the amusement park in the nearby boardwalk town of North Wildwood.

This charming and well-run bed and breakfast country inn is one recommended to us by our readers. It is one of the few in Cape May that welcomes children; in fact, the owners go out of their way to make kids feel at home. Although not a "budget" destination in the height of summer, families traveling on a budget like to visit in late spring or early fall when the weather is still warm and the rates more affordable. Guests are given complimentary beach tags and towels for the beach, which is only a few blocks from the hotel. You can leave your car behind and hop on one of the inn's bicycles, available to guests at no charge.

Season: Year-round.

Accommodations: Rooms are nicely furnished with homemade quilts and are air-conditioned. Most include a mini-refrigerator and private bathrooms; some have a whirlpool tub and a popcorn maker.

Special Features: Hearty breakfast, afternoon tea with sweets, and sodas and popcorn are included in the price. There is a library well-stocked with books and magazines, a fireplace, and player piano. Another parlor has games, puzzles, and a TV. Twice daily housekeeping service.

Cost: Large room with private bath $95 to $210 per night double occupancy. Rates range from winter weekday to summer weekend. Each additional person $20 per night.

Nearby: Lifeguards and calm surf can be found at Bay Beach. Undeveloped and secluded Cape May Point State Park has a fun lighthouse to climb and makes for a great day trip. Children enjoy hunting for "Cape May Diamonds," which are quartz crystals polished by waves. Sunset Beach is a popular site to search for these faceted gems, or head for the souvenir shop in town.

Note: Also in Cape May is the Chalfonte Resort; see the chapter on resorts, page 17. For stays of a week or more, call Coastline Realty at 800–377–7843 or 609–884–5005 and Tolz of Cape May at 800–444–7001 or 609–884–7001.

EAST HAMPTON, NEW YORK

MAIDSTONE PARK COTTAGES

Address: 22 Bruce Lane, East Hampton, New York 11937 (off Three Mile Harbor Road)
Telephone: 516–324–2837; 718–347–4829

These surprisingly affordable cottages are set amid an upscale resort area known for its magnificent beaches, magnificent mansions, and equally magnificent prices. Located five miles northeast of East Hampton Village, the cottages have charming old-country surroundings. Swimming and sunbathing at breathtaking Gardiner's Bay beach is just a short walk away. Ocean beaches are a short drive from the cottages, as is fishing from the jetty at Three Mile Harbor.

Season: May through September.

Accommodations: Shingled one- and two-bedroom cottages have full kitchen, color TV with cable, carpeting, ceiling fans, brick patios with picnic tables and grills for each cottage, chaise lounges, and beach chairs. The one-bedroom sleeps three people, the two-bedroom sleeps up to five.

Special Features: Beach passes for all twelve town beaches are provided.

Cost: One-bedroom cottages $570 per week; two-bedroom cottages $685 per week. If you stay more than one week, successive weeks are discounted. Rates lower in May and June.

Nearby: It is a short walk to swim in the bay and a short drive to the ocean, tennis, and golf. Charter fishing is available at nearby Montauk. Whale watching, golf, and tennis are also close by.

CAPE COD, MASSACHUSETTS

Cape Cod, a seventy-mile-long peninsula that juts straight out to sea from the southeastern corner of Massachusetts, has 300 miles of shoreline, much of which is white sand. The Cape is known for its houses of gray cedar shingles, lobsterman's shacks, grassy dunes, sand castles, and wild-berry ice cream from the dollhouse streets of commercial Provincetown. While summer is certainly the best time of year for swimming, fall is a popular and less expensive season on Cape Cod. The warmest ocean water and gentlest waves in Massachusetts are found on the Cape's Atlantic side.

The Cape begins south of Plymouth, where the *Mayflower* landed in 1620. Stop there to see Plimouth Plantation, where costumed docents relive the day-to-day routine of America's first settlers amid thatched-roof cottages. Nearby is a replica of the *Mayflower*; children can visit below decks to see the conditions endured by the refugees. On the way to the Cape, stop at the Edaville Railroad in Carver (508–866–4526) for a narrow-gauge train ride through working cranberry bogs.

The Cape Cod National Seashore, between Chatham and Provincetown, encompasses more than forty miles of protected beach, trails, and dunelands. Since 1961 these beaches have been spared the crowded development prevalent elsewhere along the Cape. You may have a bit of a walk from your parked car, but you will be sure to find a secluded beach, even during the summer. From late June through Labor Day the beaches charge a $5 user fee, and lifeguards are on duty at this time. Easily accessible and popular with families is Marconi Beach. The national seashore maintains miles of bicycle trails and self-guided nature trails that are open all year; pick up a map at the Salt Pond or Province Lands visitor centers. Ranger-guided activities held in spring, summer, and fall include sharing nature with children, shellfishing demonstrations, canoe discovery trips, tidal flats walks, and programs that lead to junior ranger certificates. Schedules are available at the park's two visitor centers or by writing Cape Cod National Seashore, Race Point Road, South Wellfleet, Massachusetts 02663. Anchoring the national seashore is the charming town of Wellfleet. With its dramatic dunes and historic town center, it makes for a wonderful base for beach-loving families. There are five dune-dotted beaches in Wellfleet; all have lifeguards. You can rent bikes, rafts, inflatable boats, and other gear at Black Duck Sports Shop in town (508–349–9801). Wellfleet also has bayside beaches including Duck Harbor, which has great tide pooling. It is gentle and recommended for families with young children. Families with older children who like to hike will enjoy the four miles of unspoiled beaches found further south along the Great Island peninsula.

Alternate a day at the beach with a day at the Wellfleet Bay Wildlife Sanctuary, a thousand-acre park managed by the state's Audubon Society. In addition to snorkeling or canoeing, you can hike along trails bordering marches and moors, take a hands-on workshop in inventive nature crafts such Japanese fish-printing, or cruise the bay on an inexpensive three-hour evening tour with a park naturalist. On board, kids can identify ocean life (such as sponges, seaweeds, and scallops), look at plankton under a microscope, run simple tests on water for salinity and temperature, or look for turtles, whales, and dolphins (508–349–2615).

Other activities rated highly by kids are the children's theater productions presented by The Cape Playhouse in Dennis on Friday in the summer (508–385–3911), the Water Wizz water park in Wareham (508–295–3255) near Buzzards Bay, and viewing the Peter Rabbit memorabilia at the Thornton W. Burgess Museum (508–888–4668). The Cape is ideal for bicyclists. The family bike path at the Cape Cod Canal Recreation Area in Bourne has two wide, flat roads closed, to traffic, which run along both banks of the canal so you can watch boats as you ride by. The Cape Cod Rail Trail runs for more than twenty-five miles from Dennis to South Wellfleet; it is New England's longest paved bike path. For more recommendations of places to visit, call the Cape Cod Chamber of Commerce at 508–362–3225 and ask for a free copy of "Kids on the Cape."

THE EVEN'TIDE MOTEL AND COTTAGES

Address: PO Box 41, Route 6, South Wellfleet, Cape Cod, Massachusetts 02663
Telephone: 800–368–0007 (Massachusetts only); 508–349–3410

A haven for families, the Even'tide has double motel rooms, suites, apartments, and cottages, and its location is ideal. Its eight acres are bordered on the east by the national seashore, which includes an extension of the Cape Cod Rail Trail, a paved bicycle path that makes it possible to reach most of Wellfleet's beaches without traveling on the highway. It is also very close to the charming town of Wellfleet and just a few minutes' drive to many beautiful ocean, bay, and freshwater beaches.

Season: Year-round.

Accommodations: All motel rooms have a refrigerator, cable TV, telephone, heat and air-conditioning, and private bath. Two-room suites have a spacious bedroom with two double beds, a cozy sitting room with table and chairs, and double-size sofabed. Queen-size rooms have one queen-size bed; portacribs and rollaways can be added. Double-size rooms have two double beds, table and chairs. Studio apartments have one or two rooms with one queen or two double beds. Equipped for housekeeping, they have a full-sized refrigerator, two-burner cooktop, and microwave oven.

Eight cottages are located off the main road, in a quiet wooded setting. All have outdoor picnic tables and barbecues, carpeted living areas, cable TV, telephone, full bath, and are furnished and equipped for light housekeeping with full kitchens. Most have woodstoves and decks; the A-frames have a private deck off the upstairs bedrooms, as well as one off the living room. Cottages are available for up to six people; one family per cottage is allowed.

Special Features: Large heated indoor pool open year-round, outdoor sunning deck, central playground and picnic area, laundry facilities.

Cost: Two-room suites $88 per night, double occupancy during high season; $55 to $58 per night off-season. Queen-size rooms $75 per night, double occupancy, high season; $47 to $51 per night off-season. Double-sized rooms $79 per night, double occupancy, high season; $51 to $54 per night off-season. Studio apartments $103 per night, double occupancy, high season; $61 to $65 per night off-season. Each additional person in same family: adults $10 per night, children $7 per night. Crib $5 per night ($15 maximum); rollaway bed $10 per night ($25 maximum). Ten-percent discount on rentals of seven nights or more.

Cottages $656 to $861 per week, high season, depending upon cottage selected; $435 to $540 per week off-season; $525 to $687 per week shoulder season.

Nearby: The hotel provides a map for a three-quarter mile hike on a path through the woods to Marconi Beach. In addition to the activities listed on page 267 at the national seashore, there is much to do in Wellfleet. Kids enjoy digging for oysters, quahogs, and steamers—check with the Shellfish Department at 508–349–0325. At night, families convene at the 1957 Wellfleet Drive-In where you can begin your evening with a round of miniature golf and then gorge on a picnic in your car while enjoying the double feature. At the Town Pier, there are Wednesday night family square dances. Contact the Wellfleet Chamber of Commerce at 508–349–2510.

COMPASS REAL ESTATE

Address: PO Box 1205, Wellfleet, Massachusetts 02667
Telephone: 800–834–0703, 508–349–1717; fax: 508–349–1662

This agency handles many seaside cottages, condominiums, and vacation homes in the Wellfleet and Truro area. All require at least a week's stay. They will send you black-and-white photographs of a variety of homes in your price range, along with descriptions of the accommodations and detailed maps of their locations.

Season: May through September.

Accommodations: Among the listings appropriate for families traveling on a budget is a two-bedroom Nellie Road cottage, which sleeps four and is a short walk from LeCount's Hollow Beach, one of Wellfleet's finest beaches. Also close to LeCount's Beach is a ranch-style home that sleeps four with pond views. A barn-style home close to Dyer Pond and a short drive from the beach is situated on a private lane. A short walk from Mayo Beach is a three-bedroom home that sleeps six. A charming cape that sleeps six to eight people has full dormered windows, and is located one and a half miles from the beach and about half a mile from a golf course in Truro.

Special Features: All are equipped for full housekeeping but their amenities vary. Most homes have a complete kitchen with a dishwasher and a microwave oven, a washer and dryer, deck, patio, lawn chairs, picnic table, charcoal grill, and color TV.

Cost: From June through September, Nellie Road cottage $600 to $750 per week depending on time of visit; ranch-style home $650 to $700 per week; barn-style home $950 per week; Cape-style home in Truro $500 per week in June and September, $900 per week in July and August (if eight people rent the house, the cost is $1,000 per week).

Nearby: In addition to the activities listed on page 266 at the national seashore, refer to the listing for the Even'tide Motel and Cottages on page 267 for activities in Wellfleet.

HOSTELLING INTERNATIONAL–TRURO

Address: PO Box 402, North Pamet Road, Truro, Massachusetts 02666
Telephone: 508–349–3889; 508–349–3726. Reservations are essential. Phone reservations are accepted with a credit card. Off-season, mail reservations to 1020 Commonwealth Avenue, Boston, Massachusetts 02215, or call 617–739–3017.

Originally a coast guard station, this hostel is the furthest out on the arm of the Cape. It is set atop a dune near the tip of the Cape Cod National Seashore, just a seven-minute walk from the beach. Large picture windows provide a spectacular view from the large kitchen and dining area. This makes a comfortable, inexpensive base for exploring the salt marshes, cranberry bogs, long beaches, and sand dunes of the seashore.

Season: Mid-June through early September.

Accommodations: There is one private family cabin in this forty-two bed hostel.

Special Features: Kitchen, linen rental.

Cost: HI members, adults $12 per night; non-members $15. Children five to twelve half price.

Nearby: The National Audubon Bird Sanctuary is a few miles away. Provincetown is ten miles away and accessible by bike. On the way you can stop and climb the Pilgrim Monument, which commemorates the pilgrim's first landing in 1620. Whale-watching expeditions depart from MacMillan Wharf. For more things to do in this area, see page 266.

KALMAR VILLAGE

Address: Shore Road, Route 6A, North Truro, Massachusetts 02652
Telephone: 508–487–0585; in winter, 617–247–0211

Kalmar Village is a family resort of authentically styled Cape Cod cottages, efficiency units, and motel rooms on a private 400-foot beach along the shore of Cape Cod Bay, directly across from the national seashore's sand dunes. The cottages are separated by green lawns with picnic tables, benches, and lounge chairs. There is a large freshwater swimming pool on the premises.

Season: May through October.

Accommodations: Cottages and efficiencies have fully equipped kitchens, bedding, towels, electric heat, cable TV, and charcoal grills. Two-room cottages have a double bed and a twin bed in the bedroom and two double sofabeds in the living area. Three-room cottages have one double bed and two twin beds in the bedrooms and a double so-fabed in the living area.

Special Features: Laundry facilities, housekeeping service, and a list of available baby-sitters. Portacribs are available at no extra charge.

Cost: The most expensive time is July 13 through August 31; the least expensive time is May 15 through June 22 and September 7 through October 21. Nightly rates available off-season. Two-room cottage $435 to $875 per week; two-room deluxe cottage $485 to $935; three-room cottage $535 to $985 per week, depending on season. Rates are for four people; additional people $60 to $100 per week.

Two-room efficiency $395 to $675 per week, $63 to $110 per night, double occupancy, depending on season. Motel room $43 to $73 per night, double occupancy, depending on season. Each additional person $45 to $60 per week, $7 to $10 per night.

Nearby: The resort is a five-minute drive from many activities such as whale watching, nature walks, shopping, and restaurants. For things to do in Truro see the listing for Hostelling International–Truro on page 270. For more things to do on the Cape, see page 266.

GIBSON COTTAGES

Address: PO Box 86, North Eastham, Massachusetts 02642
Telephone: 508–255–0882. Reserve before January for summer months.

These comfortable shingled cottages are set in a quiet wooded area on the private sandy beach of a beautiful, clean freshwater lake. Rowboats and sailboats are provided at no charge to guests, and the lake is ideal for swimming and fishing. In addition to these lakeside pursuits, the national seashore, ocean, and bay beaches are a short drive away.

Season: From late June through Labor Day, cabins are rented by the week. From April through June and September through November there is a two-night minimum stay.

Accommodations: Housekeeping cottages have one, two, or three bedrooms. Each cottage has a screened porch or deck, fully equipped kitchen, bathroom with shower, and baseboard heat. TVs are available for $25 per week.

Special Features: A twenty-mile bicycle path leads from the cottages.

Cost: In summer, one-bedroom cottage $600 per week, two-bedroom cottage $650 per week, three-bedroom cottage $700 per week. Off season (before the last week in June or after Labor Day), rates are lower, depending on the month; usually, about $400 for the one-bedroom cottage to $500 per week for the three-bedroom cottage.

Nearby: Cottages are within walking distance of a general store and library. The Eastham 1869 Schoolhouse Museum (off Route 6, opposite the visitors center of the National Seashore) is an authentic one-room schoolhouse. The Oldest Windmill on the Cape, built in 1793, is also on Route 6, opposite Town Hall. For more things to do on the Cape see the introduction on page 266.

HOSTELLING INTERNATIONAL–MID-CAPE

Address: 75 Goody Hallet Road, Eastham, Massachusetts 02642
Telephone: 508–255–2785, 508–255–9762. Reservations are essential July through August. Phone reservations are accepted with a credit card. Off-season, mail reservations to 1020 Commonwealth Avenue, Boston, Massachusetts 02215, or call 617–739–3017.

This hostel's cozy cabins are surrounded by three acres of wooded land in a quiet rural area, just a fifteen-minute walk from Cape Cod Bay and four miles from the wide ocean beaches of the national seashore. The nearby Salt Pond National Seashore Visitor's Center provides hiking and biking maps of the national seashore and has ranger-led tours.

Season: Late May through early September.

Accommodations: Two family cabins are part of this fifty-bed hostel.

Special Features: Bicycle rental, baggage storage area, kitchen, linen rental, and on-site parking.

Cost: HI members, adults $12 per night; nonmembers $15. Children ages five to ten half price.

Nearby: For more things to do in Eastham see listing for Gibson Cottage, page 271. For more things to do in the area, see pages 266 and 267.

THE BREAKWATERS

Address: Box 118, 432 Sea Street Beach, Hyannis, Massachusetts 02601
Telephone: 508–775–6831

These weathered gray housekeeping cottages are set on two acres on the beach in a quiet residential area on Nantucket Sound. Accommodations are situated between a pool and a calm sandy beach. All units have private decks or patios with views of the sound. The heated pool has lifeguards, and swimming lessons are offered every morning for children. Each unit has a barbecue grill, picnic table, and lounge chairs.

Season: May through mid-October.

Accommodations: Cottages are fully equipped for housekeeping and have one to three bedrooms that sleep two to eight people. They also have cable TV, complete kitchens, and private phones.

Special Features: Housekeeping service is available in season at no extra charge.

Cost: The least expensive units are the one-bedroom cottages, which have twin beds or one king-size bed in the bedroom, a sofabed in the living room, a small kitchen, and a full bathroom: $375 per week or $68 per night May and October; $475 per week or $72 per night in spring and fall; $650 per week in early summer (June 15 through 29); and $925 per week in high summer. Children stay free when sharing a cottage with their parents.

Nearby: Hyannis Center's shops and restaurants are one mile away. Boats to Nantucket and Martha's Vineyard leave daily from its wharf. The town of Hyannis has a miniature golf course called Cape Cod Storyland. The Cape Cod Railroad departs from the downtown Hyannis Station at Main and Center streets for a two-hour tour of Historic Sandwich Village and the Cape Cod Canal. Kids also enjoy watching (and sampling) potato chips being made at Cape Cod Potato Chips on Breed's Hill Road in Independence Park, near the Cape Cod Mall. For other activities on the Cape see page 266.

YARMOUTH SHORES COTTAGES

Address: 29 Lewis Bay Boulevard, West Yarmouth, Massachusetts 02673
Telephone: 508–775–1944

Yarmouth Shores is a small, family-oriented colony of thirteen cottages on two and a half acres of land with more than 300 feet of gently sloping private beach. Many children stay here and enjoy the fun play area with swings on the premises. Many children's amusements are within four miles of the cottages, including the Aqua Circus, miniature golf, a wild animal farm, and horseback rides.

Season: May 15 through October 15.

Accommodations: Housekeeping cottages have a living room with fireplace, fully equipped modern kitchen, bedrooms with twin beds, bathrooms with stall shower, electric heat, outside shower for sand removal, and picture windows with views of the bay.

Special Features: Guests can bring their own TV and bed linens. One blanket is provided for each bed. Rollaway beds free for one extra guest per unit; cribs are available for a small fee.

Cost: Two-bedroom cottages $475 per week in season, $262 to $288 per week off-season. Three-bedroom cottages $588 per week in season,

$288 to $367 per week off-season. Four bedroom cottages $730 per week in season, $325 to $435 per week off-season.

Nearby: The Aqua Circus of Cape Cod on Route 28 in Yarmouth has daily sea lion and dolphin shows. The Pirate's Cove Adventure Golf in South Yarmouth rates high with the young set. The Hyannis Center, fishing, golfing, boating, movies, summer theater, restaurants, and churches are all minutes away by car. For other activities in Hyannis see The Breakwaters, page 272. For more things to do on the Cape see page 266.

MARTHA'S VINEYARD, MASSACHUSETTS

The idyllic island of Martha's Vineyard is generally not a place to look for bargains, especially during high season. We have listed a few of the least expensive accommodations, however, because the Vineyard provides an old-fashioned beach vacation with wide pristine beaches, clean salty air, historic towns, summer book fairs, and winding lanes with springtime blossoms of beach plum and blackberries. Families can find bargain rates well into June as well as in late September, when the days are usually still warm enough for swimming.

If the cottage or hotel you choose does not have access to a private beach, the best public beach on Martha's Vineyard for those with young children is State Beach, between Oak Bluffs and Edgarton. It has a long, flat shore, and the water has a sandy bottom. Older kids will like the high waves at the public Katama Beach on the island's south shore, but it can get quite crowded. Rent surfboards, boogie boards, sea kayaks, sailboards, and small sailboats at Wind's Up! (508–693–4252).

On the Vineyard, bicycles are the best way to get around. Rent them at Wheel Happy (508–627–5928) or R. W. Cutler (508–627–4052) for $10 to $15 per day. In Oak Bluffs, stop by the Flying Horses carousel (508–693–9481), the oldest in the country. Be sure to visit the Vineyard's breathtaking Clay Cliffs at Gay Head, Felix Neck Wildlife Sanctuary, and the Cape Pogue Wildlife Refuge.

CAUSEWAY HARBORVIEW

Address: Skiff Avenue, Box 450, Vineyard Haven, Martha's Vineyard, Massachusetts 02568
Telephone: 800–253–8684; 508–693–1606

Causeway Harborview has twenty-four apartments and a cottage high on a hill, just a few minutes' walk to downtown Vineyard Haven. Facing the harbor and Nantucket Sound, the spacious landscaped property features a large pool, picnic sites with barbecues, and many views of the water. The apartments and cottages are a short drive to the Vineyard's public beaches. Although more expensive than other listings in this book, these rates offer a good value for this extremely expensive island.

Season: Year-round.

Accommodations: Each of the apartments and cottages has color TV, a fully furnished kitchen, a full bath, homey furniture, and linens.

Special Features: Weekly housekeeping service.

Cost: In summer (June 19 to September 21), four-room, two-bedroom apartment or cottage for four people $975 to $1,010 per week; six-room, three-bedroom apartment or cottage for six people $1,105 per week. Mid-season (April 16 to June 19 and September 21 to November 14), two-bedroom apartment or cottage $480 to $500 per week; three-bedroom apartment or cottage $525 per week. Off-season (November 15 to April 15), two-bedroom apartment or cottage $380 per week; three-bedroom apartment or cottage $435 per week. Each additional person $10 per day.

Nearby: The inn is within driving distance of golf, tennis, horseback riding, twenty miles of paved bicycle paths, world-famous fishing, and sailboarding. Swimming is available around the island at eight public beaches. For specifics, see page 274.

SANDCASTLE VACATION RENTALS

Address: PO Box 2488, Edgarton, Massachusetts 02539
Telephone: 508–627–5665

If you can stay at least a week and can plan at least six months ahead, renting a private home on the island can be the most affordable and comfortable way to experience the Vineyard, especially if you share accommodations with another family.

Season: May through December.

Accommodations: This agency handles approximately 600 homes, cottages, and estates on the island. Accommodations, which range from "simple to elegant," have all the amenities of home, and are fully equipped for moving right in.

Cost: Prices for homes start at $1,000 per week; the average well-located three-bedroom home is between $1,200 to $2,000 per week.

Nearby: For specific island activities see page 274.

HOSTELLING INTERNATIONAL–MARTHA'S VINEYARD

Address: Edgarton-West Tisbury Road, Box 158, West Tisbury, Martha's Vineyard, Massachusetts 02575
Telephone: 508–228–0433. Reservations are essential. Phone reservations are accepted with a credit card. Off-season, mail reservations to 1020 Commonwealth Avenue, Boston, Massachusetts 02215, or call 617–739–3017.

This inexpensive hostel provides easy access to the beaches and traditional towns of this idyllic resort island. Rent bicycles and explore the island's network of trails that run through the towns, through wilderness areas, and along the coast.

Season: April through early November.

Accommodations: The hostel has five rooms with seventy-eight beds. Families of four or more can have one of the smaller rooms to themselves.

Special Features: Kitchen, baggage storage area, linen rental, and on-site parking.

Cost: HI members, adults $12 per night; nonmembers $15. Children five to twelve half price.

Nearby: Swimming is available around the island at eight public beaches. For specifics, see page 274.

BLOCK ISLAND, RHODE ISLAND

At the summer beach resort of Block Island, which is an hour-long ferry ride from Rhode Island's coast, a family needs no car—just bikes, bathing suits, thongs, and sunscreen. The island, a compact seven miles in length, is blessed with many sandy beaches, gently rolling hillsides dotted with wildflowers, open pastures, and hundreds of freshwater ponds. Spectacular cliffs reminiscent of the white cliffs of Dover line the islands southern corner.

State Beach has amenities such as bathrooms, lifeguards, and concessions; it can get quite packed throughout the summer. Crescent Beach is one of the island's nicest, stretching for over two miles along the eastern shore. The surf is calm, there are lifeguards, and you can rent water sports equipment. Mansion Beach has no amenities but is ideal for swimming, with a sandy bottom and waves for bodysurfing. Here you'll find amazing tide pools with crabs, starfish, and sand dollars. Families with young children head for freshwater Sachem Pond, where the waters are calm and warm.

You can bring your own bike or rent one at reasonable rates. Cycling is recommended on the island's West Side where there is less traffic, great vistas, and many inviting picnic or fishing spots. The island has excellent fishing; it is known especially for its striped bass, blues, and flounder. There are boats for rent and several charter boats for hire. Many of the restaurants here serve local lobsters and clams. Other island activities include tennis, scuba diving, sailboarding, snorkeling, sailing, and visiting the wildlife refuges. The bird sanctuary Lapham's Bluestone makes for a shady sidetrip when you need a break from the beach, and Rodman's Hollow is a nice spot to park the bike and take a hike—you may see a white-tailed deer. Ferries to the island depart from Point Judith and Newport, Rhode Island; Montauk Point, New York; and New London, Connecticut.

PHELAN REAL ESTATE

Address: PO Box B-2, 226 Water Street, Old Harbor, Block Island, Rhode Island 02807
Telephone: 401–466–2816; fax: 401–466–2931

If you can stay at least a week and can plan six months ahead, renting a vacation home on the island is one of the most comfortable ways to vacation here. This agency handles approximately seventy homes, cottages, and apartments, all of them on the beach or a short distance away.

Season: June through September.

Accommodations: All accommodations are fully equipped for moving right in. Phelan will send you a black-and-white photo catalog with complete descriptions of the rentals along with a map detailing their locations.

Special Features: Many of the homes have outdoor showers to remove sand, large decks, grassy lawns, washers and dryers, and playrooms.

Cost: Homes within walking distance of the beach that accommodate four people start at $800 per week. All houses have security deposits ranging from $200 to $300.

SURF HOTEL

Address: Dodge Street, Box C, Block Island, Rhode Island 02807
Telephone: 401–466–2241

Located in the heart of downtown, the back steps of this Victorian-style hotel, built in 1876, lead directly down to rose-laden Crescent Beach.

The beach, which stretches for three miles, is calm and great fun for children.

Season: Memorial Day weekend through Columbus Day weekend.

Accommodations: Rooms, a good many with ocean views, are small but clean and colorful. Rooms for families have shared bathrooms.

Special Features: Playground, basketball hoop, dogs and parrots in the antique-filled lobby (which also sports a giant chess set), library, television, and communal refrigerator. There are outdoor grills for guests to cook on. The hotel restaurant provides a complimentary light breakfast.

Cost: In July and August there is a six-night minimum stay. During this time, room with shared bath $500 to $560 per week depending on view, double occupancy; each additional person or crib $100 per week. In late June, room with shared bath $80 to $90 per night, double occupancy; each additional person or crib $15. Memorial Day through mid-June and early September through mid-October, room with shared bath $60 to $70 per night, double occupancy; each additional person or crib $10.

Nearby: Within walking distance of Old Harbor.

ISLAND MANOR RESORT

Address: Chapel Street, Box 400, Block Island, Rhode Island 02807
Telephone: 401–466–5567

Just one block from town and the beaches, this establishment has efficiency units that sleep four people each. The host family has lived on the island for more than twenty-five years and eagerly shares its knowledge of the best spots for fresh- or saltwater fishing, snorkeling, swimming, surfing, cycling, and dining.

Season: Year-round.

Accommodations: Efficiency units sleep four with a queen-size sofabed and a double Murphy bed, private bath, equipped kitchenette, and cable TV.

Special Features: Portacribs are available at no extra charge.

Cost: In summer, efficiencies $808 per week, double occupancy; each additional person $15 per night. Children under twelve stay free. Significantly lower rates in spring, fall, and winter.

THE SOUTHERN MAINE COAST

Maine's southernmost coast may not have the rugged, windy, "down east" feel, but it offers sandy beaches and vacation amenities that vanish north of Portland. The summer colonies of the Yorks (York Village, York Harbor, York Beach, and Cape Neddick), Ogunquit, Kennebunkport, and Wells have protected inlet beaches of hard-packed sand, and abundant cottages and motels. The water is clean (although chilly), the surf is gentle, and the crowds manageable, except for hot summer weekends.

York Beach is a hub of activity with many seaside cottages and houses for rent (see rental agencies on page 282). From May through mid-June, you can sometimes reserve a last-minute booking at a considerably reduced rate. Three-mile-long Long Sands is York's best beach for body surfing; canvas rafts are available for rent right at the beach. Short Sands is a bit gentler and has public restrooms and a lifeguard; on Wednesday evenings in July there are live band concerts here. Cape Neddick Beach has tide pools that are fun to explore. Adjacent to Short Sands is a kiddie amusement area called Fun-o-rama and a theater for rainy days. The Goldenrod candy shop (207–363–2621) is a sweet tooth's dream with specialty candies, some for only a penny, and salt-water taffy kisses. A block away is York's Wild Animal Kingdom (800–456–4911), with elephant rides and a great reptile section. York's historic Nubble Lighthouse can be viewed from Sohier Park or from a sightseeing cruise aboard the *Finestkind*, which departs down the coast in Ogunquit (207–646–5227). Much of eighteenth-century life has been preserved in York Village, where families can tour the dungeons of the Old Gaol Museum, an authentic schoolhouse from 1745, and Jefferd Tavern, where there are daily hearth-cooking demonstrations.

Ogunquit Beach is backed by the Ogunquit River, which is sheltered and waveless. Hiking along the Marginal Way in Ogunquit and through the Rachel Carson Wildlife Reserve is fun with older kids. Kennebunkport has the picture-perfect Maine look, with white clapboard houses, manicured lawns, a rocky shoreline dotted with sandy beaches, beach cottages, and harbors dotted with lobster boats. Goose Rocks Beach is Kennebunkport's best beach for young children, with fine sand, calm surf, and a gradual underwater slope. You can pick strawberries in June, blueberries in July and August, apples in September, and pumpkins in October. There are many bike paths, including an off-road trail from the Kennebunk beach area through marshlands and woods to town; bikes can be rented in Kennebunkport. Deep-sea fishing and whale watching can be arranged, and there are golf courses at Kennebunk Beach, Arundel, and in Kennebunkport. Kennebunk's Seashore Trolley Museum (207–967–2712) has a fun trolley ride, many examples of Victorian-era horse cars, and vintage streetcars from the 1960s.

Half an hour's drive south from Kennebunk in Kittery are many factory outlets, including the Children's Place clothing outlet. Freeport, less than an hour away, has L. L. Bean, Coach, Patagonia, J. Crew, and Ralph Lauren outlets.

Note: We cover Maine's northern coastal area of Acadia, which includes Mount Desert Island and Bar Harbor, in the National Parks chapter.

THE HISTORIC GARRISON HOUSE RESORT

Address: 1099 Post Road, Wells, Maine 04090 (The resort is between Ogunquit and Kennebunkport. Take exit 2 off I-95; turn left onto Route 109 to U.S. 1. It is on the ocean side, one mile south.)
Telephone: 800–646–3497; 207–646–3497. July and August are peak season and require reservations. June and September have excellent weather and lower rates.

Situated on the coast only one mile from Wells Beach, the historic Garrison House is a ten-acre resort overlooking the ocean and the Carson bird and wildlife sanctuary. The resort specializes in accommodating families comfortably and affordably. Fifteen motel units, seventeen cottages, and two-room suites with full kitchens all have panoramic views of the ocean and tidal inlet, and surround a large, heated swimming pool. Parents can relax while their children enjoy the swing set, play basketball, badminton, or baseball, fly kites, and swim.

Season: May to November.

Accommodations: Two-bedroom cottages sleep four to six people and have a full kitchen, a spacious living room, a sun deck, air-conditioning and heat, and cable TV. All linens, towels, and blankets are provided. Motel efficiencies have two double beds, heat, air-conditioning, full baths, cable TV, telephones, and a compact kitchen with a microwave oven. Standard motel rooms have two double beds, heat, air-conditioning, a small refrigerator, cable TV, and telephone. Two room suites have one bedroom with a queen-size bed, a full kitchen with a microwave oven and dishwasher, a living room/studio with a double bed, sofabed, sitting area, telephone, heat, air-conditioning, and cable television.

Cost: Two-bedroom cottage for four $325 to $425 per week off-season, $475 to $575 per week in July and August. Two-bedroom cottages for family of six $425 to $485 per week off-season, $725 per week in July and August. Motel efficiency $55 to $75 per night, double occupancy, off-season; $85 per night, double occupancy, in July and August, with three-night minimum stay. Motel rooms $35 to $45 per night, double occupancy, off-season; $55 to $75 per night, double occupancy, in July and August, with a two-night minimum stay. Two-room suites for family of four $95 per night in July and August with a three-night minimum stay; off-season $55 to $75 per night, double occupancy.

Nearby: The resort is on the trolley line and within walking distance of restaurants and tennis courts.

SAND DOLLAR REAL ESTATE

Address: PO Box 87, Kennebunkport, Maine 04046
Telephone: 207–967–3421

Season: Rental season June through mid-October. Call after Valentine's Day for the upcoming summer's available cottages.

Accommodations: This rental agency handles over 100 beach vacation rentals in the Kennebunkport area. All properties are extremely well maintained and ready for normal housekeeping.

Cost: One-bedroom cottage $600 per week; two-bedroom cottage $750 per week; larger homes up to $2,000 per week, depending on size and location.

SEASIDE RENTALS

Address: PO Box 278, Cape Neddick, Maine 03902
Telephone: 207–363–1825

Season: Rental season June through mid-October. The office is open mid-December through mid-October.

Accommodations: This rental agency handles more than 350 properties, ranging from small apartments to large homes. Most appropriate for budget-minded families are the houses and cottages near York Beach and Ogunquit. All properties are extremely well maintained and clean. Seaside will send you a catalog with its full array of listings and will follow up with color photographs of the rentals you are considering.

Cost: Average home near the beach for up to six people $600 to $800 per week during the summer.

SENTRY HILL RENTALS

Address: 43 York Street (office), PO Box 593 (mail), York Harbor, Maine 03911
Telephone: 207–363–0904; fax: 207–363–0834

Season: Spring through fall.

Accommodations: This agency handles vacation cottages and homes at York Beach and homes or condominiums either on the beach or a short walk away from Wells, Moody, and Ogunquit beaches. All accommodations have full kitchens; some have gardens, decks, pools, or access to private beaches.

Cost: Homes that sleep six to eight people at York Beach average $600 to $800 per week. Homes that sleep six people on the beach or a short walk away from Wells, Moody, and Ogunquit beaches start at $800 per week. Condominiums that sleep four that have ocean views or are a short walk from these beaches start at $755 per week. Off-season rates are half-price.

LEARNING VACATIONS AND DAY TRIPS

*L*earning vacations can take many forms. They can be as simple as a day trip to a living history village or cowboy poetry festival, or as involved as participating in a week-long archaeological dig for Indian relics. Teens and preteens, in particular, can benefit from a structured vacation with an educational dimension.

Many of our listings reflect the character of American culture, from its history and mythology to its icons, inventions, and cultural mix. We describe many of the unique attractions that children and adults can enjoy and learn from together—places that offer an excellent value, both educationally and financially. Many worthwhile organizations offer family learning vacations, but we have listed only those that fall into a more affordable price range.

NATIONWIDE

NATIONAL WILDLIFE FEDERATION

Address: 1400 Sixteenth Street, Washington, DC 20036–2266
Telephone: 800–245–5484; 703–790–4363

The National Wildlife Federation offers "Conservation Summits" to teach people about natural history and ecology in some of the most beautiful areas of the United States. Its hands-on, experiential programs are structured so that every member of the family has a program geared to their abilities and interests. Preschoolers have touch-and-feel expeditions and nature crafts; five- to twelve-year-olds have games and wildlife investigations; teens are offered more physically challenging activities, such as orienteering and hiking. Adult activities include lectures, workshops, and day hikes. The word is out about the high quality and low cost of these programs, and more than half of the participants return from year to year, so book early.

Each year the headquarters selects several different outdoor settings for the program. Past choices have included Big Sky in Montana, Alaska, the Blue Ridge Mountains in North Carolina, and New Hampshire. Classes are led by naturalists and professors who are experts in their field. A Teen Adventure Program for ages thirteen to seventeen combines outdoor adventure, group interaction, and exploration; activities include orienteering, day hikes, outdoor skill sessions and field trips, and challenges to mental and physical abilities. The Junior Naturalist Program for ages five to twelve has activities including outdoor games, nature hikes, arts and crafts, wildlife investigations, stream studies, and bird walks. The morning preschool program for ages three and four has touch-and-feel expeditions, nature crafts, short hikes, and lots of hands-on activities. Many of the activities are created for families to enjoy together, such as sing-alongs, square dancing, and slide shows on natural history.

Accommodations: Housing options may include lodges, apartment-style suites, hotels, and bed and breakfasts. The Federation's accommodations change from year to year, depending on where the programs take place. It uses the facilities of other organizations, such as college dormitories, resorts, and lodges. Meals are almost always included.

Cost: Fees are divided into two types. *Program fees*, including all classes, field trips, special afternoon events, evening activities, transportation for all adult and youth field trips, and instructors, $325 to $375 per adult per week. *Housing fees*, including lodging, meals, tax, meeting space, and recreational activities on the grounds, $300 to $650 per adult per week. Children usually pay one-third to one-half less. The Conservation Summits are a special program for National Wildlife Federation members, but it's easy and inexpensive to become a member of NWF; call 800–588–1650 for information.

SIERRA CLUB

Address: 85 Second Street, San Francisco, California 94105
Telephone: 415-977-5522; fax: 415-977-5795; Web site:
www.sierraclub.org/outings

The Sierra Club offers more than 300 diverse and exciting outings throughout the United States and even more worldwide. Parents with younger kids or those with minimal camping and nature study experience will most enjoy the trips designed with families in mind. Children twelve and older can participate in most of the other programs that the hundred-year-old institution offers.

The Family Outings are planned specifically to introduce parents and kids to the wonders of the outdoors and the pleasure of camping. Recent outings have included Acadia Toddler Tromp, Havasupai Indian Reservation Grand Canyon, and Fins and Family on the island of St. John in the U.S. Virgin Islands. Trips include opportunities to explore nature, hike, swim, and fish. Everyone shares in the camp chores, outdoor skills, and observation of plants, animals, and ecology. Single-parent families, grandparents (special outings are planned for grandparents and grand-children), and other relatives are welcome.

Families also can participate in service outings to help with projects such as constructing nature trails, and there is plenty of time to enjoy recreational opportunities after the work is done.

Accommodations: The style of lodging varies. Campers may stay in lodges or cabins, pack animals may transport food and equipment, or the group may drive to a campsite and takes day hikes from there.

Cost: Most trips last seven to ten days and cost $325 to $700 per adult, $215 to $475 per child. Service outings $225 per adult, $150 per child.

THE WEST

YOSEMITE FIELD SEMINARS

Address: c/o The Yosemite Association, PO Box 230, El Portal,
California 95318
Telephone: 209-379-2321; fax: 209-379-2486

Family outings in Yosemite range from the rugged—a guided family backpacking trip—to the very relaxed—Catered Family Camping. The backpacking trip covers eleven miles over three days, so the pace is pretty easy; the first day of the trip is spent on short hikes from a base camp to get acclimatized to the 8,600-foot elevation before heading out with packs on your backs. The Catered Family Camps celebrate nature the easy way. You bring your own tent and set it up and the staff cooks great camp meals. Each day the group explores different areas of Tuolumne Meadows. Many other seminars are offered throughout the summer months, but are best for older teens and their parents.

Season: Summer only.

Accommodations: A list of gear is provided for the backpacking trip; catered campers need to bring their own tents and sleeping bags.

Cost: Backpacking trip: adults $165, kids 6 to 11 $85; Catered Camping: adults $190, children five and up $110.

COWBOY POETRY FESTIVAL

Address: PO Box 888, 501 Railroad Street, Elko, Nevada 89803
Telephone: 702–738–7508; fax: 702–738–2900

Cowboys and cowgirls bring the romance of the Old West to life at Elko's cowboy poetry festival, the granddaddy of all of the cowboy poetry festivals that have sprung up around the country. Well-told tales of true grit, lost loves, and life on the range (with plenty of humor thrown in) will enthrall even the most jaded of teenagers. The Western Folklife Center sponsors this five-day event in late January. Cowboy poets, musicians, and artists from seventeen western states and Canada take part in presentation, workshops, exhibits, dances, films, videos, and performances. Each year has a specific focus, such as family life on the ranch, Canadian Cowboys, or the Celtic influence in the West. The Western Folklife Center operates out of the old Pioneer Hotel, built in 1913; it has a retail store and interpretive center of folk life with a focus on cowboys. The center has a catalog of books, music, audiotapes, and videotapes of cowboy and cowgirl poets, stories about the American West for children and adults, and cowboy poetry memorabilia.

Cost: Daytime passes are free for children under twelve and $7.50 to $15 for adults; concert tickets $20 and up per person, regardless of age. Special week-long and weekend passes available.

Where to Stay

Children stay free in their parents' room at Elko's Motel 6; rooms with two double beds $42 per night. Rollaways are not available. Book early. Address: 3021 Idaho Street, I-80 East, Elko, Nevada 89803. Telephone: 702–738–4337.

ROCKY MOUNTAINS AND SOUTHWEST

YELLOWSTONE INSTITUTE

Address: PO Box 117, Yellowstone National Park, Wyoming 82190
Telephone: 307-344-2294

Families planning to visit Yellowstone would be wise to book one of the institute's family programs, in which they can discover what makes Yellowstone so distinctive. Rangers teach about the park's history, wildlife, ecology, plants, and geology through leisurely walks, hikes, and discussions. Free time is built into the program so that families can relax or explore on their own. Campfires and evening programs regularly take place after dinner. Several family classes are offered each summer, with five or six families accommodated in each. Most classes last three days. Many families take a class, then head out on their own to explore Yellowstone with their newfound knowledge. The classes usually are based at a group camp, but participants can opt for other accommodations nearby. The institute's pamphlet, *Field Courses and Nature Study Vacations,* describes all available classes for adults and families. Family programs offered in the past have included "Family Days in the Thermal Basins" and "Exploring the Park with a Ranger." Four-day family horse-packing trips include horses, food and tents; you bring your own sleeping bags.

Accommodations: Most classes stay in campgrounds, which you may need to book separately; be sure to ask. If you do not wish to camp you can request accommodation information when you book. Participants are responsible for their own meals.

Cost: Three-day course $135 per adult, $70 per child. Camping is extra, usually about $8 to $10 per night. Horse trips $575 per person. Discounts available to members of the Yellowstone Institute.

BUFFALO BILL HISTORICAL CENTER AND THE CODY NITE RODEO

Named for Buffalo Bill Cody in 1896, Cody's current attractions are the Buffalo Bill Historical Center and the Cody Nite Rodeo. The Chicago, Burlington, and Qunicy Railroad, filled with passengers bound for Yellowstone and big game hunting, began serving the town in 1901. Homesteaders were drawn to the area by Cody's name, and the growing city became the county seat in 1909. Tourism remains a big industry, as thousands of people still pass through Cody on their way to Yellowstone.

Buffalo Bill Historical Center

The Buffalo Bill Historical Center, with one of the nation's finest collections of western Americana, is made up of four museums. In addition to its permanent collections it has rotating exhibitions throughout the year, special events, and films.

The **Buffalo Bill Museum** has an enormous western collection, much of it relating to Buffalo Bill's career as a Pony Express rider, Civil War soldier, buffalo hunter, army scout, and most of all, a showman. Visitors can see a stagecoach used in the Wild West Show, Annie Oakley's gloves and guns, and Wild Bill Hickok's handgun. Other items include posters and showbills, gifts to Buffalo Bill from foreign heads of state, photographs, playbills, and pocket watches. His boyhood home sits on the center's grounds.

The **Plains Indian Museum**'s vast collection covers the twenty-seven Indian tribes inhabiting the area from the Mississippi River to the Rocky Mountains, and from central Texas to central Canada. Examples of exquisitely beaded saddles, elaborate war bonnets, bows and arrows, carved leather bowls, and intricately patterned body adornments show the viewer the importance of beauty and symbol in the lives of the Plains Indians. A large tepee hall exhibits numerous full-size tepees and a section of a tepee village.

Among the firearms in the **Winchester Arms Museum** are crossbows, hand cannons, and an 1860s rifle popular with frontiersmen. It documents the historical development of firearms in general but focuses on those manufactured by Winchester.

Western painter Frederic Remington's art studio has been reconstructed at the **Whitney Gallery of Western Art**. Paintings by Remington and other western greats, such as Charles M. Russell and George Catlin, give the viewer a glimpse of the romantic West. The collection begins with works by artists, such as Catlin, who accompanied explorers and recorded what they saw in drawings and paintings. It continues with works of landscape painters, such Albert Bierstadt, who depicts the striking natural beauty of the frontier world. The museum also includes paintings of Indians and the everyday life of settlers; outstanding collections of Remington and Russell contain more than one hundred works by each artist. Contemporary artists are represented as well.

Address: 720 Sheridan Avenue, Cody, Wyoming 82414
Telephone: 307–587–4771

Cost: Two-day tickets, adults $8; students thirteen and over $4; children six through twelve $2, five and under free; senior citizens $6.50. Open daily May through October; closed Monday in March, April, and November. Group tour rates available by request.

Cody Nite Rodeo

The Cody Nite Rodeo happens every night at 8:30 from June through August and features cowboys from all over the United States, Australia, and New Zealand. Try to get tickets for seats in the "Buzzard Roost" for great views of cowboys psyching up to straddle a two-thousand-pound bull and of animals exploding out of the chutes. These cost only $1 to $2 more than grandstand seats.

Address: Stampede Grounds, 421 West Yellowstone Avenue, Cody, Wyoming 82414 (on the western edge of town)

Telephone: 307–587–2992

Cost: Regular grandstand tickets, adults $9, children seven to twelve, $4; Buzzard Roost seats $10 and $6. Children six and under free.

Nearby: Visitors should plan a quick stop in the reconstructed frontier village Trail Town, with homestead cabins that date from 1880 to the early 1900s. The most popular cabin is "Hole in the Wall," where Butch Cassidy and the Sundance Kid holed up together (1831 Demaris Drive, Cody, Wyoming 82414; 307–587–5302; open 8 A.M. to 8 P.M.).

Where to Stay

Pahaska Tepee Resort (see page 26) has housekeeping units and lodge rooms that can be rented by the night. The Lockhart Inn was the historical home of author Caroline Lockhart, who owned and edited Cody's weekly newspaper from 1919 to 1924. Families are most comfortable staying in the attached motel units or a fully equipped family cabin that sleeps up to five people for $75 per night, double occupancy, plus $10 for each additional person, including breakfast. The motel rooms, decorated in a western motif, have two double beds and private baths. Breakfast is included. Address: 109 West Yellowstone Avenue, Cody, Wyoming 82414 (near the rodeo, about two miles from the historical center). Telephone: 307–587–6074.

SNAKE RIVER INSTITUTE

Address: PO Box 128, Wilson, Wyoming 83014
Telephone: 307–733–2214; fax: 307–739–1710

Snake River's courses, available to both children and adults, explore and celebrate the cultures and communities of the American West. Its summer children's classes are guaranteed to please: The Institute uses the suggestions of a group called the "Antelope Advisors," made up of young people in grades one to nine, when they develop their program. Courses typically last one to five days, running from 9 A.M. to 3 P.M., and most are based in Jackson Hole.

Kids can learn the basics of fly fishing or photography, make a field journal and illustrate nature, or search for fossils while they learn about geology. Children taking "Landtracks" learn to find, track, and record animal facts, make plaster casts of tracks, and use watercolors and various other media to create their own artistic impressions. More than half of participants come from all over the country; families tend to have their own cars and stay in campgrounds, condos, motels, and ranches in the area.

Cost: Children's classes for first to ninth graders cost about $30 per day, which includes class and snack; some classes have materials fees. Adult classes about $75 per day.

Where to Stay

The family-owned and -operated Sundance Inn is a block from the shops and restaurants of the town square in Jackson Hole and includes a delicious continental breakfast in its rates, with home-baked muffins and breads, fresh fruit, yogurt, cereal, fresh squeezed orange juice, tea, and coffee. Lemonade and cookies are offered at "social hour" every afternoon. Two family rooms are available with a double and two twin beds: double $49 to $99, with highest rates during peak summer season; $10 extra for up to two children in parents' room. Two-room suites are also available, one with a kitchenette for $50 more.

CROW CANYON ARCHAEOLOGICAL CENTER

Address: 23390 County Road K, Cortez, Colorado 81321 (ten miles
from the entrance to Mesa Verde National Park)
Telephone: 800–422–8975; fax: 970–565–4859

Crow Canyon offers a year-round archaeological program dedicated to research and education for adults and high-school and junior-high students, but family vacationers should take note of Family Week for parents, grandparents, and kids in grade seven or higher. They start the week with hands-on activities examining Anasazi artifacts and reconstructing the lives of the Indians who owned them. Junior-high kids have two half days in the field as well as lab work and other programs. High-school students and adults spend their days in the field and lab. On Friday everyone gathers together for a tour of Mesa Verde National Park to tie together all aspects of the week-long program. Evening lectures are offered throughout the week.

Day-long programs are offered through the summer and are open to families who are touring the Southwest, but you must make reservations. Hands-on activities teach participants about the ancient Puebloan culture, and there is a tour of a laboratory and Crow Canyon's research sites.

Accommodations: Shared accommodations are in log hogans or in the Crow Canyon Lodge. Both share modern shower facilities and include three meals a day. The center tries to accommodate families together on campus, but sometimes finds it necessary to house participants in male and female groups.

Cost: Adults $795, students $474; includes seven days of lodging, meals, and all instruction and activities. Day-long program: adults $30; kids 12 to 18 $20, children under twelve $15.

ANDERSON RANCH ARTS CENTER

Address: 5263 Owl Creek Road, PO Box 5598, Snowmass Village, Colorado 81615
Telephone: 970–923–3181; fax: 970–923–3871

Anderson Ranch is set in the mountain resort of Snowmass Village near Aspen, and its setting is as magnificent as the artistic expression the program yields. Summer workshops are offered for both adults and children age six and up, and they concentrate on expanding creativity and growth in whatever medium a student—beginner or expert—selects. Kids can choose classes such as outdoor clay sculpture, printmaking, or inventions, while parents can pick from ceramics, woodworking, photography, drawing, painting, or interdisciplinary studies taught by accomplished working artists. Kids' classes run Monday through Thursday or Friday and can be morning only, afternoon only, or all day. All children's class sizes are limited to fourteen. Adult workshops normally last one to two weeks.

Accommodations: The ranch is a mixture of renovated log cabins, barns, and new buildings. Families stay in condominiums, while adult students are housed in a campus dorm.

Special Features: Sunday and Tuesday night slide lectures by visiting faculty; exhibitions by current faculty. Some airline discounts can be arranged through the ranch's travel agency.

Cost: Children's workshops $75 for one week's instruction. One-week adult workshops $375 to $495. Nonrefundable registration fee of $30 for all students. Accommodations in nearby condominiums $690 per week for a two-bedroom unit.

WHITE MOUNTAIN ARCHAEOLOGICAL CENTER

Address: HC 30, Box 30, St. Johns, Arizona 85936 (six miles south of Lyman on route 180/191)
Telephone: 520–333–5857

Budding archaeologists should take note of this unusual opportunity: Parents and kids age nine and over can work side by side with professional archaeologists to preserve and uncover a prehistoric pueblo occupied from A.D. 1000 to 1400. The Raven Site Ruin, inhabited by the Mogollon people to the south and the Anasazi people to the north, has a breathtaking setting that overlooks the Little Colorado River. The pueblo contains more than four hundred rooms and two kivas that are being excavated grid by grid and level by level. Many of the rooms will be restored to their original condition. Miles of petroglyph trails run throughout this area, and week-long guests help with the surveying.

The scientists who run this program have found children to be skilled and responsible team players, and all participants work beside the scientists, excavating the ruins, surveying petroglyph trails, working in the lab, and helping with restorations. A field laboratory and museum are on the dig site. Your visit can be as long or short as you like. The week-long program includes all aspects of fieldwork, while the daily program takes in just part of it. There is a campfire most nights. A gift shop on the premises features education materials, books, and the work of top-quality Native American crafts people; on occasion the artists visit the ruins and demonstrate their crafts.

For those just wanting a look around, daily guided petroglyph hikes and one-hour site tours are offered.

Season: May through mid-October.

Accommodations: Four private rooms each have a double bed; two bunk rooms have four to six beds. Shower rooms adjoin the bunkhouses. Tent camping is available.

Cost: Daily program, adults $61, kids nine through seventeen $37;

fees include lunch. Group overnight rate $83 for adults includes meals, lodging, and program; $61 ages nine to seventeen (need eight people). Tour of site $3.50 for adults, $2.50 for seniors and children twelve to seventeen; under twelve free. Petroglyph hike $18 for adults and $15 for kids. Motel in town of Reeds 800–814–6451 (discounts if you mention you are part of program).

TEXAS FOLKLIFE FESTIVAL

Address: 801 South Bowie Street, San Antonio, Texas 78205 (in HemisFair Park in downtown San Antonio)
Telephone: 210–458–2224

Texas has attracted people from all over the world at different times and for different reasons. The state's varied and distinctive cultures are the focus of the four-day Texas Folklife Festival presented each August in San Antonio by the Institute of Texan Cultures. Food, crafts, music, and dance from forty different ethnic and cultural groups create an explosion of sight, sound, and taste. This high-quality event has celebrated Texas's cultural diversity for more than twenty-five years. Sample German bratwurst, Mexican burritos, Belgian waffles, Southern soul cooking, and cowboy chuck wagon fare while you listen to Texas blues, Tex-Mex and mariachi music, German and Czech polkas, cowboy ballads, and country and western bands.

Sunday is kids' day. Kids get in free with an adult, and entertainment and activities—music, storytelling, dancing, puppet shows—are geared especially for them. Throughout the festival are many frontier activities for kids to try; roping a calf, making a hoecake, and grinding peanuts for peanut butter. There's even a watermelon-seed-spitting contest. The institute has a large "Back 40" with a tepee and one-room schoolhouse, where many of the children's activities take place.

The Institute of Texan Cultures also provides exhibitions, programs, and publications year-round. In the exhibition halls, kids are encouraged to touch the interactive displays, which focus on pioneer life and the contributions of various ethnic groups. The *Gone to Texas Puppet Theater* presents plays on a variety of Texas topics, and music performances take place throughout the exhibition hall.

Both the festival and the institute are located in spacious HemisFair Park. Kids will want to wander by its fountains and take a quick trip to the top of the Tower of the Americas for a panoramic view of the area. An excellent children's playground is found in the park near the institute.

Season: The festival begins in the evening on the first Thursday in

August and runs through Sunday afternoon. The institute is closed on Monday.

Cost: Institute admission: adults $4, children three to twelve and seniors 65 and older $2; children 2 and under free. Special rates for sightseeing and tour groups. Call 210–558–2291 to book a tour. Texas Folklife Festival admission (includes admission to the Institute) at the gate: adults $8, children six to twelve $2, children under six free. Tickets can be purchased in advance in a reduced price.

Nearby: Don't miss the Alamo or the Riverwalk, a section of river lined with shops, restaurants, and garden pathways, during a stay in San Antonio.

Where to Stay

The Mayan Guest Ranch, about an hour away, has a reasonably priced rooms.

The Clarion Suites, about twenty minutes from town, has a pool, complimentary continental breakfast, and one-bedroom suites with kitchenettes for $79 to $109 a night. Address: 13101 East Loop 1604 North, San Antonio, Texas 78233. Telephone: 210–655–9491.

The Bullis House Inn, in a historic Texas mansion, has a number of affordable rooms that sleep three, four, or six people $59 to $69 per night, double occupancy. Children under eighteen are $6 additional. Cribs are available at no charge for kids under three. Rates include continental breakfast, and guests have the use of a small kitchen, dining area, and picnic tables. A swimming pool is open mid-April to mid-October. Address: 621 Pierce Street, San Antonio, Texas 78208. Telephone: 210–223–9426.

CENTRAL UNITED STATES

RED EARTH FESTIVAL

Address: Red Earth, Inc., 2100 NE 52 Street, Oklahoma City, Oklahoma 73111
Telephone: 405–427–5228

The largest, most authentic, and colorful of all Native American gatherings and festivals is Red Earth, held the second weekend in June in Oklahoma City's Myriad Convention Center. It features dancing and traditional music presentations, storytelling, and exhibitions. The dance competitions and exhibitions are a mainstay of the festival and attract more than a thousand of the most accomplished Native American dancers from the United States and Canada. There are exhibitions of War, Jingle Dress, Grass, and Fancy Dress dances. Other events include the Red Earth Run 5-K race, a Native American film and video competition, and a juried art show that features textiles, jewelry, pottery, clothing, cultural items, and contemporary paintings and sculptures. Speakers address the cultural traditions and heritage of Native American art and life. There's face painting, storytelling, and crafts for kids.

Cost: Tickets to the dance competition free for children under twelve; adults $6. Evening dance performances, adults $10, children $5.

Nearby: Cowboy Hall of Fame. Address: 1700 North East 63rd Street, Oklahoma City, Oklahoma 73111. Telephone: 405–478–2250.

Where to Stay

Radisson Inn offers a shuttle to the festival. It has large rooms with two double beds and extensive recreational facilities, including three outdoor swimming pools open during the summer; indoor pool open year-round; tennis; a jogging track, a health spa; and restaurants. Rates for two adults, two children $60 to $109 per night. Address: 401 South Meridian, Oklahoma City, Oklahoma 73108. Telephone: 800–333–3333; 405–947–7681.

INDIAN CITY U.S.A. AND AMERICAN INDIAN EXPOSITION

Address: PO Box 695, Anadarko, Oklahoma 73005
Telephone: 405–247–5661

Anadarko is the place to be during the first week of August for the American Indian Exposition at the city fairgrounds. With parades, a war dancing competition, all-Indian archery competitions, Indian rodeo, and nightly tribal dances, anyone fascinated with Native American culture will be deeply satisfied. When the activities at the fairgrounds slow down, visit Indian City U.S.A.'s outdoor displays of authentic Indian villages and dance performances, and indoor exhibits of artifacts, clothing, memorabilia, and photos. The reconstructed dwellings have been restored authentically under the supervision of the Department of Anthropology at the University of Oklahoma.

Season: Year-round.

Nearby: Also in Anadarko is the National Hall of Fame for Famous American Indians, the Delaware Tribal Museum, the Philomathic Pioneer Museum, and the Southern Plains Indian Museum and Crafts Center.

Where to Stay

Quartz Mountain Resort, one of Oklahoma's state resort parks, is within driving distance (see pages 37 to 38).

MORE INDIAN ACTIVITIES IN OKLAHOMA

Oklahoma has the highest population of Native Americans of any state in the United States. Through the centuries some sixty-seven different Indian tribes have lived in Oklahoma, including Cherokee, Choctaw, Seminole, Creek, Cheyenne, Apache, Pawnee, and Chickasaw, and descendants from each of those tribes still reside in the state. The state travel and tourism office (800–652–6552 or 405–521–2409) publishes a list of the thirty-seven tribes that maintain council houses in Oklahoma, including dates of their powwows. A powwow is a gathering of many tribes for singing, dancing, feasting, and selling and trading arts and crafts. Visitors are welcome at many of them. During the summer there is a powwow somewhere in the state every weekend. Be sure to note the powwow etiquette tips included in the brochure before you head out.

LAURA INGALLS WILDER PAGEANT

Address: Laura Ingalls Wilder Memorial Society, 105 Olivet Avenue, De Smet, South Dakota 57231
Telephone: 605–854–3383

If you're anywhere near De Smet, South Dakota, in late June and early July, visit this "Little Town on the Prairie" for the Laura Ingalls Wilder Pageant, held for three weeks near the original Ingalls homestead site. Wilder's popular books (made into a highly successful TV show) chronicle the life of a delightful pioneer family on the Great Plains. The outdoor pageant is based on the book *By the Shores of Silver Lake* and is performed by an all-volunteer cast, including lots of children. The performance begins at sundown; plan to arrive early for children's horse-drawn wagon rides. The last performance has home-cooked meals for sale before the pageant. If you miss the pageant, the Laura Ingalls Wilder Society conducts tours of sites described in the books throughout the summer.

Six of Laura Ingalls Wilder's books are set in De Smet. Their first winter the family lived in a surveyor's house, later moving into the house that "Pa" built in 1887; tours of both places are conducted year-round. The homes contain memorabilia and artifacts from the family; the five original cottonwoods that Pa planted still stand, and the surveyor's house contains the original chest of drawers that Pa built, where Laura accidentally discovered her Christmas present in *The Long Winter*.

The Laura Ingalls Wilder gift shop next door to the surveyor's house is filled with wonderful books, posters, postcards, pictures, toys, and memorabilia relating to the Laura Ingalls Wilder books. Visitors also can tour sixteen other sites mentioned in the Little House books, including the schoolhouse where Laura and her sisters attended school and the cemetery where her parents are buried. The society will send you a catalog of its merchandise on request.

Cost: Tickets to the pageant: adults $5, children $2. Guided tours of the Laura Ingalls Wilder sites $5 per adult, $2 for children ages five to twelve, under five free. Visitors receive a map of all sites. The society is open from 9 A.M. to 7 P.M. seven days a week during June, July, and August. Special hours during winter months.

Nearby: The World's Only Corn Palace (604 North Main Street, Mitchell, South Dakota; 605–996–7311), an exotic Moorish-inspired structure decorated each year with murals composed of thousands of bushels of corn, grain, and grass grown by local farmers, is seventy-five miles away.

Where to Stay

The Prairie House Manor Bed and Breakfast, two doors down from the Ingalls homestead, has rooms available for families of all sizes. All units have a private bath and TV, and a full breakfast is included in the price. Rates $35 to $75 per night, depending on the size of your group and room. Address: 209 Poinsett Avenue, De Smet, South Dakota 57231. Telephone: 605–854–9131.

INTERNATIONAL MUSIC CAMP SUMMER SCHOOL OF FINE ARTS

Address: 1725 Eleventh Street, SW, Minot, North Dakota 58701
Telephone: 701–263–4211 (summer); 701–838–8472 (winter)

On the border between North Dakota and Manitoba in the International Peace Gardens of the Turtle Mountains, the International Music Camp Summer School of Fine Arts has week-long sessions for adults and children age ten and up. Select from intensive courses in band, chorus, piano, guitar, piping and drumming, dance, art, creative writing, and much more. Sessions run Sunday to Saturday during June and July. A few classes are shorter (three days) or longer (two to four weeks). This is basically a study camp; classes range from beginning through advanced levels and are divided according to ability instead of age.

Recreational activities include record hops, movies, volleyball, softball, swimming, concerts, and arts and crafts. Student performances on Saturdays are free and open to the public. Friday night concerts are held in the International Peace Gardens. If you time your visit right you can catch the Old Time Fiddlers Contest in early June. The International Peace Gardens has ten miles of paved roads that are great for biking; bring your own wheels.

Season: Summer.

Accommodations: There are separate dorms for kids and grownups so that adults don't have to adhere to the lights-out policy for the youngsters. Dorms are large rooms with thirty to sixty beds in each and are chaperoned. Each dorm has its own set of bathrooms. Families that wish to stay together can use the camping facilities within walking distance of the school. There is a small additional fee for a campsite, but campers have full access to special recreational activities and cafeteria meals.

Cost: Approximately $200 per week per person for room, board, instruction, and recreational activities.

Nearby: Lake Metigoshe, twenty miles from the camp near Bottineau, has boating, fishing, cabins, and simple resorts.

INDIANA UNIVERSITY BLOOMINGTON

MINI-UNIVERSITY

Address: Indiana Alumni Association, PO Box 4822, Bloomington, Indiana 47402–4822
Telephone: 800–824–3044; 812–855–0921

Mini-University, an award-winning vacation college on the Bloomington campus of Indiana University, has a week-long program geared for families with kids ages four to sixteen. Adults (and older teens) can choose from an enormous list of classes and stimulating discussions in the arts, business and technology, human growth and development, science, international affairs, health, fitness and leisure, or humanities. While the adults tune up their intellectual skills, kids four to sixteen enjoy themselves at Camp Shawnee Bluffs on Lake Monroe. They are taught and supervised by trained counselors; activities include swimming, boating, hiking, field games, archery, tennis, and more. Children ages one to three are cared for at a state-licensed nursery near campus.

Many activities are planned outside of the classroom, and guests have plenty of free time to pursue their own interests. Evening activities for adults always include arrangements for children's supervision.

Accommodations: Housing is available on and off campus. The Teter Quadrangle offers dormlike housing with shared baths; rooms have two twin beds, linens, air-conditioning, and phone. Parents can request a mattress for one child and pay for just a food package if they wish. Hotel accommodations are available on and off campus.

Cost: Class registration: adults $115, children under eighteen $95 for the week. Dorm housing (including meals) $230 per adult single occupancy, $195 double occupancy. Children eight and over $155, children under eight $130. Children's meals-only rate $90, under eight $65.

CONNER PRAIRIE

Address: 13400 Allisonville Road, Fisher, Indiana 46038 (northwest of Indianapolis)
Telephone: 800–966–1836; 317–776–6000

Time has rolled back to 1836 at Conner Prairie with the sights, sounds, and smells of life in the small village of Prairietown, where village inhabitants go about their daily work. Wander about the village and chat with the "residents"; you'll hear the small-town chatter and conversation common to any prairie village of the 1830s. The more your children ask questions of the residents, the more they'll get out of their visit. But beware: the costumed characters you'll be talking to know only of life in their own era. Talk to them about airplanes or automobiles and they'll think you a bit "touched in the head."

Three different historical sites make up Conner Prairie: the 1836 village, the William Conner home, and the Pioneer Adventure area. The village has forty-two buildings, including a store, schoolhouse, log cabins, and inn, all staffed with costumed interpreters who go about their business cooking, tending store, repairing rifles, and so on. William Conner was one of Indiana's first residents, and his house, which is original to the site, was recently restored.

Kids will want to headquarter in the Pioneer Adventure Area, a hands-on activity center where they can try the different activities they've heard about while visiting the village and house. They can dip a candle, weave a basket, make soap, or create corn husk dolls. There are many 1830 games available to play, such as stilts, a game similar to darts, and horseshoes. They can also practice washing clothes with a scrub board.

Season: April to November.

Cost: Admission fees $9.50, children six to twelve $7, children under five free. Senior citizens $7. Admission to William Conner home additional $2.

Where to Stay

A bed-and-breakfast establishment, The Frederick-Talbot Inn, has special rates for Conner Prairie guests. Regular rates $89 to $169 per night double occupancy, including a full breakfast buffet. Telephone: 800–566–BEDS. The Waterfront Inn in Cicero (about a twenty-minute drive) has rooms overlooking the water with kitchenettes for $74 to $94 per night. Children under twelve stay free in their parents' room; each additional person is $6 per night. Address: 409 West Jackson, Cicero, Indiana 46034. Telephone: 317–773–5115.

LINCOLN BOYHOOD NATIONAL MEMORIAL AND STATE PARK

Address: Box 216, Lincoln City, Indiana 47552 (state park); Box 1816, Lincoln City, Indiana 47552 (memorial)
Telephone: 812–937–4710 (state park); 812–937–4541 (memorial). Theater reservations, 800–346–4665 within Indiana; 800–264–4423 outside Indiana.

Lincoln State Park and its neighbor, the Lincoln Boyhood National Memorial, combine the outdoors with history in a way that will interest even the most reticent young student. With well-staged historical musical dramas, a working pioneer farm, an interpretive center, and lots of outdoor activities, families can learn about the life and times of the sixteenth U.S. president while they enjoy numerous recreational diversions.

A 1,500-seat covered amphitheater in the state park stages repertory productions of *Young Abe Lincoln* and *Big River*, a musical about the life of Huckleberry Finn, nightly during the summer. The Lincoln Boyhood National Memorial, across the street, has an interpretive center with displays about Abraham Lincoln and a film describing the Lincoln family's time in Indiana. The Lincoln Living Historical Farm is a recreation of an early-nineteenth-century farm; from April through September people dress in period attire and plant, plow, cook, harvest, spin, and quilt just as they did in Lincoln's time. Another trail takes visitors to the cemetery where Lincoln's mother is buried and to a memorial marking the site of one of Lincoln's family homes. The self-guided Boyhood Nature Trail takes guests past species of trees that Lincoln's father, a master woodworker, might have used.

The state park, with its rolling hills and shady forest, is on Lake Lincoln and has a wonderful swimming beach, fishing, and boat rental. In summer a naturalist program sponsors free activities such as sand castle building contests and animal identification; choices are posted weekly.

Cost: $2 to $5 per person. Seniors and children sixteen and under free. Rowboats and canoes $1.75 per hour, $9 per day. Paddleboats $4 per day, $2 per half hour; mandatory life jacket rental $1 per person.

Nearby: Holiday World Theme Park, the oldest theme park in the country, is nearby in Santa Claus, Indiana. Mega-maze in Dale is an enormous life-size maze with a miniature golf course in the middle.

THE SOUTH

OZARK FOLK CENTER

Address: PO Box 500, Mountain View, Arkansas 72560
Telephone: 501–269–3851

Celebrating the way of life in the Ozark Mountains pre-1920, the Ozark Folk Center is dedicated to preserving and perpetuating traditional Ozark Mountain crafts and music. Craft demonstrations and music shows are a staple on the grounds of the folk center, and workshops and performances take place throughout the year for kids and adults.

The Young Pioneer Program gives visiting children the chance to do the kinds of things the kids of the Ozarks used to do: pottery making, corn shucking, rope and paint making, spelling bees, making and using feather pens, and Ozark games. It takes place five days a week, three times a day in June, July, and August. If you visit in fall or spring, try to visit on a Saturday; this is the only day the Young Pioneer Program operates during those months.

"Youth Weeks," which take place twice throughout the summer, usually in June and August, provide a hands-on tour of the folk center crafts area for young people seven to sixteen. Kids get to make and take home a candle, a pinch pot, a printed card, and other projects. The two-and-a-half to three-hour tour is conducted daily and is included in the price of a child's admission ticket to the crafts area. At the end of the tour kids receive a special "Certificate from Yesteryear."

Cost: Crafts area and evening music show tickets can be purchased separately or as a package. There are many package deals, depending on the number of days you stay. Daily craft tickets: adults $7, children six to twelve $4.50; family tickets $17.25. Music tickets: adults $7, kids six to twelve $4.50; family tickets $17.25. Combination tickets: adults $12.75, children six to twelve $6.75; family tickets $31.25. Three-day passes are available, as are season passes. If you stay in the Ozark Folk Center Lodge you can get further discounts.

Where to Stay

The Ozark Folk Center Lodge (800-264-3655; 501-269-3871), located on the folk center grounds (address on previous page), has comfortable rooms with two double beds; windows and doors open onto the Ozark National Forest. Lodge guests have use of the swimming pool and game room, and the restaurant features home-style southern cooking. Rooms for four $45 to $60 per night depending on season; summer rates are highest.

CRATER OF DIAMONDS STATE PARK

Address: Route 1, Box 364, Murfreesboro, Arkansas 71958
Telephone: 501-285-3113

Hunt for gemstones at the Crater of Diamonds State Park, the only mine open to the public in North America where you can pocket what you find. Spend a few hours or a week searching a thirty-six acre field for diamonds; more than 70,000 already have been found. Although diamonds are the main attraction, other semiprecious gemstones you might come across include amethyst, garnet, jasper, agate, and quartz. Digging tools can be rented and free gem identification and certification are provided by the park staff. The field is plowed monthly to turn up new specimens. Historical structures, old mining equipment, washing pavilions, and restrooms are located at the mine.

A short walk away from the mine area is a shady trail leading to the Little Missouri River, providing a cool break from the sunny mine. You can fish for bass, catfish, and bream along the bank, but you'll need a fishing license (available in Murfreesboro, two miles away). Special programs and slide shows are presented daily throughout the summer. The park has campgrounds, a restaurant, a visitor information center, gift shop, laundry facilities, and a playground.

Cost: Admission to the mine area, adults $4, children six to twelve $1.50. Children under six free if accompanied by an adult. Screens, shovels, lawn chairs, stools, buckets, and knee pads are available for rent Memorial Day through Labor Day for $1.25 to $2.50 each per day.

Where to Stay

If you're not going to camp in the park, consider the Swaha Lodge, a few hundred yards from the swimming beach and marina of Lake Greeson. One- and two-bedroom condominiums are available February through December, and rustic cabins are available May through October. Condominiums $75 to $140 per night. Eleven simple cabin units have kitchenettes, air-conditioning, and one or two bedrooms, $40 to $65 per night. Address: PO Box 226, Murfreesboro, Arkansas 71958. Telephone: 510–285–2272.

NATCHITOCHES FOLK FESTIVAL

Address: Louisiana Folklife Center, Box 3663, Northwestern State University, Natchitoches, Louisiana 71497
Telephone: 318–357–4332

Dance the Cajun waltz, stuff yourself on gumbo, and turn the kids loose at the children's tent during the third weekend in July, when more than thirty Cajun, country blues, bluegrass, and zydeco bands take over the historic town of Natchitoches (pronounced *nak*-a-tish). Held in the air-conditioned coliseum of Northwestern State University, the festival features music, dancing, crafts, food, and a children's festival. Events on three different stages run throughout the day; headliner acts fill a main stage area that can hold an audience of 4,500 people. Talks and demonstrations take place nearby. The town of Natchitoches is like a small version of New Orleans and a microcosm of Louisiana, blending the influence of six different ethnic groups—African-American, French, Spanish, Indian, Anglo-Irish, and French-African Creole—into its rich culture. The festival attempts to present folk traditions through storytelling, music, food, and crafts.

There is a special area for kids; past years have had storytellers spinning folk tales, African stilt walkers, wooden toys, pottery, Indian toys and blowgun making workshops, and demonstrations of arrowhead chipping.

More than fifty traditional artists and crafts people are invited to the festival to demonstrate and sell their work, selected for its authenticity and quality (no macramé plant hangers and crudely tooled leather belts here). Some of the more unusual crafts on view over the years have included nail art, in which nails of different sizes pounded into wood create patterns and pictures; flint knapping, which is chipping flint to make arrowheads and tools; Mississippi mud art, in which mud gathered from the Mississippi River is sculpted into dolls' heads and other objects; and garfish jewelry created from the fish's scales.

And the food! Indulge in crawfish, roast pig, meat pies, Creole gumbo, and pralines, and then dance it all off. There are dance areas with lessons in both Cajun and country dancing; band after band plays everything from the latest zydeco to the oldest Cajun waltz and hottest Texas two-step.

Natchitoches, the oldest permanently inhabited area in the Louisiana

Purchase Territory, still has many eighteenth-century buildings, as the town was not burned down during the Civil War. Walk through the historic district of the town and admire the structures; many have elaborate grillwork. Be sure to tour the fort and take a boat and trolley tour.

Cost: Adults $5 to $7 per show, children under twelve $3 per show. All-show booklets, available in advance, offer a slight discount.

Where to Stay

Natchitoches does not have many budget overnight accommodations. Its historic downtown is filled with beautiful bed-and-breakfast establishments, most of which do not accept children; we list a child-friendly one below. A Super 8 Motel at the edge of town has rooms for four people at $50 per night. Address: 801 Highway 3110 Bypass, Natchitoches, Louisiana 71457. Telephone: 318–352–1700.

The Holiday Inn charges $65 per night for rooms with two double beds; rollaways are $6 per night. Kids under 18 stay free in their parents' room. Book by the end of May for the folk festival. Address: Highway 1 South Bypass, Natchitoches, Louisiana 71457. Telephone: 318–357–8281.

The Breazeale House Bed and Breakfast is a splurge. Its third-floor area has two bedrooms, a den, and a bath. Rollaway beds can be added to accommodate larger families. One family can have the entire area for $130 per night, which includes a hearty breakfast and use of the swimming pool. The house is within walking distance of the historic downtown area and about a five-minute drive from the university. The host, a grandmother, enjoys having children stay with her in this magnificent historic home, which was featured in the movie *Steel Magnolias*. Book early. Address: 926 Washington, Natchitoches, Louisiana 71457. Telephone: 318–352–5630.

OKEEFENOKEE SWAMP EXPLORATION

Address: 711 Sandtown Road, Savannah, Georgia 31410–1019
Telephone: 912–897–5108

The Okeefenokee National Wildlife Refuge's vast watery wilderness is teeming with wildlife and vegetation. Three- and four-day educational tours of the swamp are operated by Wilderness Southeast, a nonprofit "school of the outdoors." The Okeefenokee Cabin/Canoe program, suited to children age eight and up, allows families to explore the swamp by canoe and return each evening to a cozy cabin with air-conditioning, showers, and full kitchens. During the day observe basking alligators, wading birds, musk turtles, songbirds, life under the lily pad, and a once-thriving logging town on a small island. A packed lunch is eaten along the way. After a dinner break back at the cabins, an evening program might involve a short hike into the swamp with flashlights to search for wolf spiders, whose eyes flash brilliant green when light hits them. The program runs in the spring and fall. Wilderness Southeast offers other high-quality programs for families and adults.

Accommodations: Cabins at Stephen Foster State Park (for more information about the park, see page 189). Food is ample, healthy, and delicious and is prepared by the staff with help from participants. Meals are taken together. Small families might share a cabin; families of four or more usually have their own cabins.

Cost: Four-day programs including meals, instruction, equipment, and accommodations, adults $525. Three-day programs $375. Fifteen-percent discount for children accompanied by one parent, twenty-five-percent discount if accompanied by two parents.

JOHN C. CAMPBELL FOLK SCHOOL

Address: Route 1, Box 14-A, Brasstown, North Carolina (seven miles east of Murphy)
Telephone: 800‑365‑5724, 704‑837‑2775

The Little Middle Folk School of this excellent school of traditional crafts, music, and folklore is offered just one week each summer, usually the last week of June. Children seven to seventeen can take up to four classes, which are divided by age group. Many participants are from the Brasstown area, but a number of others come with parents who take courses that same week or who explore the area while the kids are occupied. Classes offered in the past have included weaving, felt making, paper arts, enameling, blacksmithing, mask making, pottery, bead weaving, woodcarving, folk toys, folk talks, and outdoor adventure. Hundreds of classes for parents are offered throughout the summer, including papermaking, quilting, wood carving, basketry, Appalachian music, ceramics, and weaving.

The 365-acre campus, in a beautiful mountain setting, has fully equipped studios, a hardwood dance floor, a nature trail, a crafts shop, and rustic lodging. It is modeled after the Danish folk school concept of learning through the "living word," or personal exposure to the teacher, instead of through books, lectures, examination, or grades.

Accommodations: Some housing is in dormitories and some in old residences on campus. One of the most beautiful is a native fieldstone house from the 1920s that has been renovated and modernized inside. Older rooms and rooms with shared baths are least expensive, and some of the rooms can accommodate three, four, or five people. All linens are provided. Meals are taken together in a dining hall; when the bell rings, it's chow time. The food is traditional farm-style. A campground with full hookups and limited facilities available.

Cost: Little Middle Folk School tuition $70 to $85. Cost for adult classes averages $250 per week. Little Middle Folk School children's classes fill especially quickly, so register early. Extra materials fees for some classes. Dorm room with four to five twin beds $215 per person for six nights, room, and board. Campground prices do not include meals and are for two persons per site: $48 per six nights, meal packages $110 per six-day week.

AUGUSTA HERITAGE CENTER

Address: Davis and Elkins College, 100 Syracuse Street, Elkins, West Virginia 26241–3996
Telephone: 304–637–1209

A week at Augusta involves almost all of the senses: the sounds of old-time fiddle tunes, voices raised in four-part harmony, or feet dancing an Irish jig or an Appalachian flatfoot on a wooden dance floor; the sight of African masks, traditional paper-cut silhouettes, and sparks flying from a blacksmith's anvil; and the smells and tastes of herbs collected in West Virginia's woods and waters, fresh mountain air, and spicy Cajun cooking. The center is well respected for its exceptional adult summer workshop program, dedicated to passing on the values and crafts of the early Appalachian settlers. A Folk Arts for Kids Program offers a five-week series of classes in traditional music, folklore, dance, and crafts.

The children's program offers classes for boys and girls ages eight to thirteen, and students have opportunities to learn from leading musicians, dancers, storytellers, and craftspeople; the instructors for both the kids' and adults' classes read like a list of Who's Who in music and crafts. Classes meet for six hours each day, with children joining their parents for meals, concerts, dances, and other evening events. Some special events for the children involve the parents as well. The subject matter varies by week. One week focuses on southern old-time music taught on a fiddle and other instruments. Those with no fiddle experience build a xylophone and learn to play tunes on it. Several other weeks introduce children to a number of Appalachian folk arts, including lively games and traditional play parties, storytelling, songs, clogging, and crafts. Another emphasizes cooking, crafts, outdoor games, riddles, ballads, Appalachian singing, and African stories.

Workshops for adults are offered on all levels and truly provide something for everyone with ninety week-long classes in music, dance, crafts, and folklore. Pick from flat-pick guitar, zydeco accordion, gospel piano, hammered dulcimer, storytelling, basketry, or clogging, to name just a few. The center also sponsors a Spring Dulcimer Week and an October Old Time Week in Appalachian music.

Public concerts and spontaneous jam sessions fill the halls, fields, and parks with blues, bluegrass, swing, Cajun, Irish, Scottish, and old-time music. There's so much spontaneous music that one dormitory is designated a quiet zone; jam sessions often go on elsewhere all night long.

The center also produces recordings by traditional West Virginia musicians and has a successful statewide West Virginia Folk Arts Apprenticeship Program that pairs students with master artists in a one-on-one study of a traditional or ethnic folk art or craft.

Season: Early July to mid-August for workshops.

Accommodations: Families with all members enrolled in a workshop or class stay in college residence halls that have two beds and a shared bath. Children can bring a sleeping bag and share a dorm room with two adults. Sheets and pillows are provided, but students must bring their own blankets and towels. Meals are served in the cafeteria and provide a wide choice of entrées, including meatless dishes and a salad bar at every meal. Three campgrounds are located within ten miles of the campus and there are several private motels nearby.

Cost: Children's and adult workshop tuition $260 to $300 per week. Room and board package $235 per week for a six-night week.

SHAKER VILLAGE

Address: 3500 Lexington Road, Harrodsburg, Kentucky 40330 (twenty-five miles southwest of Lexington)
Telephone: 606–723–5411

Known for their spare, elegant furniture, the Shakers were a religious sect that settled in the United States in the early part of the nineteenth century. They were named for the writhing, shaking dance motions used in their rituals, and they invented a surprising number of household items, including the flat broom, the circular saw, and the washing machine. Shaker Village was originally an experimental agricultural station. By the last half of the nineteenth century the Shakers had faded away, but modern interest in their buildings and way of life has revived their heritage. Thirty-three buildings have been painstakingly restored in accurate historical detail, and visitors can walk at their own pace through a village to observe broom makers, spinners, weavers, quilters, and coopers hard at work. The rooms are filled with the simple and elegant Shaker furniture coveted by today's antique dealers.

On a tour of the village, guides in nineteenth-century dress will acquaint you with the Shaker beliefs and way of life. Demonstrations of broom making and other activities, such as sheep shearing, spinning, and weaving, help children make a connection between past and present. If you visit April through October, you can also watch daily demonstrations of Shaker domestic life, including candle dipping, butter churning, open-hearth cooking, natural dyeing, and farming with historic tools and methods.

A dining room is open for breakfast, lunch, and dinner throughout the year. From Memorial Day through October a summer kitchen is open for lunch; both have a children's menu and delicious Kentucky country fare.

During late spring through early fall the Shaker Village sternwheeler runs daily excursions on the Kentucky River. One-hour boat rides are led by an interpreter playing the life of a nineteenth-century Kentucky River traveler, who talks about life on the river, the Civil War, and the Shakers.

Accommodations: Overnight lodging is available year-round in fifteen restored Shaker buildings. Furniture is spare and simple and there are no closets, only pegs along the walls of the rooms to hold clothes and other possessions. Candle sconces have been wired for electricity; otherwise the walls are completely bare. Rooms have air-conditioning, heat, and private indoor bathrooms. For spring, summer, and fall visits, reserve accommodations at least two weeks in advance.

Cost: Entrance fees to the village, adults $9; children twelve to seventeen $4.50, six to eleven $2.50. Boat rides and horse and wagon rides extra; package deals and family rates available. Rooms rates, double occupancy (kids seventeen and under stay free in parents' room) $50 to $80 per night; suites and a house also available.

Nearby: Hiking trails extend from the village, which is seven miles from Kentucky's oldest city, Harrodsburg. Fort Harrod State Park has an outdoor drama called *The Legend of Daniel Boone* in the summer. Kentucky Horse Park, near Lexington, is thirty miles away.

COLONIAL WILLIAMSBURG

Address: PO Box 1776, Williamsburg, Virginia 23187-1776
Telephone: 800–HISTORY

Colonial Williamsburg is one of the oldest living history museums in the United States. Many Americans who once visited it as children return with their own children to tour its historic district and special exhibits that bring eighteenth-century Colonial America to life. Horse-drawn carriages clip-clop through the streets, militia drills and fife and drum corps march about, master artisans demonstrate their art, and costumed characters reflect upon the social, economic, and political climate. Five hundred buildings range from dank jail quarters and simple homes, shops, and taverns to elegant government buildings. After dark Colonial Williamsburg has candlelight concerts, eighteenth-century plays, games, and "gambols," an old form of entertainment.

Special children's activities are offered at various times throughout the year. You might happen upon fife and drum presentations or magic shows, or take a children's tour in which a child in period dress tells about becoming an apprentice to one of the master tradesmen in the village. Ticket holders receive a copy of the *Visitor's Companion*, listing weekly outdoor events and the midday cannon firing. Study a copy to plan your day effectively.

Cost: The best value is the Patriots Pass, which is good for a year and includes admission to all major exhibits: adults $33, kids six to twelve $19, kids under six free. Basic Plus tickets are good for two days but do not get visitors into all of the sights: adults $29, kids six to twelve $17. Evening concerts and dramas $10 for children and adults, $5 for Patriots Pass holders. All admission tickets include the use of the Colonial Williamsburg transportation system, a copy of the *Visitor's Companion*, and admission to the introductory film *Williamsburg, the Story of a Patriot*. Special children's tours, $10 per child; parents free when accompanied by a child.

Where to Stay

Colonial Williamsburg has a number of "official" hotels, the most economical of which is the Governor's Inn, three blocks from the restored area. Its room rates vary depending on season and how full the hotel happens to be when you call for the dates you want. Rooms with two double beds, $50 to $85 per night. Rollaways and cribs are available. Rates include use of the outdoor pool and a shuttle to the restored area. Address: 506 North Henry Street, Williamsburg, Virginia 23185. Telephone: 800–HISTORY.

THE NORTHEAST

PENN STATE ALUMNI COLLEGE

Address: 105 Old Main Building, Pennsylvania State University, University Park, Pennsylvania 16802
Telephone: 814–865–LION (5466); fax: 814-865-3589

You don't have to be a graduate of Penn State to attend this four-day academic, recreational, and social program. Adults choose from a variety of lectures, discussions, and hands-on activities, while children of all ages are entertained and educated in either day camp, a sailing day camp, a sports camp, or a day-care center, depending on their age. Families stay in air-conditioned dorms or in a nearby hotel. Tuition and fees include instructional costs, material, several meals, and snacks.

Children under six are cared for in an off-campus day-care center. Six- to thirteen-year-olds can participate in a special thematic day camp featuring computers, chemistry, archaeology, etc. Children eight to sixteen can join a sailing day camps with van transportation and bag lunches provided. Teenagers can attend the adult program or participate in a variety of sports camp such as ice hockey, tennis, golf, lacrosse, and soccer.

Adult instruction is offered by university faculty. Past sessions have included workshops and seminars on landscape architecture, military history, lab tours, theater, investments, demonstrations of sheep shearing and colt training, discussions on how to get your book published, and much more. Each day is divided into morning and afternoon sessions, with several choices for each. In the evening families are free to explore the town or campus or participate in star gazing and ice cream socials. The Central Pennsylvania Festival of the Arts takes place over the weekend preceding the program and many families take advantage of an early check-in to enjoy the festival.

Penn State also offers Family History Weekends throughout the year. Contact the number above for more information.

Season: The program usually takes place in mid-July.

Accommodations: Select from air-conditioned suites with two bedrooms and a bath or a hotel nearby. Accommodations fee includes breakfast and lunch.

Cost: Tuition $350 for Penn State alumni, $380 for nonmembers (which covers alumni association membership costs). Includes breakfasts, lunches, parking, field trips, opening dinner picnic, and theater nights. Day camp $250 per session. Rates for full-day sports camps vary.

Dorm accommodations $50 per night for a double room plus meal ticket (three breakfasts, three lunches, one brunch).

CHAUTAUQUA INSTITUTION SUMMER SCHOOL

Address: PO Box 1098, Chautauqua, New York 14722 (between Buffalo, New York and Erie, Pennsylvania)
Telephone: 716–357–6348 (late June through late August); 716–357–6255 (post-season)

This charming Victorian village offers a stimulating mix of fine and performing arts, education, recreation, and religion. Set on the shore of Chautauqua Lake in western New York State, the Chautauqua Institution is a National Historic District. The institution offers a broad selection of courses, a lecture series, religious programming, classical and popular music, and theater. More than 300 courses are offered for adults and children in subjects including amateur astronomy, storytelling, humor writing, tap dance, foreign language, magicianship, and a young artists program. Most classes last one week and range in length from one to three hours, so you can take more than one class if you wish. There is a Children's School for two-and-a-half- to six-year-olds, and a Boys' and Girls' Club day camp with a full program of recreational interests for six- to fifteen-year-olds. Activities include swimming, sailing, canoeing, arts and crafts, music, games, and sports. After class, head to the beach for a swim.

Special Features: Special scholarships for families with demonstrated need.

Cost: Families attending the Chautauqua Institution have three different costs: the gate ticket, which allows access to beaches, concerts, lectures, and other programs. (Separate tickets must be purchased for opera and theater performances.) 1997 one-week gate tickets, adults $170; children ages thirteen to seventeen $70; twelve and under free. You can also buy admission to the grounds by the day or evening. Evening concerts include the Chautauqua Symphony Orchestra and such artists as Roy Clark; Peter, Paul, and Mary; and the Manhattan Transfer in an open-air, 5,000-seat amphitheater. Recreation includes four beaches, a sports club with boat rentals, softball field, shuffleboard, badminton, volleyball, lawn bowling, tennis, and golf.

Course fees vary: five-day course $40 to $100; Children's School: $75 to $85 per week, less for a second child; Boys' and Girls' Club: $95 to $105 per week, less for second child.

Where to Stay

Participants arrange their own accommodations. Choose from a wide variety of hotels, inns, guest houses, rooms, condominiums, houses, and apartments. A campsite and other off-grounds accommodations are located nearby.

On-grounds accommodations prices range from $85 per week for a room to $2,200 per week for a house. Apartments are generally the best deal for a single family staying a week. For vacation packages and other information call the Accommodations Referral Service at 716–357–6204.

NATIONAL BASEBALL HALL OF FAME AND MUSEUM

Address: 25 Main Street, PO Box 590, Cooperstown, New York 13326
Telephone: 607–547–7200; 607–547–2044

Starting with the entrance turnstile and the life-size carved wooden statues of Babe Ruth and Ted Williams at the door, this three-floor museum of baseball memorabilia has a distinct ballpark flavor. The displays and exhibits pay tribute to the greatest heroes of America's most beloved sport. For sheer atmosphere and nostalgia, top prize goes to the Ballparks Room, with actual dugout benches, grandstand seats, and turnstiles from such places as Forbes Field, Crosley Field, and the Polo Grounds. Lockers that once belonged to Joe DiMaggio, Mickey Mantle, Lou Gehrig, and Hank Aaron are found throughout the second floor.

Rare old photos and displays of artifacts trace the origin of the game and an exhibit called Baseball Today showcases the highlights and heroes of the last five years to give young baseball fans a frame of reference. The Hall of Fame Gallery is filled with simple bronze plaques honoring the more than 225 members who have been selected for their talent and dedication to the sport.

Statistics nuts can spend hours playing with the computers in the Records Room. A complete statistical and audiovisual history of each inductee is available via touch-screen technology.

Other highlights include a two-hundred-seat movie theater, television monitors featuring continuous showings of *This Week in Baseball,* a display of historic baseball cards, and special exhibitions on subjects such as baseball's contributions to World War II and the history of the Negro League.

Season: Year-round.

Cost: Adults $9.50; children seven to fifteen $4, under seven free. Combination tickets for the Farmers Museum and the James Fenimore Cooper House (see below) are available.

Nearby: The lovely village of Cooperstown, named for American novelist James Fenimore Cooper, is at the foot of Otsego Lake, with beautifully preserved historic houses lining the streets. Two other museums are worthy of a visit: the James Fenimore Cooper House contains an excellent collection of American folk art and American Indian art. The Farmers Museums and Village has displays on rural life in America and a working village full of old-time blacksmiths, weavers, and printers. Three-way tickets can be purchased for the Hall of Fame, the Farmers Museum, and the James Fenimore Cooper House. Boat rides on the lake leave from a dock about two blocks from the Hall of Fame. The U.S. Soccer Hall of Fame is thirty minutes away in Oneonta.

Where to Stay
Fieldstone Farm (see page 48).

MYSTIC SEAPORT

Address: 75 Greenmanville Avenue, Mystic, Connecticut 06355-0990
Telephone: 203–572–5315

Today Mystic Seaport is a seventeen-acre indoor and outdoor museum of U.S. maritime history. Kids can climb aboard its historic vessels, including the *Charles W. Morgan*, the last wooden whaling ship in America; a full-rigged training ship built in 1882; and the wooden steamboat *Sabino*. They can interact with friendly interpreters in period dress and working craftsmen who forge iron, carve figureheads, and make barrels. Chantey singers, cooking on a fireplace hearth, and on-site boat building add to the atmosphere.

Families should make sure to stop at the Children's Museum, where kids can play with an extensive collection of nineteenth-century replica toys and games. At the boat-building area kids can build and launch their own boats, and a special area set aside for children under seven contains replicas of nineteenth-century clothes for dress-up play.

The busy village area of the museum gives visitors an impression of a historic seafaring community. Kids also will particularly enjoy the Buckingham House, which features demonstrations of fireplace cooking, the Shipsmith iron working demonstration, the Mystic Press printing demonstration, and the Shipcarvers Shop, with woodcarving demonstrations.

From mid-May through October, the 1908 *Sabino* takes passengers on short Mystic River cruises for an extra fee. Passengers learn about the history of the boat and the river.

If your kids start to whine, take them to the blubbering room on whale ship *Morgan*'s lower deck. They'll be amazed at the tiny berths and confining quarters where up to twenty-two sailors lived with very little light or ventilation.

An enticing array of high-quality annual events await visitors throughout the year. Best for kids are Kids Liberty Days, with scavenger hunts, crafts, and family programs. The week after Christmas is another great time to visit because there are special activities, games, crafts, and entertainment just for families.

Season: Year-round.

Cost: Hours, activities, and prices are seasonal, and many price packages are available; call ahead for details. General admission in summer averages $16 for adults, $8 for youth six to fifteen, and free for children five and under.

OLD STURBRIDGE VILLAGE

Address: 1 Sturbridge Village Road, Sturbridge, Massachusetts 01566-0200
Telephone: 508–347–3362; fax: 508–347–5375

Massachusetts's Old Sturbridge Village is a re-creation of an 1830s New England rural community. About an hour west of Boston, it features more than forty historic buildings, a working farm, sawmill, covered bridge, and special programs. A staff of working artisans explain how everyday life was lived—shoemakers stitch shoes, tinsmiths decorate ornate lanterns, and blacksmiths form farm implements. Children can play historic games on the commons, such as graces, hoops, and cup and ball. At scheduled times throughout the year, children can participate in activities in the Museum Activities Building at no extra charge. An old-fashioned schoolhouse is complete with a schoolmaster who is known to ask visiting students to read, recite, or mind their manners.

Many of the events of special interest to families are scheduled during the summer. Family Fun Weekends are held throughout the summer with entertainment, a toy hot-air balloon flight, musket firing, music with dancing dolls, singing, and dancing. The Fourth of July is a lively affair with people in period dress, a parade, a reading of the Declaration of Independence, picnicking on the common, and live music. There is a haying contest in July, a summer garden day in early August, and other special programs designed for children.

The price of admission includes a second consecutive day free, so families can take their time and participate in all of the activities that interest them.

Season: Year-round.
Cost: Adults: $15, children six to fifteen $7.50; kids under six free.

PLIMOUTH PLANTATION

Address: PO Box 1620, Plymouth, Massachusetts 02362 (Route 3, exits four or five)
Telephone: 508–746–1622

Children will get a blank stare if they ask a costumed interpreter at Plimouth Plantation about anything having to do with modern life, or for that matter, of life past 1627. Interpreters even speak in seventeenth-century dialects. This living museum of seventeenth-century New England harkens back to the time of the Colonists who settled in New England and of the Native Americans they encountered. Buildings in a re-created pilgrim village, where people assume the roles of the town's residents, contain accurate historical reproductions of household objects, and visitors are encouraged to touch just about anything they want. The town militia often practices its drills each day around the village, women cook over an open hearth, housewives and servants milk cows, and there are baby animals to tend to in the spring.

Next to the village is a Wampanoag Indian Homesite, where Native American interpreters in period dress go about their business. Children can ask them questions about their lives; in fact, the more the children ask, the more they will get out of their visit. A new interactive exhibit in the Visitor Center takes visitors through Native and English relationships through 1690. Kids will love the computer technology throughout the exhibits.

A reproduction of the *Mayflower* on the Plymouth waterfront near Plymouth Rock, about two miles away, is also part of the museum. In the summer a trolley runs back and forth between them. The ship is set up as it might have been in 1621, just a few days before it set sail for its return voyage to England.

Children's activities are scheduled throughout the year, with a heavier concentration during the summer months. Activities might include writing with quill and ink, dressing like a pilgrim in doublets and breeches, and learning to play Native American games. Older kids will like the games-making workshop, archaeological programs, and navigational and map-making workshops. Before you go, request a calendar of events so you can plan to visit when there are special programs for your kids.

The grounds house a cafeteria, picnic area, bike shop, gift shops, and a crafts center with artisans at work. The gift shops sell some reproductions of seventeenth-century children's games, such as one called "The Voyage of the *Mayflower*," and other children's books and toys.

Season: April through November.

Accommodations: Plimouth Plantation is 45 miles south of Boston and about twenty minutes from Cape Cod; see page 00 for accommodations ideas on the Cape.

Cost: Adult admission $18.50; children under eighteen $11, under six free. Trolley $3.50 for an all-day ticket. Become a member (family memberships $70) and you'll get free family admission, various discounts, and publications—a good buy, especially for larger families.

COUNTRY DANCE AND SONG SOCIETY'S FAMILY WEEK

Address: 17 New South Street, Northampton, Massachusetts 01060
Telephone: 413–584–9913; fax: 413–585–8728

The Country Dance and Song Society is a nationwide association of people who enjoy traditional, historical, and contemporary American and English folk dance, song, and instrumental music. Families at three camps—one in Massachusetts, one in West Virginia, and one in New York—enjoy dancing, traditional crafts, singing, swimming, storytelling, and more during week-long family programs.

Pinewoods Camp, in the woodlands near Plymouth, Massachusetts, has cozy cabins nestled under the pines near lakes. The largest lake is a mile long and its clear blue water is suitable for swimming and canoeing. Four dance pavilions are set in the pine forest. Housing is in small bunk rooms with bathrooms nearby.

Buffalo Gap, near Capon Bridge, West Virginia, is located on two hundred acres of a forested mountainside, part of which has been cleared for the camp's buildings. The property has a two-acre lake with swimming, a slide and diving board, and enormous dance pavilions. Each family is housed in a bunkroom built to hold twelve.

Camp Kinder Ring is located on one hundred acres in Hopewell Junction, New York, sixty-five miles north of New York City in the Hudson River Valley. It has a beautiful beachfront on Sylvan Lake with swimming, canoes, sailboats, and paddleboats available. The camp has several spaces for dancing and socializing. Each family is housed in a bunk room with bathrooms attached.

The programs at all three camps follow the same format, combining music, dance, crafts, songs, and storytelling for children only as well as for families together. Two classes per day are arranged by age group and another class is arranged by interest. Children age four and up enjoy singing games and circle dances. For older children the program includes sword dance, contradancing, and English country dance. Crafts classes for kids offer wood carving, quilting, or other activities. **Accommodations:** Housing is different at each camp (see above). Meals are served in a dining hall and everyone pitches in with the work for perhaps a half hour each day.

Special Features: Kids four to twelve have daily classes of their own, while teens and adults can choose among classes in English country dance, square dance, clogging, carving, dance band, storytelling, and more. Twice a day the entire group gathers for singing, stories, and dancing.

Cost: Adults $500 per week; children thirteen to seventeen $450, ten to twelve $375, seven to nine $325, four to six $275, two and three $175, and under two $35. Rates include lodging, food, tuition, and all activities. A special campers' week, in which the participants develop the program, costs less: adults $400 per week, children thirteen to seventeen $350, nine to twelve $300, seven and eight $260, four to six $220, two and three $140, and under two $30.

APPALACHIAN MOUNTAIN CLUB'S FAMILY EDUCATION PROGRAMS

Address: 5 Joy Street, Boston, Massachusetts 02108. Programs take place in New Hampshire, the Berkshires, and the Catskill Mountains
Telephone: 617–523–0636

The Appalachian Mountain Club conducts top-quality workshops for adults and excellent family education programs for parents and children and grandparents and grandchildren. Sessions over a full weekend include family backpacking trips and workshops such as "Discovering the Natural World with Children." Shorter weekend morning programs are for families with children age six and up and include such topics as life in a stream and pond, the world of insects, and wildflowers, wild animals, and the wilderness. Children also are welcome on any of the club's easier guided hikes, a series that takes beginning and experienced hikers on a guided introduction to the flora, fauna, archeology, and history of the White Mountains in New Hampshire.

Accommodations: Family programs are offered at the AMC's Pinkham Notch Visitor Center in New Hampshire, Bascom Lodge atop Mount Greylock in the Berkshires of Massachusetts, and at Valley View Lodge, a privately run facility in the heart of the Catskills' high peaks region.

Cost: Fees for a weekend range from $80 to $135 for adults and $40 to $55 for children. The price includes lodging, guides where needed, and most meals. AMC members receive a ten-percent discount (family membership is $65 per year).

NATURE PROGRAMS AT PINKHAM NOTCH

Address: Box 298, Gorham, New Hampshire 03581
Telephone: 603–466–2721

Appalachian Mountain Club's nature programs at Pinkham Notch include Family Discovery Weekend, Teen Wilderness Adventures (an overnight for ages twelve to eighteen), and Mountain Discovery Camp (a day camp for ages seven to twelve). Programs vary in length from a weekend to several weeks and include canoeing, birding, low-impact camping, nature crafts, map and compass reading, and wildflowers. There are also many day and evening programs such as nature walks appropriate for families that are free of charge offered daily during the summer and weekends during the rest of year. The AMC will send you a catalog of current programs on request. Make reservations to stay overnight at Pinkham Notch when you book the program.

Season: Year-round.

Accommodations: Bunkrooms of different sizes; family rooms are available. Bathrooms are shared.

Cost: Program fees range from $10 for a day program to several hundred dollars for the camp and overnight teen programs. Fees include lodging, instruction, equipment, and meals. AMC members receive a ten-percent discount; family membership $65.

APPALACHIAN MOUNTAIN CLUB'S HUT-TO-HUT HIKES

Address: 5 Joy Street, Boston, Massachusetts 02108
Telephone: 617–523– 0636 (AMC main number); 603–466–2727 (reservations)

The Appalachian Mountain Club operates eight alpine huts in New Hampshire, each a day's hike apart along the Appalachian Trail. Hikes to two of the huts, Zealand Falls and Lonesome Lake, are well within the ability of beginning hikers. The hut-to-hut hikes open the overnight hiking experience to families that otherwise would need to pack a tent, stove, cooking gear, and food. The huts provide comfortable shelter and fresh, hot dinners and breakfasts. Hikers bring sheets or a sleeping bag, lunch, snacks, and other personal gear.

Lonesome Lake Hut, which stands in a birch and balsam forest, has lake swimming and a nearby beaver colony. Lonesome is the most popular family hiking destination because the hike is short (1.7 miles) and it has a refreshing lake. Individual bunk rooms for four, six, or eight people can be reserved for a family group. Special rates are available in summer that include lodging, breakfast and dinner, and special daily "Family Discovery" programs led by staff and volunteers include natural history activities, guided walks, and evening talks.

Zealand Falls Hut is at the eastern edge of the new Pemigewasset Wilderness along Whitewall Brook. The cascading waters and crystal-clear pools are popular swimming spots for families. Most hikers begin at a trailhead 2.7 miles away for an easy hike in. The hut accommodates a total of thirty-six people in twin bunk rooms.

Season: June through August.

Cost: Overnight lodging, breakfast, and dinner, adults $62, children $32 per night. The price is lower midweek in June and July, and is discounted further for club members. Rates for lodge and breakfast only are available. Family membership in the Appalachian Mountain Club is $65 per year and entitles you to discounts for all AMC lodges, huts, and education programs. The huts are most popular on weekends and in August. Lonesome Lake Hut offers low package rates throughout the summer season that are $13 to $18 lower than the regular rates and include lodging, dinner, and breakfast.

FLETCHER FARM SCHOOL FOR THE ARTS AND CRAFTS

Address: 611 Route 103 South, Ludlow, Vermont 05149
Telephone: 802-228-8770

Every summer since 1947, a converted farmhouse, 200-year-old barn, corn crib, and sugar house have been bustling with workshops and classes at the Fletcher Farm School for the Arts and Crafts. Special classes such as drawing and painting, dancing, wood carving, weaving, and creative arts are offered for children, with a few designated especially for "young adults" or teenagers. Adults can also take week-long classes on basketry, early American decorations, wood carving, stained glass, or rug hooking, to name just a few of the 100 selections available. Parents who don't want to take a class can enroll their kids and explore the area's great beauty, golf courses, lakes, and quaint villages. The school, surrounded by hundreds of acres of forest land and meadows, is operated by the Society of Vermont Craftsmen.

Season: June, July, and August, with most classes offered in July and August.

Accommodations: Adults may board on the campus of the school but families need to stay in one of the many condos or campgrounds nearby. Day students can purchase a meal package in the cafeteria for $20 per day. For information on where to stay, contact the Ludlow Area Chamber of Commerce, 802–228–5318.

Cost: Tuition for a five-day course $170; $85 for a two-day course. Some courses have a materials fee.

THE CHEWONKI FOUNDATION

Address: RR 2, Box 1200, Wiscasset, Maine 04587
Telephone: 207–882–7323; fax: 207–882–4074

Many of Chewonki's outdoor programs take place in Maine, but you'll find their family groups canoeing the waters of the Okeefenokee Swamp in Georgia, the Everglades in Florida, and the Mistissini Reserve in Quebec. Their goal is to enhance appreciation and respect of the natural world and their canoeing, kayaking, and sailing trips are led by professional staff members who have a background in natural history and are certified in first aid, CPR, and water safety. They provide all equipment. Most trips are for ages twelve and up, but a few (such as Introduction to Canoe Camping on Big Wood Pond and Attean Pond) are for families with kids age eight and up. Most of the Maine trips take place in summer, while Canoeing the Florida Everglades takes eight days in late February to explore the mangrove-lined channels and inland bays. Expect to see manatees, alligators, and turtles.

Accommodations: Participants usually camp; Chewonki staff oversees the cooking and you're apt to have hearty meals with home-baked desserts. The Foundation provides tents, and can supply waterproof river bags, sleeping bags, and pads for a small rental fee.

Cost: Fees vary depending on length of trip: adults $360 for four days, kids one and over $270 for four days. Six-day trips, adults $540, kids $450.

STATE PARK CABINS AND RESORTS

*S*tate parks have some of the lowest-priced resorts and cabins in the United States. Established in areas of great natural beauty, state parks are found on the edge of towering mountain peaks and crystalline lakes, nestled among rolling green hills, presiding over vast prairies and harsh desert landscapes, and marking sites of historical significance. Every state in the union has parks that are open to the public, and more than half offer remarkably low-priced cabin accommodations and resort facilities.

While private resorts might have several hundred scenic acres, most state parks have thousands of acres of unspoiled wilderness, usually selected for their breathtaking scenery. Many are situated on lakes, rivers, and seashores, offering a wide selection of reasonably priced recreational activities. At the very least, you can expect to find swimming, boating, or excellent hiking trails. Most state park resorts also feature golf, tennis, boating, lawn games, nature centers, and horseback riding, among other activities.

Many of the first state parks were developed in the 1930s through the efforts of the Civilian Conservation Corps (CCC), one of Franklin Delano Roosevelt's most successful New Deal programs. Stone and log lodges and cabins contain the legacy of a conservation program that did much to preserve the natural and historical treasures of many states in the nation. Other, newer parks have since been developed, with up-to-date lodgings and modern amenities.

All states will provide you with information on their state park accommodations, either through their tourist office or the state park office. Generally the parks are busiest on summer weekends and holidays and throughout the months of July and August. Some parks start taking reservations as early as a year in advance. Because state park cabins and resorts are such a bargain, they are popular and fill up quickly. Cancellations occur, however, so there's always a chance of getting in. Do your homework and make sure you know the reservation system required by each state.

ALABAMA

Address: Alabama Department of Conservation and Natural Resources, Division of State Parks, 64 North Union Street, PO Box 301452, Montgomery, Alabama 36130-1452
Telephone: 800–ALA–PARK (nationwide reservations); 334–242–3333

Alabama has one of the best resort parks in the system. Gulf State Park Resort, with a full-service hotel on the white sands of the Gulf of Mexico and comfortable cabins on the shores of freshwater Lake Shelby next door, is an excellent value. It is described in greater detail on pages 43–44.

Five other parks have hotels or lodges, and eleven more have cottages or chalets. All hotel and cabin guests have free lake fishing, boat launching, use of the swimming pool and beach areas, and tennis courts. Six of the parks have golf courses, two have full-service marinas, and most have hiking, nature trails, tennis and basketball courts, and playgrounds.

Accommodations: Older, rustic cabins have simple furnishings, fully equipped kitchens, heat, air-conditioning, and linens. Modern cabins are comfortably furnished and have linens, air-conditioning, and fully equipped kitchens. Certain parks require a one-week minimum stay during summer.

Cost: Rates have seasonal adjustments, and the lowest and highest rates quoted here may vary, but not by much. Be sure to inquire about special getaway and golf vacation packages that are offered time to time. Rates also vary from park to park. Rustic cabins $40 to $75 per night. Modern cabins $40 to $124 per night, depending on number of people and time of year.

ARKANSAS

Address: Division of State Parks, Arkansas Department of Parks and Tourism, One Capitol Mall, Little Rock, Arkansas 72201
Telephone: 501–682–1191

Arkansas's premier resort park is Degray Lake Resort State Park, on the north shore of a 13,800-acre fishing and water sports lake. Its full-service marina, golf course, pool, tennis courts, bike rentals, and many special events make it a popular destination. Families can stay in comfortable lodge rooms or in houseboats along the lake. Another family favorite, Lake Ouachita State Park, is situated at the lake's eastern tip. Historic A-frame cabins overlook the lake, which offers swimming, waterskiing, scuba diving, boating, and fishing for bream, crappie, catfish, and trout. A total of nine state parks have cabins, and four have lodges where children under age twelve stay free with an adult. Most parks present special guided hikes, lake tours, and historic demonstrations during the summer. Arkansas's first state park, Petit Jean, is described in detail on pages 186–187, and an Ozark Folk Center listing is on pages 302–303.

Accommodations: Many of the one-, two-, and three-bedroom cabins have fireplaces, and nearly all have fully equipped kitchens. A few parks have "Rent-A-Camps" outfitted with tents, coolers, lanterns, and other camping gear, perfect for those who want an outdoor experience without having to bring all the equipment with them.

Cost: Cabins $35 to $95 per night depending on size of cabin (one, two, or three bedrooms) and season. Each additional person (over twelve) $5 per night in lodge rooms and cabins. Rent-A-Camps $25 per night. Advance reservations necessary; call or write the individual park. Reservations for April through October accepted beginning January 1 of the same year. Winter lodgings $10 lower than regular rates, except for special events periods.

DELAWARE

Address: Department of Natural Resources and Environmental Control, Division of Parks and Recreation, 89 Kings Highway, PO Box 1401, Dover, Delaware 19903
Telephone: 302–284–4526 State Park Office; 302–284–3412 Killen Pond State Park

Killen Pond State Park is Delaware's only state park with cabins. Its location at the edge of a small lake means it is filled with activities to keep any family busy exploring the water by boat (canoes, rowboats, and pedal boats can be rented during the summer), swimming in the 25-meter pool, hiking, biking, and enjoying the playground, fitness trail, games court, and ball fields. Families who like to fish can drop a line for largemouth bass, carp, perch, bluegill, and pickerel.

Accommodations: Six cabins are exactly the same, with a double and bunk beds in the bedroom, a small kitchen/dining area, and a living area. Guests need to bring their own linens, pots, pans, dishes, and utensils.

Cost: From Memorial Day to Labor Day, by the week only, $230. Per night rest of the year, $34 to $45.

FLORIDA

Address: Department of Environmental Protection, 3900 Commonwealth Boulevard, Mail Station 535, Tallahassee, Florida 32399-3000
Telephone: For a free state parks guide, 904–488–9872

Curious about manatees, the gentle endangered creatures once thought to be mermaids? Blue Springs State Park, near the St. Johns River, has a spring-fed water system for wonderful swimming and canoeing and is one of the few natural manatee habitats in the United States. Eight of Florida's state parks have cabins ranging from primitive to deluxe. Most offer swimming, hiking, and naturalist programs such as guided walks or campfire talks. We profile another terrific park, St. Joseph Peninsula Park, on page 258.

Accommodations: Primitive cabins have electricity, bunk beds, and a shared bathhouse. Other cabins all have linens and kitchens and range from basic to very modern and comfortably appointed.

Cost: Primitive cabins $20 to $30 per night; other cabin prices vary by park. Most parks have cabins that cost $50 per night; several also have cabins for $55 to $110 per night, depending on degree of luxury and size.

GEORGIA

Address: Georgia State Parks, 205 Butler Street, Atlanta, Georgia 30334
Telephone: 404–656–3530 (information); 800–864–7275(reservations)

Twenty-six of Georgia's parks have cottages and five have lodges, all situated to provide scenic views of the lakes, mountains, valleys, and other spectacular natural riches in the state's park system. All cottages have fully equipped kitchens and many have porches and decks over-looking these vistas. For example, Cloudland Canyon State Park strad-dles a deep canyon cut into the mountains. At the bottom of the canyon are waterfalls accessible by hiking trails. A swimming pool and tennis courts are available for guests. Red Top Mountain State Park is about thirty-five minutes from Atlanta on a 2,000-acre peninsula in the middle of Lake Allatoona. Cottages border the lake; there is also a swimming beach, lodge, restaurant, seven-mile nature trail, and marina with boat rentals, including houseboats.

See pages 188 and 39 for detailed descriptions of Crooked River State Park Cabins in St. Mary's and F. D. Roosevelt State Park.

Accommodations: One-, two-, and three-bedroom cottages have complete kitchens and linens. All cottages have heat and air-conditioning. Lodge rooms are available in five state parks.

Cost: Cottages $40 to $95 per night, depending on size and time of week. Lodge rooms $50 to 75 per night. During summer months, res-ervations accepted by the week only. Maximum stay fourteen days. Res-ervations can be made up to eleven months in advance, but often there are last-minute cancellations.

HAWAII

Address: PO Box 621, Honolulu, Hawaii 96809
Telephone: 808–587–0300 for cabins on Hawaii and Maui; 808–293–1736 for Oahu; 808–335–6061 for Kauai

With warm tropical waters, lush vegetation, and breathtaking scenery, Hawaii is a favorite vacation spot year-round. Seven of its state parks offer housekeeping cabins. The Hawaii State Parks office manages the cabins on the islands of Hawaii and Maui and concessionaires run the cabin rentals in state parks on the islands of Oahu and Kauai; they all offer the best-priced lodging anywhere in the island chain. Permits are granted for a maximum visit of five days. See page 206 for a description of the cabins in Hana, Maui, and other general information.

Accommodations: The housekeeping cabins come with all house-keeping equipment and bedding. A few are duplex-style. Several parks have barracks that serve as a group camp: they can accommodate up to 64 people in several barracks buildings with a community kitchen. One park has simple A-frames that are similar to camping cabins and accom-modate up to four people.

Cost: Most cabins $45 per night for up to four people, $55 up to six people. Barracks $55 per night for up to eight people, $5 per person up to 64 people. A-frames $20 per night.

ILLINOIS

Address: Illinois Department of Natural Resources, Office of Public Services, 524 South Second Street, Suite 610, Springfield, Illinois 62701-1787
Telephone: 217–782–7454

Once a popular pirate roost and now a popular state park, Cave-in Rock State Park Resort is near a bluff overlooking the Ohio River in the Shawnee National Forest. Cabin guests can enjoy the panoramic views that the pirates once used. It has four duplex guest houses with eight suites, each with a private deck overlooking the river. A family-style restaurant serves breakfast, lunch, and dinner, featuring such specialties as southern fried catfish and homemade desserts. Extensive hiking trails, playgrounds, boating, and fishing are out the front door. Another family favorite, Starved Rock Park, has a historic lodge, canoe rentals, and other water sports on the Illinois River, and two types of cabins to rent. A spectacular waterfall within hiking distance of the lodge is especially dramatic when it freezes in winter.

A total of seven Illinois state parks have resorts with historic lodges, many of which were built in the 1930s and feature hand-hewn beams and rock fireplaces. All have been carefully restored. A number of the resorts have cabins on the grounds, and all have enough recreational opportunities to keep any family busy.

Accommodations: Lodge rooms usually have one or two double or king-size beds and sofabeds. Cabins vary in size and do not always have kitchens. Deluxe cabins have fireplaces. Rollaway beds and cribs are available at most parks.

Cost: Summer rates (March through November) are higher; double rooms $50 to $75 per night, each additional person $5 per night. In winter, $45 to $60 per night. Children twelve and under stay free in parents' room.

INDIANA

Address: Indiana Division of State Parks, Indiana Department of Natural Resources, 402 West Washington Street, Room 298, Indianapolis, Indiana 46204
Telephone: 800–622– 4931; 317–232–4124

Indiana's eight state parks with inexpensive housekeeping cabins can be found along lakes, creeks, reservoirs, and hillsides. Most offer boating, swimming, fishing, hiking, and naturalist programs. Several have horseback riding rental, bike trails, and cross-country skiing. They begin taking reservations exactly one year in advance. Weekly reservations are required in June, July, and August. See descriptions of Pokagon State Park on Lake James and Lincoln State Park on pages 31 and 184.

Accommodations: Cabins offer bedrooms, living areas, kitchens, and modern bathroom facilities. Extras vary from park to park; some provide linens and have fully equipped kitchens, while others do not.

Cost: Weekly rates $210 to $525; nightly rates $22 to $80, depending on size, location, and season. Most cabins cost about $400 per week.

IOWA

Address: Iowa Department of Natural Resources, Wallace Building, Des Moines, Iowa 50319
Telephone: 515–281–5145

The most popular of Iowa's eight state parks with cabins is Backbone, named for a unique limestone geological formation that sticks up out of the middle of a river like the backbone of an enormous dragon or dinosaur. Backbone has sixteen original cabins built in the 1930s by the Civilian Conservation Corps, as well as four newer two-bedroom cabins. People come to fish, swim, and picnic in summer, and cross-country ski and ice fish in winter. Iowa's state parks boast excellent playgrounds that have undergone extensive renovations and expansion in recent years.

Accommodations: Primitive cabins have a central bathhouse and do not have kitchens. Older cabins have kitchens but lack air-conditioning and heat and are open only in the summer. Modern cabins have kitchens and private baths.

Cost: Primitive cabins $15 per night, $80 per week; older cabins $25 per night, $150 per week; modern cabins $40 per night, $225 per week.

KENTUCKY

Address: Kentucky Department of Parks, 500 Mero Street, 11th floor, Frankfort, Kentucky 40601-1974
Telephone: 502–564–2172

Kentucky's impressive state lodgings include sixteen state resort parks with lodges and all but one have fully equipped housekeeping cottages, too. Many have boating, miniature golf, fishing, horseback riding, planned children's activities, and swimming pools. Lake Cumberland State Resort Park, profiled on pages 41-42, has even more things to do. In addition, many of the state parks have historic sites, outdoor museums, dramas, reenactments, and special events. When requesting information, ask for the brochure and listing of special events at the different parks.

Accommodations: All cottages have fully equipped kitchens, air-conditioning, and linens. Nine different cottage types range from efficiencies to deluxe three-bedroom units. The newest and most deluxe are called executive cabins, each with modern appliances such as a dishwasher and microwave oven, stylish appointments, a fireplace, and two bathrooms; they sleep eight to twelve people. A typical cabin for four would be a two-bedroom with a living room, bath, fully equipped kitchen, and all linens. Many cabins are duplexes. Most lodge rooms have two double beds, and suites are available.

Cost: Two-bedroom cottages $79 to $95, lodge rooms $45 to $65, depending on season and location. Children sixteen and under stay free. Reservations accepted up to thirteen months in advance.

LOUISIANA

Address: Louisiana Office of State Parks, PO Box 44426, Baton Rouge, Louisiana 70804-4426
Telephone: 504–342–8111

One of Louisiana's most popular state parks is Bayou Segnette State Park on the west bank of New Orleans, overlooking a bay. Cabins have screened porches or decks and their own private boat docks. The park has a wave pool, swimming pools, playgrounds, picnic sites, and nature trails. It's a terrific place to headquarter to combine a city visit to New Orleans with an outdoors experience. See page 187 for more on this park.

Another favorite, Chico State Park, has several different types of cabins and is on a lake with water sports and excellent fishing. Its rustic lodge, built in the 1940s, sleeps twelve people in two double beds, and four bunk beds. It's fully equipped with a kitchen, dining area, living room, air-conditioning, and heat.

Seven of Louisiana's state parks have cabins and two of the parks have lodges suitable for a large family group or several families. Many have beautiful locations on lakes, bayous, or reservoirs. People looking for a family reunion site would be wise to look into Louisiana's six different group camps, which have dorm-style accommodations, private swimming pools, and large kitchens. They sleep 50 to 160 people and cost $60 to $320 per night, depending on the size and facilities.

Accommodations: Four types of cabins are available throughout the state park system: cabin type #1 sleeps up to eight people and is brand new; cabin type #2, a bit older, also sleeps up to eight people; cabin type #3 sleeps up to six people; and cabin type #4, more rustic still, sleeps four to six people. All cabins feature fully equipped kitchens, heat, and air-conditioning, and some have fireplaces. All bed linens are provided, but guests must bring their own towels. Fully equipped lodges sleep ten to twelve people.

Cost: Cabin type #1, $65 per night; #2, $60 per night; #3, $50 per night; #4, $45 per night. Lodges $90 per night. Reservations for April 1 to September 30 accepted beginning January 2; reservations for October 1 through March 31 accepted beginning July 1. People reserve by phone for the first twenty-four hours on the first day reservations are allowed and mail in reservation requests after that.

MAINE

Address: Bureau of Parks and Land, 22 State House Station, Augusta, Maine 04333-0022
Telephone: 207–287–3821

One of Maine's most beautiful state parks, Baxter State Park in Millinocket (207–723–5140), has simple cabins. Baxter is a wilderness area set aside by a former Maine governor with the stipulation that it be preserved as a sanctuary for wildlife and a recreation area for those who love nature. Hiking, fishing, bird watching, and mountain climbing are popular pastimes; the park contains Maine's highest peak, just short of a mile in height. Cabins and campsites are available and are situated on two large ponds. One has a swimming dock and rental canoes are available for exploring and fishing.

Accommodations: Cabins accommodate two to four people. Cooking facilities are outside and consist of grills and picnic tables. Gas lighting and firewood is provided, and cabins are heated by woodstoves.

Cost: Two-bedded cabins $30, three-bedded cabins $40, four-bedded cabins $50 per night. Reservations must be made in advance by writing the park at 64 Balsam Drive, Millinocket, Maine 04462. Canoes $1 per hour or $8 per day.

MARYLAND

Address: Maryland Forest, Park, and Wildlife Service, Trawes State Office Building, 580 Taylor Avenue, Annapolis, Maryland 21401
Telephone: 301–974–3771

Rental cabins are available at five state parks in Maryland, most with swimming, boating, nature programs, and hiking. Herringbone Manor and New Germany state parks have lake swimming, boat rentals, hiking, and fishing in summer and cross-country skiing in winter. Elk Neck State Park has swimming and boating along a river, and Jane's Island State Park has boating and fishing along the bay.

Accommodations: Most cabins are equipped for housekeeping with complete kitchens. Different sizes sleep four, six, or eight people. All park cabins have private baths except those at Elk Neck, which use a central washhouse.

Cost: Four-person cabins $70 per night, $350 per week; six-person cabins $450 per week; eight-person cabins $450 per week. Reservations can be made up to one year in advance. Contact the park you are interested in directly by phone (the office above can provide phone numbers). Weekly reservations only for Memorial Day through Labor Day.

MASSACHUSETTS

Address: Division of Parks and Forests, 100 Cambridge Street, Boston, Massachusetts 02202
Telephone: Mohawk Trails, 413–339–5504; Savoie Mountain, 413–663–8469

Only two state parks in Massachusetts have cabins: Mohawk Trails State Forest in the Connecticut River Valley and Savoie Mountain State Park in the Berkshires. Both have fishing, swimming, kayaking, canoeing, hiking, and mountain biking (bring your own bikes) nearby.

Accommodations: Cabins have one to three rooms and are rather primitive. Larger cabins have cold running water and an indoor sink; all cabins have a fireplace and grill out front and bunk beds, table and chairs, and a wood stove inside.

Cost: Cabins $8 to $10 per night. Reservations accepted up to six months in advance and are by the week only in July and August, with a two-night minimum stay the rest of the year.

MICHIGAN

Address: Department of Natural Resources, State Parks Division, Box 30257, Lansing, Michigan 48909
Telephone: 517–373–9900; 517–373–1270

Several of Michigan's state parks have well-maintained bike trails, and families headquarter at the parks to explore the area on bicycles. Eighteen of Michigan's state parks have simple cabins. Many overlook lakes, rivers, or streams, and swimming, boating, and fishing are popular pastimes. In addition you can find horseback riding, cross-country skiing, sailboarding, and even a state park with a field dog training section.

Accommodations: "Wilderness" cabins are somewhat primitive and come in a variety of sizes. All have twin beds or bunks, woodburning stoves (no electricity), table, and chairs. There are pit toilets and outside pumps for water. More comfortable "mini-cabins" are found next to the campground areas and have electricity, two sets of bunks, table, chairs, and electricity, outdoor grill, picnic tables, and fire ring, and are a short walk from bathhouses. Bring your own bedding and kitchen utensils.

Cost: Cabin fees, based on capacity and location, $25 to $60 per night. Mini-cabins are $30 to $50 per night.

MINNESOTA

Address: Minnesota Department of Natural Resources, DNR Information Center, 500 Layafette Road, St. Paul, Minnesota 55155-4040
Telephone: MISTIX reservations, 800–765–CAMP; state park office, 612–296–4776

The land of 10,000 lakes has several state parks with cabins and one with a historic lodge and inn. Children under twelve stay free, and cabins vary by park. Some are very large, such as the two-story, six-bedroom cabin at Saint Croix that rents for an unbelievably low $100 per night. Itasca, established in 1891, is the oldest Minnesota state park and has the widest selection of lodgings. It is here that the mighty Mississippi River begins its 2,552-mile journey to the Gulf of Mexico. Accommodations are in the historic Douglas lodge complex built by the Civilian Conservation Corps, featuring cabins, an inn, a lodge, and a family hostel. Cabins at Scenic State Park come with their own private boat or canoe. Reservations are made though the MISTIX Corporation, a private reservation company.

Accommodations: Primitive two-bedroom cabins have kitchens, living rooms, dining rooms, and bathhouses. More modern cabins have fully equipped kitchens, fireplaces, and full baths.

Cost: Primitive two-bedroom cabins $50 per night, more modern cabins $50 to $80 per night.

MISSISSIPPI

Address: Department of Wildlife, Fisheries and Parks, PO Box 451, Jackson, Mississippi 39205-0451
Telephone: 601–364–2120

Each cabin has its own fishing pier at Percy Quinn State Park, one of this state's family favorites, and also one of the largest. Guests staying in one of the twenty cabins can explore the lake on paddleboats or canoes, drop a line from a fishing boat, swim in the pool, and play golf or miniature golf. Another very popular state park is Buccaneer State Park with camping (no cabins) and a full-scale water park.

Most of Mississippi's twenty-two parks with cabins are built around water. You'll find the cabins along small creeks, immense lakes, and the sandy beaches of the Gulf of Mexico. Water sports are plentiful, and canoeing, swimming, boating, and waterskiing can keep you cool when the temperatures rise.

Accommodations: All cabins have air-conditioning and heat, and are furnished with linens and fully equipped kitchens. Cabins are classified by their architectural style: "deluxe" are the most modern, "standard" were constructed in the fifties and sixties, and "rustic" were constructed by the Civilian Conservation Corps in the thirties with stone or rough-hewn wood. Cabins accommodate two to twelve people, with the majority holding four to six guests.

Cost: Cabins for two $30 to $45 per night; for four or six $30 to $50 per night. Motel rooms $50 for a family of four.

MISSOURI

Address: Missouri Department of Natural Resources, Division of Parks, Recreation and Historic Preservation, PO Box 176, Jefferson City, Missouri 65102
Telephone: 800–344–6946

All eleven of Missouri's state parks are on the edge of sparkling lakes, fast-running rivers, or more leisurely winding streams. Recreational opportunities abound—you'll find excellent fishing, swimming, and boating, plus hiking trails, swimming pools, caves, and even forests with Indian petroglyphs. One of the state's oldest and most popular parks is Bennet Springs, where nearly one hundred million gallons of water gush daily. The bubbling pool feeds a stream with excellent fishing for rainbow trout. Canoeing is popular on the nearby Niangua river, and there are cabins, a swimming pool, dining lodge, and visitors center.

Accommodations: Housekeeping cabins have linens and fully equipped kitchens. Sleeping cabins and motel rooms have linens. All cabins and rooms are air-conditioned. Most are open April 15 through October 31, although a few are open longer.

Cost: Prices vary according to number of persons and number of bedrooms. Housekeeping cabins $40 to $105 per night, motel rooms $35 to $55, sleeping cabins $30 to $65. To reserve, call or write the individual park of your choice; the Division of Parks will send you the list. Two-day minimum stay for summer reservations.

NEBRASKA

Address: Nebraska State Parks Commission, PO Box 30370, Lincoln, Nebraska 68503
Telephone: 402–471–0641

Nebraska, with its endless ranch lands, fertile farmland, and rolling hills, has accommodations in seven state parks. Many of the parks have horse rentals, fishing, swimming, and boating. Platte River State Park features unusual tepee accommodations along with inexpensive camper cabins. This former children's summer camp, now operated by the state, offers horseback riding, a swimming pool, and boating on a small lake. Another family favorite, Eugene Mahoney State Park, has a lodge, swimming pool and water slide, horseback riding, paddleboat rental, a driving range, and miniature golf. Western-style Fort Robinson State Park has cabins, lodge rooms, several larger houses to rent, horse rentals, a chuck wagon cookout, swimming, stagecoach rides, train tours, and a trail ride breakfast. Two Rivers State Park offers guests the chance to sleep in an authentic caboose that has been refurbished to sleep six.

Accommodation: Fully equipped cabins have two to five bedrooms. Camper cabins are sleeping accommodations only. Canvas tepees are decorated with Indian artwork and set on a carpeted wooden platform; they sleep six to eight people and have grills and picnic tables outside.

Cost: Simple two-bedroom cabins $40 to $50 per night, tepees $10 per night, camper cabins $20 to $30 per night.

NEW JERSEY

Address: Division of Parks and Forestry, CN 404, Trenton, New Jersey 08625
Telephone: 609–292–2797

Sixteen miles of the Appalachian Trail runs along the ridge of Stokes State Forest, and as you might imagine, the hiking is spectacular. The park has two lakes, Ocquittunk and Stoney. Rustic housekeeping cabins are next to Lake Ocquittunk, and lake swimming under the watchful eye of a lifeguard is possible seven miles away at Stoney Lake. Boaters can bring their own craft and use Lake Ocquittunk. A total of six of New Jersey's parks have family cabins, one park has group cabins, and most have boating, fishing, swimming, children's playgrounds, and nature trails.

Accommodations: Most cabins accommodate four to six people and several parks have cabins that sleep eight to twelve people. All cabins have toilets (but not necessarily showers or bathtubs), kitchen facilities, living rooms, and sleeping quarters. Some require guests to bring their own linens and cookware. Primitive camp shelters have four bunks. Enclosed lean-tos are also available.

Cost: Four-bunk cabins $28 per night, $196 per week. Six-bunk cabins $50 per night, $294 per week. Eight-bunk cabins $56 per night, $392 per week. Twelve-bunk cabins (at one park only) $70 per night, $490 per week. Lean-tos $15 per night, camp shelters $20 per night. Cabin reservations are by lottery.

NEW YORK

Address: New York State Parks, 1 Empire State Plaza, Albany, New York 12238
Telephone: cabin reservations, 800–456–CAMP; state park offices, 518 – 474– 0456

One of New York's most beautiful state parks is Letchworth, south of Rochester, which is sometimes referred to as the Grand Canyon of the East. Its eighty-two cabins are within hiking distance of three magnificent waterfalls. Grounds include a swimming pool, hiking trails, an Indian museum, white water rafting, balloon rides, and an inn with a restaurant. Several types and sizes of cabins are available, from rustic one-room affairs to fully equipped two- and three-bedroom units. Allegany State Park, near Jamestown, has more than 400 cabins spread over 64,000 acres. The park is so large it is divided into two sides; the most popular with families is the Red House Side, which has boating, swimming, miniature golf, bike rental, and horseback riding. Both sides have man-made lakes, and naturalists take visitors on beaver colony tours and star-gazing expeditions. Cabins in these facilities are simple, with shared bathhouses.

Accommodations: Cabins must be reserved by the week during the summer and by the day the rest of the year. Modern two-bedroom cabins have kitchens and bathrooms; guests bring their own kitchenware and linens. More primitive cabins have cots, kitchens, and shared bathhouses.

Cost: Cabin prices $17 to $50 per night and $122 to $340 per week, depending on size and amenities.

OHIO

Address: Department of Natural Resources, Fountain Square, Building C-1, Columbus, Ohio 43224
Telephone: 800–BUCKEYE (information); 800–282–7275 (lodge reservations)

The natural settings for the lodges in Ohio's eight resort parks have been chosen to reflect the focal point of each particular park. Maumee Bay, at the edge of Lake Erie, has incomparable water views, a beach area, bike trails, tennis courts, and an eighteen-hole Scottish-style golf course, among other highlights. Mohican Lodge is set on the Clear Fork Branch of the Mohican River and has an indoor and outdoor pool, tennis, ball courts, and more. All of the lodges have restaurants, swimming pools, tennis courts, conference facilities, and playground equipment. Many also have exercise facilities, golf courses, bike trails, sports, and games.

Sixteen of Ohio's state parks have cabins on lakes and rivers or in woods and mountains; twenty-three of the parks have Rent-A-Camp programs, where guests are provided with a tent set up with cots, sleeping pads, cooler, propane stove, and lantern. Naturalist programs with slide presentations, movies, nature hikes, and animal talks operate at most of the parks. Family favorite Pymatuning State Park Cabins is profiled on page 185.

Accommodations: "Housekeeping" cabins usually sleep six people in two bedrooms and a sofabed in the living room. Most have screened porches, private baths, fully equipped kitchens, and linens. More rustic "standard" cabins are less elaborately equipped and vary from park to park. "Sleeper" cabins do not have kitchens or linens. "Rent-A-Camps" have an already-set-up tent and camping gear. Lodge rooms vary by park; most are double rooms, some are rooms with lofts.

Cost: Housekeeping cabins $80 per night, $400 to $445 per week. Rustic cabins approximately $65 per night, $350 to $375 per week. Sleeping cabins $50 to $70 per night, $225 to $340 per week. Rent-A-Camp sites $25 per night. Lodge rooms $70 to $95 per night. Parks accept reservations one year in advance.

OKLAHOMA

Address: 500 Will Rogers Building, Oklahoma City, Oklahoma 73105–4492
Telephone: 800 – 654–8240; 405–521–2464

Oklahoma's five state resort parks each capture the scenic, cultural, and historical highlights of their location. All five offer swimming pools, golf, tennis, playgrounds, restaurants, fishing, boating, nature trails, camping, and a year-round recreation program. Guests stay in a lodge or inn, cabins, or campsites. Lake Murray Resort and State Park has turn-of-the-century decor in a country inn on the lake. Family fun includes a three-mile shoreline hike, swimming beach and pool, boating, waterskiing, horseback riding, miniature golf, and an eighteen-hole golf course. Lake Texoma Park has record-setting fish, golf, more water sports, and an indoor fitness center. Western Hills Guest Ranch features southwestern hospitality.

Nine state parks with such names as Tenkiller, Robbers Cave, Roman Nose, and Boiling Springs feature cabins for up to six people. Choose from timber or native stone, lakeside and river-view cabins. Many of the parks offer junior naturalist programs for children that feature hands-on interpretive lessons under the guidance of a naturalist.

Accommodations: All cabins are air-conditioned with fully equipped kitchens, private baths, sofabeds, and linens; most have one or two bedrooms. Resort cabins have TVs and phones; park cabins do not. Lodges are similar to motel rooms.

Cost: One-bedroom park cabins $40 per night; at the other end of the scale, cabins sleeping ten to fourteen people on Lake Murray $195 per night. Most cabins about $55 per night. Children eighteen and under stay free in parents' room.

PENNSYLVANIA

Address: Bureau of State Parks, PO Box 8551, Harrisburg, Pennsylvania 17105-8551
Telephone: 800–63–PARKS; Web site www.dcnr.state.pa.us

Pennsylvania has 275 cabins in twenty-six different state parks; all can be rented in June, July, and August. During the summer, many offer swimming, boating, fishing, and hiking; in winter, you'll find ice-skating, sledding, cross-country skiing, and ice fishing at many parks. Other special features include nature programs, exercise trails, and historical trails.

Accommodations: "Modern" cabins were built in recent years and have furnished bedrooms, living room–dining room areas, bathrooms with shower, and electric heat. "Rustic" cabins were built in the 1930s out of logs, stone, or boards, and are generally closed from mid-December to early April. Houses, usually former residences that have been renovated, have an average of three bedrooms, plus modern kitchens, full baths, and large living rooms. Most sleep six to ten people.

Cost: Modern cabins sleeping six $60 to $70 per night, $250 to $275 per week. Rustic cabins $23 to $55 per night, $90 to $230 per week. Houses $78 to $85 per night, $310 to $335 per week.

SOUTH CAROLINA

Address: South Carolina State Parks, 1205 Pendleton Street, Columbia, South Carolina 29201
Telephone: 803–734–0156

South Carolina has some outstanding state parks with comfortable cabins on its sunny Atlantic coastline. Another favorite park on a freshwater lake, Santee, is known for its excellent fishing and cabins perched on piers over the water. Oconee Station State Park has the oldest structure in the South Carolina upcountry, once used as an Indian trading post. A total of fourteen state parks have cabins amid Blue Ridge Mountain scenery, beside sparkling inland lakes, and along sunny beaches. We profile Hunting Island State Park Cabins on page 241, Myrtle Beach State Park Cabins on page 238, and Edisto Beach State Park Cabins on page 240.

Accommodations: Most cabins are completely furnished, heated, air-conditioned, and supplied with linens and cooking equipment. Sizes vary, accommodating four to twelve people. Cabins must be rented by the week from April 1 through October 31 and by the weekend or for three consecutive nights the rest of the year. Shorter stays can be arranged if there are vacancies.

Cost: Rates vary considerably from park to park. Average price for cabin sleeping six people $35 to $110 per night; weekly rates $200 to $575. Reservations required; ask for the brochure that describes this simple process.

SOUTH DAKOTA

Address: South Dakota Game, Fish and Parks, Division of Parks and Recreation, 523 East Capital, Pierre, South Dakota 57501-3182 Telephone: 605-773-3391

Buffalo roam freely through most of enormous Custer State Park in South Dakota's Black Hills near Mount Rushmore. Guests can stay in one of several lodges, housekeeping cabins, motel units, or sleeping cabins. The park contains three large streams for fishing and four lakes. Three of the lakes have lovely sandy beaches for swimming, and the fourth is for waterskiing. A fun-filled junior naturalist program for children seven to twelve is available. For lodging information, call 800–658–3530.

Lewis and Clark, another family favorite, is a water lover's paradise, with a full-service marina offering boating, sailing, and waterskiing. Hiking, biking, and horse trails run through the park. Lodgings include camper cabins, twenty-six-foot travel trailers, housekeeping cabins, and motel rooms; for Lewis and Clark lodging information, call 605–668–2985.

Eleven of South Dakota's state parks have rustic log camping cabins along rivers, in the prairies, or in woodland areas. You can receive a brochure describing each one.

Accommodations: Camping cabins have one large room with a set of bunks and a double bed, a small table, and benches. All have electricity, bathhouses nearby, and heat and air-conditioning. Each cabin is equipped with an outdoor picnic table and a fire ring. Custer and Lewis and Clark accommodations vary widely; contact each park for details.

Cost: Camping cabins $35 per night per cabin; trailer $60; reservations are accepted starting January 1. Other cabins at Custer and Lewis and Clark $60 to $100 per night; lodge rooms $75 to $100 per night.

TENNESSEE

Address: Tennessee Department of Environment and Conservation, Division of Parks, 401 Church Street, Nashville, Tennessee 37243
Telephone: 888–TN–PARKS

Fall Creek Falls State Park in middle Tennessee boasts the highest waterfall east of the Mississippi, a championship golf course, an inn, several villas, a restaurant, and spectacular mountain scenery. West Tennessee's Reelfoot Lake State Park was formed by a series of earthquakes in 1799 that caused the Mississippi to alter its course, creating a cypress swamp with lily pads and water flowers. The motel-inn and restaurant are perched right over the water and offer spectacular vistas.

Of Tennessee's fifty-one state parks, eighteen have comfortable cabins and seven have gracious inns. Depending on the park, visitors can enjoy horseback riding, scenic boat cruises, fishing, canoe and paddleboat rentals, swimming, golf, tennis, bike rentals, hiking trails, cave exploration, and outdoor dramas. Several of the parks have unusual recreational facilities, such as Frisbee golf courses (Meeman-Shelby, Forest, and Cedars of Lebanon) or skeet and trap ranges (Henry Horton). Some even host historical reenactments, and fourteen parks include regional museums.

Accommodations: Cabins have kitchens, fireplaces, and all linens. Deluxe cabins have fully equipped kitchens, air-conditioning, wood stoves with complimentary firewood, rollaway beds, phones, and TVs. Smaller, rustic cabins do not have air-conditioning, phones, or TVs. Villas can accommodate ten or more and have three bedrooms, two baths, a kitchen, and dining and commons area.

Cost: Prices differ from park to park. Inn rates range from $56 to $65 for doubles on in-season weekends to $40 off-season. Cabin rates range, in season, from $50 for rustics to $100 per night for deluxe. Villas from $95 to $135 per night. Children stay free in parents' room, and there is no charge for rollaway beds. Parks accept reservations a year in advance.

TEXAS

Address: Texas Parks and Wildlife Department, 4200 Smith School Road, Austin, Texas 78744
Telephone: 512–389–4890

The Lone Star State has eight state parks with cabins that accommodate one to six people, and four parks with lodges. One architecturally notable lodge is pueblo-style Indian Lodge, built of adobe by the Civilian Conservation Corps. This full-service hotel has a restaurant and handmade cedar furniture. Balmorhea State Park also has adobe units, plus a large swimming area warmed by hot springs. Bastrop State Park's many rustic stone-and-timber cabins were built by the CCC; they are thought to be some of the finest of that era. Its swimming pool, nine-hole golf course, playground, and biking trails make it a perennial family favorite.

Accommodations: Guests can stay up to fourteen days, and cabins vary considerably from park to park.

Cost: Cabins range from $35 to $95 per night to accommodate two to six people. Reservations taken up to eleven months in advance.

VIRGINIA

Address: Virginia State Parks, 203 Governor Street, Suite 306, Richmond, Virginia 23219
Telephone: 804–786–1712 (general information); 804–933–PARK (reservations)

First Landing/Seashore State Park and Natural Area is the most visited of Virginia's seven state parks with cabin accommodations and it's easy to see why. Seventeen miles of hiking trails wind through lagoons, past large cypress trees and rare plants, and along the shore. A well-done visitor's center has exhibits explaining this coastal environment. The park also has a bike trail and boat rentals. Fairy Stone State Park, home of the lucky "fairy stones" near the Blue Ridge Parkway, has a 168-acre lake for swimming and boating and a variety of outdoor family programs. We profile family favorite Hungry Mother State Park on page 192.

Accommodations: Up to two additional cots per cabin are available for a nightly charge. Maximum occupancy per cabin, with the rental of two cots, is as follows: One-room cabins sleep up to three people, one-bedroom cabins sleep up to four people, two-bedroom cabins sleep up to six people. All have combination living/dining rooms with equipped kitchens, private baths, and linens.

Cost: One-room cabins $60 per night, $270 per week; one-bedroom cabins $67 per night, $310 per week; two-bedroom cabins $80 to $90 per night, $412 to $530 per week, depending on the park. Cots $3 per night.

WEST VIRGINIA

Address: West Virginia Division of Tourism and Parks, 1900 Kanawha Boulevard East, Charleston, West Virginia 25305
Telephone: 800–CALL–WVA will connect you with any park

Cass Scenic Railroad State Park has thirteen two-story guest cabins that once housed loggers who worked for the lumber industry in the state. The railroad that originally transported logs now operates as a tourist train; two different rides run during the summer. A hiking and biking trail begins at Cass; it runs seventy-six miles to North Cladwell with spectacular scenery and quaint little towns along the way. West Virginia has eighteen parks with top-notch resort and cabin facilities. Four parks with lodges have golf courses; the off-season package deals are an especially good buy. Other parks have horseback riding, boating, fishing, scenic chair lifts, picnicking, and hiking. Many have nature programs with free activities and events just for kids.

We profile the excellent resort park at Cacapon on pages 45–46.

Accommodations: Cabins fall into four categories: "Modern" cottages and cabins have fireplaces, complete kitchens, private baths, and heat, and sleep two to eight people. "Standard" log cabins have modern kitchens, private baths but no heat, and accommodate two to six people. "Economy" cabins have one big room with a small bath, kitchen area, built-in bunks, and a loft; most hold four people. "Rustic" cabins have gas lamps, a woodburning kitchen stove, and gas refrigerator, with water and bath facilities outside. Most hold four to six people.

Cost: Cabins rent by the week only June 1 through Labor Day; nightly rentals available the rest of the year. Prices vary: per week, modern cabins $375 to $625; standard cabins $290 to $470; economy $242 per week; rustic cabins $165 to $315. Make reservations up to one year in advance at individual parks.

APPENDIX I: BUDGET MOTELS

*M*any cost-conscious families stretch their vacation dollars by using no-frills budget motels when they need lodging enroute to a vacation destination or in popular tourist areas where they won't be spending much time in their rooms. The following motels offer all of the basic amenities, including air-conditioning, private baths, and televisions, and quite a few have extras such as free continental breakfasts, swimming pools, and restaurants. The typical double room in a budget motel costs $40 to $50 per night, double occupancy, and children under seventeen almost always stay free in their parents' rooms. Since many budget hotels and motels have rooms with two double beds, this option can work well for families with one child or two younger children. Larger families can add a rollaway bed for a small additional fee. Most budget motels have a toll-free reservation line and will send you a directory of their locations, amenities, and prices.

Budget Host Inns 800–283–4678	Comfort Inns and Suites 800–228–5150
Budgetel Inns 800–428–3438	Courtyard by Marriott 800–321–2211

Days Inn
800–329–7466

Econo Lodge
800–553–2666

Hampton Inn
800–426–7866

Holiday Inn Express
800–446–4656

Knight's Inns
800–843–5644

Motel 6
505–891–6161

Thriftlodge/Travelodge
800–578–7878

APPENDIX II: U.S. TOURIST OFFICES

Alabama Bureau of Tourism and Travel
401 Adams Avenue, Suite 126
Montgomery, Alabama 36103
800–252–2262, 334–242–4169
Fax: 334–242–4554
E-mail: alabamat@mont.mindspring.com
Web site: http://alaweb.asc.edu/ala__tours/tours.html

Alaska Division of Tourism
PO Box 110801
Juneau, Alaska 99811
907–465–2010
Fax: 907–465–2287
E-mail: GoNorth@commerce.state.ak.us
Web site: http://www.state.ak.us

Arizona Office of Tourism
2702 North Third Street, Suite 4015
Phoenix, Arizona 85004
800–842–8257, 602–230–7733
Fax: 602–277–9289
Web site: http://www.arizonaguide.com

Arkansas Department of Parks and Tourism
One Capitol Mall
Little Rock, Arkansas 72201
800–628–8725, 800–828–8974, 501–682–7777
Web site: http://www.state.ar.us/html/ark__parks.html

California Division of Tourism
801 K Street, #1600
Sacramento, California 95812
800–862–2543
Web site: http://www.gocalif.ca.gov

Colorado Department of Tourism
PO Box 3524
Englewood, Colorado 80155
800–255–5550
Fax: 718–591–7068

Connecticut Vacation Center
865 Brook Street
Rocky Hill, Connecticut 06067
800–282–6863, 860–258–4355
Fax: 860–258–4275
Web site: http://www.valnet.com/Intertrek/Visitor/Connecticut/
ConnecticutVisit.html

Delaware Tourism Office
99 Kings Highway, Box 1401
Dover, Delaware 19903
800–441–8846, 302–739–4271
Fax: 302–739–5749
Web site: http://www.state.de.us/govern/agencies/dedo/index

Washington D.C. Convention and Visitors Association
1212 New York Avenue NW
Washington, DC 20005
202–789–7000
Fax: 202–789–7037
Web site: http://www.washington.org

Florida Division of Tourism
126 West Van Buren Street
Tallahassee, Florida 32399
904-487-1462
Fax: 904-921-9158
Web site: http://www.state.fl.us/commerce/

Georgia Department of Industry and Trade
PO Box 1776, Department TIA
Atlanta, Georgia 30303
800-847-4842, 404-656-3590

Hawaii Visitors Bureau
Waikiki Business Plaza
2270 Kalakaua Avenue #801
Honolulu, Hawaii 96815
808-923-1811
Fax: 808-922-8991
Web site: http://www.visit.hawaii.org

Idaho Department of Commerce
PO Box 83720
Boise, Idaho 83720
800-635-7820, 208-334-2470
Web site: http://www.state.id.us/tourism.html

Illinois Bureau of Tourism
100 West Randolph #3-400
Chicago, Illinois 60601
800-226-6632, 312-814-4732
Web site: http://www.enjoyillinois.com

Indiana Tourism Division
One North Capitol Avenue #700
Indianapolis, Indiana 46204
800-289-6646, 317-232-8860
Web site: http://www.ai.org/tourism

Iowa Department of Tourism
200 East Grand Avenue
Des Moines, Iowa 50309
800-345-4692, 515-242-4705
Web site: http://www.state.ia.us/tourism/

Kansas Travel and Tourism Division
700 SW Harrison Street, Suite 1300
Topeka, Kansas 66603
800–252–6727, 913–296–2009
Fax: 913–296–5055
Web site: http://www-dev.cecase.ukans.edu/kdoch/html/tour1.html

Kentucky Department of Travel Development Visitors Information
Service
500 Mero Street
Frankfort, Kentucky 40601
800–225–8747, 502–564–4930
Fax: 502–564–5695
Web site: http://www.state.ky.us/tour.tour.htm

Louisiana Office of Tourism
PO Box 94291
Baton Rouge, Louisiana 70804
800–33–GUMBO, 800–334–8626, 504–342–8119
Web site: http://www.state.la.us/crt/tourism/htm

Maine Publicity Bureau
PO Box 2300
Hallowell, Maine 04347
800–533–9595, 207–623–0363
Fax: 207–623–0388
Web site: http://www.state.me.us/decd/tour/

Maryland Office of Tourism Development
217 East Redwood Street, 9th Floor
Baltimore, Maryland 21202
800–543–1036, 410–333–6611
Web site: http://www.mdisfun.org

Massachusetts Office of Travel and Tourism
100 Cambridge Street, 13th Floor
Boston, Massachusetts 02202
800–447–6277, 617–727–3201
Web site: http://www.magnet.state.ma.us/travel/travel.html

Michigan Travel Bureau
PO Box 3393
Livonia, Michigan 48151
800–543–2937, 517–373–0670
Web site: http://travel-michigan.state.mi.us

Minnesota Office of Tourism
121 Seventh Place East
St. Paul, Minnesota 55101
800–657–3700, 612–296–5029
Web site: http://tccn.com/mn.tourism/mnhome.html

Mississippi Division of Tourism Development
PO Box 1705
Ocean Springs, Mississippi 39566
800–927–6378
Fax: 800–873–4780
Web site: http://www.mississippi.org

Missouri Division of Tourism
PO Box 1055
Jefferson City, Missouri 65102
800–877–1234, 314–751–4133

Travel Montana
PO Box 200533
Helena, Montana 59620
800–847–4868, 406–444–2654
Fax: 406–844–1800, 406–444–2808
Web site: http://travel.mt.gov

Nebraska Travel and Tourism Department
PO Box 98913
Lincoln, Nebraska 68509
800–228–4307, 402–471–3796
Fax: 402–471–3026
Web site: http://www.ded.state.ne.us/tourism.html

Nevada State Board on Tourism
Capital Complex
Carson City, NV 89710
800–638–2328, 702–687–4322

New Hampshire Office of Travel and Tourism
PO Box 1856
Concord, New Hampshire 03302
800–FUN–IN–NH, Ext. 162; 603–271–2343 Ext. 162
Web site: http://www.visitnh.gov/

New Jersey Division of Travel and Tourism
20 West State Street, CN 826
Trenton, NJ 08628
800–537–7397, 609–292–2470
Web site: http://www.state.nj.us/travel/index.html

New Mexico Department of Tourism
491 Old Santa Fe Trail
Santa Fe, NM 87503
800–545–2040
Fax: 505–827–7402
Web site: http://www.newmexico.org/

New York State Travel Information Center
1 Commerce Plaza
Albany, New York 12245
800–225–5697, 518–474–4116
Web site: http://www.iloveny.state.ny.us

North Carolina State Board of Tourism
430 North Salisbury Street
Raleigh, North Carolina 27603
800–VISIT NC, 800–847–4862, 919–733–4171

North Dakota Tourism
604 East Boulevard
Bismarck, North Dakota 58505
800–435–5663, 701–224–2525
Fax: 701–328–4878
Web site: http://www.ndtourism.com

Ohio Division of Travel and Tourism
PO Box 1001
Columbus, Ohio 43216
800–282–5393, 614–466–8844
Fax: 513–794–0878
Web site: http://www.travel.state.ohio.us

Oklahoma Tourism and Recreation Department
500 Will Rogers Building
Oklahoma City, Oklahoma 73105
800–652–6552, 405–521–3981
Web site: http://www.otrd.state.ok.us/

Oregon Tourism Commission
775 Summer Street NE
Salem, Oregon 97310
800–547–7842, 503–986–0000
Fax: 503–986–0001

Pennsylvania Office of Travel Marketing
Department of Commerce
453 Forum Building
Harrisburg, Pennsylvania 17120
800–847–4872, 717–787–5453
Web site: http://www.state.pa.us/Visit/info-trav.html

Rhode Island Tourism Division
7 Jackson Walkway
Providence, Rhode Island 02903
800–556–2484 (printed material only), 800–250–7384, 401–277–2601
Fax: 401–273–8720

South Carolina Department of Parks, Recreation and Tourism
PO Box 71
Columbia, South Carolina 29202
800–346–3634, 803–734–0122
Fax: 803–273–8270
Web site: http://www.prt.state.sc.us/sc

South Dakota Department of Tourism
711 East Wells Avenue
Pierre, South Dakota 57501
800–732–5682, 605–773–3301
Fax: 605–773–3256
E-mail: sdinfo@goed.state.sd.us
Web site: http://www.state.sd.us

Tennessee Tourism Division
PO Box 23170
Nashville, Tennessee 37202
800–836–6200, 615–741–2158
Fax: 615–741–7225
Web site: http://tennessee.net/tennessee/

Texas Department of Tourism
PO Box 12728
Austin, Texas 78711
800–888–8839, 512–462–9191
Web site: http://www.texas.gov/tourist.html

Utah Travel Council
Council Hall
Capitol Hill, Department TIA
Salt Lake City, Utah 84114
800–200–1160, 801–538–1030

Vermont Department of Travel and Tourism
134 State Street
Montpelier, Vermont 05602
800–837–6668, 802–828–3237
Fax: 802–828–3367, 802–828–3233
E-mail: vtinfo@dca.state.vt.us

Virginia Division of Tourism
1021 East Cary Street
Richmond, Virginia 23219
800–847–4882, 804–786–4484
E-mail: 75143.1111@CompuServe.Com
Web site: http://www.virginia.org/cgishl/
VISITVA/Tourism/Welcome

Washington Tourism Development Division
PO Box 42500
Olympia, Washington 98504
800–544–1800, 360–586–2012
Web site: http://www. tourism.wa.gov.forthewashington

West Virginia Division of Tourism and Parks
2101 Washington Street East
Charleston, West Virginia 25305
800–225–5982, 304–345–2286

Wisconsin Division of Tourism
PO Box 7976
Madison, Wisconsin 53707
800–432–8747, 608–266–2161
Web site: http://tourism.state.wi.us/agencies/tourism

Wyoming Division of Tourism
I-25 at College Drive
Cheyenne, Wyoming 82002
800–225–5996, 307–777–7777
Fax: 307–777–6904
Web site: http://www.state.wy.us/state.welcome.html

INDEX

VACATIONS STATE BY STATE

Alabama
Gulf State Park Resort, 43–44
State Park accommodations, 43–44, 322
Arkansas
Buffalo Outdoor Center, 185–186
Crater of Diamonds State Park, 302
DeGray Lake Resort Park, 323
Gaston's White River Resort, 38–39
Lake Ouachita State Park, 323
Ozark Folk Center, 301
Ozark Folk Center Lodge, 302
Petit Jean State Park, 186–187
Scott Valley Resort and Guest Ranch, 84–85
State Park accommodations, 186–187, 302, 323
Swaha Lodge, 302–303
Arizona
Bright Angel Lodge and Cabins, 128
Don Hoel's Cabins, 175
Grand Canyon Lodge North Rim, 131–132
Grand Canyon National Park, 127–132
Kay El Bar Guest Ranch, 76–77
Lazy K Bar Ranch, 77
Maswik Lodge, 129
Moqui Lodge, 130
Pfeifer's Slide Rock Lodge, 175
Slide Rock State Park, 175–176
White Mountain Archaeological Center, 292–293
Yavapai Lodge, 129–130
California
Bahia Resort Hotel, 208–209
Beach Cottages, 210
Bonanza King Resort, 168–169
Capitola Venetian Court, 215
Coffee Creek Ranch, 66–67
Convict Lake Resort, 166–167
Curry Village, 96–97
Dana Inn and Marina, 209
Disneyland, 14–16

Drakesbad Guest Ranch, 65–66
Emandal Farm, 146
Family Vacation Center, University of California at Santa Barbara, 145–146
Glorietta Bay Inn, 211
Greenhorn Creek Guest Ranch, 64–65
High Sierra Camps, 97–98
Housekeeping Camp, 97
Hunewill Circle H Guest Ranch, 67–68
Inn at Schoolhouse Creek, 220–221
Konocti Harbor Resort and Spa, 19–20
Lair of the Golden Bear, 149–150
Lost Whale Bed and Breakfast Inn, 220
Mendocino vacation home rentals, 220–21
Miramar Resort Hotel, 212–213
Montecito-Sequoia Lodge, 148–149
Monterey Peninsula, 213–217
Pigeon Point Lighthouse Hostel, 217–218
Pinecrest Lake Resort, 167–168
Point Montara Lighthouse Hostel, 218
Point Reyes Hostel, 219
Richardson's Resort, 18–19
San Diego, 207–211
San Jose Family Camp, 148
Santa Cruz County, 213–217
Santa Cruz County Beach Vacation Rentals, 216–217
Seaway Hotel, 214–215
Skylake Yosemite Family Camp, 147
Trinity Alps Resort, 20–21
Tuolumne Meadows Lodge, 94
Vacations by the Sea, 216
Wawona Hotel, 93–94
White Wolf Lodge, 95
Yosemite Lodge, 95–96
Yosemite National Park, 90–98
Colorado
Anderson Ranch Arts Center, 291–292
Aspen Grove Family Camp, 150–151
Canyon Ranch, 69–70
Coulter Lake Guest Ranch, 70

Crow Canyon Archaeological Center, 290–291
Deer Forks Guest Ranch 71–72
Early Guest Ranch, 73
Estes Park Center, 25–26
Grand Lake Lodge, 121
H-Bar-G Ranch Hostel, 122
Harmel's Ranch Resort, 70–71
Lazy L and B Ranch, 72–73
Lazy J Resort and Rafting Company, 172–173
Rimrock Dude Ranch, 73–74
Rocky Mountain National Park, 120–122
Snow Mountain Ranch, 24–25
Trails End Ranch Family Camp, 151–152
Two Bars Seven Dude Ranch, 74–75
Valhalla Resort, 121–122
YMCA of the Rockies, 24–26
Connecticut
Mystic Seaport Museum, 313–314
Delaware
Beacon Motel, 263–264
Lewes vacation rentals, 264
Killen Pond State Park, 323–324
State Park accommodations, 323–324
Florida
Adventures Unlimited, 191
Amelia Island vacation rentals, 247
Bahia Honda State Park, 253–254
Bluewater Bay, 42–43
Captiva Island, 254–256
Clearwater Beach Hostel, 257
Conch Key Cottages, 252–253
Disney World, 14–16
Driftwood Resort, 250–251
Everglades National Park, 134–136
Flamingo Lodge Marina and Outpost Resort, 135–136
Florida Keys, 251–254
Gulf Breeze Cottages, 255–256
Gulf of Mexico (Panhandle), 256–258
Homosassa Springs State Wildlife Park, 190–191
accommodations, 191
Key West Hostel, 252
Ocean Gallery, 249–250
Pointe Santo, 256
Rivard of South Walton, 257–258
Sanibel Island, 254–256
St. Augustine, 247–250
St. Augustine Hostel, 249
St Joseph Peninsula State Park Cabins, 258
State Park accommodations, 253–254, 258, 324
Traveler's Palm, 254
Georgia
Best Western Jekyll Inn Oceanfront Resort and Villas, 245–246
Cloudland Canyon State Park, 325
Coast of, 243–247
Crooked River State Park Cabins, 188
F.D. Roosevelt State Park, 39
Hostel in the Forest, 246–247
Jekyll Island vacation rentals, 246
Lighthouse Point Beach Club, 244–245

Okefenokee Swamp Exploration, 304–305
Red Top Mountain State Park, 325
Sea Island vacation rentals, 244
State Park accommodations, 39, 188–190, 324–325
Stephen Foster State Park, 189–190
Tybee Island vacation rentals, 244–245
Hawaii
Hale Pau Hana Resort, 203–204
Hawaii Volcanoes National Park, 103–105
Maui, 202–206
Namakani Paio Camping Cabins, 105
Napili Sunset, 205
State Park accommodations, 206, 325
Volcano House, 104
Waianapanapa State Park Cabins, 206
Idaho
Hill's Resort, 172
Redfish Lake Lodge, 171
Illinois
Cave-in Rock State Park Resort, 326
Hobson's Bluffdale Vacation Farm, 83
Shaw-Waw-Nas-See 4-H Camp, 153
Starved Rock State Park, 326
State Park accommodations, 326
Indiana
Chain O' Lakes Canoe Trips, 184
Conner Prairie, 299
Frederick-Talbot Inn, 300
French Lick Springs Resort, 31–32
Indiana University, Bloomington Mini University, 298–299
Lincoln Boyhood National Memorial and State Park, 300–301
Potawatami Inn, 31
Pokagon State Park, 31
State Park accommodations, 326–327
Iowa
Backbone State Park, 327
State Park accommodations, 327
Kansas
Flint Hills Overland Wagon Train, 78–79
Kentucky
Lake Cumberland State Resort Park, 41–42
Mammoth Cave Hotel, 136–137
Mammoth Cave National Park, 136–137
Shaker Village, 307–308
State Park accommodations, 41–42, 327–328
Sunset Point Motor Lodge, 137
Woodland Cottages, 137
Louisiana
Bayou Segnette State Park, 187
Breazeale House Bed and Breakfast, 304
Chico State Park, 328
Natchitoches Folk Festival, 303–304
State Park accommodations, 187, 328–329
Maine
Acadia National Park, 140–143
Alden Camps, 59–60
Attean Lake Lodge, 199–200
Baxter State Park, 329
Beech Hill Road House, 142
Camp Wyonegonic Family Camp, 164
Chewonki Foundation, 320

Hall Quarry Road House, 141–142
Harbour Woods, 142–143
Historic Garrison House Resort, 280–281
Kawanhee Inn, 200
Oakland House Seaside Inn and Cottages,
    60–61
Sand Dollar Real Estate, 281
Seaside Cottages, 141
Seaside Rentals, 281
Sebago Lake Lodge and Cottages, 198–
    199
Sentry Hill Rentals, 282
State Park accommodations, 329
Southern coast of, 279–282
Southern coast vacation rentals, 281–282
Maryland
Elk Neck State Park, 330
Herrington Manor State Park, 194
Jane's Island State Park, 330
New Germany State Park, 330
State Park accommodations, 330
Swallow Falls State Park, 194
Massachusetts
Appalachian Mountain Club's Family
    Education Programs, 317–318
Appalachian Mountain Club's Hut-to-Hut
    Hikes, 318–319
Becket-Chimney Corners YMCA Family
    Camps, 162–163
Breakwaters, 272–273
Cape Cod, 266–264
Causeway Harborview, 274–275
Compass Real Estate, 269
Country Dance and Song Society's Family
    Week, 316–317
Even'tide Motel and Cottages, 267–269
Gibson Cottages, 271–272
Hostelling International-Martha's Vineyard,
    276
Hostelling International-Mid-Cape, 272
Hostelling International-Truro, 270
Kalmar Village, 270–271
Martha's Vineyard, 274–276
Mohawk Trails State Park, 330
Old Sturbridge Village, 314–315
Plimouth Plantation, 315–316
Sandcastle Vacation Rentals, 275
Savoie Mountain State Park, 330
State Park accommodations, 330
Yarmouth Shores Cottages, 273–274
Michigan
Al-Gon-Quian Family Camp, 156
Camp Michigania Walloon, 157
Crystal Mountain Resort, 32–33
Isle Royale National Park, 133
Lavalley's Resort and Antiques, 183–184
Maple Lane Motel and Resort, 183
Miller's Cabins, 183
Mission Point Resort, 33–34
Rock Harbor Lodge, 133
Sleeping Bear Dunes National Lakeshore,
    182–183
State Park accommodations, 331
Wolk Lake Ranch Resort, 83–84
YMCA Storer Camps, 155–156

Minnesota
Black Pine Beach Resort, 177–178
Camp Lincoln/Camp Lake Hubert Family
    Camp, 157–158
Gunflint Northwoods Outfitters Canoe
    Trips and Cabins, 180
Itasca State Park, 331
Saint Croix State Park, 331
Scenic State Park, 331
State Park accommodations, 331–332
Timber Bay Lodge and Houseboats, 178–
    179
Village Inn and Resort, 34–35
Mississippi
Buccaneer State Park, 332
Gayle's Cottages, 259
Percy Quinn State Park, 332
State Park accommodations, 332
Missouri
Bennet Springs State Park, 333
Eagle Hurst Resort and Dude Ranch, 80
Emminence Canoes, Cottages, and Camp,
    176
Merramec River, Float Trips on, 177
Ozark Mountain Resort Swim and Tennis
    Club, 30
State Park accommodations, 332–333
Still Waters Condominium Resort, 29–30
Montana
Chico Hot Springs, 27–28
Cliff Lake Lodge, 173–174
Glacier National Park, 105–108
Glacier Park Lodge, 107
Holland Lake Lodge, 174–175
Lake McDonald Lodge, 106–107
Many Glacier Hotel, 106
Rising Sun Motor Inn, 107
Sweet Grass Ranch, 75–76
Swiftcurrent Motor Inn, 108
Village Inn, 108
Nebraska
Eugene Mahoney State Park, 333
Fort Robinson State Park, 333
Oregon Trail Wagon Train, 79–80
Platte River State Park, 333
State Park accommodations, 333
Two Rivers State Park, 333
Nevada
Cowboy Poetry Festival, 286
New Hampshire
Anchorage, 198
Camp Merrowvista, 163
Franconia Inn and Hillwinds Lodge, 55–56
Inn at East Hill Farm, 56–57
Lakeshore Terrace, 197
Loch Lyme Lodge, 53–54
Rockhouse Mountain Farm, 57
Rockwold-Deephaven Camp, 54–55
Twin Lake Village, 52–53
New Jersey
Cape May vacation rentals, 265
Chalfonte, 50–51
Queen Victoria, 264–265
State Park accommodations, 334
Stokes State Forest, 334

New Mexico
Brush Ranch Camps, 152–153
New York
Allegany State Park, 334–335
Camp Chingachgook on Lake George, 161
Canoe Island Lodge, 47–48
Chautauqua Institution Summer School, 311–312
Fieldstone Farm, 48–49
Golden Acres Farm and Ranch, 85–86
Lake Taghkanic State Park, 195
Letchworth State Park, 334
Maidstone Park Cottages, 265–266
National Baseball Hall of Fame and Museum, 312–313
Pinegrove Dude Ranch Resort, 86–87
Rocking Horse Ranch, 87–88
Silver Bay Association, 46–47
State Park accomodations, 195, 334–335
Timberlock, 49–50
Weona Family Camp, 162
North Carolina
Alan Shelor Beach Rentals, 235
Carolina Designs Realty, 232–233
Carolina Temple Apartments, 236–237
Crystal Coast, 233–235
Crystal Coast Rentals, 234
Hatteras Island vacation rentals, 235–236
High Hampton Inn and Country Club, 40–41
John C. Campbell Folk School, 305–306
Ocracoke Island vacation rentals, 235–236
Outer Banks, 231–233
Outer Banks Hostel, 231–232
Seafarer Family Camps, 160–161
Sun Realty's Beach Vacation Homes, 232
Wrightsville Beach vacation rentals, 237
North Dakota
International Music Summer School of Fine Arts, 297–298
Laura Ingalls Wilder Pageant, 296
Prairie House Manor Bed and Breakfast, 297
Ohio
Camp Christopher Family Camp, 159
Circle K Ranch, 81
Cleveland Area YMCA Family Camps, 158
Maumee State Park, 335
Pymatuning State Park Cabins, 185
State Park accommodations, 185, 335
Oklahoma
Indian Activities in, 296
Indian City U.S.A. and American Indian Exposition, 295–296
Lake Murray Resort and State Park, 336
Lake Texoma State Park, 336
Quartz Mountain Resort, 37–38
Radisson Inn, 295
Red Earth Festival, 294–295
State Park accommodations, 336
Western Hills Guest Ranch State Park, 336
Oregon
Bar M Ranch, 68–69
Best Western Oceanview Resort, 222
Crater Lake Lodge, 99

Crater Lake National Park, 98–100
Ka-Nee-Ta Resort, 21–22
Mazama Village Motor Inn, 99–100
Odell Lake Lodge, 169–170
Seaside vacation rentals, 222
Pennsylvania
Mountain Springs Lake Resort, 193–194
Penn State Alumni College, 310–311
State Park accommodations, 337
Rhode Island
Block Island, 276–278
Island Manor Resort, 278
Phelan Real Estate, 277
Surf Hotel, 277–278
South Carolina
Beach Colony Resort, 239
Coast of, 237–243
Edisto Beach State Park Cabins, 240
Edisto Island vacation rentals, 241
Hickory Knob State Resort Park, 40
Hilton Head Island Forest Beach Vacation Villas, 242–243
Hunting Island State Park Cabins, 241–242
Isle of Palms vacation rentals, 240
Kiawah Island vacation rentals, 240
Myrtle Beach State Park Cabins, 238–239
Oconee State Park, 337
Santee State Park, 337
Seabrook Island vacation rentals, 240
State Park accommodations, 40, 238–239, 240–242, 337–338
South Dakota
Badlands National Park, 134
Cedar Pass Lodge, 134
Custer State Park, 338
Lewis and Clark State Park, 338
State Park accommodations, 338
Tennessee
Big Ridge State Park, 189
Cumberland Mountains State Park, 188–189
Fall Creek Falls State Park, 339
Reelfoot Lake State Park, 339
State Park accommodations, 188–189, 339
Texas
Balmorhea, 339
Balstrop State Park, 339–340
Big Bend National Park, 132–133
Chain-O-Lakes Resort and Conference Center, 28–29
Chisos Mountains Lodge, 132–133
Island Retreat, 230–231
Mayan Ranch, 78
Padre Island National Seashore, 229–231
Port Aransas, 229–231
State Park accommodations, 339–340
Tarpon Inn, 230
Texas Folklife Festival, 293–294
accommodations, 294
Utah
Arches National Park, 123–126
Canyonlands National Park, 123–126
Cedar Breaks Condos, 126
Entrada Ranch, 125–126
Homestead, 23–24
Moab, 124–126

Recapture Lodge and Pioneer House, 22–23
Vermont
Fletcher Farm School for the Arts and Crafts, 319–320
Harvey's Lake Cabins and Campground, 195–196
Indian Joe's Courts 196–197
Rodgers Country Inn, 58
Smugglers Notch, 51–52
Wildflower Inn, 58–59
Virginia
Big Meadows Lodge, 139
Camp Friendship, 159–160
Chincoteague Island, 259–263
Chincoteague Island Vacation Rentals, 261–262
Colonial Williamsburg, 308–309
Fairy Stone State Park, 340
First Landing/Seashore State Park, 340
Hungry Mother State Park, 192
Island Motor Inn, 262–263
Lewis Mountain, 139
Refuge Motor Inn, 262
Shenandoah National Park, 137–139
Skyland Lodge, 138
State Park accommodations, 340
Washington
Baker Lake Resort, 170
Beach Haven Resort, 224
Coast of, 227–229
Iron Springs Ocean Beach Resort, 228
Kalaloch Lodge, 100–101
Klipsan Beach Cottages, 228–229
Lake Quinault Lodge, 101–102
Log Cabin Resort, 102–103
Ocean Crest Resort, 227
Olympic National Park, 100–103
Puget Sound Islands, 222–226
Roche Harbor Resort & Marina, 225–226
Sol Duc Hot Springs Resort, 103
Vashon Island Ranch Hostel, 226
West Virginia
Augusta Heritage Center, 306–307
Blackwater Falls State Park, 192–193
Cacapon Resort, 45–46
Cass Scenic Railroad State Park, 341
Oglebay Resort, 44–45
State Park accommodations, 341
Wisconsin
Barefoot Bay Resort, 35–36
Camp Nebagamon Family Camp, 154
Edwards YMCA Camp on Lake Beulah, 154–155
Meadowbrook Resort, 181
Pine Beach Resort, 182
Polynesian, 36–37
Sunset Resort, 180–181
Woodside Ranch, 82
Wyoming
Buffalo Bill Historical Center, 287–289
Canyon Lodge and Cabins, 118
Cody Nite Rodeo, 287–289
Colter Bay Tent Cabins, 111
Colter Bay Village Cabins, 110–111

Deer Forks Guest Ranch, 71–72
Elk Refuge Inn, 112–113
Grand Teton National Park, 108–113
Grant Village, 117
Jackson Lake Lodge, 110
Lake Lodge and Cabins, 117
Lake Yellowstone Hotel and Cabins, 116
Lazy L & B Ranch, 72–73
Mammoth Hot Springs Hotel and Cabins, 118–119
Old Faithful Inn, 114–115
Old Faithful Lodge and Cabins, 115
Old Faithful Snow Lodge Cabins, 115–116
Pahaska Tepee Resort, 26, 289
Roosevelt Lodge and Cabins, 119–120
Signal Mountain Lodge, 112
Snake River Institute, 290
Two Bars Seven Ranch, 74–75
Yellowstone Institute, 287
Yellowstone National Park, 113–120

GENERAL INDEX

Acadia National Park, Maine, 140–143
Adirondack State Park, 161
Amelia Island, Florida, 247
America River Touring Association, 166
American Wilderness Experience, 166
Arches National Park, Utah, 123–126
Assateague Island, Virgina, 260–263
Atlantic Beach, North Carolina, 233–235
Audiotapes, 13
AuTrain Lake, Michigan, 183–184

Badlands, South Dakota, 134
Bar Harbor, Maine, 140–141
Bass Lake, California, 147
Beach vacations, 201–282
Beaches of South Walton, Florida, 257–258
Beaufort, North Carolina, 233–235, 238, 241
Berkshire Mountains, Massachusetts, 162–163
Best Hikes with Children in Utah , 123
Big Bend National Park, Texas, 132–133
Birch Lake, Minnesota, 178
Block Island, Rhode Island, 276–278
Boundary Waters Canoe Area, Minnesota, 180
Brainerd Lakes Area, Minnesota, 177–178
Branson, Missouri, 29–30
Budget, travel, 4
Budget motels, 9
Budget motels, list of, 342–343
Burt Lake, Michigan, 156

Canyonlands National Park, Utah, 123–126
Cape Cod, Massachusetts, 266–274
Cape Cod National Seashore, Massachusetts, 266–270
Cape Fear Coast, North Carolina, 236–237
Cape Hatteras National Seashore, North Carolina, 231, 235–236
Cape Lookout National Seashore, North Carolina, 233
Cape May, New Jersey, 14–15, 264–265

Cape Neddick, Maine, 279, 281
Capitola Beach, California, 215–216
Captiva Island, Florida, 245–256
Catskill Mountains, New York, 85–86
Charleston, South Carolina, 237–238, 240
Chautauqua Lake, New York, 311
Chincoteague Island, Virginia, 259–263
Chocktawhatchee Bay, Florida, 42–43
Class VI River Runners, 166
Clear Lake, California, 19–20
Cody, Wyoming, 287–289
Colonial Williamsburg, Virginia, 308–309
Conservations Summits, 283–284
Consumer Reports Travel Letter, 5
Cooperstown, New York, 313
Crater Lake National Park, Oregon, 98–100
Crystal Coast, North Carolina, 233–235
Crystal Lake, New Hampshire, 57
Complete Guide to America's National Parks, 89
Corpus Christi, Texas, 229–230
Cumberland Island National Seashore, Georgia, 243–244

Dinosaur National Monument, Utah, 125
Discover Grand Teton, 109
Discover Yellowstone, 113
Duck, North Carolina, 231–233
Day Trips and Learning Vacations, 283–320
Discount books, 6
Disneyland, California, 14–16
Disney World Florida, 14–16
Driving tips, 12–13
Dude Ranchers' Asociation, 64
Dude ranches, 62–88

East Hampton, New York, 265–266
Edisto Island, South Carolina, 238, 240–?41
Estes Park, Colorado, 25–26, 120
Everglades National Park, Florida, 134–136
Exchanging your home, 9–10
Expeditions, Inc., 166
Expenses, bugeting for, 4
Exploring the Grand Canyon, 127

Family camps, 144–164
Family hostels, 10–11
Family Fun in Yellowstone , 113
Family Guide to Rocky Mountain National Park , 120
Florida Keys, 251–254
Food, saving money on, 7–8
Fort Macon State Park, North Carolina, 234–235
Franconia Notch State Park, New Hampshire, 55–56
Frequent flyer programs, 6

Georgia, coast of, 243–247
Glacier National Park, Montana, 105–108
Grand Canyon National Park, Arizona, 127–132
Grand Teton National Park, Wyoming, 108–113
Grand Teton Official Handbook, 109

Grayton Beach, Florida, 257–258
Gulf Coast, Mississippi, 259
Gulf Islands National Seashore, Mississippi, 259
Gulf of Mexico (Panhandle), Florida, 256–258
Gulf Shores, Alabama, 43–44, 258

Hapuna Beach State Recreation Area, Hawaii, 206
Hatteras Island, North Carolina, 231, 235–236
Hawaii Volcanoes National Park, Hawaii, 103–105
Hilton Head Island, South Carolina, 242–243
Home exchanges, 9
Home rentals, 10
Hostelling International, 11
Hostels, 11
Hunting Island, South Carolina, 238, 241–242
Huntington Beach and State Park, South Carolina, 237
Hyannis, Massachusetts, 272–274

International Peace Gardens of the Turtle Mountains, North Dakota, 297–298
Intervac U.S., 10
Isle au Haut, Maine, 140
Isle of Palms, South Carolina, 238, 240
Isle Royale National Park, Michigan, 133

Jackson Hole, Wyoming, 109, 112–113, 290
Jekyll Island, Georgia, 243, 245–246
Jockey's Ridge State Park, North Carolina, 231–232

Kalaloch, Washington, 100–101, 227
Kennebunkport, Maine, 279–281
Kiawah Island, South Carolina, 238, 240
Kill Devis Hills, North Carolina, 231–233
Kitty Hawk, North Carolina, 231–233
Kokee State Park, Kauai, 206

Lake Altus-Lugert, Oklahoma, 37–38
Lake Beulah, Wisconsin, 154–156
Lake Cumberland, Kentucky, 41–42
Lake Delton, Wisconsin, 182
Lake George, New York, 46–48, 161
Lake Hubert, Minnesota, 157–158
Lake James, Indiana, 31
Lake Tahoe, California, 18–19
Lake Webb, Maine, 200
Lake Wentworth, New Hampshire, 197
Lake Winnisquam, New Hampshire, 198
Lakeshore and riverside vacations, 165–200
Lassen Volcanic National Park, California, 65–66
Lewes, Delaware, 263–264
Long Beach Peninsula, Washington, 227
Lower Whitefish Lake, Minnesota, 177

Mackinac Island, Michigan, 33–34
Maine, Southern Coast of, 279–282
Makaekahana State Recreation Area, Oahu, 206
Malaquite Beach, Texas, 229

Mammoth Cave National Park, Kentucky, 136–137
Martha's Vineyard, Massachusetts, 274–276
Maui, Hawaii, 202–206
Meals, saving money on, 7–8
Mendocino, California, 220–221
Mesa Verde National Park, Utah, 291
Moab, Utah, 123–126
Monterey Bay Aquarium, California, 214
Monterey Peninsula, California, 213–217
Mount Desert Island, Maine, 140–143
Mustang Island State Park, Texas, 229–230
Myrtle Beach, South Carolina, 237–239

Nags Head, North Carolina, 231–232
National Park vacations, 89–143
National Parks: The Family Guide , 89–90
National Wildlife Federation, 283–284
Nebagamon Lake, Wisconsin, 154
Norris Lake, Tennessee, 189
North Coast, California, 217–221
Northeast Kingdom, Vermont, 58–59, 195–197

OARS (Outdoor Adventures Specialists), 166
Ocean Shores, Washington, 227
Ocracoke, North Carolina, 231, 235–236
Off-season travel, 5
Ogunquit, Maine, 279–282
Okefenokee Swamp, Georgia, 189–190, 243–244, 304–305
Orcas Island, Washington, 223–224
Olympic National Park, Washington, 100–103
Orlando, Florida, 15–16
Outer Banks, North Carolina, 231–233
Ozark Mountains, Arkansas, 38, 185–186, 301
Ozark Mountains, Missouri, 29–30
Ozark National Riverway, Missouri, 176

Padre Island National Seashore, Texas, 229–231
Packing tips, 11
Pecos Wildnerness, New Mexico, 152–153
Planning, early, 2–3
Plymouth, Massachusetts, 266
Point Reyes National Seashore, California, 219
Port Aransas, Texas, 229–231
Priest Lake, Idaho, 172
Puget Sound Islands, Washington, 222–226

Quetico Wilderness Area, Canada, 180

Resorts, 17–61
River rafting, 166
Riverside and lakeshore vacations, 165–200
Roanoke Island, North Carolina, 231
Rocky Mountain National Park, Colorado, 24–26, 120–122
ROW (River Odysseys West), 166

St. Augustine, Florida, 247–250
St. Joseph's Peninsula, Florida, 256–258

San Diego, California, 207–211
San Juan Islands, Washington, 222–226
Sanibel Island, Florida, 245–256
Santa Barbara, California, 145–146, 212–213
Santa Cruz County, California, 213–217
Savannah, Georgia, 241, 244–246
Sea Island, Georgia, 243–244
Seaside, Oregon, 222
Seabrook Island, South Carolina, 238, 240
Shadow Lake, 58
Sharing Nature with Children, 90
Sharing the Joy of Nature, 90
Shenandoah National Park, Virginia, 137–139
Short Hikes and Easy Walks in Grand Teton, 109
Sierra Club, 285
Sleeping Bear Dunes National Lakeshore, Michigan, 182–183
Snow Lake, Indiana, 31
South Carolina, coast of, 237–243
Souvenirs, 7
Squam Lake, New Hampshire, 54–55
State Park cabins and resorts, 10
state by state, 321–341
State tourist offices, 344–352
Strom Thurmond Lake, South Carolina, 40
Superior National Forest, Minnesota, 178–179
Suwanee River, Georgia, 189–190

Table Rock Lake, Missouri, 29–30
Tahoe area, California, 18–19
Tourist offices, list of, 344–352
Travel Smart, 5
Traveling by car, 12–14
Trinity Alps, California, 20–21, 66, 168
Tybee Island, Georgia, 243–245

Unicorn Expeditions, 166
U.S. Tourist Offices, list of, 344–352

Vacation Exchange Club, 10
Vashon Island, Washington, 223, 226
Vero Beach, Florida, 250–251

Walloon Lake, Michigan, 157
Washington, coast of, 227–229
Wellfleet, Massachusetts, 267–269
Wells, Maine, 279–282
Western Folklife Center, Nevada, 286
White River, Arkansas, 38
Williamsburg, Virginia, 308–309
Wisconsin Dells, Wisconsin, 36–37, 181–182
World Wide Web, 4
Wrightsville Beach, North Carolina, 236–237

Yellowstone Institute, Wyoming, 287
Yellowstone National Park, Wyoming, 113–120
York Beach, Maine, 279, 282
Young Naturalist, The, 90
Yosemite Field Seminars, 285–286
Yosemite National Park, California, 90–98, 147, 285–286

REPLY FORM

Let us know . . .

If, in your travels through the United States with your family, you discover a bargain destination or a vacation that we did not mention in this book, please fill out this form and tell us about it. We will research your suggestion for possible inclusion in future editions of *The Best Bargain Family Vacations in the U.S.A.*

Name and address of lodging _____

_____

Date of your visit _____

Age(s) of your children _____

Rates per night or per week _____

What did you and/or your children like about this place? _____

_____

_____

_____

_____

Have any of the places we've recommended changed for better or worse since this book was written? _____

_____

_____

_____

_____

Your name _____

Address _____

_____

Phone _____

Send to Laura Sutherland and Valerie Wolf Deutsch
       Best Bargain Family Vacations in the U.S.A.
       c/o St. Martin's Press, Inc.
       175 Fifth Avenue
       New York, New York 10010